LINGUISTIC STUDIES
OF NATIVE CANADA

EUNG-DO COOK AND JONATHAN KAYE
Editors

Linguistic Studies of Native Canada

UNIVERSITY OF BRITISH COLUMBIA PRESS – VANCOUVER
1978

© The Peter de Ridder Press 1978
All rights reserved

Published 1978 by the University of British Columbia Press
For sale only in North America

This book has been published with the help of a grant
from the Canadian Federation for the Humanities,
using funds provided by the Canada Council.

> Canadian Cataloguing in Publication Data
> Main entry under title:
> Linguistic Studies of Native Canada
>
> ISBN 0-7748-0066-6
> 1. Indians of North America – Canada –
> Languages – Addresses, essays, lectures.
> 2. Eskimo language – Addresses, essays, lectures.
> I. Cook, Eung-Do, 1935 –
> II. Kaye, Jonathan, 1942 –
> PM231.L55   497   077-002137-9

International Standard Book Number 0-7748-0066-6

Printed in Great Britain by
William Clowes & Sons Limited
London, Beccles and Colchester

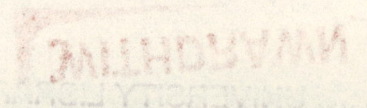

CONTENTS

INTRODUCTION 1

J. K. CHAMBERS
    Dakota Accent 3

EUNG-DO COOK
    Palatalizations and Related Rules in Sarcee 19

PHILIP W. DAVIS AND ROSS SAUNDERS
    Bella Coola Syntax 37

JAMES L. FIDELHOLTZ
    Micmac Intransitive Verb Morphology 67

DONALD G. FRANTZ
    Copying from Complements in Blackfoot 89

JAMES E. HOARD
    Obstruent Voicing in Gitksan: Some Implications for Distinctive Feature Theory 111

TH. R. HOFMANN
    Equational Sentence Structure in Eskimo 121

JONATHAN KAYE
    Rule Mitosis: The Historical Development of Algonquian Palatalization 143

TERRY J. KLOKEID
    Surface Structure Constraints and Nitinaht Enclitics . . . 157

J. H. MASSENET
    Une 'conspiration' en Eskimo 177

DAVID H. PENTLAND
    Proto-Algonquian *sk in Woods Cree 189

GLYNE L. PIGGOTT
    Some Implications of Algonquian Palatalization 203

PATRICIA A. SHAW
    On Restricting the Power of Global Rules in Phonology: A Case from Dakota 227

GREGORY E. THOMSON
    The Origin of Blackfoot Geminate Stops and Nasals . . . 249

H. CHRISTOPH WOLFART
    How Many Obviatives: Sense and Reference in a Cree Verb Paradigm 255

REFERENCES 273

INTRODUCTION

This volume has as its inspiration, as its title implies, the monumental work *Linguistic Structures of Native America*. It differs from that work, however, in a number of important respects. *LSNA* contains thirteen descriptions of languages native to North America. The coverage ranges from Greenlandic Eskimo to Aztec, from Delaware to Yuma. The studies are, with one exception, descriptions of the particular languages, each being somewhere between a "thumb-nail sketch" and a full-blown monograph. Bloomfield's famous "Sketch" is the exception, being a detailed reconstruction of proto-Algonquian.

The aim and scope of our volume is rather different. We have substituted the word "studies" for "structures" in the title quite self-consciously. The papers found in this book are not sketches or exhaustive descriptions by any means. Nor does this book purport to describe the current state of research on the native languages of Canada (for such coverage see the articles by Kaye, Cook, Grubb, and Paillet in the forthcoming *The Languages of Canada* edited by J. Chambers).

In collecting these articles we were looking for work of a particular kind: its nature is intensive rather than extensive, i.e. a detailed look at a particular aspect of the structure of the language rather than a sketch. Furthermore, the aspect being described is something that has not appeared in print before. By and large, the articles contained here are based on field work carried out by the author(s). The object of such studies is to show their relevance with regard to current problems in linguistic theory. One need only look at recent work on Klamath to see the enormous impact that such studies can have on the development of linguistic theory. Some of the articles do not deal with theoretical problems as such but rather provide a sufficiently detailed account of some aspect of a language to enable our readers to draw their own theoretical conclusions.

It is possible to classify the articles in this volume according to a number of criteria. Both synchronic (e.g. Chambers, Frantz, Fidelholtz) and diachronic (e.g. Pentland, Thomson, Kaye) studies are presented. The volume contains papers on phonetics (Hoard), phonology (Cook, Piggott), syntax (Frantz, Davis and Saunders) and semantics (Klokeid, Wolfart). In terms of linguistic families, the following are represented: Salish (Davis and Saunders), Athapaskan (Cook), Wakashan (Klokeid), Tsimshian (Hoard), Siouan (Shaw, Chambers), Algonquian (Piggott, Fidelholtz, Kaye and Wolfart), and Eskimo (Massenet, Hofmann).

Since the present political boundaries of Canada are not relevant insofar as the native languages are concerned, it should be clear that the scope of this book is not motivated from this point of view. Rather we are presenting the current thinking of many of the scholars now engaged in the study of the native languages of Canada. It is hoped that this volume will help to bring about a sense of common purpose in this area, to promote increased attention to what has been in the past a most neglected area of study.

To conclude this introduction we should point out certain gaps in the coverage of this anthology. Neither Iroquoian nor Kutenai are represented among the studies of this book. There is also a decided lack of papers from French Canadian authors. What is desired further is the participation of native linguists. None of the authors contributed to this volume has native intuition of the language, although some speak it quite fluently. Given the current state of research in Quebec and the efforts made in many native communities, there should be little difficulty in remedying the defects in future works of this nature. In fact several linguists who could not meet the deadline for this volume expressed their desire to contribute to a future volume should such a plan be forthcoming.

Eung-Do Cook Jonathan Kaye
Calgary *Montreal*

DAKOTA ACCENT

J. K. CHAMBERS

Siouanists have traditionally maintained that accent in the Dakota languages is unpredictable.[1] This position has been taken most unequivocally by linguists working within the strictures on abstractness in neo-Bloomfieldian structuralism. For example, Hans Wolff (1950:172) simply states it as a fact, without further discussion: "Stress appears phonemic in all existing Siouan languages.... Stress is therefore reconstructed as phonemic in Proto-Siouan." Linguists who do not adhere to those strictures have been rather more equivocal, even while maintaining the same position. Boas and Swanton (1911:884) say, "The placing of accent is said sometimes to constitute the only difference between words, but it is possible that other vocalic modifications, not hitherto observed, may be involved."[2] Matthews also holds that "on a purely phonological basis, the position of accent is phonemic." He does, however, qualify this traditional position in a footnote, stating that "it seems probable that the position of the accent can be described on a morphological basis" (1955:59).

In what follows, I take the unequivocal position that accent is predictable in Dakota. In §1, the Dakota Accent Rule is stated, along with evidence of its application to data which is representative of the great majority of forms in the language. The application of the rule in these cases is straightforward and noncontroversial, and thus establishes the credibility of the rule. In §2, analyses of data which are *superficial* exceptions to the Dakota Accent Rule are presented, with the purpose of showing that the Rule does indeed apply but is made opaque by the application of later rules, which are themselves either well known rules of Dakota or, when they are not well known, reasonably well motivated rules. It is apparently the "exceptionality" of forms like those in the second section that led earlier linguists to conclude that accent was phonemic. However, the analysis required to support my position that it is predictable is by no means unduly abstract, and furthermore leads to a number of significant generalizations about the morphophonemic structure of the language that were missed by earlier analyses. There remain, of course, some forms in the language which cannot be accounted for by my analysis, such as *ũkcé* 'to fart' and *ũkce* 'shit' (which would both have final accent if the Dakota Accent Rule were exceptionless). However, I know of only a handful of such exceptions, and even if the number of exceptions that come to my attention should quintuple (as it very well may) I would have no qualms whatever about admitting them as true exceptions, or inherently accented formatives. Nothing more will be said about exceptional formatives. My purpose is to establish the main or productive accent pattern in Dakota, and to suggest its ubiquity. All the data are from Deloria (1932) or the sources cited in footnote 2, unless otherwise noted.

1. THE DAKOTA ACCENT RULE (DAR)

One of the most striking features about Dakota to a linguist who knows that its accent is purportedly phonemic is the overwhelming preponderance of accents falling on the second syllable of stems. In collections of connected texts like Deloria's (1932, 1954), for example, this rule is sometimes exceptionless in page after page, apart from the trivial 'exceptionality' of monosyllabic stems. My proposal, then, is that Dakota accent is determined by the following simple rule:

(1) DAR $V \rightarrow \acute{V} \ / \ [(C_o \ V) \ C_o \underline{\quad\quad}$

The rule accounts for monosyllabic accent as well as second-syllable accent by the familiar disjunctive ordering convention expressed by parentheses.

1.1 Among the plain roots that plainly undergo the DAR is the verbal subclass that Boas was wont to consider "the second main group" of verbs. These roots are distinguished from other verb roots by their manner of reduplication and by the fact that they can end in any vowel, whereas the 'first' group can end only in -*a* (see §2 for some detail about the other, *a*-final verbs). They also include all of the verbs which infix personal pronouns. Examples illustrating bisyllabic roots of this class are listed below. (For many other examples, see Boas and Deloria 1932:101–02, and 1941:31ff.) Note that the glosses provided here are for the roots; the formatives are homophonous with third person singular non-future verbs, that is, 'he/she/it V's':

(2)a. c^{h}eslí   to shit
   b. c^{h}ok'í   to roast in ashes

c. apʰé   to wait for
d. naxmá   to hide
e. x'ãyã́   to be dying
f. pazó   to reveal
g. hĭgnú   to singe hair off hide
h. sutʰṹ   to be ripe

In terms of accent placement, verbs like these are perfectly regular. Boas, however, tended to consider them a minor subgroup, apparently because many of them are derived by compounding. He conceded that many of the elementary roots were no longer meaningful in the language: thus in (2)a, cʰe is unknown but *sli* remains with the meaning 'to squeeze out'; in (2)b, cʰo exists independently with the meaning 'flesh' but k'ĭ is meaningless. Some, like (3) below, remain meaningful in both elements:

(3) cʰokṹ to plan to kill someone
     cʰo 'flesh' + kũ 'to covet'

The problem would seem to be whether to treat verbs like (2) and (3) as compounds or as unanalysable roots, Neither of these alternatives is entirely satisfactory. On the one hand, treating them as compounds entails allowing the DAR to operate on both underlying roots, thus accenting both syllables, and then introducing an ancillary accent rule to delete the first of the two accents. This latter rule would merely 'correct' the double application of the DAR, and moreover would not be generally applicable to compounds in the language, which retain some accent on both elements but lower (rather than delete) the pitch of the second accent. On the other hand, treating them as plain roots simply ignores the fact that many of them are analysable. A third alternative, more satisfactory than either of these, is to mark non-productive compounds of this sort with the special boundary '|', as follows:

(4) cʰe|sli, cʰo|kĭ, cʰo|kũ, etc.

This boundary will originate in the rule of word formation in the lexicon which derives compound roots, thus reserving the word boundary '#' for compound stems, which are the result of syntactic transformations like PREDICATE RAISING. In the latter compounds, the DAR applies to both elements. In the former, it applies to the whole formative: that is, the boundary '|' does not block the DAR from applying across it, and no ancillary accent rule is necessary. Moreover, the boundary '|' can be used to trigger PRONOUN INFIXING in the subset of these roots that take infixed personal pronouns, which must be marked diacritically anyway.[3]

1.2 Among the prefixes which are accent-affecting is the set of personal pronouns. The following is a paradigm of a transitive verb illustrating the invariable second-syllable accent:[4]

(5) a. cʰikté   I kill you
               cʰi 'I-you' (syncretism) + kte 'kill'
    b. mayákte   you kill me
               ma 'me' + ya 'you' + kte 'kill'
    c. ũyáktepi   you kill us (that is, him and me)
               ũ 'us' + ya 'you' + kte 'kill' + pi 'plural'
    d. ũníktepi   we kill you
               ũ 'we' + ni 'you' + kte 'kill' + pi 'plural'
    e. wicʰáwakte   I kill them
               wicʰa 'them' + wa 'I' + kte 'kill'
    f. wakté   I kill him
               ∅ 'him' + wa 'I' + kte 'kill'
    g. makté   he kills me
               ∅ 'he' + ma 'me' + kte 'kill'
    h. nikté   he kills you
               ∅ 'he' + ni 'you' + kte 'kill'

(Riggs 1890 is the source of (5)g.) Personal pronouns are also stress-affecting when they are infixed, as in roots like *mani* 'to walk': *mawáni* 'I walk', *mayáni* 'you walk', *maní* 'he walks', etc. Thus the personal pronouns always count as syllables in the domain of the DAR.

A second class of accent-affecting prefixes is the set that Boas lumped together as "locatives" (Boas and Deloria 1941:39-45; also Boas and Swanton 1911:900-1, where they are called "prepositional prefixes"). Although they are formally a small set, they seem to have a multitude of functions, as illustrated by (6) and (7), where for example the prefix is an instrumentalizer in (6)a, a nominalizer in (6)e, and has no discernible effect whatever upon the meaning of the root in (6)f. The main point of the list is to illustrate that these prefixes count in the application of the DAR:

(6)   *Plain root*   *Prefixed root*
    a. kahĩte   to sweep   icáhĩte   (i+kahĩte) broom (Riggs 1890)
    b. yũká   to recline   iyũka   to go to bed
    c. tũwá   to look   atũwã   to look for something

d.	cʰaštʰų́	to name	ocʰáštʰų̃	to be famous
e.	owá	to paint	oówa	a painting
f.	cʰăkú	road	ocʰắku	road

Roots can also take more than one prefix of this type, as in the following example:

(7) kašká   to tie fast   iyákaška (i+a+kaška) to imprison

In (7), both of the prefixes must be within the domain of the DAR.

A somewhat better defined set of accent-affecting prefixes are the "instrumentals" (Boas and Deloria 1932:113-14, and 1941:45-52). When these are combined with roots they derive a verb of causative meaning with the type of action specified, as illustrated in (8):

(8)a. wiyákpa   to shine, glisten (Riggs 1890)
       pawíyakpa to polish, cause to shine by pushing
   b. okó   a crack, hole, aperture (Riggs 1890)
       paóko   to push apart, cause a crack by pushing
       yuóko   to pull apart, cause a crack by pulling

Instrumentals co-occur with other instrumentals in some cases, and both count in the application of the DAR:

(9)   ksa   to be severed
   a.   kaóksa   to cause something to be severed inside a hole by striking (i.e., a tooth is knocked out, a roof is caved in)
            ka + o + ksa 'by striking + within a place + sever'
   b.   okáksa   to sever by striking, the action occurring within an area
            o + ka + ksa

The glosses for (9) are Boas's.

1.3 Among the classes of morphemes that have traditionally been considered suffixes in Dakota, the only one that is accent-affecting is the set which might be called 'bound main verbs'. This set includes -*ya* 'to cause indirectly or unintentionally', -*kʰiya* 'to cause directly', and -*ši* 'to order' (for more complete lists, see Boas and Swanton 1911:906-8, 931; Boas and Deloria 1932:103-4; and 1941:73-75, 100). Examples of these three elements, again illustrating the regular application of the DAR, are as follows:

(10)a. yeyá   he sends (someone)
                ya^5 'go' + ∅ 'he' + ya 'cause'

b. yewáya   I send (someone)
ya + wa 'I' + ya
c. yek^{h}íya   he makes (someone) go
ya + ∅ + k^{h}iya 'cause directly'
d. yewák^{h}iya   I make (someone) go
ya + wa + k^{h}iya
e. yeší   he orders (someone) to go
ya + ∅ + ši 'order'
f. yewáši   I order (someone) to go
ya + wa + ši

Although formatives like *-ya*, *-k^{h}iya*, and *-ši* have the semantic force of verbs and occur with personal prefixes as in (10)b, d and f, they differ from all other verbs in being necessarily bound. A phonological correlate of this morphological difference is the accent, for while the morphological complexes with bound main verbs are accented by the DAR, as we have seen, compounds which combine free verbal elements occur with more complex contours, as in (11):

(11)a. škálomàni   he goes playing about
škat^6 'play' # omani 'travel, go about'
b. manúwac^{h}ĭ   he tried to steal (something)
manŭ 'steal' # wac^{h}ĭ 'try'

In these compounds, both constituents are accented, and the accent is on the syllable that would be accented if the verb occurred freely. That is, the assignment of accent is no problem if one assumes that the constituent structure of the compounds is as follows:

(12)   # # škat # omani # #

The DAR will thus apply to both elements enclosed by word boundaries, accenting the monosyllable *škat* and the second syllable of *omani*. One further rule is required to adjust the second of two accents in compounds, as follows:

(13)   COMPOUND RULE $\acute{V} \rightarrow \grave{V} \;/\; \#\# \ldots \acute{V} \ldots \# \ldots \underline{\quad} \ldots \#\#$

The COMPOUND RULE applies to compounds of various other classes as well, such as compound nouns like (14)a, b, noun-adjective compounds like (14)c, and noun-verb compounds like (14)d:

(14)a. pté-oyàte   Buffalo Tribe
pte 'buffalo' # oyate 'people, nation, tribe'

b. pʰeží-wokʰèya   a grass-house
c. hayápi-waštèšte   Sunday-best clothes
                                hayapi 'garments' # wašte 'good' (reduplicated)
d. asãpi-yuslì   to milk
                                asãpi 'milk' # yusli 'to squeeze out'

On the other hand, compounds involving bound main verbs cannot undergo the same derivational history. Their accent would, however, be determined correctly if one assumed an internal occurrence not of '#', as in (12), but of '|', the boundary which was proposed for the verb sublass specifically to allow the DAR to apply across it. Thus (10)c, for example, has the following constituent structure:

(15)   # ya | kʰiya #

The DAR will correctly apply to the material bounded by '#', without regard for the internal boundary. This further use of '|' naturally raises the question of whether it is merely an ad hoc device of no particular interest, or whether it is necessary in order to capture (perhaps crudely) a real structural distinction. If it were merely associated with the bound main verbs as a type of diacritic, it would seem to be the former. If on the other hand there is reason to believe that there are two distinct compounding processes in Dakota which derive structures like (12) and (15), respectively, then it would have a reasonable claim to the latter. In fact, there are two distinct processes in the grammar, for while it is true that bound verbs always and only surface as compound formatives as in (10), free verbs can combine either as derived compounds of the type shown in (11) or as compound formatives parallel to those with bound verbs, as in:

(16)a. škalómani   he goes about to play
                       škat + omani (see 11a)
b. kosínaxni   to be in a hurry to wave
                     koz⁷ 'wave' + inaxni 'be in a hurry'

The status of '|' is definitely not diacritical, since the elements compounded in (16)a are identical to the elements compounded in (11)a, with a subtle difference in the semantic result and an obvious difference in the accent. The application of the DAR to compound formatives suggests that they are the result of a (lexical) word formation rule, whereas its application to the component elements of derived compounds suggests that they are the result of a syntactic transformation. The boundaries, then, characterize processes associated with different components of the grammar.

1.4 Bound main verbs are distinguished from all the other "suffixes" because they alone are accent-affecting. The others, which are more properly called enclitics, include verbal trappings with the expected functions: to mark plurality, futurity, intensity, and so on. In the examples given here to show that the DAR does not apply to them, the enclitics are separated from the stems by the boundary '=':

(17) a. tʰípi   they dwell
∅ '3 pers.' + tʰi 'dwell' = pi 'plural'

b. wicʰáša kĩ hípi   The men have come
'man' 'the' 'come = plural'

c. íkta   he will wear (something)
∅ '3 pers.' + ĩ 'wear' = kta 'future'

d. t'íkta   he is going to die
∅ '3 pers.' + t'a⁸ 'die' = kta

e. báka   he more or less blames him
∅ '3 pers.' + ba 'blame' = ka 'rather'

f. cʰíkešni   he is disinclined to do it
∅ '3 pers.' + cʰĩ 'want' = ka 'rather' = šni 'not'

g. éxca   (it's) this one here
e 'here' = xca 'very'

h. étu   it is here
e 'here' = tu verbalizer

The enclitic boundary, like the word boundary, blocks the DAR.

1.5 A number of surface forms that are apparent exceptions to the DAR are demonstrably nonexceptional if the DAR applies before the various rules of COALESCENCE. A number of processes reducing two initial syllables to one have been observed, although they have not yet been systematically incorporated into Dakota phonology (see Boas and Deloria 1941: 6-10 for dozens of examples). The following forms will illustrate the ordering relation between the DAR and the COALESCENCE rules:

(18)   Surface form   Underlying elements

a. tʰáze   tʰa + aze
udder   ruminant + breast

b. hécʰũšni   he + ecʰũ = šni
that cannot be done   that + to do + not

c. tʰówašte   tʰa + wo + wašte
his goodness   his + quality + good

d. wóγa	wa + yuγa	
to husk corn	with a knife + to husk	

Notice that the surface form for each of these occurs with accent on the first syllable, contrary to the DAR. Then notice that the underlying morphology for each of them includes a second syllable which coalesces with the first in the surface form: $a + a > a$ in (a), $e + e > e$ in (b), $a + wo > o$ in (c), and $a + yu > o$ in (d). If the DAR applies to the underlying rather than the surface form, these examples are perfectly regular. That is, the DAR accents the second syllable, as usual, and then COALESCENCE merges two syllables retaining the accent, as in the following derivation of (18)a:

(19) *underlying* # tʰa + aze #
      DAR   tʰa   áze
      COALESCENCE   tʰáze
      surface   [tʰáze]

COALESCENCE thus makes the DAR opaque. 'Exceptions' of this type were well known to Boas, and further observations of coalescence were almost certainly what he had in mind when he spoke of predicting accent after determining certain "vocalic modifications, not hitherto observed." But the hypothesis that accent might turn out to be predictable once all the coalescences are sorted out seems naive, since they do not account for all surface exceptions. However, the largest class of apparent exceptions that remains can be shown to be perfectly regular too, by the analysis advanced in §2.

2. THE *a*-TYPE ROOTS

The *a*-type roots, mentioned briefly in §1.1, constitute a large set of bisyllabic formatives with the distributional peculiarity that all of them end in *-a*. They make a significant class of apparent exceptions to the DAR since they all have the accent on the initial syllable. My point in this section is to show that the terminal, unaccented *-a* is not a part of the root at all,[9] which means that they are underlying monosyllables and therefore receive their accent regularly by the DAR. The argument that *-a* is not part of the root consists of an explication of some processes which these roots enter into: in all instances the root shows up as a monosyllable.

2.1 Noun roots as well as verb roots belong to this class. When the nouns occur as the first member of a compound, the *-a* is not included. Examples, contrasting the simple surface form of the noun and the *a*-less compounded form, are as follows:

(20) *Simple form*   *Compounded form*
    a. šŭka dog, horse   šŭk-mánitu   wolf (dog-god)
                                  šŭk-c^{h}ícala   colt (horse-child)
    b. hắpa mocassin   hăp-ítake   mocassin tongue

Some roots undergo certain characteristic morphophonemic changes when the terminal -*a* is not present. For example, roots with a voiced C preceding -*a* in the simple form show up with a voiceless C, as in the following example:

(21) máza metal   mas-íyap^{h}e   hammer (metal striker)
                       mas-íyokatã   nails (metal-to drive in)

A second alternation replaces /t/ preceding -*a* in the simple form by [l]:

(22) p^{h}éta fire   p^{h}el-íleye   kindling (fire-to cause to burn)

Another alternation deletes the final C of the root before consonant clusters:

(23)a. p^{h}éta fire   p^{h}e-šníža   sparks (fire-withered)
     b. šŭka dog, horse   šŭ-blóka   stallion (horse-male)

These surface alternations and a few others will be further exemplified in the following discussion of some other morphological processes, but a detailed analysis of them would take us too far afield from the morphological point that I am interested in. They are included because they are characteristic of the class of roots under discussion.

With respect to the main point, notice that the -*a* does not function as part of the root in compounds, and that these compounds are the type that take word accent rather than compound accent. That is, they are the result of the lexical compounding rule.

2.2 A second process involves the incorporation of object nouns into the verbal element. Incorporation is not obligatory, but is a morphological process with semantic consequences, as illustrated by the contrasting glosses on (24)a, and (24)b below, which are made up of the same formatives in non-incorporated and incorporated surface structures:

(24)a. *Non-incorporated*
       owắka kĭ yužáža   He is washing the floor.
       floor the (he)washes
    b. *Incorporated*
       owắk-yužaža   He is mopping (= floor-washing)

Notice that when the noun is incorporated the root occurs without the final *a*. Other examples illustrating the non-occurrence of *-a* with incorporated roots are as follows:

(25) *Simple form*   *Incorporated form*
 a. cʰápa beaver   cʰap-kʰúwa   He is beaver-hunting.
 b. tʰápa ball   tʰap-kápsica He is ball-hitting.

The following examples show the alternation of voiced final C with their voiceless counterparts in the incorporated forms:

(26) a. máγa garden max-kášla He is garden-hoeing.
  b. cáγa ice   cax-kázo   He is skating.
              (*lit.* marking the ice, ice-marking)

Examples showing the alternation of *t* and *l* are given in (27); (27)c extends this rule by showing that *c* alternates with *l* under the same conditions:

(27) a. pʰéta   fire   pʰel-kʰícãye   He is fire-tending.
  b. kʰắta   plum   kʰăl-yúšpi   He is plum-picking.
  c. wakšíca dishes wakšíl-yužaža   He is dish-washing.

Again the non-occurrence of the terminal segment is predictable in incorporated formatives derived by a rule of word formation.

2.3 Certain verb compounds involving *a*-type roots also illustrate the non-occurrence of *-a* in the first member, exactly parallel to the examples with nouns given in §2.1. A couple of examples are given in (16) above, including a further illustration of one of the morphophonemic alternations.

2.4 Reduplication of verbs of this class also illustrates the separability of the final *-a* from the root. The general rule for reduplication is that the entire simple form excluding *-a* is repeated.

(28) *Simple form*   *Reduplicated form*
 a. cʰépa to be fat   cʰepcʰépa to be very fat
 b. sápa   to be black   sapsápa
 c. šóka   to be thick   šokšóka
 d. tʰóka to be different tʰoktʰóka

As in (21) and (26), voiced C's preceding the -*a* in simple forms surface as their voiceless counterparts in reduplicated forms:

(29) a. núya   to be gnarled   nuxnúya
    b. píža   to be wrinkled   pišpíža
    c. púza   to be dry   puspúza

As in (23), the final C is deleted when the second element begins with a cluster:

(30) a. bléza   to be sane   blebléza
    b. ksápa   to be wise   ksaksápa
    c. ptéca   to be short   pteptéca
    d. spáya   to be wet   spaspáya
    e. xlóka   to be hole-y   xloxlóka

As in (22) and (27), when the final C is /t/ it surfaces as [l] under certain conditions:

(31) a. k^háta   to be hot k^halk^háta
    b. kítã   to be stubborn   kilkítã

Comparison of the forms in (22), (27), and (31) will show that the /t/ → [l] alternation is conditioned by a following [−coronal] consonant. On the other hand, when a final /t/ precedes a [+coronal] consonant, it alternates with [k]:

(32) a. zŭta   to be parallel   zŭkzŭta
    b. žáta   to be forked   žakžáta
    c. súta   to be hard   suksúta
    d. títã   to be forceful   tiktítã

Clearly, the rule which gives these alternations of /t/ with [l] and [k] has the result of eliminating /t/ as the first element in a derived consonant cluster. The segment /c/ is similarly precluded as the first element in a derived cluster, as has already been suggested by the /c/ → [l] alternation shown in (27)c. In fact, the alternations involving /c/ are exactly parallel to those involving /t/: /c/ → [l] before a [−coronal] consonant, as shown in (33), and [k] before a [+coronal] consonant, as shown in (34):

(33) a. k^héca   to be like that k^helk^héca
    b. k^híca   to scrape off top layer k^hïlk^híca
    c. p^híca   to be rather good p^hilp^híca
    d. xíca   to awaken someone   xilxíca

(34) a. tʰéca   to be new   tʰektʰéca
     b. cʰéca   to be similar   cʰekcʰéca
     c. šíca   to be bad   šikšíca
     d. žíca   to be rich   žikžíca
     e. níca   to lack   nikníca

In all of these examples, the terminal -*a* does not show up when the root undergoes a word formation process.

2.5 The word formation rules of compounding, incorporation and reduplication, then, all provide evidence for distinguishing the terminal -*a* from the rest of the root, or, more precisely, from the root proper. Such roots should therefore be entered in the lexicon in their *a*-less, C-final forms, as *šũk* 'dog horse', *tʰap* 'ball', *nuɣ* 'to be gnarled', *ptec* 'to be short', *žat* 'to be forked' and so on. The environment in which the morphophonemic rules apply to give the alternations listed above always involves the boundary '|'. Conversely, it might be said that the word formation boundary and the terminal -*a* are mutually exclusive, and that the morphophonemics only apply when the -*a* is not attached. The insertion of -*a* is therefore predictable whenever a C-final root occurs before either of the boundaries = or # (that is, the enclitic boundary and the word boundary, respectively). Unlike the verbs discussed in §1.1, the *a*-type roots cannot stand alone as stems, but require the insertion of -*a* as a stem-formative. Only then can they co-occur with enclitics or stand as unaffixed stems in the syntagm. The stem-formative can be inserted by a simple rule, as follows:

(35) STEM FORMATION $\emptyset \rightarrow a \:/\: C \_\_\_ \begin{Bmatrix} = \\ \# \end{Bmatrix}$

Such a rule does not seem very plausible as a phonological rule of epenthesis, because unlike rules of epenthesis it does not apply in an environment which would otherwise violate a phonotactic constraint in the language. Words do occur in Dakota with consonant finals, although such words are infrequent. Rule (35) seems to have status as a morphological rule, however, as the term "stem formation" would imply. Such status is consistent with its relation to other rules in the language. As far as I know now, rule (35) can be ordered before any of the patently phonological rules in the grammar. For at least two of the phonological rules, STEM FORMATION must come first. One of these is the rule that changes /a/ to [e] before certain morphemes (see note 5). The stem-formative *a* undergoes this rule, and hence must be inserted before the rule applies. The other one is VELAR PALATALIZATION (Shaw 1975, in this volume), by which /k/ becomes [c] in the environment between non-low front vowels and a following vowel. The stem-formative often completes the environment, and thus feeds palatalization. On the other hand there is no phonological rule which must precede STEM FORMATION other than the DAR.

2.6 The analysis of terminal -*a* as a stem-formative rather than a segment of the root proper makes a significant claim about the restructuring of this branch of Siouan. Historically, all such *a*'s are segments of the root. However, the analysis of *a* as a stem-formative explains an otherwise curious discrepancy in the evolution of Dakota from Proto-Siouan, namely, the tendency of Proto-Siouan final vowels to occur in Dakota as /a/, no matter what the normal reflexes of such vowels are in other environments. Thus the historical neutralization of final vowels to /a/ correlates with the re-analysis of such vowels as a separate morpheme. Some examples of the etymological neutralization of various root-final vowels are given in the following list, with proto-forms from Matthews (1970:107–8) unless otherwise noted:

(36)   *Proto-Siouan*   *Dakota*
  a. *í > a   *xapí   (yu)γápa   strip, pull off
  b. *i > a   *k'ési   k'éza   scratch
               *péti (Wolff 1950:169) pʰéta   fire
               *rúti   yúta   eat
               *wǎki   wǎká   lie, be
  c. *é > a   *hǎské (Wolff 1950:176) hǎska   tall
               *t'e   t'a   die
  d. *e/*i > a { *xote (Matthews) } xóta   grey
               { *xoti (Wolff)   }
  e. *e > a   *mǎxe   iwǎya   inquire
               *rúše   yúza   grasp
               *šóte   šóta   muddy
               *tape (Wolff 1950:169) tʰápa   ball
               *wyéxe   cʰéγa   kettle
  f. *ó > a   *xro   xna   rattle

Historically, Matthews notes that in the branch of Siouan that includes Dakota "there has been a general tendency to move the stress to the penultimate [i.e., the first] syllable of the stem" (1970:98). This tendency and the tendency to neutralize final vowels converge, if we assume that the DAR was operative at an early stage in the development of the Dakota branch. As Proto-Siouan roots came to be reanalysed in Dakota as monosyllabic, the accent was placed on the vowel of the root proper, constituting an accent shift diachronically, and the low functional load of the final vowels permitted a wholesale merger into the least marked vowel in the inventory.

NOTES

[1] Dakota is used throughout as a generic term for a branch of the Siouan family comprised roughly as follows:

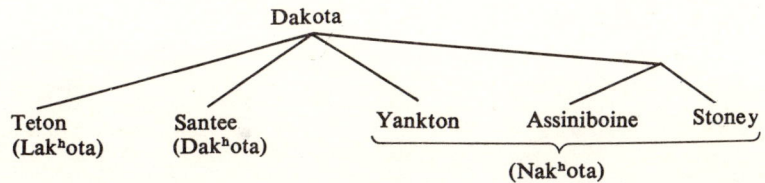

Teton, from which the data in this paper are drawn, is spoken in southern Saskatchewan and in several areas of the midwestern United States. Santee is spoken in southern Manitoba, and Yankton in northern Saskatchewan, as well as in the midwestern States. Stoney is spoken throughout Alberta, and Assiniboine in Montana. Generalizations based on Teton data in this paper are hypothesized to hold for all the Dakota dialects.

Notation is generally straightforward, except that c is used for č, that is, to symbolize the [−anterior, +coronal] affricate. Segments marked by a prime (as t', k') are glottalized.

I am grateful to Patricia Shaw, Jonathan Kaye, and Ed Cook, who did what they could to make this a better paper than it is, and to David Rood, who elicited some additional forms for me.

[2] Boas never did follow up the suggestion made here. His later sketch (Boas and Deloria 1932) does not discuss accent at all, and his grammar (Boas and Deloria 1941), while pointing out a number of regularities, concludes: "It is difficult to give a generally valid rule" (1941:22).

[3] Pronoun infixing is usually explained in terms of the fact that these verb roots are (historically) compounds, so that the effect of infixing is to 'prefix' the pronouns to the main verbal element in the usual way. Thus, $c^howkũ$ 'to plan to kill someone', has paradigmatic forms:

    $c^howákũ$ $c^ho|wa+kũ$ I plan to kill someone
    $c^hoyákũ$ you plan to kill someone
    $c^hoũkũpi$ we plan to kill someone

(The latter two forms are from Riggs 1890.)

[4] The order of personal pronouns in the VP is governed by a surface structure constraint (Shaw 1974:215). Pronoun order is III-I-II, regardless of function.

[5] Certain a's become e when followed by a particular set of morphemes. For details, see Boas and Deloria 1941:29; and Shaw 1975 (in this volume).

[6] Root-final t alternates with l except before the stem-formative a. See §2 below, especially the examples cited in (22), (27), and (31).

[7] Root-final consonants are voiceless except before the stem-formative a. See (21), (26), and (29) below for further examples.

⁸ Certain *a*'s become *i* when followed by a particular set of morphemes, a process probably related to the one mentioned in note 5.
⁹ This claim is implicit in Boas, since he continually refers to roots of this type as CVC and CCVC, that is, in terms of their canonical shape with the terminal *-a* deleted. However, he always includes the *-a* when he cites specific roots, and includes it in his discussions of the morphophonemics.

PALATALIZATIONS AND RELATED RULES IN SARCEE*

EUNG-DO COOK

The University of Calgary

0. The purpose of this paper is to discuss the palatalization processes in Sarcee with particular reference to such notions as rule ordering and abstractness of underlying representations. In the first three sections, I shall deal with palatalizations as synchronic processes, and in the last section I shall discuss a diachronic process of palatalization and its implications for the development of the Athapaskan stem-initial consonants.

The palatalization rules, which will be presented in some detail, interact with other rules of the grammar. While the mainstream of discussion will focus on the palatalizations, other rules which interact with the palatalizations will be discussed as much as they are relevant to the main problem.

1. One of the palatalizations, which I call 'S-Palatalization', is the contraction of *s* with the following stem-initial *y* yielding *š*:[1]

(1)a. dìšá ← di + s + ∅ + ya   'I will start off'
         asp   subj C   stem   (C = classifier)
    b. dìyá ← di + ∅ + ∅ + ya   'he will start off'
(2)a. xààníšúd ← xa + i + ni + s + ∅ + yud   'I will chase them'
         adv obj mod subj C stem
    b. xààniwúd ← xa − i − ni − ni − ∅ − yud   'you will chase them'

In (1)a the subject morpheme is *s* which contracts with the following *y*, while in (1)b the subject morpheme is phonologically zero and S-Palatalization does not apply. In examples (2), S-Palatalization applies in the same way as in examples (1), but there are a few other rules that are required for the derivation of the sentences in (2). In (2)b, the subject is *ni* (2p.sg.) which is deleted by a rule which need not concern us here (see Cook 1971a, 1971c). In (2)a, the vowel *i* (indefinite object) assimilates to the preceding vowel. I shall call this 'I-Assimilation' for future reference. Finally, the derivation of (2)b requires a rule which converts stem-initial *y* to *w* ($y \rightarrow w\ /\ \_\_\_\_$ u). Because of this latter rule, which I call 'Back Gliding', and of S-Palatalization the initial consonant of stem 'to chase' is realized always as *š* or *w*, but never as *y*. This raises an interesting question which will be discussed along with another similar problem in section 2. I shall now return to S-Palatalization:

R1 S-Palatalization: s + y → š

Apparent counter-examples to S-Palatalization, i.e. surface phonological representations which are opaque[2] with respect to R1, would include (3a) and (3b), among others, where the sequence of *s* + *y* remains on the surface:

(3)a. ídísyił   'I will stumble'
   b. nátsìnìsyiłt   'I banged my head against you'

It is, however, not difficult to see why these two do not constitute counter-examples if one examines the inputs to R1 given below:

   a. i + di + s + l + yił
   b. na + tsi + ni + s + l + yiłt

The so-called classifiers of Sarcee are ∅, *d*, *l*, and *s*.[3] The classifier is ∅ in examples (1) and (2) and *l* in the examples (3). I have argued elsewhere (Cook 1971b) why the classifier in (3) should be *l* underlyingly, although it is never realized as *l* on the phonetic surface; it is deleted following a consonant (as in (3)) or is assimilated to a preceding vowel. What is apparent from the underlying structures of (3)a and (3)b is that the classifier *l* blocks S-Palatalization. This fact can be accounted for by ordering 'L-Deletion' after S-Palatalization as illustrated by the following derivations:

di + s + ya	Input	i + di + s + l + yił
diša	S-Palatalization	
—	L-Deletion	idisyił
dìšá	Other rules	ídísyił

These two rules as they stand now are in nonfeeding order, and if the order is reversed L-Deletion would feed S-Palatalization. But this rule order would yield ungrammatical strings. This is what will also happen, if the two rules are unordered, since the underlying structure meets the structural description of L-Deletion first, the output of which then feeds S-Palatalization.

The l-classifier is not the only segment which may occur between the subject morpheme *s* (1p.sg.) or *as* (2p.pl.) and the stem-initial consonant; either the s-classifier or the d-classifier may also occur in place of the l-classifier. As we shall see, the intervening s-classifier does not, but the intervening d-classifier does, block S-Palatalization. Consider the following examples:

(4)a. máguŝō ← ma + gu + s + s + yo   'I will learn it'
              obj   theme subj C stem
   b. γáguŝō ← γa + gu + ∅ + s + yo   'he will learn it'

Since the subject morpheme in (4)a is *s* which is homophonous with the ·s-classifier, a geminate cluster of *ss* precedes the stem initial *y*. This geminate cluster is reduced to a single consonant (the details of which are discussed in Cook 1971c) by a rule which I call 'C-Reduction', after which S-Palatalization is applied as illustrated by the following derivation.

ma + gu + s + s + yo	Input
ma + gu + s + yo	C-Reduction
maguŝo	S-Palatalization
máguŝō	Other

The two rules seem to apply in feeding order, but they are not necessarily in a feeding relationship, since S-Palatalization applies whether or not the geminate cluster is reduced. In other words, the rules can be applied in the reverse order, in which case the subject *s* must delete after S-Palatalization. The rule which deletes *s*, however, is not motivated otherwise, whereas C-Reduction is, hence the order shown in the above derivation.

The *d*-classifier, on the other hand, contracts with the stem-initial *y* yielding an affricate *dž* by the so-called 'D-Effect' which is a well-known process in the Athapaskan languages (see Howren 1971).

A second group of apparent counterexamples to S-Palatalization includes (5)a and (5)b where *s* and *y* remain intact on the phonetic surface even though there is no intervening *l* or any other consonant:

(5)a. nìsyíɬ ← ni + s + ∅ + yiɬ   'I am crazy'
              mod subj C stem
   b. mīk'ánìsyìs ← mi + k'a + ni + s + ∅ + yis   'I'll break it'
              obj   pp   asp subj C stem

Notice the sequence of *s* plus *y* in the above strings to which S-Palatalization is apparently applicable but not applied. One might consider that stems like *yiɬ* 'to be crazy' and *yis* 'to break' are exceptions to S-Palatalization and should be marked as such in the lexicon. This is certainly not an interesting solution, nor an insightful one. A more interesting solution to the problem is to derive the stem-initial *y* from underlying *γ*. The choice of *γ* as the underlying segment is not an arbitrary one, but is based upon yet another

process which I call 'Glide-Formation' by which the underlying ɣ becomes
y before i and w before u:

$$\text{R2 Glide Formation:} \quad ɣ \rightarrow \begin{Bmatrix} y\ /\ \underline{\quad}\ i \\ w\ /\ \underline{\quad}\ u \end{Bmatrix}$$

This process, which operates both in stem phonology and prefix phonology, is illustrated by the following examples:

(6)a. nìsyíɬ ← ni + s + ∅ + ɣiɬ   'I am crazy'
             mod subj C stem
   b. gúswūl ← gu + s + ∅ + ɣul   'I am scratching it'
             obj subj C stem
   c. dúùyīsʔíh ← du + i + ɣi + s + ∅ + ʔih   'I do not see'
             neg theme asp subj C stem
   d. dúùɣāàʔih ← du + i + ɣi + aa + ∅ + ʔih   'we do not see'
             neg theme asp subj C stem

This means, of course, that ɣ underlies the stem-initial of (5)a = (6)a and of (5)b. The reason that the *sy* sequence remains unaffected by S-Palatalization is obvious in the light of the ordering relationship of S-Palatalization and Glide Formation. In other words, examples presented in (5) do not constitute counterexamples if S-Palatalization and Glide Formation apply in that order where ɣ represents the stem-initial consonant.

To digress a little, consider (6)c and (6)d. In (6)c R2 applies as expected to ɣ of prefix ɣi, whereas the same segment in (6)d is not affected by this rule, since R2 is bled by another rule which I call 'I-Deletion' (i → ∅ / __ a).[4] It is interesting to note the ways in which the three pairs of rules interact in the derivation of apparent counterexamples. The first group of apparent counterexamples are accounted for in terms of S-Palatalization and L-Deletion in that order, i.e. nonfeeding order. The reverse order would feed S-Palatalization, but that does not happen. The second group of counterexamples are accounted for in terms of S-Palatalization and Glide Formation in that order, i.e. again in nonfeeding order. In the case of (6)c and (6)d, I-Deletion and Glide Formation apply in that order, i.e. bleeding order.

To recapitulate, the underlying stem-initial consonant of verb stems 'to be crazy' (5)a, 'to break' (5)b, and 'to scratch' (6)b is posulated as ɣ, although there is no allomorph which contains stem-initial ɣ because the initial consonant is always realized as y or w as the case may be. This fact may be due to pure coincidence that the vowel which follows the stem-initial happens to be either *i* or *u* without involving any ablaut.[5] Since the surface representation is always *y* or *w*, one might question the validity of this analysis. The representation of ɣ is abstract to the extent that it never alternates with *y* in paradigms like 'to be crazy' or with *w* in paradigms like 'to scratch'; on the other hand, ɣ is not an abstract representation in that it appears elsewhere on the phonetic level. As mentioned above, the lack of alternation between ɣ and *y* or *w* as stem-initial consonants is coincidental to the lack of vowel ablaut in such verb paradigms as 'to be crazy' and 'to scratch'. If these verb stems were to inflect by ablauting *i* to *a*, the stem-initial ɣ would certainly show up before *a*, hence ɣ alternating with *y* or *w*. This assumption is supported by the alternation between ɣ and *y* before *a* and *i* respectively as shown in verb paradigms like (7). This provides further reason to believe that ɣ is the most reasonable segment to represent the underlying stem-initial consonant.

(7)a. dāsyás ← di + as + l + ɣas   'ye will run'
              asp subj C   stem
    b. ɣāsyīs ← ɣi + as + l + ɣis   'ye are running'

2. If what the principle of internal reconstruction indicates is correct, the stem-initial ɣ which has been postulated as the underlying segment must be a historical reality. I can offer additional synchronic as well as diachronic evidence to attest the initial ɣ. From the analysis given above, I would like to single out a fact which bears upon the issue on hand. As shown in the analysis of (1) and (2), the underlying stem-initial *y* causes the preceding *s* to be palatalized (S-Palatalization), whereas the *y* which derives from underlying ɣ as shown by the analysis of (5) does not cause S-Palatalization. In other words, while it is apparent that there are two sources, namely *y* and ɣ, for all cases of surface *y*, there is good reason to believe all surface *w*'s derive from underlying ɣ as far as stem-initials are concerned. First of all, the only vowel that occurs after the initial *w* is *u* (while *i* is not the only vowel which occurs after the initial *y*). In other words, there is not a single sequence of the form [wi], [wa], or [wo]. Secondly, in Sapir's notes as well as in my own, [ɣʷ] is occasionally found where [w] is normally expected, suggesting the development of [w] from ɣ via [ɣʷ]. Thirdly, there are less than a dozen verb stems whose initial is realized as [w] or [ɣʷ] always followed by a stem vowel *u* which does not alternate, and there is only one stem, namely 'to chase' (2), whose initial is [š] or [w].

Those stems whose initial is always [w] or [ɣʷ] do not present any real problem as it is quite reasonable to assume that the underlying initial is ɣ to which Glide Formation applies. The case of stem 'to chase', however, does not render itself a simple solution. From a strictly synchronic point of view, three solutions are possible, one with stem-initial y, another with ɣ, and a third with w. The underlying stem-initial assumed in (2) is ɣ. With the underlying ɣ, let us consider the derivation of the two sentences given in (2):

xa + i + ni + s + ɣud	Input	xa + i + ni + ɣud
xa + i + ni + šud	S-Palatalization	—
—	Back Gliding	xa + i + ni + wud
xa + a + ni + šud	I-Assimilation	xa + a + ni + wud
xàànìšúd	Other rules	xàànìwúd
'I'll chase them'		'you'll chase them'

What is particularly interesting in the above derivation is the structure provided by the sequence $s + \gamma ud$, wherein S-Palatalization and Back Gliding obtain a mutually bleeding relationship. In other words, if S-Palatalization applies, as it does in the above derivation, the string results in *šud*, on the other hand Back Gliding could apply to the same string, yielding *swud*. This means, of course, that the two rules S-Palatalization and Back Gliding work correctly only in that linear order. The only unattractive feature of this solution is that there is no strong evidence that Back Gliding is a synchronic rule.

As an alternative analysis, let us assume that ɣ is the stem-initial instead of y and that R1 (S-Palatalization) is revised as follows:

$$s \left\{ \begin{matrix} \gamma \\ w \end{matrix} \right\} \rightarrow š$$

In this solution Back Gliding is no longer relevant as shown in the following derivations:

xa + i + s + ɣud	Input	xa + i + ni + ɣud
xa + i + s + wud	Glide Formation	xa + i + ni + wud
xa + i + šud	S-Palatalization	
xa + a + šud	I-Assimilation	xa + a + ni + wud
xàànìšúd	Other rules	xàànìwúd

This solution sounds quite reasonable in that no Back Gliding is required and Glide Formation and S-Palatalization apply in a feeding order. The most unattractive feature of this solution is the assumption that *s* contracts not only with y, but also with w as shown above.

A more transparent solution is to posit *w* as the underlying stem-initial consonant. Obviously, neither Glide Formation nor Back Gliding is necessary, but S-Palatalization must be in the revised form as in the second solution. What makes this solution attractive is the underlying stem initial *w* which shows up on the phonetic surface in one allomorph of the verb. As we have seen already in the first solution the underlying *y* never appears in any allomorph of the verb stem, since S-Palatalization contracts the *y* with a preceding *s* or Back Gliding converts it to *w*. Similarly, in the second solution, the underlying γ never surfaces due to S-Palatalization and Glide Formation. This is why the third solution is the least abstract.

It is not easy to make a choice among these three solutions from a purely synchronic point of view. It is interesting to note that Sapir and Li treated the verb stem ('to chase') as one of the γ-initial stems, i.e. an analysis comparable to our second solution. This seems to be the most reasonable solution from the point of view of internal reconstruction, apparently reasonable enough for Sapir and Li to accept. However, what is assumed of diachronic development suggested by the analysis of stem 'to chase' in the second solution is wrong as indicated by the following comparative data. Consider the imperfective forms which are cognates:

Sarcee	wud (Sapir 1922, Cook 1973)	
Chipewyan	yur (Li 1933b)	
Galice	yad (Hoijer 1973)	(tones unmarked)
Hupa	yod (Golla 1970)	
Navajo	yood	

It is clear that the above Sarcee stem-initial *w* develops from Athapaskan *y* rather than γ. This *y* in Sarcee becomes *w* before vowel *u* (Back Gliding) or contracts with a preceding *s* (S-Palatalization). This fact, incidentally, is what causes the skewed distribution of *y* (which occurs before all vowels except the high back) and explains why the D-effect rule does not involve any stem-initial *w*. This means that the surface stem-initial *w* has two historical sources as shown below:

Pre-Sarcee[6]
*γ → *w* before *u*, *y* before *i*, γ elsewhere
*y → *w* before *u*, *y* elsewhere

The comparative evidence brought forward proves how wrong what is assumed from internal data alone could be. Furthermore, this confirms the correctness of the nonfeeding rule order of R1 and R2, which accounts for the data that are opaque with respect to R1.

The following summarizes how S-Palatalization interacts with other rules:

S-Palatalization
L-Deletion
Glide Formation
Back Gliding

An interesting point is that the rule ordering shown above is nonfeeding and the relationship between I-Deletion and Glide Formation is bleeding. No two rules that have been presented so far are in a feeding relationship.

3. As we have seen, S-Palatalization contracts *s* and *y* across a morpheme boundary, whereas the domain of a second type of palatalization which I call 'C-Palatalization' is an entire word as it affects every specified segment in the word.

The process of C-Palatalization, to state it informally, is a recursive regressive assimilation of a nonpalatal sibilant (including affricatives) to a corresponding palatal sibilant. What is typically observed is that if a stem of the canonical form $C_1V(C_2)$, or very rarely $C_1V(C_2)(C_3)$, has a palatal sibilant, e.g. *š*, *dž*, *tš*, any preceding (but not following) nonpalatal sibilant or sibilants, e.g. *s*, *z*, *ts*, become palatalized. The following exemplifies this process:

(8)a. šítšídzàʔ ← si + tšiz + aʔ   'my duck'   Cf. tšíz   'duck'
   b. sìtšógò ← si + tšogo   'my flank'   Cf. sìtsáɣà 'my hair'

In (8a) the noun stem begins in a sibilant, namely *tš* which causes palatalization of *s* of *si* 'my' to *š*. Notice that the nonpalatal sibilant which follows the palatal sibilant is not affected (the final fricative *z* becomes affricated before a vowel), hence the process is regressive, i.e. from right to left. Consider the following verbs:

(9)a. nāšɣátš ← na + ∅ + s + ∅ + ɣatš   'I killed them again'
              asp obj subj C   stem
      Cf. yīsɣá 'I killed them'
   b. mítš'ìdìšwùšt ← mi + ts'i + di + ∅ + s + wušt
                    obj   pp   asp subj C stem
      'someone whistled at him'

The stem-final *tš* of (9)a causes the palatalization of *s* (1p.sg.subj.) to *š*, and the second last stem consonant of (9)b, namely *š* causes palatalization of the classifier *s* to *š*, which in turn causes the palatalization of *ts'* of postposition *ts'i* to *tš'*.

Although C-Palatalization applies, in principle, to every sibilant that precedes the right-most palatal sibilant in the word, it has been observed that the force of palatalization becomes gradually weaker as it gets farther from the palatal sibilant which originally triggers the process. Notice in (10)a that the process covers all the relevant sibilants, while in (10)b it does not reach to the left-most sibilant, namely *ts'*.

(10)a. šátš'ìgùsišáy   'you forgot me'
    b. mīts'ìdīšīšwùšt   'I whistled to him'

The main problem associated with C-Palatalization arises from such data as those in (12) in which š (palatal) appears where *s* (nonpalatal) is expected. Examples like those in (12), therefore, constitute opacity with respect to C-Palatalization, which falls under Definition (ii) as defined originally by Kiparsky (1971) and revised recently by Kaye (1974).

(11)a. dínísyāl   'I am round'
    b. dínásyāl   'ye are round'
(12)a. ìnīšyá   'I am named'
    b. ìšīšwú   'I am ready'

A simple solution in which examples like (12) are treated as exceptions would not answer such a diachronic question, no matter how well it may be justified on purely synchronic grounds, as how such exceptions have come to exist. As usual, the kind of opacity shown in (12) is due to the fact that the segment which caused C-Palatalization has been eliminated by a subsequent rule or rules. With this general historical process in mind, we may consider the following two possibilities. First, one may assume (however unlikely) that the stem of (12) has an underlying final consonant which is a palatal sibilant. That such an assumption is false can be attested by stems like *yih* (imperfective) and *yin* (perfective) 'to sing' whose nonpalatal sibilants occurring in the prefix complex are palatalized despite the fact that the stem-final consonant is not a palatal sibilant. Pursuing further along the same line of reasoning, one might still look for the possibility that stems like *yih/yin* have an underlying final cluster of CC, the second of which being a palatal sibilant. This, however, is not the case either, since the second consonant, if it occurs at all, marks an aspect category and in the case of *yih* (← *yiṇ*) and *yin*, the distinction between the imperfective and the perfective is made by alternating syllable types, a light syllable for the imperfective and a heavy syllable for the perfective (see Cook 1972). Second, it may be assumed that the stem-initial *y* which causes C-Palatalization as in (12) is underlyingly different from the initial *y* which does not as in (11).[7] Therefore, I propose that the stem-initial consonant of (12) which causes C-Palatalization derives from a dorso-palatal fricative, namely γ^y.[8] With this underlying stem-initial consonant, we shall see how the examples in (12) are generated:

(12)a. i + ni + s + γ^ya   Input
      i + ni + š + γ^ya   C-Palatalization
      inīšya 'I'm named'   Other rules
  b. i + si + s + γ^yu   Input
      i + ši + š + γ^yu   C-Palatalization
      išišwú 'I'm ready'   Other rules

An immediate question at this point is what is the 'other' rule that applies after C-Palatalization in the above derivation. It is apparent that γ^y is 'depalatalized' in the derivation of (12)a, while γ^y became a glide in the derivation of (12)b. In other words, this rule causes γ^y to merge with γ neutralizing the underlying contrast, i.e. both γ and γ^y become y before i, w before u, and γ elsewhere as illustrated by examples like in (12) and (13):

(13)a. nādžánādìsyì   'I will be refreshed'
  b. nādžánādìšyáy   'he has become refreshed'

This suggests that Glide Formation (R2) presented in the preceding section is part of a larger rule which may be formulated something like the following:[9]

$$\left\{\begin{array}{c}\gamma\\\gamma^y\end{array}\right\} \to \left\{\begin{array}{l}y \,/ \underline{\quad} \, i\\w \,/ \underline{\quad} \, u\\\gamma\end{array}\right\}$$

Quite clearly, one can assume the above synchronic rule reflects historical developments of the underlying γ^y. Although no comparative data are presented here to attest the historical reality of γ^y, there is good reason to believe that the above analysis actually reflects historical facts and that it seems to shed new light on the Proto-Athapaskan consonantal system originally proposed by Sapir (1915 and 1931) and later studied by Li (1933a) and Hoijer (1963), and most recently revised by Krauss (1964). Among the three sets of Athapaskan initial consonants, Sapir shows the following correspondences between the Athapaskan and Sarcee:[10]

III.	Athapaskan	Sarcee
1.	x^y	š
2.	y	y
3.	gy	dž
4.	ky	tš
5.	ky'	tš'

The regular sound change observed above is from the dorso-palatal to the alveo-palatal with the exception of the second consonant. What strikes me first in the above correspondences is that all Athapaskan dorso-palatals have become Sarcee (alveo) palatal sibilants which cause C-palatalization except the second, namely y. In other words, the second consonant of Series III is an exception to the regular sound change which has never been adequately explained in my knowledge. Secondly, as shown in Athapaskan Series I and II which are merged in Sarcee, the fricatives contrast between the voiceless and the voiced, i.e. s and z contrast in I and š and ž contrast in II:

I & II.	Athapaskan	Sarcee
	s, š	s
	z, ž	z
	dz, dž	dz
	ts, tš	ts
	ts', tš'	ts'

This structural fact suggests that y in Series III does not fit into the picture, since neither the Athapaskan fricative pair y and x^y, nor the Sarcee counterpart, y and š, contrast in voicing only. Therefore, the second Athapaskan consonant in Series III that fits into the structural symmetry is y^y, one which has been postulated as an underlying stem-initial consonant of Sarcee on the basis of C-Palatalization and Glide Formation. This, of course, means that Athapaskan y^y remains as y^y in Sarcee rather than changed to ž which is what one would expect from the regular change observed in Series III. (This problem will be discussed in the following section.) This analysis, however, does not rule out the existence of Athapaskan y which remains as y in Sarcee as discussed in the preceding section. What I am suggesting is that the Sarcee reflex of the Athapaskan y causes S-Palatalization, the output of which, in turn, causes C-Palatalization, whereas the Sarcee reflex of the Athapaskan y^y causes C-Palatalization only.

Having drawn this conclusion, I was delighted to note Hoijer's interpretation of Sapir's PA *y in a footnote (Hoijer 1963:5):

[5]P.A. probably had two y-phonemes: one a front palatal voiced spirant (the voiced equivalent of *xy) and the other a semivowel. These appear to have fallen together in some of the daughter languages. *Our P.A. *y represents the spirant, not the semivowel* (emphasis added).

Clearly, Sarcee is one of those 'daughter languages' in which the 'two y-phonemes have fallen together' on the phonetic surface, while they are still distinctive in a deeper level.

4. With the above analysis, I now propose to revise Sapir's Series III stem-initial consonant correspondences as follows:

	Athapaskan	Sarcee
1.	x^y	š
2.	γ^y	γ^y ($\to$ [ɣ, y])
3.	g^y	dž
4.	k^y	tš
5.	$k^{y'}$	tš'

This analysis leaves two puzzling questions unanswered. First of all, why does the Athapaskan $*\gamma^y$ not correspond to Sarcee ž, which is what is expected according to the regular correspondences shown in other dorso-palatals? Second, if this analysis is correct, what is the status of voiced fricatives in Proto-Athapaskan? These are the questions I shall attempt to answer in this section.

To state the conclusion first, Athapaskan $*\gamma^y$ does in fact correspond to Sarcee ž as well as to γ^y ($\to$ [ɣ, y, w]) in Sarcee![11] This conclusion is drawn from the examination of such verbs as the following set:

(14) a. nìšíšγá 'I grew up'
 b. nìšāšγá 'ye grew up'
(15) a. šìšdžó 'I am (got) old'
 b. šídžó 'you are old'
 c. šāàdžó 'we are old'
(16) a. nīšó 'I will raise him'
 b. nīśó 'you will raise him'
 c. nāàžó 'we will raise him'

The alternation between the two vowels, namely *a* and *o* are quite frequent in older Sarcee as shown in Sapir's field notes, and *a* of contemporary Sarcee often corresponds to *o* of older Sarcee. Therefore, we shall disregard this difference in the above three sets of sentences. As observed in many Athapaskan languages, related 'themes' (e.g. neuter vs active, intransitive vs transitive (causative), etc.) are derivable from a common stem by affixing the so-called classifiers and/or other derivational prefixes.[12] The three different verbal themes in (14)-(16) above, therefore, are derived from the same stem with the three different classifiers: in (14) theme 'to grow up' is expressed by the stem alone (i.e. with the ∅-classifier), in (15) theme 'to get old' is analyzable in terms of the *d*-classifier plus stem -γ^yo, the initial affricate dž being the result of D-effect (i.e. d + γ^y → dž), and in (16) the transitive/causative theme 'to raise (to make X grow)' is analyzable in terms of the *s*-classifier plus the stem (see below for the alternation of the surface initial *š* and *ž*). In short, it is quite reasonable to assume that the three verbal themes are derived (historically at least) from the same stem with three different classifiers.

There are two facts that suggest the underlying stem-initial consonant is y^y (which never shows up on the surface) rather than y (which does show up). First, the effect of C-Palatalization is transparent in three sets of sentences, e.g. *s*- (1p.sg.subj.) and *si*- (perfective) are realized by *š*- and *ši*- respectively. This means, according to the analysis presented in the preceding section, that the stem-initial segment is y^y rather than y. Secondly, according to the D-effect process, *d* plus y yields *g*, while *d* plus y^y yields *dž*, which is what we have for the sentences in (15).

These facts lead one to assume the following are underlying representations of the three derivationally related themes:

(i) $\emptyset$ + y^ya 'to grow'
(ii) d + y^yo 'to get old'
(iii) s + y^yo 'to raise' (to make X grow)

Assuming the above are correct underlying representations of a synchronic analysis, let us examine how the three different surface stem-initial consonants are derived. As mentioned above $d + y^y$ sequence (ii) becomes *dž* by the D-effect rule and no further problem remains for the theme 'to get old'. The stem-initial y of (14) is accountable in terms of depalatalization (see R3) by which underlying y^y becomes y before *a* as illustrated by the derivation of sentence (12)a in section 3. This leaves us with the alternating stem-initials *š* and *ž* of (16). The crucial problem is that there is no reasonable synchronic rule that would derive *ž* from underlying y^y. This means that the underlying stem-initial consonant of (iii) is no longer y^y in modern Sarcee. In order to account for the alternation between *š* and *ž* as shown in (16), (iii) must be represented underlyingly as follows:

(iii) s + žo

The classifier *s* devoices *ž* to *š*, and then gets deleted, hence (16)a and (16)b; the classifier gets deleted before devoicing the stem-initial if *aad* 'we' precedes,[13] hence (16)c.

What should be noted here is the historical change of y^y to *ž*. It is obvious that not all pre-Sarcee stem-initial y^y changed to Sarcee *ž*; the change has taken place only when the *s*-classifier precedes. In other words, the pre-Sarcee stem-initial y^y has not changed after classifiers $\emptyset$, *d*-, or *l*-. The fact that sentences with theme 'to grow up' ($\emptyset + \gamma^y o$) do not have any alternating initial $\check{z}$ attests to this fact. Furthermore, there are only three other themes whose stem-initial consonant alternates between $\check{s}$ and $\check{z}$ under exactly the same condition as theme 'to raise' (s + $\gamma^y o$). The following sentences further illustrate this point:

(17)a. nīkānī́šā   'I am bothering you'
    b. nīkāgìmììžā   'we are bothering them'
(18)a. mátš'ìgùšíšāy   'I forgot about it'
    b. mátš'ìgùšììžáy   'we forgot about it'
(19)a. mágùšìšāt   'I learned it'
    b. mágùšììžāt   'we learned about it'

In all these sentences the stem-initial consonant is undoubtedly $\check{z}$. This, however, does not necessarily mean that the $\check{z}$ corresponds to pre-Sarcee γ^y. There are, however, two quite good reasons to believe that the initial $\check{z}$ does in fact correspond to pre-Sarcee γ^y. First of all, there are only four verb stems (so far recorded) in which $\check{s}$ and $\check{z}$ alternate initially, and in all these cases, the co-occurring classifier is s or $\emptyset$. Secondly, a more interesting fact is that Sapir recorded one sentence (20)a and I recorded one sentence (20)b where γ shows up in place of $\check{z}$ and $\check{s}$, the theme being identical or derivationally related (one cannot tell for sure from the glosses) to that of (19):

(20)a. mágùnāàyāh   'we know about it' (Sapir)
    b. mágùnììyāt   'we know about it' (Cook)

The two sentences are identical, the phonological difference of the subject prefix (āà vs ìì) (see note 13) and of the final consonant (h vs t) being insignificant. Two explanations are possible for the stem-initial y of (20). First, there are two themes based on the same stem, one with the $\emptyset$-classifier, namely $\emptyset + \gamma^y at$ 'to know', another with the s-classifier, namely s + $\gamma^y at$ 'to learn'. Alternatively, the sentences in (20) are archaic forms whose underlying stem-initial has not yet undergone the change ($\gamma^y \rightarrow \check{z}$).[14] In any case, it is apparent that the stem-initial in question must have derived historically from pre-Sarcee γ^y.

To summarize, the Athapaskan or pre-Sarcee γ^y has been split in Sarcee into γ^y and $\check{z}$, the former being realized by y, w, or γ depending on the quality of the following vowel, the latter by $\check{s}$ or $\check{z}$ depending on the devoicing effect of the preceding s-classifier. With this analysis, now can revise again Series III of the Athapaskan-Sarcee initial consonant correspondences as given below in which *y^y corresponds to ž as expected from purely structural point of view:

III.	Athapaskan	Sarcee
1.	x^y	š
2.	y^y	$\begin{Bmatrix} y^y \ ([y, w, \gamma]) \\ ž \ ([š, ž]) \end{Bmatrix}$
3.	g^y	dž
4.	k^y	tš
5.	$k^{y'}$	tš'

The above account of initial ž still leaves one question unanswered. Sapir recorded two verb stems (-žiž 'to rattle',[15] -žił 'to shout') which constitute themes with the Ø-classifier only. I do not know what pre-Sarcee consonant this initial ž corresponds to. The paucity of stem-initial as well as stem-final ž (see Cook 1972) has not been adequately explained not only in Sarcee but also in Chipewyan. According to Li (1946), Chipewyan has the following fricative pairs:

| Surds | x | xw | θ | s | š | ł |
| Sonants | γ | γʷ | ð | z | y | l |

Notice that y is paired with š where there is no ž in the language. There is morphological reason for this pairing to the extent that š alternates with y as stem-initials, e.g. šen 'song' vs se-yen-é 'my song' (Li 1946:400). Stem-finally, however, š does not alternate with y while other fricative pairs do in what is known as the alternation between light and heavy syllables, a light syllable being closed by a surd and a corresponding heavy syllable by a sonant, marking the imperfective and the perfective respectively (Li 1946:399-400). In other words, š and y constitute a pair which is an exception to the syllable alternation rule.[16] All of these rather puzzling facts both in Sarcee and Chipewyan do not seem to be accidental and may very well be attributable to a common fact. If and when this fact is uncovered, the status of y^y will become clearer.

The question raised at the beginning of this section, regarding the phonemic status of PA voiced fricatives, cannot be answered in this paper. The internal evidence drawn from Sarcee suggests that voicing is distinctive in PA fricatives, whereas other comparative evidence such as discussed in Howren (1969) and Cook (1974) supports Krauss' (1964) view that voicing is redundant in PA fricatives.

NOTES

* This work is supported in part by the Canada Council grant S71-1469. I am grateful to Michael E. Krauss whose corrections, critical comments, and supplementary data have undoubtedly improved the quality of this paper. I regret that I could not make more use out of his insights, especially, into the Proto-Athapaskan-Eyak correspondences. Also I wish to thank Jonathan Kaye and Earl Hofer who offered me useful comments and suggestions upon reading an earlier version of this paper. Needless to say, any remaining errors are my own.

[1] The orthography used in citing Sarcee examples is neither phonemic nor phonetic, but a convenient system which eliminates a great deal of phonetic redundancy. The symbols are identical to those of Cook (1971a). It may be worthwhile to mention that I use o in place of Sapir's and Li's ϱ for no other reason than typographic convenience.

[2] The notion of opacity and transparency is introduced by Kiparsky (1971). The examples discussed in this section fall under Definition (i) of Kiparsky, and examples which fall under Definition (ii) will be presented with respect to C-Palatalization in 3. Kaye (1974) has recently revised the second type of opacity (Definition (ii) of Kiparsky) relating it in an interesting way to the notion of 'recoverability' and naturalness.

[3] The classifier s corresponds to the Athapaskan ł-classifier. This morpheme and the 1p.sg.subj. morpheme, which may occur in the first and the second position respectively, preceding a stem, happen to be homophonous. There are cases where both may occur in juxtaposition, and there are strings in which only one of them occurs. There is some evidence that the phonological behavior of the classifier s is different from that of the subject s. This problem, however will not be discussed here since it does not directly bear upon the problem on hand.

[4] The vowel i is deleted before a, but it assimilates to a preceding vowel, a or u (I-Assimilation). This I-Deletion rule, however, is different from a rule which deletes the i of si- (perfective). The reduction of si- to s- is quite common in the Athapaskan languages, but the synchronic and diachronic nature of this process is not well understood.

[5] Different aspects are usually marked by vowel ablaut, tonal alternation, and/or suffixing. If the stem-vowel is u the inflection does not involve vowel ablaut (see Cook 1972).

[6] Sapir (1931) recognizes contrast between voiced and voiceless fricative, whereas Krauss (1964) does not consider voicing is distinctive. I use the term 'pre-Sarcee' instead of 'Athapaskan' as I can not determine the (historical) status of the voiced velar fricative (see the last section).

[7] One might of course suspect that $š$ of (12) is the result of S-Palatalization ($s + y \rightarrow š$), i.e. the stem-initial of (12) would be a cluster of $yγ$. This possibility, however, is ruled out by the fact that no morpheme otherwise begins in a CC cluster and that no morpheme which may be represented by y occurs between the subject prefix and the stem.

[8] The reason that $γ^y$ instead of x^y is chosen is due to the assumption that no voiceless fricative occurs underlyingly as a stem-initial consonant. Li's stem list contains a few stems whose initial consonant is a voiceless fricative, namely $š$, which, however, is derivable from underlying $ž$ in terms of 'Devoicing' or from underlying y in terms of S-Palatalization. In an alternative analysis, it may be assumed that all stem-initial fricatives are voiceless underlyingly, and all voiced fricatives are derivable by a voicing rule. If Krauss' reconstruction of PA consonants (1964) is correct, the latter would correspond to the diachronic reality. More will be said on this in section 4.

[9] Alternatively, we may simply add a rule of depalatalization ($γ^y \rightarrow γ$) which applies after C-Palatalization and before Glide Formation, in which case R2 remains as is (see Hofer 1974). In this analysis, the underlying $γ^ya$ of (12)a becomes $γa$ by Depalatalization, and the underlying $γ^yu$ of (12)b becomes $γu$ by Depalatalization, then finally wu by Glide Formation. In other words, Glide Formation is fed by Depalatalization. It is clear that what the underlying $γ^y$ does is nothing but to trigger C-Palatalization. The apparent theoretical problem of abstract phonology involved in $γ^y$ here is not the main concern of this paper.

[10] Phonetic symbols are slightly modified to maintain consistency.

[11] If we accept the abstract analysis presented in 3, the Athapaskan $γ^y$ corresponds to Sarcee $γ^y$ (underlyingly) from which $γ$, w, and y are derived.

¹² See Golla (1970) for a most comprehensive account of these phenomena.
¹³ The phonological irregularity involving 2p.pl.subj. is not well understood. On the surface, this morpheme often appears as *āà* or *īì*, but preceding an l-initial verb a D-effect is observed, suggesting an underlying *d*, i.e. *āàd* or *īìd*. Perhaps, this *d* is deleted along with the s-classifier *before* the latter devoices the following stem-initial fricative.
¹⁴ Other archaic pronunciations include ł which has changed to *s* before a consonant. One speaker quite often alternates between ł and *s* (for *s*-classifier) and between *ał* and *as* (for 2p.pl.subj.).
¹⁵ Krauss (personal communication) suggests the following Minto data as possible cognates: *-zrosr* 'to rattle', *srosr* 'drum', *-zrusr* 'to clatter'.
¹⁶ According to Krauss (personal communication) Minto apparently has a similar problem. He says that while *š* is rare, there is no *ž*, and that *š* and *y* are paired in a way but do not show regular alternations like other fricative pairs, e.g. *x* vs *γ*, ł vs *l*, etc.

BELLA COOLA SYNTAX

PHILIP W. DAVIS and ROSS SAUNDERS

0.0 In this paper we are concerned with the syntax of Bella Coola, a Salishan language spoken at Bella Coola (*nuxalk*), British Columbia.[1] In earlier times the language was spoken as far west as Kwatna, approximately fifty miles from Bella Coola on Kwatna Inlet, and as far east as Stuie (*stuix*), approximately forty miles east on the Bella Coola River. To the north, Bella Coola was spoken in Kimsquit (*nuλ'l*) at the mouth of the Dean River; and to the south it was spoken at Tallio (*ʔac'āxɬ*) on the South Bentinck arm of the Dean Channel. Voegelin and Voegelin (1964) cite 200-400 as an estimate of the present number of native speakers. The total number of registered Bella Coolas in 1966 was 574, and of these only the middle aged and older speak the language. This number is closer to 200.[2]

0.1 The specific portions of the syntax dealt with here are three structures involving embedded sentences: 'adjectival clauses' (1.1 and 2.1), 'relative clauses' (1.2 and 2.2), and 'complex sentences' (1.3 and 2.2). These exhibit many of the principal syntactic phenomena of Bella Coola.

Given the current tentativeness of theorizing about language, we do not feel constrained to employ consistently and thoroughly one or another theory. One generally agreed assumption about language is the distinction between an overt and covert structure, whether that is expressed as the deep-surface structure distinction of Chomsky 1965, the more semantic and surface structure distinction of generative semantics, the (hyper)-semological-lexological distinction of stratificational grammar, or the semantic-surface structure distinction of Chafe 1970. This much, at least, is common to current ideas of language, and it is the distinction between an underlying and a surface structure that is the basis for the description here. We adopt a set of underlying structures that seems best suited to the expression of Bella Coola grammar and relate them to surface structures via transformational processes.

0.2 Bella Coola is a VSO language. Compare the following sentences:

(1) k'xis tiʔimlktx cixnascx[3] 'The man sees the woman'
(2) sp'tis tiʔisimmĺkitx wawac'uksc 'The boy is hitting the dogs'

The verbs,[4] here *k'x* 'see' and *sp* 'hit', exhibit a set of affixes that agree with the subject – *ʔimlk* 'man' and *ʔimmĺki* 'boy' – and object – *xnas* 'woman' and *wac'uks* 'dogs' – of (1) and (2).[5] The affixes appear to mark not only a subject and direct object but also the subject and indirect object as in

(3) naptis cixnascx waʔimlkuksc xtismɫktx
    'The woman is giving the men the fish'

The peripheral term, *tismɫktx* 'the fish', is marked by the preposition *x-*. The subject-object affixes then copy onto the verb the information of person and number from the first two adjacent terms. The agreement of (3) is between subject and indirect object, but in

(4) sp'is cixnascx tiʔimlktx xtistntx
    'The woman is hitting the man with the stick'

the middle noun is again the direct object, and the peripheral term, *tistntx* 'the stick', is the instrument. The second nouns of (1)-(4) are treated identically in Bella Coola as are the third nouns of (3) and (4). We assume this same formal treatment to indicate a semantic identity. We will call the second terms of (1)-(4) the Agent; the third terms, e.g. *tiʔimlktx* in (4), the Patient; and the fourth terms, e.g. *xtistntx* in (4), the Adjunct. The designation of Bella Coola as VSO is then correct with the equation of S with Agent and O with Patient.

0.3 Utterances in Bella Coola are basically predicative. Sentences (1)-(4) all contain an Agent and Patient or those plus an Adjunct, but they are otherwise structurally identical to sentences with only an Agent:

(5) ƛ'apaw waƛ'mstac   'The people are going'
(6) staltmxaw waʔimlkuksc   'The men are chiefs'
(7) waks tiƛ'aptx   'Who is going?'

where *ƛ'ap* 'go', *staltmx* 'chief', and *waks* 'who?' are predicated of their respective Agents. The first term of (1)-(7) specifies new information; the remaining ones, given information. Both the following sentences are grammatical

(8) ƛ'ap tiʔimlktx   'The man is going'
(9) tiʔimlktx tiƛ'ap   'The one who is going is the man'

but only (9) – with *tiʔimlktx* in the position appropriate for new information – answers the question of (7). (8) and (9) are not paraphrases. Where both Agent and Patient are present, we may find both

(10) sp'is cixnascx tiʔimlktx   'The woman is hitting the man'
(11) tiʔimlktx tisp'is cixnascx   'The one the woman is hitting is the man'

Only (11) answers

(12) waks tisp'is cixnascx   'Who is the woman hitting'

(8) and (10) answer the questions 'What is the man doing?' and 'What is the woman doing to the man?'. It is also possible to make the distinction of sentences (8)-(9) and (10)-(11) with an Adjunct. On the basis of these observations, the first term of each sentence is labeled the Comment. A Comment associated with an Agent but no Patient announces a property predicated of that Agent. Where Agent and Patient occur, the Comment predicates a relationship between them. The term Agent then is not precise. It is interpreted consistently as actor or instigator only when Patient follows. Otherwise, it is interpreted as having some property attributed to it without the Agent's instigation. See (5) and (6). In (5) we assume 'going' is predicated as a property of 'people'.

The elemental underlying structure is assumed to be

(13)
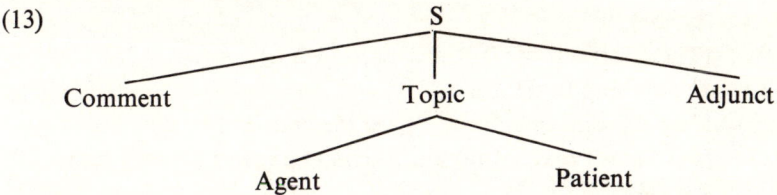

Patient within Topic and Adjunct within S are optional constituents. The remaining ones are obligatory. Grouping Agent and Patient within Topic is based semantically on the observation that the Comment predicates of the Agent (and Patient) but not the Adjunct. Formally, the agreement rules affect these two to the exclusion of Adjunct; only Adjunct is marked by a preposition; and finally, a Lexical Suffix Copy rule (see Davis and Saunders 1973) applies in one way to an Agent or Patient and in another way to the Adjunct. All this is taken as evidence that Agent and Patient are constituents of Topic. Sentences in Bella Coola seem to be of the structure (13) or to be derivable from combinations of it by successive embeddings.

1.0 We now turn to consideration of three syntactic constructions within Bella Coola. In 1.1-1.3 we present examples of them, and in 2.1-2.2 we discuss possible descriptions.

1.1 Consider the following sentences with adjectival clauses:

(14)(i) k'xic tija tiʔimlktx   'I see the good man'
   (ii) k'xic tiʔimlk tijatx   'I see the good man'

The two are paraphrases. Formally, the *-tx* is restricted to one occurrence, while the *ti-* occurs as many times as there are modifying Comments of *ʔimlk*; thus,

(15) k'xic tija ticācti tiʔimlktx   'I see the good, young man'

but not

(16) *k'xic tijatx tiʔimlktx

The adjectival clause also occurs where the modified term is Agent of an intransitive verb (17), Agent of a transitive verb (18), Patient of a transitive verb (19), and Adjunct (20):

(17)(i) k'xic tiƛ'ap tiƛ'mstatx   'I see the person [who is] going'
       (see-I/him Proximal-go Proximal-person-Article)
   (ii) k'xic tiƛ'msta tiƛ'aptx
       (see-I/him Proximal-person Proximal-go-Article)

(18)(i) *k'xic tiqup'ɬt tiƛ'mstatx[6]
   (ii) k'xic tiƛ'msta tiqup'ɬttx   'I see the person [who] punched him'
       (see-I/him Proximal-person Proximal-punch-past-he/him-Article)
       (The *-t* variant of *-is* is discussed in 2.1.)

(19)(i) *k'xic tiqup'ɬit tiƛ'mstatx
   (ii) k'xic tiƛ'msta tiqup'ɬittx   'I see the person they punched'
       (see-I/him Proximal-person Proximal-punch-Past-they/him-Article)

(20)(i) *k'xic tisnapixʷ tisnāx̣tx[7]
   (ii) k'xic tisnāx̣ tisnapixʷtx
       'I see the slave you are giving him'
       (see-I/him Proximal-slave Proximal-
       Preposition-give-you/him-Article)

The paraphrases of (14) and (17) are absent in (18)-(20). Only one sequence of modifier and modified occurs.

It may appear that the presence or absence of paraphrases is to be predicted in terms of transitive or intransitive Comments, but

(21)(i) *k'xic tiƛ'ap ʔałcixnascx tiƛ'mstatx
   (ii) k'xic tiƛ'msta tiƛ'ap ʔałcixnascx
       'I see the person [who is] going with the woman'

(22)(i) *k'xic tija ʔałcixnascx tiƛ'mstatx
(ii) k'xic tiƛ'msta tija ʔałcixnascx
'I see the person [who is] good for the woman'

show the absence of paraphrase in these sentences to be a function of two or more constituents within the non-Comment portion of the modifier in the adjectival clause. In the transitive structures of (18)-(20) there are always (at least) an Agent and Patient; and the paraphrase is always absent. In the intransitive structures of (14) and (17) an optional Adjunct is possible and where it occurs the paraphrase relation is absent. In

(23)(i) k'xic tistaltmx tiʔimlktx   'I see the man [who is] chief'
(ii) *k'xic tiʔimlk tistaltmxtx

paraphrase is again not possible; but it is not attributable to the pattern given above. Here, there may be reason to distinguish between lexical items that are Nouns and those that are non-Nouns (including verb and adjective). With these distinctions, one structural and one lexical, it is possible to predict where paraphrases may occur and where they may not, and in the latter case, which sequence of modifier and modified is grammatical. Syntactically, each lexical item will be considered as marked for class membership [±Noun].

1.2 Relative clause constructions are illustrated by the following:
(24)(i) ʔałk'jukił swas tija tiʔimlktx   'We know the man who is good'
(ii) ʔałk'jukił swas tiʔimlk tijatx
(25)(i) ʔałk'jukił swas tiƛ'ap tiʔimlktx
'We know the man who is going'
(ii) ʔałk'jukił swas tiʔimlk tiƛ'aptx
(26)(i) *ʔałk'jukił swas tiqup'ɬt tiʔimlktx[8]
(ii) ʔałk'jukił swas tiʔimlk tiqup'ɬttx
'We know the man who punched him'
(27)(i) *ʔałk'jukił swas tiqup'łit tiʔimlktx
(ii) ʔałk'jukił swas tiʔimlk tiqup'łittx
'We know the man whom they punched'
(28)(i) *ʔałk'jukił swas tisnapixʷ tisnāxtx[9]
(ii) ʔałk'jukił swas tisnāx tisnapixʷtx
'We know the slave whom you are giving him'

Paraphrase is possible in relative clause constructions under the same conditions as in adjective clauses. Compare (14), (17-20), and (23) with (24)-(28) and

(29)(i)   k'xic swas tistaltmx tiʔimlktx   'I see the man who is chief'
   (ii)   *k'xic swas tiʔimlk tistaltmxtx

Sentences (24)-(28) are paralleled by a set in which the relative *wa* is replaced by *ka* 'which':

(30)(i)   ʔałk'jukił skas tija tiʔimlk
        'We know which man is good'
   (ii) ʔałk'jukił skas tiʔimlk tija
(31)(i)   ʔałk'jukił skas tiƛ'ap tiʔimlk
        'We know which man is going'
   (ii) ʔałk'jukił skas tiʔimlk tiƛ'ap
(32)(i) *ʔałk'jukił skas tiqup't tiʔimlk [10]
   (ii) ʔałk'jukił skas tiʔimlk tiqup't
        'We know which man is punching him'
(33)(i) *ʔałk'jukił skas tiqup'it tiʔimlk
   (ii) ʔałk'jukił skas tiʔimlk tiqup'it
        'We know which man they are punching'
(34)(i) *ʔałk'jukił skas tisnapix^w tisnāx̣ [11]
   (ii) ʔałk'jukił skas tisnāx̣ tisnapix^w
        'We know which slave you are giving him'

The sentences with *ka* work syntactically as those with *wa* do with two differences. The first is their behavior with respect to the occurrence of Demonstrative/Article. Neither may occur with *ka*. The relative element *ka* seems to refer to an indefinite object and as such is incompatible with the definiteness of the grammatical categories of Demonstrative/Article (cf. n. 3 for comment on indefiniteness imparted by the absence of the deictic suffixes). The relative element *wa* identifies a specific object and must occur with a member of this grammatical opposition. The second difference between *ka* and *wa* lies in the modified items with which they may occur. The relative *ka* occurs with inanimate, animate, nonhuman, and human nouns, but *wa* is restricted to modifying human nouns.

1.3   The following complex sentences occur:
(35)(i)   ʔałnapił sƛ'apaw waʔimlkuksc
        'We know that the men are going'
  (ii) ʔałnaptił waʔimlkuksc sƛ'apaw
        'We know the men are going'
(36)(i)   ʔałnapił sƛ'apaw
        'We know that they are going'

(ii) ʔałnaptił sƛ'apaw
'We know they are going'
(37)(i) ʔałnapił sƛ'apnu
'We know that you are going'
(ii) ʔałnaptułnu sƛ'apnu
'We know you are going'

(35i) and (35ii) are not paraphrases. The first may be used of strangers; what is known is that the men are going, not specifically who they are. In (35ii) the meaning is something like 'We know the men [plus the fact that they] are going'; it cannot be said of strangers. The alternate Agent-Patient affix of (35ii) also reflects the fact that *ʔimlkuks* is directly involved as Patient. (36i) and (36ii) parallel (35i) and (35ii). In (37) the syntactic parallel is continued with a nonthird person Patient: 'We know that you are going' versus 'We know you [plus the fact that you] are going'. The modification of the (ii)-forms of (35)-(37) is nonrestrictive and contrasts with the restrictive modification of the adjectival clauses.

2.0   We now turn to a formal description of the sentences in 1.1-1.3; and that description must be taken as tentative. The underlying structures are based on our feeling for the language – about 'how things work' – and native speaker reactions. The transformational rules are for the most part 'motivated'; that is, they have application to two or more distinct structures. But it is always possible for a series of incorrect solutions to support each other and to appear correct overall. The following comments are then to be taken as one systematicization of certain syntactic phenomana in Bella Coola without claim of ultimate correctness.

2.1   Although sentences (14, 17-20) and (24)-(28) may be similarly glossed, we forgo drawing from this the conclusion that they are exact paraphrases and must derive from identical underlying structures.

Sentences (14) and (17)-(20) are assumed to have an underlying structure analogous to (38) for (14) *k'xic tija tiʔimlktx* 'I see the good man'. The structure of S_2 is based on earlier discussion of the predicative character of Bella Coola utterances. In the adjectival clause, the given Topic (Agent) of S_2 is *ʔimlk* 'man', and it is predicated of this term that it is 'good'. Similarly, for the remaining sentences of this class.

To derive a surface structure from the underlying one an Equi-Constituent Deletion rule applies as in English and elsewhere in Bella Coola (cf. Davis and Saunders 1973) deleting *ʔimlk* in S_3. This yields (with tree-pruning. Cf. Ross 1969a) the derived structure (39).

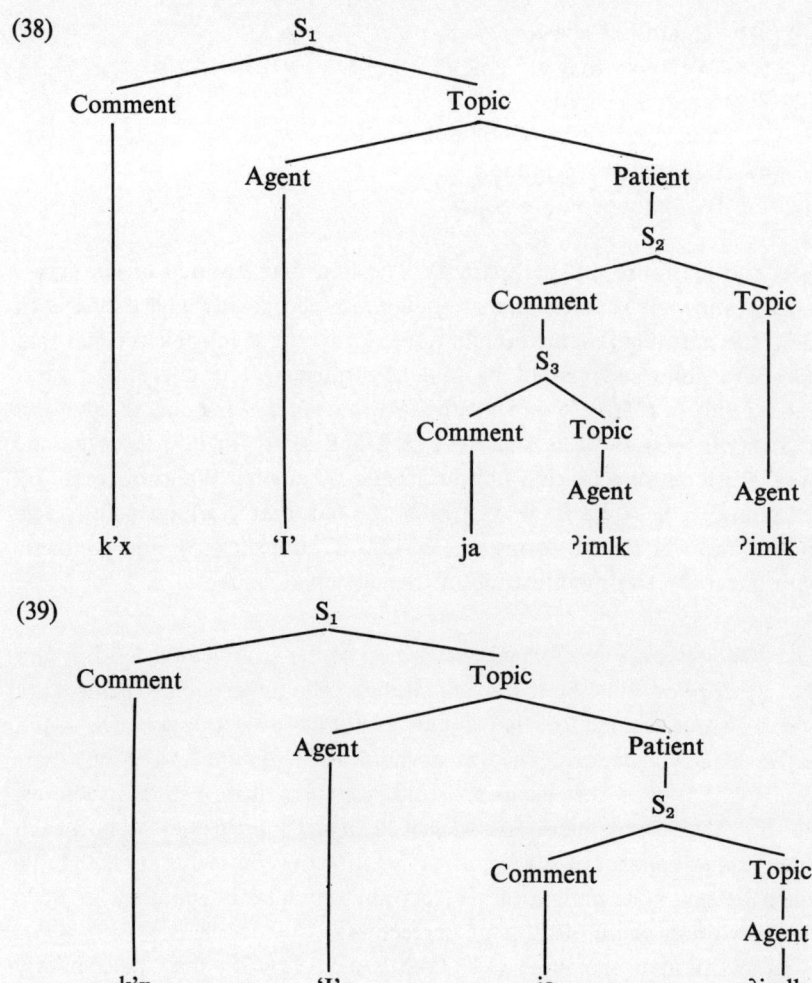

Agent-Patient Agreement now produces *k'x-ic*. Any pronoun dominated by Agent or Patient is deleted; this Pronoun Deletion rule removes 'I' from the Agent of S_1.

Notice that Agent Agreement does not apply to the derived S_2 in (39), although we might expect it to and to affix an *-s* according to our observation in fn. 5 that *-s* is the normal third person singular marker of an Agent in embedded sentences. But observe that Agent affixes are also absent for the other persons and numbers in this structure:

(40)(i)   k'xtic waja waʔimlkuksc   'I see the good men'
    (ii) *k'xtic wajanaw waʔimlkuksc

One account of this is the following. We may have recourse to the notion of global rules (Lakoff 1970) such that Agreement holds between Comments and Topics only if the Comment is *not* dominated by some S that does not also dominate the Topic in the underlying structure; if such an S is deleted by tree-pruning such that the condition is met in a derived structure, then Agreement may not apply. Since the Comment-Topic structure of S_2 in (39) is derived, the Agent Agreement rule is inapplicable. Looking at (38), this means that Equi-Constituent Deletion must apply before Agent Agreement because the structural condition for the application of the latter rule is met there in S_3, but it does not correctly apply affixing -*s*. Examination of sentences (69)-(72) below provide support for this.

A difficulty remains with the occurrence of the deictic particles. We assume that Distal/Proximal and Demonstrative/Article are properties introduced within the underlying structure. As in classical transformational generative grammar, these may be introduced via a set of context-free rules for Agent and so forth, so that a Complex Symbol is produced. A morphophonemic rule then gives them shape. Given this, the single, rightmost occurrence of -*tx* may be achieved by a rule spelling out Demonstrative/Article to the right of Agent in (39). *ʔimlk* of S_3 in (39) has been deleted before this rule applies. The result of ordering Equi-Constituent Deletion before this Deixis Spelling rule is a single deictic suffix in S_2. The multiple occurrence of the Distal/Proximal prefixes may be derived by a feature spreading rule adding [+Proximal, −Female] (in this case) to all Comments with the embedded S_3. Notice that disagreement of deixis within an adjectival or relative clause is not possible:

(41) *k'xic taja tiʔimlktx
(42) *k'xic swas taja tiʔimlktx

Feature spreading accounts for this co-occurrence restriction. Distal/Proximal is not spread to Comments of all embedded sentences. See, for example, (35)-(37). Only those structures comparable to (38), where some item is deleted, are so affected. This correctly characterizes the sentences of 1.1 and 1.2, but not those of 1.3. The spreading of Distal/Proximal may be expressed in three ways: first, as a part of Equi-Constituent Deletion; second, as a global rule functioning in derived structures where Equi-Constituent Deletion has applied; and third, as a rule functioning where an *s*- is not affixed as in *s-ƛ'apaw* and so forth in (35)-(37). Having established the existence of Deixis Spreading, we leave its precise formulation unspecified.

Sentence (18), *k'xic tiƛ'msta tiqup'łttx* 'I see the person [who] punched him', has the following underlying structure:

(43)

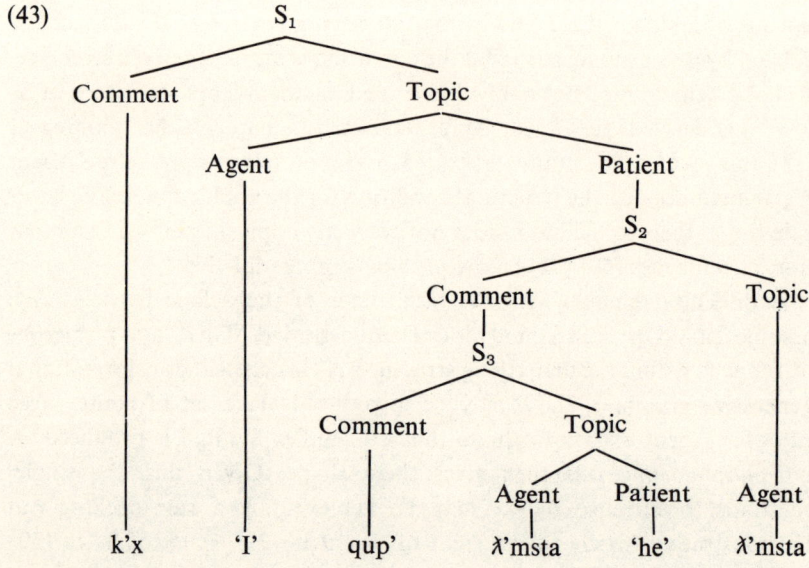

As before we employ Equi-Constituent Deletion with respect to the two occurrences of *ƛ'msta*. But notice that the affix of *qup'* is *-t*, not the normal 'he/him' *-is*. Where a third person singular or plural Agent (co-occurring with a third person singular Patient) of a transitive verb is to be deleted, the affix is *-t*. Where the Patient is singular, no other affix occurs; where it is plural, the additional increment *-an* appears:

(44) ʔałk'jukił tiƛ'msta tiqūxp'łtantx [12]
      'We know the person who punched them'

Where third person Agents occur with Patients of the first or second person in S_3 of (43), we again find the normal Agent-Patient affixes (cf. n. 5):

(45)(i)   k'xit tiʔimlk tiqup'cstx
          'They see the man [who is] punching me'
   (ii)   k'xit tiʔimlk tiqup'cttx
          'They see the man [who is] punching you'
   (iii) k'xit tiʔimlk tiqup'tułstx
          'They see the man [who is] punching us'
   (iv)   k'xit tiʔimlk tiqup'taptx
          'They see the man [who is] punching you all'

Sentence (19) has the structure:

(46)
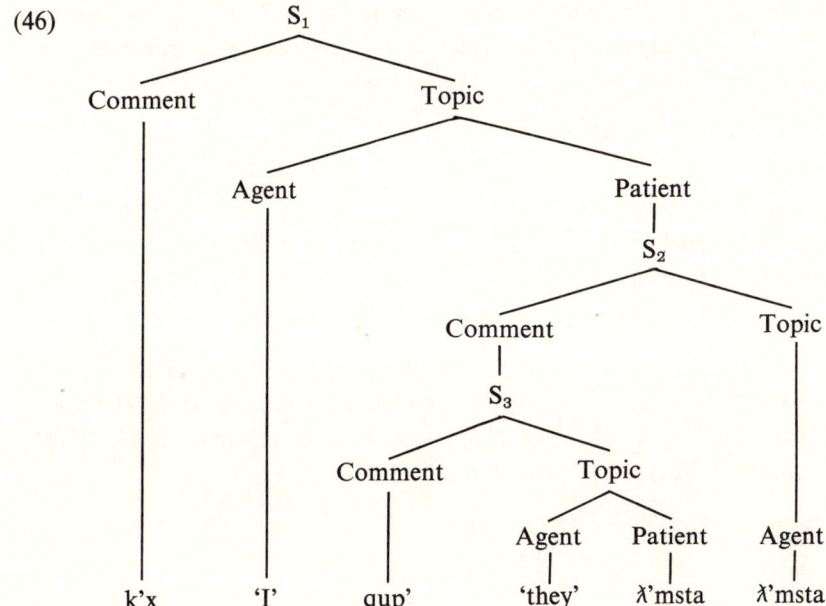

and the normal Agent-Patient affix for the third person plural Agent and third person singular Patient (-*it*) occurs.

The syntactic structure attributed to sentences (18) and (19) seems to occur only where the modified term – the Topic of S_2 in (43) and (46) – is third person. That is, Bella Coola lacks restrictive modification of first and second person pronouns which are then considered to be definite in reference. Restrictive modification of third person pronouns occurs. See (64)-(67). First and second person pronouns occur only with the non-restrictive modification of (35ii); for example,

(47)(i)   k'xcant sjac   'They see me and that I am good'
(ii)   kx'tułnu ssp'łct xtiʔimlktx   'We see you [whom] the man hit'
(iii)   k'xtułt ssp'ił tiʔimlktx   'They see us [who] hit the man'
(iv)   k'xtap sƛ'apap   'They see you all [who] are going'

and so forth. The structure of these sentences is discussed in 2.2.

To account for the presence of the suffixes of (18) and (19), we must assume Agent-Patient Agreement to apply before Equi-Constituent Deletion.[13] The reverse order would result in making Agent-Patient

Agreement inapplicable, since one of the constituents required for its application (either Agent or Patient) would be deleted. The *-t* and *-tan* of (18) and (44) are neutralizations of *-is/-it* and *-tis/-tit*, respectively. Factors affecting Agreement in embedded sentences with transitive Comments are then:

(48)   Person of the Agent
    (i)   Third   (ii)   Nonthird

(49)   Person of the Patient
    (i)   Third   (ii)   Nonthird

(50)   Identity
    (i)   The Agent is to be deleted.   (ii)   The Patient is to be deleted.

A combination of (48i), (49i), and (50i) produces *-t* and *-tan*. (48i), (49i), and (50ii) or (48i), (49ii), and (50i) produces the more usual suffixes of n. 5. (48ii) and (50i) or (49ii) and (50ii) produces sentences on the model of (47).

Sentence (20) has the structure:

(51)

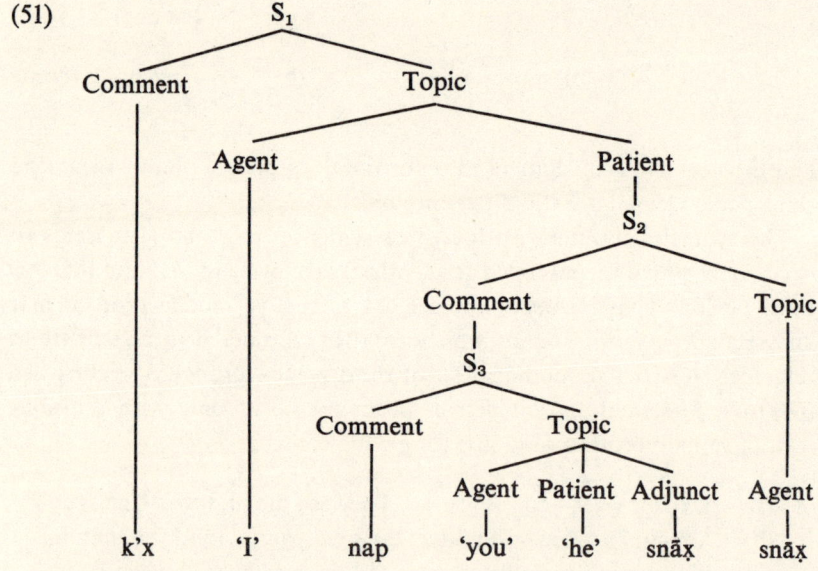

A rule is now required to raise the Topic-Agent of S_2 in (51) – and also in (38), (43), and (46) – obligatorily wherever a non-Comment constituent remains within the modifying S_3 after Equi-Constituent Deletion has applied and optionally, elsewhere when the Comment of S_3 is [−Noun]. Topic Raising does not occur where the Comment is [+Noun]. See (29).

Since pronouns count as constituents in the environment of Topic Raising, the rule is assumed to apply before Pronoun Deletion. For (51) this produces (with tree-pruning) the derived structure:

(52)
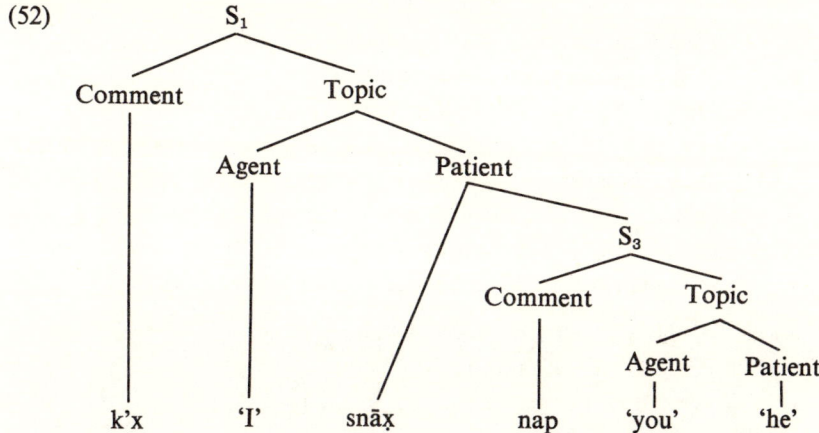

Analogous derived structures are produced from (38), (43), and (46).

The other transformational rules apply as before, but two additional comments are required. The first concerns the -s- of *tisnapix^w* in (20). This appears whenever a portion of an Adjunct co-occurring with the preposition x- has been deleted. It is assumed to be a permutation-copy (and allomorph) of x-. We return to its discussion below.

The second comment concerns the transitive structure of S_3 in (43), (46), and (47). The following sentences occur where an overt Agent, Patient, or Adjunct is present, e.g., 'I know the man [who] punched the woman' in place of 'I know the man [who] punched her/him':

(53) ʔałk'jukił tiʔimlk tiqup'łt cixnascx
 'We know the man [who] punched the woman'
(54) ʔałk'jukił tiʔimlk tinapt cixnascx xtisnāxtx
 'We know the man [who is] giving the woman the slave'
(55) ʔałk'jukił tiʔimlk tiqup'łis cixnascx
 'We know the man the woman punched'
(56) ʔałk'jukił tiʔimlk tinapix^w xtisnāxtx
 'We know the man you are giving the slave to'
(57) ʔałk'jukił tisnāx tisnapix^w cixnascx
 'We know the slave you are giving the woman'

Expressions of (53) and (54) where the modified term is Agent of an embedded S as in

(58)(i)   *ʔałk'jukił tiʔimlk tiqup't cixnascxtx
  (ii)   *ʔałk'jukił tiʔimlk tiqup't cixnastx
  (iii)   *ʔałk'jukił tiʔimlktx tiqup't cixnascx
  (iv)   ʔałk'jukił tiʔimlk tiqup'ttx cixnascx

show that the Demonstrative/Article feature of the modified term may be spelled out in these sentences, but also that restrictions on its occurrence exist. Sentences (58i) and (58ii) show that Deixis Spelling cannot apply such that Topic Raising leaves the suffix behind; sentence (58iii) shows further that Deixis Spelling cannot correctly apply after Topic Raising. Sentence (58iv) indicates the correct location for the Demonstrative/Article suffixes in these sentences. Compare now the sentences of (59) where the modified term is the Patient within an embedded S as in (55) and (56):

(59)(i)   *ʔałk'jukił tiʔimlk tiqup'istx cixnascx
  (ii)   ʔałk'jukił tiʔimlk tiqup'istx
         'We know the man he/she is punching'
  (iii)   ʔałk'jukił tiʔimlk tisp'istx xtistntx
         'We know the man he/she is hitting with a stick'

(59i) with an overt, nondeletable noun Agent cannot have an overt Demonstrative-Article suffix. (59ii) and (59iii) can. The determining factor seems to be the presence or absence of an overt, surface constituent between the term affected by Equi-Constituent Deletion and the Comment. In (59i), the Patient ʔimlk has been deleted, and there is an overt, surface Agent xnas present between the Patient and Comment qup'. In (59ii) the Patient ʔimlk has been deleted, but the Agent is a pronoun that is deleted in the surface representation. Compare further (60), where the deleted term is an Adjunct:

(60)(i)   *k'xił tistn tisisp'ittx waʔimlkuksc
         'We see the stick the men hit him with'
  (ii)   *k'xił tistn tisisp'ittx cixnascx
         'We see the stick they hit the woman with'
  (iii)   *k'xił tistn tisisp'ittx waʔimlkuksc cixnascx
         'We see the stick the men hit the woman with'
  (iv)   k'xił tistn tisisp'ittx
         'We see the stick they are hitting him/her with'

The sentences of (60) seem to confirm this characterization of the possible occurrence of Demonstrative/Article. But the ungrammaticality of

(61)   *ʔałk'jukił tiʔimlk tinapttx cixnascx xtismłktx
       'We know the man [who] is giving the woman the fish'

shows that constitutes to the right of the lexical item to be deleted must also be considered. The presence of two as in (61) renders the occurrence of -*tx* unacceptable in *tinaptx*. This contrasts with the acceptable sentences of (58iv) and (59iii) and

(62)(i)   ʔałk'jukił tiʔimlk tijatx ʔałcixnascx
'We know the man [who is] good for the woman'
(ii) ʔałk'jukił tiʔimlk tiƛ'aptx ʔałcixnascx
'We know the man [who is] going with the woman'

with one constituent (either Patient or Adjunct) to the right of the deleted item.

One way of characterizing this is to relate the occurrence of the suffixes following the Comment to the operation of Topic Raising. In sentences (58)-(60) and (62) Topic Raising is obligatory; but where the modifying S_3 has an intransitive structure and Topic Raising is not obligatory we find

(63)(i)   *ʔałk'jukił tiƛ'aptx tiʔimlktx   (iv) ʔałk'jukił tiʔimlk tiƛ'aptx
(ii) *ʔałk'jukił tiƛ'aptx tiʔimlk   (v)   *ʔałk'jukił tiʔimlktx tiƛ'ap
(iii) ʔałk'jukił tiƛ'ap tiʔimlktx   (vi) *ʔałk'jukił tiʔimlktx tiƛ'aptx
'We know the man [who is] going'

The Demonstrative/Article suffixes occur once and follow the modifying Comment only when Topic Raising has applied; otherwise, they correctly follow the modified term. We may incorporate prediction of the suffixes within the process of Topic Raising. Where Topics are raised the [+Demonstrative] or [+Article] feature is added to the Comment over which the Topic is raised. Against this we observe that such a formulation requires we know where Equi-Constituent Deletion has applied; it must have information of the derivation. Secondly, the environment determining the occurrence of Demonstrative/Article is not sensitive to the deleted pronouns as Topic Raising is. See (59ii) and (60iv). An alternative way of characterizing these occurrences is to relate them to the operation of Equi-Constituent Deletion as Deixis Spreading may be. This will obviate the need for transderivational information, since we know the position of the item to be deleted and also its nonpronoun constituent environment. Then, under the conditions outlined above, we may assume that Deixis Spreading is expanded beyond the Distal/Proximal prefixes to include the Demonstrative/Article suffixes. This alternative fails, however, to express the pattern that Topic Raising is obligatory in all structures in which Demonstrative/Article spreading occurs. Either formulation has deficiencies, and we leave the choice between them, or of some third possibility, unmade.

52   PHILIP W. DAVIS AND ROSS SAUNDERS

Let us now consider the following additional sentences:

(64)   ʔałk'jukił tijatx
        'We know the good one'
(65)(i) ʔałk'jukił tiqup'łttx
        'We know the one[who] punched him/her/it'
   (ii) ʔałk'jukił tiqup'łt cixnascx
        'We know the one [who] punched the woman'
(66)(i) ʔałk'jukił tiqup'łistx
        'We know the one he/she punched'
   (ii) ʔałk'jukił tiqup'łis cixnascx
        'We know the one the woman punched'
(67)(i) ʔałk'jukił tisnapłixʷtx
        'We know the one you gave him/her'
   (ii) ʔałk'jukił tisnapłixʷ cixnascx
        'We know the one you gave the woman'

The structure of these sentences is that of those previously considered. The difference lies in the choice of lexical item as modified S_2 Topic. In place of choosing a noun – ʔ*imlk* or *X'msta* – as Topic, a third person pronoun 'he' occurs in (64)-(67); in (64) for example

(68)

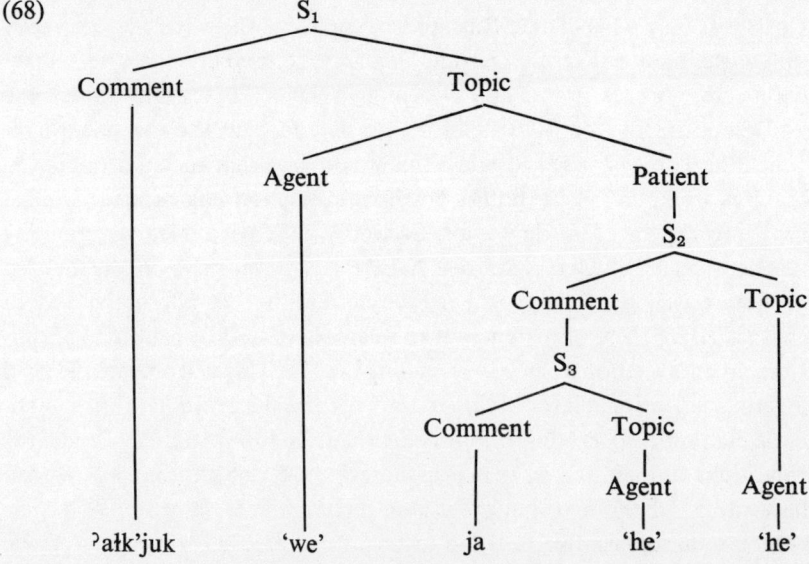

The Agent pronoun 'he' of S_3 is deleted by Equi-Constituent Deletion, and the Agent pronoun of S_2 is deleted after Agent-Patient Agreement as elsewhere yielding (64). Sentences (65)-(67) are derived in analogous fashion.

Let us now add these sentences:

(69)(i) ja cixnascx ʔuɬtiʔimlktx
  'The woman is good to the man'
 (ii) *ʔaɬk'jukiɬ tisijas cixnascx tiʔimlktx
 (iii) ʔaɬk'jukiɬ tiʔimlk tisijas cixnascx
  'We know the man the woman is good to'
 (iv) ʔaɬk'jukiɬ tisijas cixnascx
  'We know the one the woman is good to'
(70)(i) X'ap cixnascx ʔuɬtiʔimlktx
  'The woman is going to the man'
 (ii) *ʔaɬk'jukiɬ tisiX'aps cixnascx tiʔimlktx
 (iii) ʔaɬk'jukiɬ tiʔimlk tisiX'aps cixnascx
  'We know the man the woman is going to'
 (iv) ʔaɬk'jukiɬ tisiX'aps cixnascx
  'We know the one the woman is going to'
(71)(i) ja cixnascx ʔaɬtiʔimlktx
  'The woman is good for the man'
 (ii) *ʔaɬk'jukiɬ tisijas cixnascx tiʔimlktx
 (iii) ʔaɬk'jukiɬ tiʔimlk tisijas cixnascx
  'We know the man the woman is good for'
 (iv) ʔaɬk'jukiɬ tisijas cixnascx
  'We know the one the woman is good for'
(72)(i) X'ap cixnascx ʔaɬtiʔimlktx
  'The woman is going with the man'
 (ii) *ʔaɬk'jukiɬ tisiX'aps cixnascx tiʔimlktx
 (iii) ʔaɬk'jukiɬ tiʔimlk tisiX'aps cixnascx
  'We know the man the woman is going with'
 (iv) ʔaɬk'jukiɬ tisiX'aps cixnascx
  'We know the one the woman is going with'
(73) ʔixq'm cixnascx wixɬtiʔimlktx
  'The woman is walking from the man'
(74)(i) sp'is tiʔimlktx tiwac'tx xtistntx
  'The man is hitting the dog with the stick'
 (ii) *ʔaɬk'xiɬ tissp'is tiʔimlktx tiwac'tx tistntx
 (iii) ʔaɬk'xiɬ tistn tissp'is tiʔimlktx tiwac'tx
  'We are looking at the stick the man is hitting the dog with'
 (iv) ʔaɬk'xiɬ tissp'is tiʔimlktx tiwac'tx
  'We are looking at what the man is hitting the dog with'

The (i)-sentences of (69)(-74) require the modification of the elemental underlying structure of Bella Coola to allow for ʔuɬ-, ʔaɬ-, and wixɬ-. The first, ʔuɬ-, means 'directed towards an object' as in (69) where some property is directed away from some point (*xnas*) to another (*ʔimlk*), and in (70) where the motion is from one point to another (ʔimlk). wixɬ- means 'directed from an object'. The deictic orientation is derived from the initial position with respect to the object. Hence, for ʔuɬ- the deixis is distal, and for wixɬ- it is proximal. Both are nonstative involving direction or motion.

ʔaɬ- is to be compared with x-:

(75) sp'is tiwac'tx xtistntx   'He is hitting the dog with the stick'
(76) sp'is tiwac'tx ʔaɬtistntx 'He is hitting the dog with the stick'

In (75) x- implies the ready presence of the stick; ʔaɬ- in (76) implies the Agent had to go and get the stick. The prepositions ʔaɬ- and x- are opposed, as ʔuɬ- and wixɬ- are, by distal versus proximal, respectively; their point of orientation is defined with respect to the Agent of the sentence. Both ʔaɬ- and x- are stative. In (72) and (76) ʔaɬ- denotes a fixed orientation of the Agent and the object of the preposition as does x- in (75). In earlier examples x- marked a term that passed from one point to another. See (3). There, it may appear to indicate motion, but that results from equating Bella Coola *nap* with English *give*, while a better equation would be English *gift*. A closer gloss of (3) would be 'The woman gifted the man with a fish'. The staticness of x- is now more apparent as is the essential sameness of the Adjuncts in (3) and (4).

The distal ʔaɬ- and ʔuɬ- are opposed by static versus nonstatic as are the proximal x- and wixɬ-. In (69) and (71) the translation of ʔuɬ- as 'to' implies some action upon the man, e.g. giving presents. The translation of ʔaɬ- as 'for' implies no action upon the man, but that the man benefits indirectly by what the woman does or by her influence.

The four prepositions may then be described by the two oppositions distal:proximal and stative:nonstative:

	Stative	Nonstative
Distal	ʔaɬ-	ʔuɬ-
Proximal	x-	wixɬ-

To incorporate these additional data into our description of the syntax, the Adjunct of (13) is specified to have further structure:

(77)

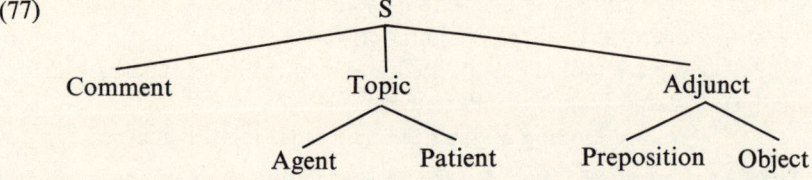

Where Equi-Constituent Deletion has removed the Object of an Adjunct, a Preposition Copy rule replicates the preposition immediately before the Comment. The copying form of x- is -s-. See (74iii) and (74iv). The copy of both distal prepositions, ʔał- and ʔuł-, is -si-. See (69iii), (69iv), (70iii), (70iv), (71iii), (71iv), (72iii), and (72iv). But wixł- has no copying form. Given (73), we would expect to find it embedded as a Comment in an adjectival clause analogous to (70iii) and (72iii):

(78) ʔałk'jukił tiʔimlk ti ____ ʔixq'ms cixnascx

where the ____ would be filled by some copy of wixł-. Since -si- copies both distal prepositions, we might expect -s- to copy both proximal ones. But

(79) *ʔałk'jukił tiʔimlk tisʔixq'ms cixnascx

is not a possible sentence. Sentences such as (78) and (79) are absent from the language, and the semantic slot is filled by constructions employing other forms; for example,

(80) ʔałk'jukił tiʔimlk tiwalis cixnascx
      'We know the man the woman is leaving'

Notice that in (69)(-72) the Comment of the embedded S_3 has an -s marking the third person singular Agent. This is because there has been no deletion of Agent or Patient of the embedded S_3 as there was in previous examples of adjectival clauses. It is the object of the Adjunct that is deleted in the (iii)- and (iv)-forms of (69)-(72). The other Agent-Patient suffixes occur where appropriate. Compare (74iii) that has the underlying structure:

(81)

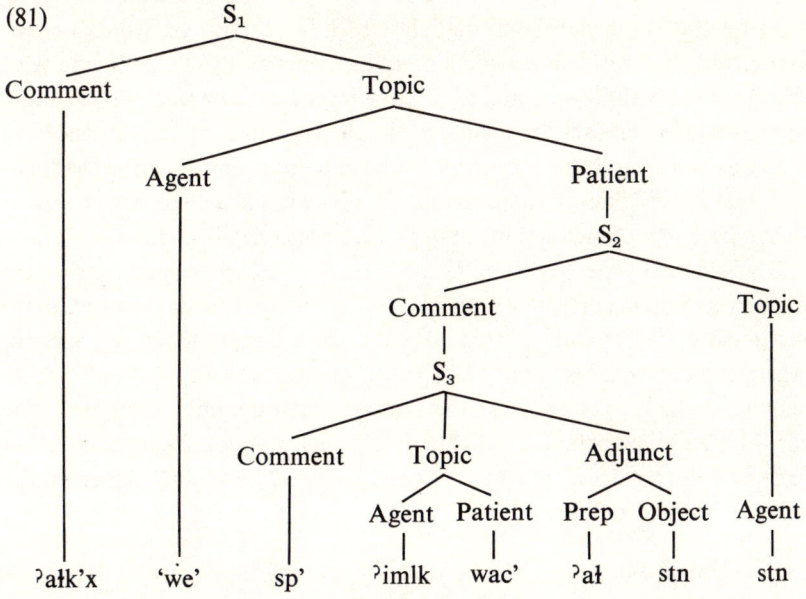

and the derived structure (82) after Equi-Constituent Deletion and Agent-Patient Agreement has applied to S_3:

(82)
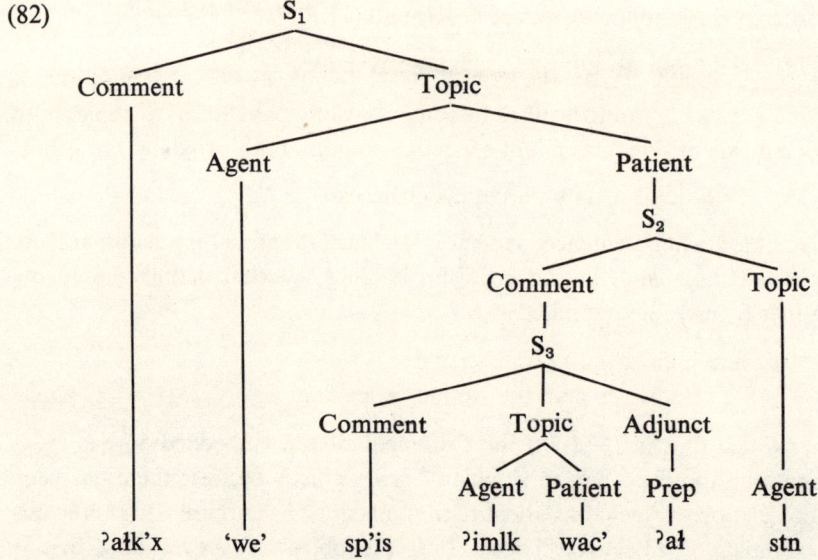

It is to this structure of S_3 in (82) and comparable ones that Preposition Copy applies.

2.2 We treat the relative clause and complex sentences together. The basis for this is the claim that the relative *wa* 'who' (and *ka* 'which') are in fact intransitive verbs functioning in all instances as a Comment, and with that difference alone – choice of relative *wa/ka* as Comment versus some other – relative clauses are syntactically identical to complex sentences.

Let us begin by discussing the complex sentences and showing that relative clause parallels exist for each type. In 1.3 we noted a distinction between nonrestrictive modification in complex sentences, the (ii)-forms of (35)-(37), and a S-Patient type, the (i)-forms of (35)-(37). The surface distinction lay in the possible occurrence of an overt noun Patient in the nonrestrictive modification type, while such was absent in the S-Patient sentences. Second, Agent-Patient suffixes other than those appropriate for a third person singular Patient may occur in the nonrestrictive modification type, while the S-Patient type complex sentence always has an Agent-Patient suffix that reflects a third person singular Patient. The two types fall together on the surface in such sentences as

(83) ʔałnapił sƛ'aps

that may mean 'We know him plus the fact that he is going' or 'We know that he is going'.

The nonrestrictive modification of complex sentences may be represented by the following underlying structure for (35ii):

(84)
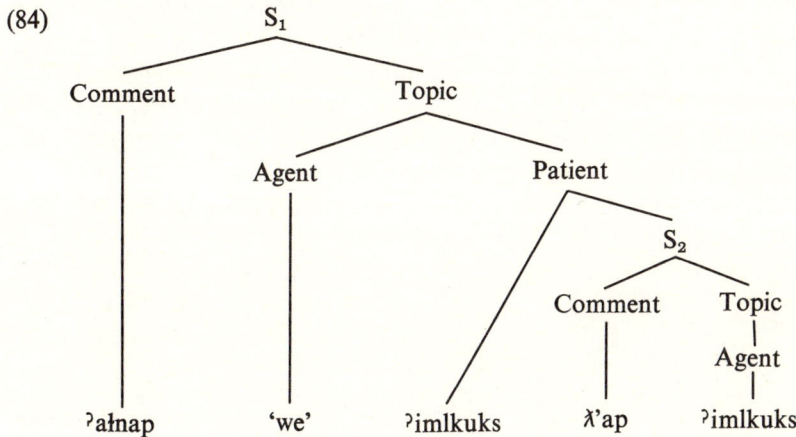

The structure of the Patient in (84) is to be contrasted with the structure of that constituent in (39). In (39), subjoining the equivalent of S_2 in (84) as a Comment predicated of a Topic expressed restriction of that Topic by new information. In (84) the structure of Patient is coordinate expressing nonrestriction; two things are known coordinately. This is comparable to other coordinate constructions:

(85)(i)   k'xił cixnascx ʔn waʔimlkuksc
        'We see the woman and the men'
 (ii)   k'xtił waʔimlkuksc ʔn cixnascx
        'We see the men and the woman'

Notice that the Agent-Patient suffix agrees with the first term of the coordinate Patient. (ʔn occurs as conjunction between lexical items but is otherwise absent in conjoined structures.) The same observation is true of the conjoined structure in (84).

The surface structure of (84) contains a single occurrence of ʔimlkuks, and

(86)   *ʔałnaptił waʔimlkuksc sƛ'apaw waʔimlkuksc

is incorrect. The Topic-Agent of S_2 in (84) is pronominalized wherever the first Patient constituent is a noun and then deleted by Pronoun Deletion. (Notice that Equi-Constituent Deletion cannot easily account for this. Recall from above that we have ordered Equi-Constituent Deletion before Agent Agreement. With that sequence we could not account for the presence of the Agent suffixes, e.g. -*aw*, in this structure.) Pronominalization applies elsewhere in Bella Coola. See Davis and Saunders 1973.

Now, the sentences of (24)-(28) with relative clauses have a structure analogous to (84). We will assume the syntactic equivalence of complex sentences and relative clauses to be demonstrated if, by assuming the structure of complex sentences for relative clauses, it can be shown that the same rules apply in the derivation of both. (87) is the structure underlying (24):

(87)
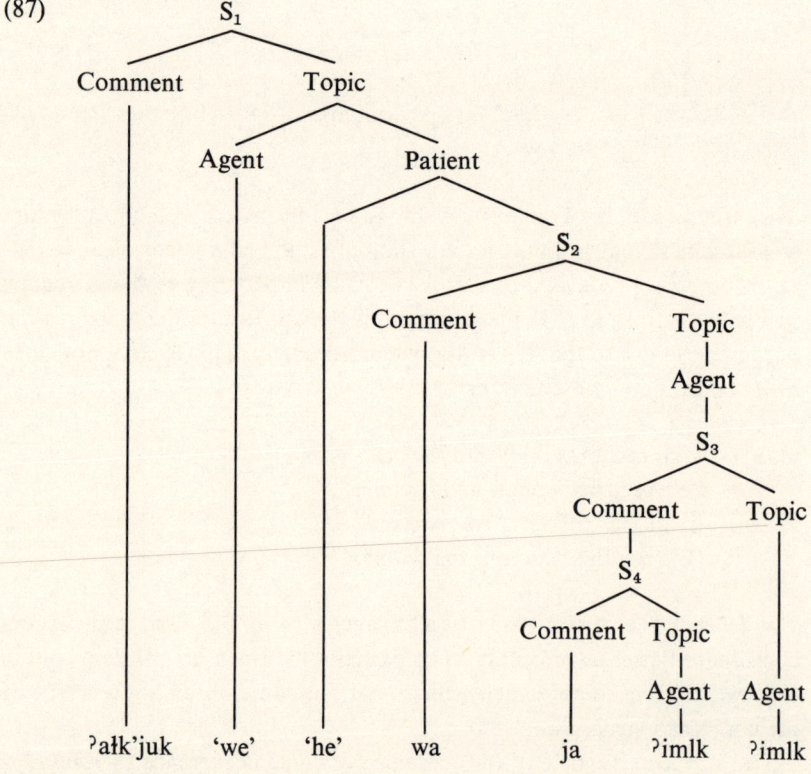

The transformational rules discussed in 2.1 apply to S_3 producing the derived structure:

(88)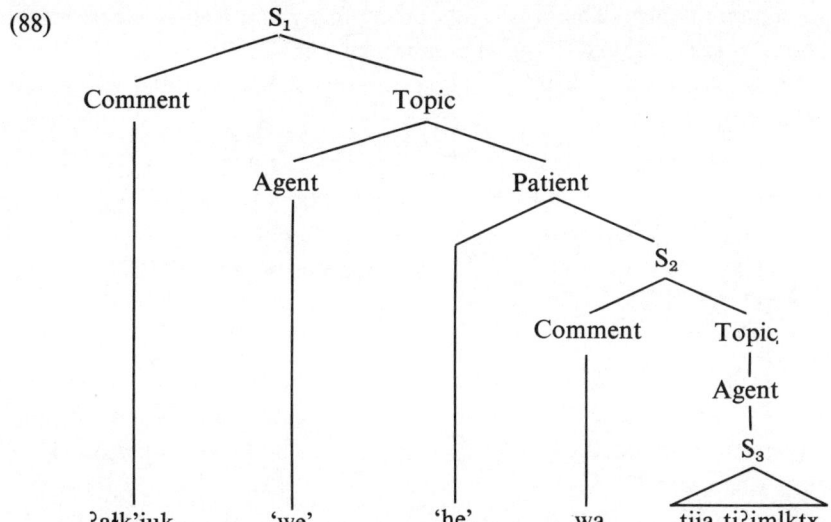

Agent-Agreement now affixes -s to wa of S_2. Sentences such as

(89) ʔałk'juktił swanaw waja waʔimlkuksc
'We know the men who are good'

show the suffix on the relative to be one of Agent Agreement. This parallels the suffix on ƛ'ap in (35ii).

One additional rule is required for both relative clauses and complex sentence constructions. Wherever an embedded S occurs such that the deictic prefixes have not been spread to its Comment, an s- is prefixed to the Comment of that S.[14] This applies to (87)-(88) and to (84). Finally, Agent-Patient Agreement applies to S_1, and the pronouns are deleted.[15]

In addition to the evidence adduced above for attributing the structure of nonrestrictive modification to relative clauses, such a structure is further required to account for the presence of Agent-Patient suffixes that vary from the third person singular Patient, e.g. (89). Relative clause sentences also occur where the first constituent of the Patient is a noun:

(90) ʔałk'juktił waʔimlkuksc swanaw waja
'We know the men who are good'

Here, Pronominalization and Pronoun Deletion have applied after Agent Agreement has suffixed -naw to wa. Again,

(91) *ʔałk'juktił waʔimlkuksc swanaw waja waʔimlkuksc

is ungrammatical. The description of the remaining relative clause structures of (25)-(28) and (30)-(34) parallel this one for (24).

Sentences occur where the Topic of the relative *wa* (and *ka*) is not restrictively modified:

(92)(i)   ʔałk'jukcant swac   'They know who I am'
    (ii) ʔałj'jukct swanu   'They know who you are'
    (iii) ʔałk'jukit swas   'They know who he is'
    (iv) ʔałk'juktułt swał   'They know who we are'
    (v)   ʔałk'juktap swanap   'They know who you all are'
    (vi) ʔałk'juktit swanaw   'They know who they are'

These have the underlying structure of (84), but the first constituent of Patient and the Topic-Agent of *wa* are pronouns. Sentences also occur where the first constituent of Patient is a noun and Pronominalization has applied; e.g.

(93)   ʔałk'juktił waʔimlkuksc swanaw   'We know who the men are'

and where the Topic-Agent of *wa* is a noun and the first constituent of Patient is a pronoun:

(94)   ʔałk'juktił swanaw waʔimlkuksc   'We know who the men are'

The S-Patient type of complex sentences – the (i)-forms of (35)-(37) – has an underlying structure similar to the following for (35i):

(95)

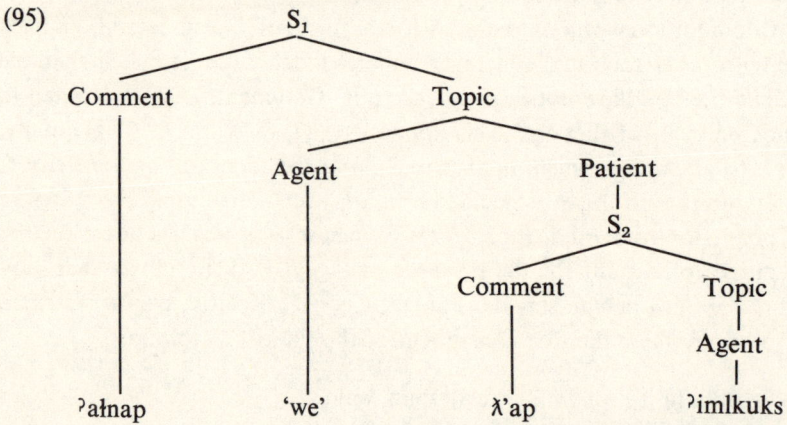

Agent Agreement suffixes -*aw* to *ƛ'ap* and an *s*- (embedded sentence) prefix is added to *ƛ'ap*. Agent-Patient Agreement then suffixes -*ił* to *ʔałnap*. Embedded sentences that prefix *s*- behave as third person singular Patients with respect to Agent-Patient Agreement.

The underlying structure (95) differs from (38), the structure underlying restrictive modification, in that (95) lacks coreferential constituents. Equi-Constituent Deletion, Deixis Spreading, and Topic-Raising do not apply to (95).

Finally, sentences also occur where the Comment of S_2 in (95) is a relative; for example,

(96) ʔałnapił swanaw waʔimlkuks waƛ'ap
     'We know that the men who are going are the ones'

The occurrence of an Agent-Patient suffix reflecting a third person singular Patient and not a third person plural one indicates that (96) has a structure analogous to (95):

(97)

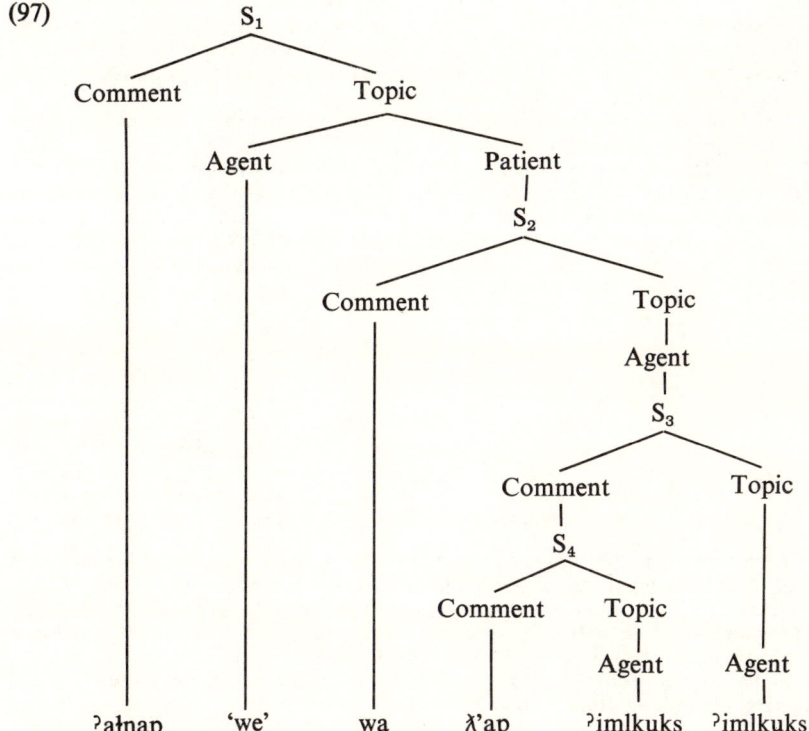

We began in 1.1-1.3 by assuming a three-way distinction of adjectival clause, relative clause, and complex sentence. Closer examination has shown that a three-way distinction in fact exists, but in different terms: restrictive modification, nonrestrictive modification, and S-Patient.

NOTES

[1] This is a revised version of a paper presented to the Eighth International Conference on Salish Languages, Eugene, Oregon, August, 1973. We wish to express here our gratitude to the National Museum of Canada, Simon Fraser University, Rice University, and the Canada Council for financial support of our fieldwork since 1966. We wish also to acknowledge the generous help given by our native informants: Andy Schooner, Margaret Siwallace, Felicity Walkus, and Charles Snow, our principal informant since 1971.

[2] The number chosen also depends on what is meant by the term 'Bella Coola'. Those of middle age, say, 35-50/55, speak a language that older speakers call 'broken.' It is the language of the older speakers that is represented in this paper. The figure 200 includes both these groups, but we will use 'Bella Coola' to designate only the language of the older group, which is significantly less than 200.

Among the older speakers we find additional variation in data across individuals, but because of the small number of speakers it is not possible to determine whether this is idiolectal or reflex of dialectal differences. It is typical of one of our informants to label as 'Kimsquit' or 'Tallio' some sentence construction with which she does not agree. The amalgamation of the villages into Bella Coola was virtually complete by 1920. The number moving from the settlements of Kimsquit and Tallio was small relative to those in Bella Coola. There are few who were reared in either of these villages still alive. It seems more likely this variation is idiolectal and perhaps further increased by the degree of influence English has had on each speaker. See now also Dorian 1973.

[3] The forms *ti---tx* and *ci---cx* bracketing *ʔimlk* 'man' and *xnas* 'woman', respectively, represent a set of deictic elements. The grammatical categories involved are Distal-Proximal, Demonstrative-Article, and Invisible-Visible. The distinction Invisible-Visible is made only in combination with Distal. Deixis intersects the grammatical categories of Singular Plural and, within the singular number, Female-Nonfemale. (The distinction is one of sex, not gender. Morphemes occurring with deixis are divided into those that refer to female animals and an unmarked group including male animals.) This intersection produces the following forms:

(i) Deixis

		Proximal		Distal		
		Article	Demonstrative	Article		Demonstrative
		I	II	IIIa	IIIb	IV
Sg.	Female	ci-cx	ci-c'ajx	ta-ił	ta-ł	ta-ʔiłaił
	Nonfemale	ti-tx	ti-t'ajx	ta-tx	ta-ł	ta-t'ax
Plural		wa-c	wa-ʔac	ta-tx^w	ta-ł	ta-t'ax^w

The referents of morphemes in construction with the deictic affixes of I are said to be near or in a known location, or seen frequently, but not necessarily visible. In construction with III the referents are either extant in the past, but not the present(IIIa) or they are not visible(IIIb). The 'past' reference of IIIa implies invisibility, and forms of III are opposed to those of IV as Invisible-Visible.

It can be seen from the display of (i) that the prefix marks the Distal-Proximal distinction, while suffixation distinguishes between Demonstrative-Article and further in III between Temporal and Spatial distance. The Demonstrative suffixes are practically identified as those that may accompany a gesture of pointing. Neither those of I nor III may do so. Further deictic segmentations can be made between Proximal and Distal space. This is marked by *-łai-* occurring immediately before the deictic suffix. It is identical for all forms of deixis except the Proximal Plural Demonstrative where it is *-ʔałai-*.

The Nonfemale Proximal prefix is also used to form gerunds:

(ii) tiƛ'ap 'going'

Gerunds may not occur with the Demonstrative/Article suffixes. Nouns, however, occur without those suffixes; without them they have indefinite reference. This makes (ii) ambiguous meaning either 'going' or 'a one[male] going'. The Plural Proximal prefix *wa-* also occurs without an accompanying suffix to mark an inanimate collective:

(iii) wa'anajkmix^w 'what[things] you want'

It is syntactically singular. Compare (iv) and (v):

(iv) 'ałnapic wa'anajkmix^w 'I know what you want'
(v)   'ałnaptic wa'anajkmix^{w}c   'I know who [all] you want'

[4] Bella Coola makes no thoroughgoing distinction between nouns, verbs, and adjectives (but see the discussion of sentences (14) and (17)-(70) below). We will use 'verb' and so forth loosely without giving them precise meaning within Bella Coola.
[5] The suffixes are partially fused, making clear distinction of a subject and object difficult. The set of noncausative, nonpassive suffixes are (cf. also Newman ca. 1935 and 1969):

(i)

		Object					
		Singular			Plural		
Subject		1	2	3	1	2	3
Singular	1	—	cinu	ic	—	tułap	tic
	2	cx^w	—	ix^w	tułx^w	—	tix^w
	3	cs	ct	is	tułs	tap	tis
Plural	1	—	tułnu	ił	—	tułap	tił
	2	cap	—	ip	tułp	—	tip
	3	cant	ct	it	tułt	tap	tił

(Verbs without additional tense, modal, or aspectual modification are undetermined within time; in our examples we gloss such verbs as simple or progressive present depending solely upon what is appropriate to the English.) Certain combinations of subject and object require further comment. Where a third person subject (singular or plural) and a second person object (singular or plural) occur with an overt subject, i.e. not a pronoun, that subject is marked by the preposition *x-* (cf. (3) and (4)):

(ii)(a) *k'xct ti'imlktx
   (b) k'xct xti'imlktx   'The man sees you'
(iii)(a) *k'xtap ti'imlktx
   (b) k'xtap xti'imlktx   'The man sees you all'
(iv)(a) *k'xtap wa'imlkuksc
   (b) k'xtap xa'imlkuksc   'The men see you all'

(In (ivb) the segment sequence /xw/ yields /x/ before /a/.) This phenomenon occurs only with this combination of persons. The (b)-constructions are incorrect for other person-number combinations.

The dashes marking some subject-object intersections in (i) occur where the referent of both subject and object is identical. In this circumstance a reflexive morpheme *-cut-* is suffixed to the stem and the subject suffixes added. They are

(v) -c   'I'   -(i)ł   'we'
     -nu 'you'   -(n)ap 'you'
     -(s) 'he/she/it'   -(n)aw 'they'

They occur elsewhere with nouns (vi), intransitive verbs (vii), and adjectives (viii):

(vi)   staltmxc   'I am chief'
(vii)   λ'apc   'I am going'
(viii) sxc   'I am bad'

They also mark possession; (vi), for example, can also mean 'my chief'. The variant forms within the plural of (v) are determined by the final segment of the stem. The vowel initial variants occur after consonants, and the consonant initial ones after vowels. The -s of the third person singular is more troublesome. In embedded sentences it always occurs with third person singular subjects. In nonembedded ones the -s at one time appeared to be stylistically determined (Newman ca. 1935:28): "One of my informants said that the -s suffix characterizes 'the way stories are told', that the zero suffix is more commonly used in conversation. Although it is true that the zero suffix is relatively rare in texts as compared with my field notes, it is not consistently avoided in telling stories ... Apparently a stylistic difference is felt between the -s and the zero suffix, the latter perhaps expressing a more informal abbreviated version of the pronominal reference." Our informants most frequently do not use -s in nonembedded sentences. Where it does occur in that position, it is affixed only to verbs, not to adjectives nor nouns – a first indication of a distinction between verb and nonverb in the language. Nonembedded sentences containing it elicit the comment that they are 'a little bit different' from the ones without it. When pressed to explain that difference, informants respond to sentences with -s with 'I'm just talking about it'. This fits Newman's observation that the -s characterizes stories. Given that it is explained as 'just talking' and that it can be used outside its appropriate stylistic matrix, it may be that a stylistic difference is in progress of being reinterpreted as a grammatical one.

Both sets of suffixes in (i) and (v) will be absent from underlying structures and assumed to be added by transformational rules that we (looking forward to the introduction of the terms Agent and Patient) call Agent-Patient Agreement for (i) and Agent Agreement for (v).

[6] (18i) is correct if glossed as 'I see him [who] punched the person' in place of 'I see the person [who] punched him'.
[7] (20i) is correct if glossed as 'I see what/him you are giving the slave' in place of 'I see the slave you are giving him/her'. The latter is intended here.
[8] (26i) is correct with the gloss 'We know who punched the man' but not with the gloss 'We know the man who punched him'. The latter is meant here.
[9] (28i) is correct with the gloss 'We know who you are giving to the slave' but not with the gloss 'We know the slave you are giving him/her'. The latter is intended here.
[10] (32i) is correct with the gloss 'We know which one punches the man' but not with the gloss 'We know which man punches him/her'. The latter is meant here.
[11] (34i) is correct with the gloss 'We know which one you are giving the slave' but not with the gloss 'We know which slave you are giving him/her. The latter is intended here.
[12] The form $q\bar{u}xp$' is a reduplication from the root qup'. For a statement of reduplication and verbal categories in Bella Coola, see Saunders and Davis 1972.
[13] Transitivity would then force the following extrinsic ordering:

(i)   Agent-Patient Agreement
(ii) Equi-Constituent Deletion
(iii) Agent Agreement
(iv) Pronoun Deletion

[14] This s- may be identified with the s- of deverbal noun derivation that occurs in Bella Coola and other Salish languages:

(i)(a) na-xc-ax   'to lie down'
   (b) s-xic-ta   'bed'
(ii)(a) q'łq^w 'to dress'
    (b) s-q'łq^w 'clothes'

If such identification is made, then embedded S's may be interpreted as being required to convert to nouns either by incorporation within a noun (i.e. via the speading of Distal/Proximal) or where that does not apply, by s-derivation.

[15] Other morphemes that occur as Comments similar to the relatives are *xsūc* 'all' and *q'ʷala* 'all gone, no more':

(i) ʔałk'juktił sxsūcaw waƛ'msta waƛ'ap
     'We know all the people who are going'
(ii) ʔałk'juktił sq'ʷalanaw waƛ'msta waja
     'We know there are no more people who are good'

Sentences (i) and (ii) have underlying structures analogous to (87).

MICMAC INTRANSITIVE
VERB MORPHOLOGY[1]

JAMES L. FIDELHOLTZ

INTRODUCTION

This article is intended to present a more or less typical example of morphological analysis, and the phonological rules which account for the morphophonemic variations involved. We will attempt to determine what are the underlying representations of the present tense, indicative mode morphemes in the Micmac of present-day Restigouche, Quebec. Micmac is an Algonquian language of Eastern Canada. We exemplify all known classes of Micmac intransitive verbs, which of course will involve a great many morphological and major and minor phonological rules; we will be unable within the scope of this article appropriately to motivate all rules we discuss. The purpose is to present the facts of a well-delimited area of Micmac morphology, and the phonological processes involved. Accordingly, little emphasis will be placed on the form of the phonological rules as such. A much more extensive analysis of these and other facts of Micmac, in most cases with more extensive motivations for the rules, can be found in Fidelholtz (1968).

We make the methodological assumption that, unless one reaches untenable positions (i.e. in cases of suppletion), two forms with the same relative position and/or the same function (and of course the same meaning) are the same morpheme – that is, phonologically identical.[2] Differences in actual shape will be assumed to be due to regular relationships between underlying and actually occurring shapes, that is, due to the application of phonological rules to these underlying forms.[3] We will try to 'undo' some of these relationships or phonological rules, and thus determine what are the underlying shapes common to superficially different forms of the same morphemes.

INTRANSITIVE VERB ENDINGS

From the paradigms of various verbs in Table 1, we can see the varying occurrent forms for the present tense person endings.[4]

Using our methodological assumption, then, we may look first of all at the second person singular morpheme (line 2 of Table 1). It seems clear that this morpheme always appears as [−n]. Lacking any reason to assume otherwise, we make the most obvious assumption, namely that the underlying form is /−n/. The only peculiarity here is in the form [telkiñ] 'you are that size', which is from assimilation of the final /l/ of the stem to the second person /n/ by a very general rule of Micmac, L-ASSIMILATION.

If we now examine the first person singular morpheme, we will find that the situation is somewhat more clouded than that we have just considered. That is, the first person singular morpheme ostensibly takes two different forms in different verbs: −0 (zero) or [−y]. Before we can explain this, it is necessary to make a brief inquiry into certain facts of Micmac noun paradigms.

If we examine the singular and plural forms of the nouns listed in Table 2, several facts become evident: firstly, Micmac nouns are divided into two classes: animate and inanimate. The animate plural (that is, nonsingular —— in nouns the dual is not distinct in form from the plural) ending is /−k/ (Table 2A), while the inanimate nonsingular ending is /−l/ (Table 2B). 2A and 2B are representative of the vast majority of Micmac nouns. But as we can see from the examples in Table 2C, some stems end in a vowel, before the plural endings /−k/ or /−l/. We must assume that this vowel is part of the stem, in order to retain the generalization that, depending on its class, the plural of any noun is either /−k/ or /−l/. In the singular, however, long vowels become short, and short vowels are lost altogether. That is, in word final position we need a rule (the FINAL VOWEL SHORTENING rule) to delete short vowels and make long vowels short. Note that this rule applies to vowels only, not glides.[5] (This is also some evidence that at the point where this rule applies, long vowels are expressed as sequences of two short vowels, so that we could simply say: in word-final position, delete one (short) vowel. See Fidelholtz (1971) for more discussion of the representation of long vowels.)

But now we can see the application of this to the first person singular. If the 1s. sing. is in fact /−i/, and if there is a rule to change some of the /i/'s to [y] (a GLIDE FORMATION rule), then the remaining /i/'s, being in word-final position, will be deleted by the FINAL VOWEL SHORTENING rule. (Note that we must also assume that the rules are ordered; we will discuss this in more

TABLE 1. *Intransitive Paradigms*

Person/no.	Abbreviation	Underlying endings	Stems				Line no.
			ayči – be such; be that way	*čič:emā* – stink	*telkil* – be that size	*wekāi* – be mad; be angry	
I	1s.	i	ayči	čič:emāy	telkil	wekāy	1
you (s.)	2s.	n	ayčin	čič:emān	telkin	wekāyn	2
he, she	3an.s.	ti	ayčit	čič:emāt	telkilk	wekāyk	3
it	3inan.s.	k	ayčik	čič:emāq	telkik	(wekāyk)*	4
DUAL							
we (inc.)	12dual	i+ū+k	ayčikw	čič:emāykw	telkilūkw	wekāyūkw	5
we (exc.)	13dual	i+e+k	ayčiek	čič:emāyek	telkilek	wekāyek	6
you	2dual	i+o+k	ayčioq	čič:emāyoq	telkiloq	wekāyoq	7
they (an.)	3an.dual	i+ti+k	ayčičik	čič:emāčik	telkilkik	wekāykik	8
they (inan.)	3inan.dual	i+k+l	ayčikl	čič:emāqal	telkikl	(wekāykl)*	9
PLURAL							
we (inc.)	12pl.	lti+ū+k	ayčultikw	čič:emōltikw	telkilultikw	wekāyultikw	10
we (exc.)	13pl.	lti+e+k	ayčultiek	čič:emōltiek	telkilultiek	wekāyultiek	11
you	2pl.	lti+o+k	ayčultioq	čič:emōltioq	telkilultioq	wekāyultioq	12
they (an.)	3an.pl.	lti+ti+k	ayčultičik	čič:emōltičik	telkilultičik	wekāyultičik	13
they (inan.)	3inan.pl.	lti+k+l	ayčultikl	čič:emōltikl	telkilultikl	(wekāyultikl)*	14

* These forms are of course semantic nonsense for this verb; but if they were possible, they would take these shapes.

TABLE 2. *Noun Plurals*

Singular	Plural	Gloss
	A (*Animate*)	
pūtay	pūtayk	bottle
čipčīč	čipčīčk	(little) bird
kopit	kopitk	beaver
lmūč	lmūčk	dog
kīkamkōn	kīkamkōnk	(jink) pole; boat pole
wow	wowkw	pot
čīkāw	čīkāwkw	bass
	B (*Inanimate*)	
nipit	nipitl	tooth
tepkik	tepkikl	night
mapos	maposl	pocket
wisawow	wisawowl	loose (diseased) feces
kīkamkōn	kīkamkōñ	(fancy) pole; flagpole
wasuek	wasuekl	flower
	C	
iktik	iktikik	other
muīn	muīnaq	bear
nikoq	nikoqol	spear
tapi	tapīk	bow
lnu	lnūkw	Indian
awkti	awktīl	road
wiñu	wiñūl	tongue

detail below.) In fact, the GLIDE FORMATION rule says, very roughly, that /i/ becomes [y] after a vowel (note the stem /wekāi−/, which becomes [wekāy−]). We then have the following derivations:

/čič:emā+i/	/telkil+i/	/wekāi+i/	
čič:emā+y	(inapplicable)	wekāy+i	GLIDE FORMATION
čič:emāy	telkil	wekāy	FINAL VOWEL SHORTENING

Note that GLIDE FORMATION is inapplicable to /telkil+i/, because /l/ is not a vowel; similarly, FINAL VOWEL SHORTENING is inapplicable to /čič:emā+y/, because /y/ is not a vowel. The actual GLIDE FORMATION rule, which is somewhat complex, will account for the fact that the second /i/ in /wekāi+i/ does not become [y]. See Fidelholtz 1968 (23-28 and *passim*) for details.[6]

We return here to the nouns for a moment to discuss two slight irregularities in the plurals. First, we expect the plural of [čīkāw] 'bass' to be *[čīkāwk] (from /čīkāw+k/), but we actually find [čīkāwkw]. In fact, we never find [−wk] or [−uk] sequences in Micmac unless the [k] is labialized, that is, followed by a [w]. Therefore the [w] is predictable by a rule we can call the K-LABIALIZATION rule. Secondly, in the plural of the word for 'bear' we expect *[muīnak] (from /muīna+k/), but we actually find [muīnaq]. If we examine the distributions of [q] and [k] in Micmac words, however, we find that [q] occurs only after an /a/ or /o/, while [k] never occurs in that environment.[7] Therefore, [q] appears to derive from /k/ by a phonological rule, the K → Q rule. Thus we can say that all [q] segments in Micmac derive from an underlying /k/ (after /a/ or /o/), and that some [kw] sequences derive also from an underlying /k/ after /u/ (some [−kw−] sequences come from underlying /−ku−/ by GLIDE FORMATION, but this is not germane to our discussion).

The third person singular inanimate appears to be quite regular – it always appears as [−k]. (See line 4 of Table 1. The slight quasi-suppletive irregularity of [telkīk] need not concern us here. See below.) In the dual and plural, however, we find that after the [k] is the inanimate plural [l], which we found in inanimate noun plurals. (We will discuss below the /i/ dual marker, and account for its frequent lack of occurrence in surface forms.)

The third person animate endings (line 3 of Table 1) seem more complex. First of all, the singular appears as either [−t] or [−k]. In fact, [−k] appears only after sonorant consonants, derived by a rule we call the T → K rule. Examples are [telkilk] 'he's that big' and [wekāyk] 'he gets mad'. Thus, the underlying form seems to be /−t/.[8] In the dual, however, we frequently find the ending [−čik] (e.g. [čič:emāčik], [ayčičik]). The [−k] here appears to be the animate nonsingular ending, just as the [−l] in the 3inan.dual forms appears to be the inanimate nonsingular ending, both of which we met earlier in the noun paradigms. We can, then, analyze the 3an.dual as [−či+k]. But now we suppose that the 3an. morpheme is /−ti/. In the 3an.s. form, FINAL VOWEL SHORTENING will give us [−t] (or [−k] after sonorants). In the dual and plural, however, the /t/, when not following a sonorant, becomes palatalized to [č] before /i/ by a very general rule we will call the T → Č rule. We can see this rule operating in the following examples:

    [pekitkopin]   'you sit a long time' (from /pekit+kopi+n/);
    [pekičāsin]   'you take a long time to get there',

on the other hand, comes from /pekit+iāsi+n/, and the T → Č rule changes the /t/ of /pekit/ to [č] (a later rule dropping the /i/ before /ā/ – see the discussion of Table 13 below – gives the actual form). Therefore the 3an. s. ending is /−ti/ $\xrightarrow{\text{FINAL VOWEL SHORTENING}}$ [−t] (sometimes, depending on the environment, $\xrightarrow{T \to K}$ [−k]), and the 3an.dual is /−ti+k/ $\xrightarrow{T \to Č}$ [−či+k] (or, after sonorant consonants, $\xrightarrow{T \to K}$ [−ki+k]).

The dual and plural in Micmac have two separate forms corresponding to the English 'we' – 'inclusive' (including second person) and 'exclusive' (excluding second person). The 'you' and 'exclusive we' dual uniformly end in [−ek] and [−oq], respectively, as we can see from lines 6 and 7 of Table 1. But, as we saw above, [q] comes from an underlying /k/, so the 2dual ending ends in underlying /−ok/. The 'we inclusive' dual ending (line 5 of Table 1) turns up as [−ikw], [−ykw], or [−ūkw]. Examples are [ayčīkw], [čič:emaykw], and [telkilūkw]. /−ūkw/ is chosen as closest to the underlying form, the /ū/ being deleted or assimilated to a stem-final /i/ in some verbs by what we call the Ū-CHANGE rule; for with this form, but not with the others, we can predict the labialization of the /k/ to [kw] by the above discussed K-LABIALIZATION rule.[9] The animate duals, then, end in underlying /−ūk/, /−ek/, /−ok/, and /−tik/, for the 12, 13, 2, and 3an.dual, respectively. Recall, however, that in /−tik/, the /k/ was analyzed as being the nonsingular animate ending; the most general assumption is that the same holds true for the other forms. Therefore duals (and plurals – see below) end in /−ū+k/, /−e+k/, /−o+k/, and /−ti+k/, respectively. The inanimate nonsingulars likewise end in /−k+l/. Note that, if correct, this further supports our analysis of the 12 nonsingular ending: unless /ū/ is present in the underlying form, it will not be possible to predict the final [w], and therefore to make the apparently correct generalization that both verbal and nominal nonsingular forms are marked by the nonsingular affixes – /k/ and /l/, respectively, for animates and inanimates. That is, the 12 ending would have to be (say) /−ikw/, with no possibility of predicting the [w].

If we consider the forms of the stem /čič:emā/ in lines 6 and 7 of Table 1, however: [čič:emāyek] and [čič:emāyoq], we find that the [y] in each case can only be accounted for by considering it to be part of the ending rather than part of the stem. Indeed, careful examination of these and other forms in Micmac shows that the [y] (from /i/) is in fact the dual morpheme. So we postulate the dual morpheme /+i+/, which remains, deletes, or changes to [+y+] in specifiable circumstances (namely, the /i/ deletes before any consonant, and after sonorant consonants (SONORANT I-DELETION), and changes to [y] by the GLIDE FORMATION rule). The underlying dual forms, then, are finally as in the third column of lines 5-9 in Table 1: /i+ū+k/, /i+e+k/, /i+o+k/, /i+ti+k/, /i+k+l/.

Likewise, it is easy to show that /−lti−/ is the plural marker, and the underlying plural endings are as in the first column of lines 10-14 in Table 1.[10] In other words, the endings we discussed above ((/−ūk/, /−ek/, /−ok/, /−tik/, and /−kl/) are the **nonsingular** endings. Each is preceded in addition

TABLE 3. *The Negative Marker* (/−u−/ > [−w−]) *and its Relation to the Dual and Plural Markers*

čič-emā− −w−ek		13 dual negative
čič:emō−lti−w−ek		13pl. negative
čič:emā− y−	ek	13dual
čič:emō−lti−	ek	13pl.

by one of two other morphemes − the dual or the plural − to distinguish between the pairs of otherwise identical nonsingular forms. The parts of the **plural** endings after the plural marker in all cases end up looking just like **dual** endings after [ayči−]-type verbs − that is, /−lti−/, as might be expected, acts like what it is − a form ending in a consonant plus /i/.

The negative marker, namely /−u−/, which sometimes becomes [w] in the same way that /i/ sometimes becomes [y] (by the GLIDE FORMATION rule), provides further evidence for our interpretation of the dual and plural morphemes − for it occurs **between** the number marker (if any) and the person endings (see Table 3 − the dual /−y−/ drops before the negative /−w−/ by a 'neighbourhood rule' extension of SONORANT I-DELETION).

Up to now, we have been concerned mainly with verbal suffixes. We will now consider phonological changes affecting the stem in subtypes of our four classes of verbs, and in other verbal classes.

Note that the vowel preceding the plural [−lti−] is often not identical to that of the stem. In particular, it is always [ŏ] or (long or short) [u]. That is, we need a rule of VOWEL BACKING to make all vowels back and nonlow before the /−lti−/ plural (but not before the /−ti−/ plural − see below). In addition to this rule, we need a rule to insert a high vowel before the plural, after a consonant stem (U-EPENTHESIS), in e.g. [wekāyulti−] < /wekāy+lti/ and [telkilulti−] < /telkil+lti−/. In most consonant stems, however, the consonant drops in many preconsonantal environments: /y/ after a nonlow vowel and all /m/'s drop before +/l, k, t/; /n/ drops before +/l/ only (namely, the plural). This rule we dub PRE-C C-DELETION.

In Tables 4, 5, 6, and 7 are listed types of verbs basically similar, respectively, to /ayči−/, /čič:emā−/, /telkil−/, and /wekāy−/.[11]

We can see that, in Table 7, underlying /sēsəpaqanēy+lti−/ becomes /sēsəpaqanē+lti−/ by PRE-C C-DELETION, and then /sēsəpaqanō+lti−/ by VOWEL BACKING. Note that PRE-C C-DELETION must follow GLIDE FORMATION in order that the /y/ of /sēsəpaqanēy−/ be deletable. [penoqōlti−] comes from /penoqwō+lti−/ by a general rule (W-VOCALIZATION) assimilating the /w/ to the following /ō/ after back consonants (/q, k/).

TABLE 4. *Stems like* /ayči−/ (220)

sneeze	/ečkwi−/ (30)	/ečkwi+lti−/ ⇒ /ečkwu+lti−/ ⇒ [ečkūlti−]
be frozen	/kelči−/ (1)	inan. → [keltə−k]
look good	/weli+alkamkusi−/ (1)	optionally → drops /−si−/ in inan.
be that color	/na+tel+amukwsi−/ (6)	optionally → drops /−si−/ and lengthens /ū/ in inan.
be blabbing	/etl+toqsi−/ (16)	inan. → [etltā−q]
be poor	/eulēči−/ (11)	inan. → [eulēč−k] (possibly by a regular rule)
be that big a lump	/tel+apskəsi−/ (1)	inan. → [telapske−k]
be burnt	/kawsi−/ (12)	inan. → [kaqte−k]
be lonesome, calm	/čikpi−/ (18)	inan. → [čikte−k]
be good	/kelūsi−/ (1)	inan. → [kelŭl−k]
grow	/pem+iki−/ (1)	inan. → [pemikwe−k]
one's shape	/tel+iki−/ (3)	inan. ⇒ [telik−k]

In Table 6, underlying /nastesin+lti/, /telkwičin+lti/, /aqamīm+lti/, and /aĪtukwīm+lti/ become respectively /nastesi+lti/, /telkwiči+lti/, /aqamī+lti/, and /aĪtukwī+lti/ by PRE-C C-DELETION, and then the respective plural stems are correctly derived by VOWEL BACKING. The /w/ is assimilated to the following /ū/ in /aĪtukūlti/ and likewise in Table 4, /ečkwu+lti/ (from /ečkwi+lti/ by VOWEL BACKING) becomes /ečkuu+lti/ by W-VOCALIZATION. Then in both cases (as well as in /penoqoō+lti/ < /penoqwō+lti/) a late very general rule of GEMINATE SEGMENT AGGLOMERATION produces a long segment from a sequence of two identical segments.

In Table 5, we find VOWEL BACKING applying to /nūqwā+lti/, /taluekē+lti/ and /esamuqwā+lti/ to give, respectively, /nūqwōlti/, /taluekōlti/, and /esamuqwōlti/. To the first and third of these, W-VOCALIZATION and GEMINATE SEGMENT AGGLOMERIZATION apply to give /nūqōlti/ and /esamuqōlti/, respectively. In the singular of /esamuqwā−/ and /taluekē−/, a NONPLURAL V-SHORTENING rule shortens the final stem vowels to /ă−/ and /ĕ−/, respectively. To retain the long /ā/ in the singular of /nūqwā−/ and /čič:emā−/, we must assume that these stems end in /aā−/, which in the singular becomes /aă−/ by NONPLURAL V-SHORTENING and then /ā−/ by GEMINATE SEGMENT AGGLOMERATION. NONPLURAL V-SHORTENING is pervasive in verbs with −/−ti/ plurals (see below), so it is possible that we should only allow it to operate generally with /−ti−/ plural verbs, and consider /esamuqwā−/ and /nūqwā−/ irregular in undergoing the rule, thus making it unnecessary to have the underlying

TABLE 5. *Stems like* /čič:emā−/ (36)

be burning	/nūqwā−/ (1)	pl. ⇒ [nūqōlti−]
what use is ___?	/tal+uekē−/ (1)	pl. ⇒ [taluekō+lti−]; /ē/ ⇒ [−long] in [−plural]
drink	/esamuqwā−/ (1)	pl. ⇒ [esamuqōlti−]; /ā/ ⇒ [−long] in [−plural]
dance	/amalkă−/ (1)	pl. → [amalkă+lti−] (?or [amalkăl+ti])
flee	/wesmuɣwă−/ (1)	pl. → [wesmu−lti−] (note peculiar behavior of extremely rare Micmac segment [ɣ] − velar, not uvular, fricative)
climb up	/toqčūkusue−/ (1)	pl. ⇒ [toqčūkusu−lti−]

TABLE 6. *Stems like* /telkil−/

	/tel+kil−/ (16)	inan. → [telkī+k]
how much does one weigh?	/tal+iksukul−/ (2)	inan. → /taliksuku+k/ ⇒ [taliksuk:w]
be caught	/nastesin−/ (66)	inan. → [nastes+k]; pl. ⇒ [nastesu+lti−]
think, believe	/tel+kwičin−/ (13)	inan. → [telkwit+k]; pl. ⇒ [telkwičulti−]
arrive, come (unexpectedly)	/pekisin−/ (1)	(inan. → [pekis+k]); pl. → [peytā−]
go in snowshoes	/aqamīm−/ (3)	inan. → [aqamĭ+k]; pl. ⇒ [aqamūlti−]
run all over	/aĭtukwīm−/ (10)	inan. → [aĭtukwĭ+k]; pl. ⇒ [aĭtukūlti−]

TABLE 7. *Stems like* /wekāy−/ (3)

[Note: except after /ā/, stem-final /y/ drops / ___ [t, k, l]. This causes the plural of /y/-stems (except the /wekāy−/ type) to be like that of /čič:emā−/]

be a blabbermouth	/sēsəpaqanēy−/ (87)	
be filthy, bad-mannered	/penoqwēy−/ (2)	pl. ⇒ [penoqōlti−]
be ready	/kiskačēy−/ (1)	inan. → [kiskatte−k]
be separated	/teppisēy−/ (1)	inan. → [teppiste−k]
bellow, holler	/ketū−/ (1)	inan. → [ketue−k]

form; e.g. /čič:emaā−/, but rather /čič:emā−/. We will leave the problem in this rather unsatisfactory state. Stem-final nonhigh short vowels drop generally before the plural morpheme (/−lti−/ or (see below) /−ti−/) by PLURAL V̆-DELETION. This gives us /toqčūkusu+lti/ from /togčūkusue+lti/, and may help account for the quite irregular /wesmu+lti/ < /wesmuɣwa+lti/. A further rule we will only mention here drops some

TABLE 8

Person/no.	/pewīke−/ sweep	/naqanāmā−/ be drinking (alcohol)	/eluēwiē−/ be crazy	/āləm−/ swim around (out of sight)
1s.	pewīkey	naqanāmay	eluēwiey	āləm
2s.	pewīken	naqanāman	eluēwien	āləmən
3an.s.	pewīket	naqanāmat	eluēwiet	ālək
3inan.s.	pewīkek	naqanāmaq	eluēwiaq	(ālək)
12dual	pewīkeykw	naqanāmaykw	eluēwieykw	āləmūkw
13dual	pewīkeyek	naqanāmayek	eluēwieyek	āləmek
2dual	pewīkeyoq	naqanāmayoq	eluēwieyoq	āləmoq
3an.dual	pewīkečik	naqanāmačik	eluēwiečik	āləkik
3inan.dual	pewīkekl	naqanāmaqal	eluēwiaqal	(āləkl)
12pl.	pewīkətīkw	naqanāmātīkw	eluēwiātīkw	āləmūtīkw
13pl.	pewītətiek	naqanāmātiek	eluēwiātiek	āləmūtiek
2pl.	pewīkətioq	naqanāmātioq	eluēwiātioq	āləmūtioq
3an.pl.	pewīkətičik	naqanāmātičik	eluēwiātičik	āləmūtičik
3inan.pl.	pewīkətikl	naqanāmātikl	eluēwiātikl	(āləmūtikl)

unstressed short vowels (especially high ones) in some consonantal environments (e.g. between velars), and gives us the inanimate /telikk/ from /teliki+k/ (Table 4) and /taliksukkw/ from the partially suppletive /taliksuku+k/ (Table 6 - stem /taliksukul/).

Another class of verb stems differs from the ones we have been discussing in that the plural morpheme added to them is /−ti−/ instead of /−lti−/.

Table 8 gives representative examples of the class of verbs with [−ti−] plurals. There are many similarities to /−lti−/ plural verbs. Note that the plural of /āləm−/ is /āləm+ti−/, which by U-EPENTHESIS becomes /āləm+u+ti−/. Then a widespread rule of PRE-TI V-LENGTHENING will give [āləmūti−]. Note that PLURAL V̆-DELETION must apply before PRE-TI V-LENGTHENING to give /pewīk+ti−/ from /pewīke+ti−/. Then, after PRE-TI V-LENGTHENING has failed to apply (since there is no vowel before /−ti−/ at that point), a rule of SHWA-INSERTION gives /pewīk+ə+ti−/. (Note that U-EPENTHESIS must precede PLURAL V̆-DELETION, or we would get /pewīke+ti−/ $\xrightarrow{\text{PLURAL V-DELETION}}$ /pewīk+ti−/ $\xrightarrow{\text{U-EPENTHESIS, PRE-TI V-LENGTHENING}}$ */pewīkūti−/.) In the singular and dual of /naqanāmā−/ and /eluēwiē−/, NONPLURAL V-SHORTENING gives, respectively, /naqanāmă−/ and /eluēwiĕ−/. In the plural /eluēwiē+ti−/, another rule of PRE-TI E → A gives /eluēwiā+ti−/. This rule could not be combined with VOWEL BACKING, since the latter would predict [ō], rather than the actual [ā], from

TABLE 9. *Stems like* /pewīke−/ (11)

be swollen	/moqpe−/ (4)	
pity	/eulitelke−/ (1)	
grow up here	/etl+ikwe−/ (3)	pl. ⇒ [etlikuti−]
work	/elukwe−/ (24)	pl. ⇒ [elukuti−]
live alone	/neuktukwalukwe−/ (5)	pl. ⇒ [neuktukwalukūti−]
fish	/weske−/ (1)	pl. stem → /wĕske−/
smoke (tobacco)	/wetma−/ (2)	identical to /pewīke−/, except with [a−]
be sick	/kesnukwa−/ (3)	identical to /elukwe−/, except with [a−]
throw, play a game, run for office	/eleke−/ (48)	pl → [elaqa+ti−]; these are all pseudo-intransitive verbs which act like TI verbs in /−eke−/ paired up with TA verbs in /−aqa+l−/
be good, generous	/welmətu−/ (10)	pl. ⇒ [welmətūti−]; 3an.s. ⇒ [welməto+q]

/ē/. Furthermore, the plural [ketkunī+ti−] (Table 10 below) shows that VOWEL BACKING is morphologically restricted to verbs taking the /−lti−/ plural, since we do not get *[ketkunūti−]. PRE-TI E → A also accounts for the plural [eknūtmuāu+ti/ from /eknūtmuēu+ti/ (from /eknūtmueu+ti/ by PRE-TI V-LENGTHENING). An extension of the rule will account for /eluēwia+q/, by K → Q from /eluēwia+k/, from /eluēwie+k/ by PRE-TI E → A, ultimately from /eluēwiē+k/ by NONPLURAL V-SHORTENING.

Tables 9, 10, 11, and 12 illustrate subtypes of verbs basically like /pewīke−/, /naqanāmā−/, /eluēwiē−/, and /āləm−/, respectively.

/etlikwe+ti/, /elukwe+ti/, and /kesnukwa+ti/ (Table 9) all show PLURAL V̆-DELETION and SHWA-INSERTION, and further show that W-VOCALIZATION (> /etlikuə+ti/, /elukuə+ti/ and /kesnukuə+ti/) and SHWA-INSERTION come after PRE-TI V-LENGTHENING. /neuktukwalukū+ti/ evinces lengthening of the /ū/ purely because of the length of the word (cf. [elukŭ+ti−] with [paqsippesīwlukū +ti−] 'be sick and tired of working. < /paqsippe+sīw+eluku+ti−/, with the identical stem, but simply as part of a long word). The stems /wetma−/ and /kesnukwa−/ are just like /pewīke−/ and /elukwe−/, respectively, except for having /ă−/ where the latter evince /ĕ−/.

The stem /welmətu−/ indicates that PLURAL V̆-DELETION can apply only to nonhigh vowels (/ayči+lti/ > ayču+lti/ shows the same thing, since, as we have seen, U-EPENTHESIS must **precede** PLURAL V̆-DELETION, the /i/ of /ayči/ can not have been deleted and a /u/ then inserted). Thus PRE-TI

TABLE 10. *Stems like* /naqanāmā−/ (87)

sleep there	/ketkunī−/ (1)	identical to /naqanāmā−/, except with [ĭ−] or [ī−], respectively
plant	/(l)ikātaqū−/ (6)	inan. → [ikātaque+k]; 2s. → [ikātaqūn]; otherwise identical to /naqanāmā−/, except with [u−] or [ū−], respectively
stutter	/(n)īnaqum−/ (1)	1s. occasionally → [inaqu]; 3s. occasionally → [inaqut]; this verb is taboo, and difficult to get forms of

TABLE 11. *Stems like* /eluēwiē−/ (181)

be a buyer	/pekwatelikē−/ (1)	
train (people)	/eknūtmueu−/ (19)	u ⇒ ∅ in sing.; e ⇒ [ā−] in pl.

TABLE 12. *Stems like* /āləm−/ (50)

[Note: forms of /alām−/ 'swim around (in sight)' are similar, except that 3nonplural forms undergo the K → Q rule]

be (there)	/eym−/ (1)	inan. → [ete−k]
die, be dead	/nepm−/ (2)	stem /m/ → ∅ optionally in 2s., 12 dual, and plural forms

V-LENGTHENING applies, giving /welmətū+ti−/ in the plural. The stem could equally well be /welmətū−/, with NONPLURAL V-SHORTENING applying in the singular. The 3an.s. [welmətoq] < /welmətu+k/ shows that a rule analogous to PRE-TI E → A (and possibly an extension of that rule) derives [ŏ] from /ŭ/ in some environments. This rule applies in the 3an.s. of all TI verbs ending in /−tu−/.

Table 10 shows that /ketkunī−/ (or /ketkunĭ−/ − see comments on /welmətu/ above) is just like /naqanāmā−/, except having /ĭ/ or /ī/ where the latter has /ă/ or /ā/, respectively.

In Table 11, we will need an ad hoc rule to delete the /−u/ (> /−w/) of /eknūtmueu−/ in the singular. This rule will, however, account for the lack of any overt /−Vw/ verb stems in Micmac.

Table 13 gives the two remaining types of intransitive paradigm. In fact, these represent only two different stems (both having roughly the meaning 'motion'), each of which occurs with a large number of prefixes. The only evidence for the initial /i/ of /iāsi/ is the fact that /č/ (which must be produced by the T → Č rule) occurs before the stem, but /t/ never does. An ad hoc late rule then drops the /i/. The verbs in /−iāsi−/ usually optionally

MICMAC INTRANSITIVE VERB MORPHOLOGY 79

TABLE 13

Person/no.	/mil+iāsi−/ play	/pem+iesi−/ walk, move
1s.	milā(s)i	pemiey
2s.	milā(s)in	pemien
3an.s.	milā(s)it	pemiet
3inan.s.	milāsək	pemiaq
12dual	milātīkw	pemātīkw
13dual	milātiek	pemātiek
2dual	milātioq	pemātioq
3an.dual	milātičik	pemātičik
3inan.dual	milātikl	pemātikl
12pl.	militaykw	pemitaykw
13pl.	militāyek	pemitāyek
2pl.	militāyoq	pemitāyoq
3an.pl.	militāčik	pemitāčik
3inan.pl.	militāqal	pemitāqal

drop the /s/ in the singular, except in the 3inan.s. The verbs in /−iesi−/ always drop the /s/ in all singular forms, and an ad hoc rule drops the final /i/ as well. Thus the /−iesi−/ verbs effectively have a singular stem /−ie−/. In the 3inan.s., the PRE-TI E → A rule gives /−ia+k/, which by K → Q yields [−iaq]. In the dual, both types change the stem /s/ to /t/, and drop the stem-initial /i/, giving in both types the dual stem /−āti+i+/. The dual morpheme /−i−/ then suffers precisely the same fate as in the /ayči−/-type verbs (cf. Table 1). In the plural, the stem in both types of verb is effectively /−itā+i−/, presumably from underlying /−iāsi+ti−/ and /−iesi+ti−/, respectively, by very complicated but rather poorly-motivated rules (the /s/ and /i/ drop, PRE-TI E → A gives /−iā+ti/, and a metathesis rule yields /−i+tā+i−/). In any case, GLIDE FORMATION will produce /y/ in all plural forms; in the 13pl. and 2pl. we will get /−itāyek/ and /−itāyoq/, while Ū-CHANGE will yield the 12pl. /−itaykw/. PRE-C C-DELETION will give /−itā+ti+k/ and /−itā+k+l/, while the T → Č and K → Q rules will produce, respectively, /−itāčik/ and /−itāq+l/ in the 3an.pl. and 3inan.pl. The latter becomes /−itāqal/ by V-COPYING.

Tables 14 and 15 present subtypes of the two classes of verbs in Table 13. /mač+itā+i−/ (< mat+iāsi+ti−/) in Table 14 shows a peculiar but regular change to /maytā+i−/ (cf., in Table 15, /weytā+i/ < /weč+itā+i−/; and /kēytu−/ 'know (TI)' < /keči+tu−/). Similar to these may be /aī+tā+i−/ and /eī+tā+i−/ (Table 15), from /al+itā+i−/ and /el+itā+i−/, respectively. Indeed, the expected forms of at least some

TABLE 14. *Stems like* /milāsi−/ (95)

stop	/naqāsi−/ (5)	3inan.s. also → [naqāyk]; 3an.dual and 3inan.dual also → [naqāsičik], [naqāsəkl; pl. ⇒ [naqaytā−]
stretch, expand	/siptaqāsi−/ (6)	pl. ⇒ [siptaqaytā−]
go, start moving	/mačāsi−/ (2)	inan. also → [mačāy+k]; pl. ⇒ [maytā−]
walk around	/alāsi−/ (1)	pl. → (possibly ⇒) [aĪtā−]
step on it	/ewkčəpukue+iāsi−/ (14)	pl. ⇒ [ewkčəpukuetā−]
come in	/piskwā(s)i−/ (3)	/si/ → ∅ always in sing.; pl. ⇒ [piskwetā−]
go up; go higher	/toqčuāsi−/ (2)	/s/ → ∅ always in sing. an.

TABLE 15. *Stems like* /pemiesi−/ (12)

come (this way)	/wečku+iesi−/ (3)	sing. ⇒ /wečkūe−/; dual ⇒ /wečkwāti−/ pl. ⇒ [wečkwitā−]
get quiet	/wanʔtaq+iesi−/ (1)	sing. ⇒ wanʔtaqaye−/; pl. ⇒ /wanʔtaqəytā−/
go up into the woods	/sōq+iesi−/ (1)	sing. ⇒ /sōqoye−/; dual ⇒ /sōqwāti−/; pl. ⇒ /sōqwitā−/
come from	/wečiesi−/ (1)	pl. ⇒ [weytā−]
go	/el+iesi−/ (2)	pl. → (possibly ⇒) [eĪtā−]

of these verbs (/mačitā+i−/, /kečitu−/) are current in more southern New Brunswick varieties of Micmac.

The plural /siptak+i+tā+i−/ $\xrightarrow{K\to Q}$ /siptaq+i+tā+i/ $\xrightarrow{\text{VOWEL COPYING}}$ /siptaqa+itā+i−/ → /siptaqaytā+i−/. Similarly, /nak+itā+i/ → /naqaytā+i−/, and in Table 15, /wanʔtak+i+tā−/ → /wanʔtaqaytā−/; in the singular, /wanʔtak+ie−/ → /wanʔtaqaye−/. In a like manner, the singular /sōk+ie−/ (Table 15) becomes /sōqoye−/ (the stem is underlying /sekok+ie(si)−/ → /seokk+ie−/ → /sōk+ie−/, by rules we will not motivate or discuss further here; see Fidelholtz 1968 (Chapter III) for further details). The dual and plural are underlying /sōk+āti−/ and /sōk+itā+i−/, respectively, which should become /sōqo+āti−/ and /sōqo+itā+i−/ as above. The /ŏ/ regularly becomes /w/ here; it appears that the /w/ is directly so produced by VOWEL COPYING (i.e. K-LABIALIZATION), for the 3inan.dual [alāqal] 'they are swimming around' < /alā+k+l/ < /alām+k+l/ shows that PRE-C C-DELETION must precede

TABLE 16. *Verbs with Two Types of Plurals*

go in snowshoes	/aqamīm−/ (1)	[aqamīmūti−] <	/aqamīm+ti−/
		[aqamūlti−] <	/aqamīm+lti−/
be burning	/nūqwā−/ (1)	[nūqwōlti−] <	/nūqwā+lti−/
		[nuqwāti−] <	/nūqwā+ti−/
be swollen	/moqpe−/ (3)	[moqpəti−] <	/moqpe+ti−/
		[moqpĭti−] <	/moqpe+lti−/
grow up here	/etlikwe−/ (3)	[etlikulti−] <	/etl+ikwe+lti−/
		[etlikuti−] <	/etl+ikwe+ti−/
pity	/eulitelke−/ (1)	[eulitelkəti−] <	/eulitelkĕ+ti−/
		[eulitelkāti−] <	/eulitelkē+ti−/
stutter	/inaqū(m)−/ (1)	[inaqūlti−] <	/inaqū(m)+lti−/
		[inaqūti−] <	/inaqū+ti−/
be a buyer	/pekwatelike−/ (1)	[pekwatelikāti−] <	
		/pekwatelikē+ti−/	
		[pekwatelikūti−] <	
		/pekwatelikŭ+ti−/ or	
		/pekwatelikwe+ti−/	

V-COPYING; but we have already seen that GLIDE FORMATION precedes PRE-C C-DELETION; therefore K-LABIALIZATION directly produces the /w/ of the 12nonsingular [−ūkw], and thus presumably also the /w/ of [sōqwitā−]. It may be possible to derive the stem /sekok−/ from an underlying /sekuk−/ (and most other [o]'s in Micmac from underlying /u/'s), but this is a vexed problem in Micmac phonology and beyond the author's present powers of demonstration. Note, however, that [o] ~ [w] alternations are very common in Algonquian languages,[12] although usually they are not completely regular; it should also be noted that in most Algonquian languages, the /o/ vowel is often close to [u] in pronunciation, and many lack /u/ (in the analyses in n. 12).

In Table 15, the stem /weču+iesi−/ becomes in the dual and plural /wečkwāti−/ and /wečkwitā+i−/, respectively, by GLIDE FORMATION. In the singular, the /i/ is assimilated to a preceding /u/ before a short vowel, giving /weču+ue−/, which gives /wečkūe−/ by GEMINATE SEGMENT AGGLOMERATION. The stems /ewkčəpukue+itā+i−/ and /piskwe+itā+i−/ in Table 14 both drop the /i/ preceding the plural /tā/, by a general but complex rule we will not discuss here, giving /ewkčəpukue+tā+i−/ and /piskwe+tā+i−/. The latter stem (and its handful of congeners) is totally irregular in the singular, either morphologically dropping the /si/ of /iāsi/, or else being suppletive with a stem of the /čič:emā−/type (which two possibilities will, of course, have the same effect).

In Table 16 are listed several types of verbs each having two different ways to form the plural. The first four simply have the option of either the

/lti/ or the /ti/ plural, and the rules discussed above apply quite regularly. The peculiarity of /eulitelke−/ is that the stem-final vowel may be taken as either long or short (since NONPLURAL V-SHORTENING will change /ē−/ to /ĕ/ in nonplural forms), and the plural is formed accordingly. The otherwise irregular verb /inaqū(m)−/ also shows either the /lti/ or the /ti/ plural; the stem may not have a final /m/, however, in the /ti/ plural, or we should expect *[inaqūmūti−], like [āləmūti−]. /pekwatelikē−/ forms one /ti/ plural regularly, but the other indicates a partial stem suppletion (or an informant performance error).

ORDERING OF THE RULES

One very important facet of phonological rules is their **ordering** with respect to one another. Ordering is crucial in many cases to the correct application of the rules we have discussed. We have already seen several cases of crucial rule ordering in the discussion above. We will call attention to a few further examples.

The GLIDE FORMATION rule must precede FINAL VOWEL SHORTENING or we would get

    1s. čič:emā+i
         *čič:emā. FINAL VOWEL SHORTENING

Likewise, the T → K rule must follow the GLIDE FORMATION rule, thus:

    3an.s. wekāi+ti
         wekāy+ti GLIDE FORMATION
         [wekāy+k]. T → K, FINAL VOWEL SHORTENING

Otherwise we get wrong results:

    wekāi+ti
         T → K
(inapplicable after /i/)
         GLIDE FORMATION, FINAL VOWEL SHORTENING
    *wekāy+t.

Again, the T → Č rule must follow FINAL VOWEL SHORTENING:

    3an.s. ayči+ti
         ayči+t FINAL VOWEL SHORTENING
         [ayčit]; (T → Č inapplicable)

otherwise:

         ayči+ti
         ayči+či T → Č
         *ayčič. FINAL VOWEL SHORTENING

MICMAC INTRANSITIVE VERB MORPHOLOGY 83

TABLE 17. *Some Rules of Micmac*

1. GLIDE FORMATION
2. T → K
3. PRE-C C-DELETION
4. L-ASSIMILATION
5. FINAL VOWEL SHORTENING
6. T → Č
7. K-LABIALIZATION (VOWEL COPYING)
8. Ū-CHANGE
9. U-EPENTHESIS
10. VOWEL BACKING
11. PLURAL V̆-DELETION
12. PRE-TI V-LENGTHENING
13. PRE-TI E → A
14. SHWA-INSERTION
15. W-VOCALIZATION
16. K → Q
17. NONPLURAL V-SHORTENING
18. GEMINATE SEGMENT AGGLOMERATION

(Note that the [y] and [č] in the stem [ayči−] come from /i/ and /t/, respectively, by the GLIDE FORMATION and T → Č rules, respectively.) Also, K-Labialization must precede Ū-CHANGE:

12dual čič:emā+i+ū+k
   čič:emā+y+ū+kw   GLIDE FORMATION
   čič:emā+y+ kw;   K-LABIALIZATION, Ū-CHANGE

otherwise:

   čič:emā+i+ū+k
   čič:emā+y+ū+k   GLIDE FORMATION
   čič:emā+y+ k   Ū-CHANGE
   *čič:emāyk.   K-LABIALIZATION (cannot apply)

We give in Table 17 a list of most of the rules we have discussed which are constrained by ordering relationships. Aside from the orderings illustrated in the discussion above (1 < 2, 1 < 3, 1 < 5, 3 < 7, 3 < 10, 5 < 6, 7 < 8, 9 < 11, 11 < 12, 12 < 14, 12 < 15, 13 < 16), we briefly present the evidence for other ordering relations found:

  1 < 8: [čič:emaykw] (see Fidelholtz 1968 (129-131) for details; Ū-CHANGE deletes /ū/ only after a glide)
  2 < 3: 3an.s. [alāq] < /alā+k/ < /alām+k/ < /alām+ti/

3 < 4: 2s. [nastesiñ] < /nastesin+n/ shows that /n/− deletion fails before /n/; /nastesulti−/ < /nastesi+lti−/ < /nastesin+lti−/ shows no L-ASSIMILATION, but does show /n/-deletion before /l/

3 < 9: [aqamūlti−] < /aqamīm+lti/; not *[aqamīmulti−]

3 < 16: 3an.s. [alāq] < /alā+k/ < /alām+k(i)/ (< /alām+ti/)

4 < 18: 2s. [telkiñ] < /telkin+n/ < /telkil+n/

5 < 7: 3an.s. [alāq] < /alā+qi/ < /alām+ti/; otherwise /alām+ti/ > /alām+ki/ > /alā+qai/ > *[alāqa]

10 < 15: [esamuqōlti−] < /esamuqoōlti−/ < /esamuqwōlti−/ < /esamuqwālti−/

15 < 18: [esamuqōlti] < /esamuqoōlti−/ < /esamuqwōlti−/

(17 < 18) 2s. [čič:emān] ?< /čič:emaa+n/ < /čič:emaā+n/.

We note in passing that the above orderings include a chain of 8 rules rigidly sequentially ordered (1 < 2 < 3 < 9 < 11 < 12 < 15 < 18; also 1 < 3). While there are remaining problems in Micmac rule order, I know of no clearcut cases in Micmac of counterexamples to the assumption of transitivity of rule ordering.

CONCLUSION

The purpose of this paper has been exposition of the facts of the indicative present of Micmac, and of the types of reasoning and data which enter into consideration in determining what underlying phonological shapes of occurring morphemes are, and in deciphering interrelationships among the varied forms of a language. Often, forms which appear to be related in meaning or function seem superficially to be phonologically unrelated; the approach we have outlined above starts with the assumption that the data exemplify as much order and regularity as possible. Thereby, many of the seeming irregularities can be seen to be regularities at a more abstract level of analysis. It can be observed that some underlying segments fail to appear in some instances (e.g. /−ū−/ in some 'we inclusive' duals), or are changed from their underlying forms (e.g. [y] comes from underlying /i/), and that in general things may not always be as they seem on the surface.[13]

NOTES

[1] This is a revised version of a paper presented at the annual meeting of the American Anthropological Association on 21 November 1970 in San Diego, California. Fieldwork was done in Summer, 1965, with a grant from the American Council of Learned Societies; Summer, 1966; and February, 1967; in each case at Restigouche, Quebec, with the invaluable assistance of my primary informant, John-Louis Jerome (*saluičič selōm*). A more extensive analysis of the data may be found in Fidelholtz 1968 (esp. Chapter IV). Much of the analysis is quite dense and will require close reading. This is a result of incorporating several goals in a necessarily relatively brief article. Since relatively little has been published on Micmac, I have essayed to present as much data as possible within broad limits of coherence: with a bit of effort, the reader will be able to generate the full indicative present declension of any of the verbs in any of the tables, should he care to do so. This goal has necessitated discussing a multitude of rules in the text; full motivation for the rules and their relative ordering is therefore lacking or abbreviated in many cases. I hope that I have nevertheless attained my second goal of scholarly adequacy. A third goal has been to indicate (perhaps somewhat unrealistically) the kinds of considerations important to a phonologist in developing his analysis. The goals are given in the order of their importance to me; nevertheless, I hope the third goal has not been totally thwarted by attention to the first two. An earlier version of this paper was commented upon by John Hewson, Mary Levy, Mary Miller, Eric Hamp, Paul Turner, Jonathan Kaye, Ernest Migliazza, and others. While I have unmercifully plagiarized their many insightful comments, the remaining faults are mine.

[2] It is certainly true of most morphemes that their meaning is clear-cut. Nevertheless, meaningless morphemes exist (e.g. perhaps *it* in 'I like *it* that John is coming.') and some morphemes have nebulous meaning, or meaning only in combination with other morphemes (e.g. *con-* in *confer, consist, congress*, etc.; or *cran-* in *cranberry*). Therefore, meaning can only be used here as a guide, although normally a very useful one.

[3] This assumption has usually been made by linguists analyzing sound systems of languages. Until recently, however, many of the solutions and relationships considered in the article (e.g. rule ordering, certain of the rules relating some of the phonetically more disparate forms, and rules deleting segments) would have been considered illegitimate. For a fuller discussion of the issues at stake, see Chomsky 1964 and Postal 1968. The basic point is that one's theoretical framework must allow him to capture the generalizations which inhere in the data.

[4] Note the abbreviations in column 2 for the 'meanings' in column 1 of Table 1. Column 3 contains the underlying forms of the respective endings, which we will attempt to motivate in this article. Columns 4, 5, 6, and 7 contain the actual forms for each of four verb stems in the various persons and numbers.

The article also uses the following abbreviations: $X \rightarrow Y$ ('X becomes Y'); $X \xrightarrow{A} Y$ ('X becomes Y by means of rule A'). The application of rules will also be indicated in some cases by a vertical listing of the changed forms of a word, with the rules producing the changes listed to the right, and between the appropriate lines. The change $X \xrightarrow{A} Y$ for example, might be as well indicated by:

$$\begin{array}{l} X \\ Y. \end{array} \; A$$

Also, an asterisk (*) before a form indicates that the form is nonoccurring or ungrammatical. The names of rules will be capitalized throughout. '>' and '<' will be used in two different ways, which should produce no ambiguity: in discussion of forms, 'A > B' and 'A < B' will mean, respectively '(some rule(s) applied to) A gives B' and 'A results from B (by the application of some rule(s))'; in discussion of rules, 'A > B' means 'A precedes B'.

There are of course other aspects of Micmac phonology which we will not discuss here. The most relevant, for those who like to pronounce what they read, are the two rules predicting voicing and aspiration of obstruent consonants (/p/, /t/, /č/, /k/, and

/s/ in Micmac). Obstruents are voiced between voiced segments (vowels and cases of /m/, /n/, and /l/ corresponding to deleted vowels), and are aspirated when either before another obstruent or word final. Thus a more nearly phonetic transcription than the one we are using would give, for example: [čipʰčičʰ], [kobitʰ], [čīgāw], for our [čipčič], [kopit], [čīkāw], respectively. Note that word-initially before a vowel, obstruents are voiceless, but also unaspirated, unlike English. Brackets '[ ]' enclose (our very broad) phonetic transcription: slant lines '/ /' enclose any representation more abstract than a phonetic transcription.

[5] The facts in Table 2 are accurate; the analysis of certain words, however, is not obvious from the forms. E.g. the correct analysis of [nikoqol] is /nikoq+l/, with an epenthetic /o/ (likewise, the correct analysis of [čič:emāqal] is /čič:emāq+l/, with an epenthetic /a/). In general, a /q/ or /k/ before a sonorant triggers the copying of a preceding back vowel (which may only be /a/ or /o/ before [q] – see below) after it as well. This rule is dubbed VOWEL COPYING; it is, however, actually a generalization of the K-LABIALIZATION rule. A more analogous example would be, say, [alukw] 'cloud', plural [alukul]; here, however, the stem-final /-u/ becomes [-w] in the singular, and thus does not drop. (Cf. the GLIDE FORMATION rule, below.) Note that in [kīkamkōn] 'flagpoles' (from /kīkamkōn+l/) we find the same assimilation of /l/ to /n/ which we found in [telkiñ] (from /telkil+n/, showing that L-ASSIMILATION is a neighborhood rule.

It has been suggested by Ken Hale (personal communication) that what I call 'short-stems' in fact simply have a morphologically different plural form – e.g. [muīn+aq] < /muīn+aq/. There is some merit in this suggestion, but for the purposes of this paper we assume the correctness of the FINAL VOWEL SHORTENING rule. A suggestion along similar lines has been made by John Hewson (personal communication) that what I postulate below as the dual marker is really a thematic vowel, or sandhi yod. While I think this approach would be ill-advised and lose some generalizations, it is worth considering; but it would take us too far afield here to do so.

Further discussion of FINAL VOWEL SHORTENING may also be found in Fidelholtz 1971:581ff.

[6] It must be mentioned here that the rules do not materialize out of thin air – this article attempts to indicate some of the lines of thought and ways of looking at the data which lead to the 'discovery' of phonological rules. Once having ascertained the generalization involved, however, the phonologist's work is not finished – a generalization is not very well motivated nor very convincing if it only accounts for a single set of data in the language. Accordingly, one must search for independent motivation for the rule. This may be of two sorts. On the one hand, a rule devised to account for a particular range of data may turn out to account for entirely unrelated facts in the language. Thus the GLIDE FORMATION rule, properly stated, accounts not only for the various realizations of the 1s. morpheme in Micmac, but for all occurrences of [w] and [y] in the language. On the other hand, a particular rule may be one we would expect to find in all languages, that is, the rule may exemplify a language universal. The rule of K-LABIALIZATION, discussed below, is perhaps such a rule. For some problems encountered in extending the domain of application of rules, and in determining the degree of generality of (and therefore the degree of motivation for) given rules, cf. Fidelholtz 1973. From the above discussion, and the fact that so far as I know the Ū-CHANGE rule (discussed below) operates only in the 12nonsingular forms, it can be seen that the motivation for this rule is very weak. Indeed, it hinges entirely on the labialization of the final /k/ in the varying shapes of this ending, and on apparent parallelism between plural forms of verbs and nouns.

[7] But see Fidelholtz (1973) for discussion of these data and some complications.

[8] Further support for the T → K rule is found in e.g. the 3an.s. negative form: [ayči(w)kw] 'he is not that way' < /ayči+w+t/.

[9] We mention here the necessity for a late ad hoc rule to shorten /ā/ before /ykw/. This rule applies to give 12dual [čič:emăykw] (Table 1) as well as to give the 12plurals [militaykw] and [pemitaykw] (see Table 13 below) from underlying /-āykw/ in each case. This rule may ultimately prove to be relevant to the correct formulation of Ū-CHANGE.

[10] [-lti-] might seem to be an exception to the T → Č rule; it is not, however; the underlying form contains another vowel between the /t/ and /i/, which effectively blocks the application of the T → Č rule. For further discussion, see Fidelholtz 1968 (31, 41-63, and passim).

[11] The following annotations are relevant to Tables 4, 5, 6, 7, 9, 10, 11, 12, 14, 15, and 16: '→' means 'becomes by a morphological (i.e. basically suppletive) process'; '⇒' means 'becomes by a regular phonological process'; '+' and '−' separate morphemes (not all morphemic cuts are indicated). Numbers in parentheses are the number of such verb stems in my data – they should be regarded as suggestive rather than definitive, as I have not e.g. separated identical stems with different prefixes. In each table, the verbs listed have their conjugation identical to the head verb of the table, except where the individual annotations in the last column indicate otherwise. The text generally does not discuss suppletive alternants (those indicated by [→]). The AI/II alternations, assumed here to be basically regular with some quasi-suppletive alternations, is the subject of a forthcoming paper. 'Inan.' is short for 'inanimate nonplural'.

[12] See e.g. Bloomfield 1946:91, 107; Bloomfield 1957:4, 21, 25, 55; Bloomfield 1962:84; Frantz 1970:12, 24; Goddard 1969:18, 64, 68, 106; D. Jones 1971:48, 55 *et passim*; W. Jones 1911:755; Taylor 1967:147f., esp. Table 1, p. 148.

[13] Once the correct generalizations have been ascertained, it is crucial that they be stated in an appropriate formalization. (See Chomsky and Halle 1968; Chapter 7 and 8.) This permits not only an evaluation of the grammar arrived at, but, more important, it allows generalizations to be captured which cannot be stated in purely verbal terms. This, however, is beyond the scope of the present article. See Fidelholtz 1968 for formal statements of most of the rules discussed here.

COPYING FROM COMPLEMENTS IN BLACKFOOT*

DONALD G. FRANTZ

1. INTRODUCTION

This is a preliminary study of the relationship between sentences such as (1) and (2), both of which have English sentence (3) as their closest equivalent:

(1) nitsíksstaa noxkówa máxka'po'takssi
 I-want my-son-3 3-might-work-conj.
(2) nitsíksstatawa noxkówa máxka'po'takssi
 I-want(trans.)-3 my-son-3 3-might-work-conj.
(3) I want my son to work.

(1) and (2) differ in that the verb glossed 'want' is inflectionally intransitive in (1) but transitive in (2). The process which accounts for such pairs, while to my knowledge previously unmentioned in descriptions of Blackfoot,[1] is seen to be quite pervasive, and interacts with other processes of Blackfoot in interesting ways, some of which bear on current issues of linguistic theory.

To readers familiar with recent work within the transformational-generative framework, the relationship between (1) and (2) is reminiscent of the process often called 'subject raising', which raises the subject of a complement to become an immediate constituent of the matrix in which the complement is embedded. Indeed, their gloss (3) is an example of the result of subject raising in English for although *my son* is the logical subject of *work*, (3) has *my son* as surface object of *want*; note that substitution of a pronoun for *my son* requires that pronoun to be objective in form:

(4) I want him to work.

Furthermore, the 'infinitive' form of *to work* can be said to be due to the removal of the subject of *work* from the complement (Kiparsky and Kiparsky 1970).

In the next section I will present evidence that (2) is not related to (1) by 'subject raising' but rather by subject COPYING. Subsequently, I will demonstrate that this copying is not limited to subjects, but is quite general. Finally, what bearing if any this process has on the set of (substantive) universal rules will be discussed.

2. COPYING VS. RAISING

In order to discuss copying, it will first be necessary to clarify the surface syntax of the Blackfoot examples.[2]

Example (1), repeated here with hyphens separating morphemes, consists of a matrix verb inflected to agree with its subject, the speaker.[3] This verb occurs with a complement clause, here

(1) /nit-wikIxtaa [n-oxko-wa m-áxk-a'po'taki-xsi]/
    1-want   my-son-3   3-might-work-conj.

enclosed in brackets. The subject of the complement is 'my son', inflected as 'third person' by suffix /wa/. The verb of the complement is inflected to agree with its subject by prefix /m/. The suffix /xsi/, as well as the fact that third person is marked by prefix rather than suffix, signals that this is a verb of the 'conjunct order', an inflectional paradigm occurring in certain classes of subordinate clauses (Frantz 1971:26-28).

In the repetition of (2) below, hyphens separate morphemes in the verb only, for the remainder of the sentence is identical to its counterpart in (1).

(2) /nit-wikIxtatw-a:-wa [noxkówa máxka'po'takixsi]/
    1-want(trans.)-SH-3

Comparing the matrix verbs of (1) and (2), note first of all that though they share the root /wikIxt/ 'want, anticipate', this root has an additional transitivizing suffix /atw/ in (2), while in (1) the root is extended only by the thematic ending /aa/. Furthermore, the verb of (2) is inflected to agree not only with its subject by prefix /nit/, but also with an object[4] by suffix /wa/. These affixes alone are not sufficient to specify whether first or third person is subject; this is accomplished by presence of the relator /a:/ 'SH' which signals that the subject person is higher on a scale that is descendingly ordered as follows: speaker, addressee, unspecified person, major animate topic, subordinate animate topic – see Frantz 1971:18-20. (The relators of Blackfoot are cognate with Bloomfield's (1946:98, 99) "theme-forming suffixes" for the transitive verb.)

What is significant for our purposes here is that (1) has an intransitive verb and (2) a transitive verb. As shown in Frantz 1971, the distribution of intransitive and transitive stems of a verb like that glossed 'want, anticipate' must be stated at a rather late point in the derivation of surface structures from underlying ('logical') structures; thus, the lexical rules of Blackfoot will replace ('spell') the predicate WANT as either /wikIxtatw/ or /wikIxtaa/ depending upon whether or not this predicate has an object at the aforementioned point in the derivation (Frantz 1971:115-20). (Complements of this verb do not count as objects in Blackfoot syntax.) Thus at the point where the selection of the verb stem to replace WANT was made in the derivations of (1) and (2), the latter must have had an object. And because the matrix verb of (2) has third person singular agreement affixes, it is clear that this object was coreferential with the subject of the complement. This must be true because, like other Algonquian languages, Blackfoot does not allow more than one specific animate entity to be third person in any one clause[4a]; thus if the object of the matrix verb and the subject of the complement verb were not coreferential, one would have been reduced to 'obviative' ('fourth person') status (Frantz 1971:41-42).

We might roughly represent the intermediate structures for (1) and (2) as (1') and (2'), respectively:[5]

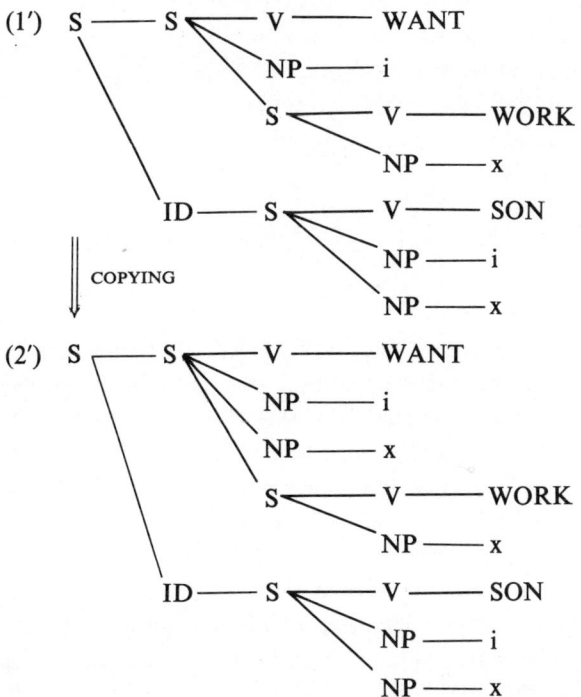

In these structures *i* is the referential index for the speaker; *x* is the index for 'my son', as indicated in the sibling S (tentatively labeled ID) which provides the identificational information for indices; this information ultimately is inserted in NPs (McCawley 1970 and 1972). (1') and (2') differ only in that the latter has an extra argument for the matrix verb, and this argument is coreferential with the complement subject. I claim that this extra argument of (2') is added by an optional[6] rule that derives structures such as (2') from corresponding structures like (1'). The claim that this extra argument is copied rather than raised from the complement is based primarily on the fact that the complement verb still is marked as having a third person subject. To make it clear that such complements are always marked for a subject, here are further examples with various combinations of persons as matrix and complement subjects:[7]

(5) kits-íksstat-o   k-áxk-so'kaas-si
    2-want(trans.)-SH(1) 2-might-strong-conj.
    'I want you to be strong.'
(6) aíksim'sstaa-wa n-oxkó-wa n-áxk-a'po'tak-ssi
    think-3   my-son-3 1-might-work-conj.
    'My son expects me to work.'
(7) nit-aíksim'sstak-k-a noxkówa náxka'po'takssi
    1-think(trans.)-SL-3 my-son-3 1-might-work-conj.
    'My son expects me to work.'
(8) nít-ssksino-a-nnaan-iawa ot-áyaaksi'n-'ss-awa
    1-know(TA)-SH-1pl.-3pl. 3-fut.-die-conj.-pl.
    'We know they are dying.'
(9) kít-ssksino-ok-oaawa   k-iká-ooy-'ss-oaawa
    2-know(TA)-SL(3)-2pl. 2-complet-eat-conj.-2pl.
    'He knows you(pl.) have eaten.'

In (5), the complement subject and its copy as matrix object are both the addressee (remember, the prefix glossed '2' indicates addressee is involved but the /o/ suffix [an allomorph of the 'SH' relator] indicates the 'higher' person [in this case, speaker] is subject). Sentences (6) and (7) differ only in that in (7) the complement subject has been copied as matrix object. (8) and (9) show that number as well as person is copied.

Because complement clauses still agree with the copied argument, the original index is evidently still in the complement at the point where agreement rules apply. All other evidence available thus far indicates that agreement is a post-cyclic rule (I will not present this evidence here, except to say that agreement applies after the formation of complex verb stems, and such stem formation is the result of cyclic rules (Frantz 1971)). We will later see some evidence that copying from complements is a cyclic rule, so we conclude that copying leaves the original argument behind for the post-cyclic agreement rules to make reference to.

The fact that there is only one surface occurrence of the noun phrase glossed 'my son' and no coreferent NP such as a pronoun, cannot be adduced as evidence that the complement subject of (1) has been raised rather than copied in (2), for Blackfoot uses no anaphoric pronouns such as those found in English. When no identificational information is inserted for an index, in Blackfoot that index has no surface realization (in contrast to the situation in English where 'bare' indices usually surface as pronouns). Thus the lack of more than one NP in (2) is exactly parallel to the same lack in (10), which clearly exhibits no copying or raising:

(10) nit-sstsipís-aawa n-óta's-a   m-áhk-it-okska's-si
     1-whip-SH-3   my-mount-3 3-might-then-run-conj.
     'I whipped my horse so he would run.'

Nor does it seem possible to determine which of the two verbs in examples such as (2) has the single surface NP as its subject. Exactly the same positional variants are possible for examples such as (1) and (10) as are allowed for (2); i.e. the single surface NP may be first, second, or last in these sentences. I have been unable to come up with any independent diagnostic for subject or object status of such NP's that might be of help here. It is not even clear, in such cases as we are discussing, that it is a decidable or even meaningful question whether the single NP is an immediate constituent of the matrix or complement. (But see discussion below under Directional Copying.)

We should consider the possibility that the examples which I am claiming involve copying from complements do not involve copying or raising at all, but that the index copies were already present as objects in the logical structures of the matrix sentences. The argument against this alternative analysis is based in part on the fact that the matrix verb in such cases must never have an object that is not coreferential with a major constituent of the complement.[8] Thus the following sentences are ungrammatical:

(11) *kits-íksstat-o   noxkówa m-áxk-axkay'-ssi
     2-want(trans.)-SH(1) my son-3 3-might-go home-conj.
     'I want(of) you that my son go home.'

(12) *kits-íksstat-o   koxkówa   m-áxk-a'pao'tomo-a-xsi
    2-want(trans.)-SH(1) your-son-3 3-might-work for-SH-conj.
    omí nínaayi
    that chief-4
    'I want (of)you that your son work for the chief.'

(11) has a surface object that is not coreferential with a complement constituent and so is ungrammatical even when spoken in a situation where the addressee has some measure of control over whether or not the proposition in the complement will become a reality (e.g. where the addressee is the son's employer). (12) is bad because even though the matrix object has a coreferent in the complement, that coreferent is within a noun phrase and not a major constituent; i.e. the NP itself is not coreferential with the matrix object.

Thus in the cases we have presented thus far, we find that the copying analysis explains both the synonymy of pairs such as (1) and (2), and the ungrammaticality of sentences such as (11) and (12).

2. COREFERENTIALITY CONSTRAINT

The alert reader may already have noted that I have presented no examples in which the subjects of matrix and complement verbs are coreferential. Such examples follow:

(13) nits-íksstaa n-áxks-oy'-ssi
    1-want   1-might-eat-conj.
    'I want to eat.'

(14) aíksim'sstaa-wa ní'sa   m-áxk-skitsstaa-xsi
    think-3   my-ol.bro.   3-might-win-conj.
    'My older brother expects/hopes to win (the race).'

(15) kít-ssksiniixpa kit-sá-waakskitsstaa-xsi
    2-know   2-neg.-fut.-win-conj.
    'You know you won't win.'

None of these data (13)-(15) exhibit subject copying. If copying took place in the derivation of these examples, the matrix sentences would then meet the structural description of the rule of reflexivization (Frantz 1971:53); the latter rule deletes an object which is coreferential with the subject of the same verb, and adds the reflexive formative (ultimately spelled /o:xsi/) to the verb stem. The result of copying and reflexivization in the derivations of (13)-(15) would produce (16)-(18) respectively.

(16) *nits-íksstat-oxsi náxksoy'ssi
    1-want(trans.)-reflex.

(17) *aíksim'sstat-oxsi-wa ní'sa máxkskitsstaaxsi
     think(trans.)-reflex.-3
(18) *kít-ssksino-oxsi kitsáwaakskitsstaaxsi
     2-know(TA)-reflex.

As indicated by the asterisks, these examples are unacceptable. We are led, then, to constrain subject copying against application when the index to be copied is coreferential with the subject of the matrix verb.

Investigation does turn up occasional reflexive examples which could be analyzed as exhibiting subject copying, though never with WANT.

(19) niit-aíksim'sstat-oxsi-wa áxk-itoxkana-íssoka'pssi-wa annoóma
     manner-think-reflex.-3   might-of all-good-3   this
     ksáxkoma
     world
     'He thinks himself to be best in the whole world.'
(20) nít-ssksino-oxsi   nits-iík-áttsa'pssi
     1-know-reflex.   1-very-crazy
     'I know I'm crazy.'
(21a) nits-iiks-íyik-aakimat-oxsi   n-áxk-a'po'tak-ssi
      1-very-hard-try(trans.)-reflex. 1-might-work-conj.
      'I'm trying very hard to work.'

The class of such examples is quite restricted. (19) would not be acceptable without the preverb /niit/ 'manner' which is in an anaphoric relation to the (apparent) complement. (20) is considered archaic. (21a) is not synonymous with (21b) and hence cannot be considered to be its copied counterpart:

(21b) nits-liks-íyik-aakimaa   n-áxk-a-'po'tak-ssi
      1-very-hard-try   1-might-work-conj
      'I'm trying very hard to work.'

It may turn out that all reflexives which appear to be the result of copying are either idioms or have a different source and really involve no copying. Tentatively, then, we will maintain the coreferentiality constraint on copying, realizing that it is probably inadequate as it stands.

4. THE SEMANTIC STATUS OF COPYING

Within the theoretical framework we are assuming, transformations are constraints on the derivation of surface structures from logical structures

(Lakoff 1969, 1970). Any two-way option in these constraints should be reflected in pairs of synonymous surface structures. Thus, because subject copying is optional with the predicate glossed 'want', (1) and (2) are synonymous.

Yet not all instances of what appear to be the same process of copying, i.e. could be described by exactly the same rule, are fully synonymous with their counterparts in which copying has not applied. This is particularly true where other than a subject has been copied, as we shall see later. But even staying within the realm of subject copying, it is possible to find pairs which informants find 'almost, but not quite' equivalent. Compare (22) and (23):

(22) iixtsimaa-wa nit-ákkaa-wa nit-saáki-aopi-ssi
     heard-3   my-friend-3   1-still-stay-conj.
     'My friend heard that I'm home.'

(23) nít-oxtsimak-k-a nitákkaawa nitsaákiaopissi
     1-heard(trans.)-SL-3
     'My friend heard (about me) that I'm home.'

The semantic difference between these is difficult to isolate, but evidently related to the fact that the transitive stem of (23) can occur without an overt complement:

(24) kít-oxtsimat-o
     2-heard(trans.)-SH(1)
     'I (have) heard about you.'

I suspect that a sentence such as (23) is slightly ambiguous, arising either by optional subject copying (and hence being synonymous with (22)) or independently from a logical structure more like that which is mapped into (25):

(25) iixt-oxtsímaa-wa nitákkaawa niistóyi, nitsaákiaopissi
     about-heard-3   my-friend   I   1-still-stay-conj.
     'My friend heard about me, that I'm home.'

There are other semantic considerations, as well. For example, with one semantic class of verbs for which subject copying is optional and usually without semantic effect, the copying apparently is more likely if the complement is emotive.[9]

(26) nít-ssksiniixpa kí'sa   ot-áyo'kaa-xsi
     1-know   your-bro.   3-sleeping-conj.
     'I know your (older) brother is sleeping.'

(27) nít-ssksino-a-wa kí'sa otáyo'kaaxsi
    1-know(TA)-SH-3
(28) nítssksiniixpa kí'sa ot-oksiná's-si
    3-cranky-conj.
(29) nítssksinoawa kí'sa otoksiná'ssi
    'I know your brother is cranky.'

Thus while (26) and (27) are synonymous and approximately equally expectable, (28) is somewhat less natural than (29) even though synonymous with it.[10]

So it is clear that a thorough study of subject copying would need to be based upon an extensive study of semantic types of complements and the verbs with which they occur. And judging from recent work by Ann Borkin (1973a,b), semantic and pragmatic factors which are much more far-ranging must be taken into consideration. For example, I would not be at all surprised to find (after appropriate testing) that (27) would be more likely than (26) in a situation where the sleeping of the brother at that particular time was judged by the speaker to be symptomatic of the brother's character.

5. COPYING OF CONJOINED NPS

As would be expected, an entire coordinate complement subject is copied; note that the matrix verb of (30) is marked as having a third person plural object:

(30) nits-íksstat-a-yawa omá noxkówa ki omá
    1-want(trans.)-SH-3pl. my-son-3 &
    nitána m-áxk-a'po'tak-ss-awa
    my-da.-3 3-might-work-conj.3pl.
    'I want my son and daughter to work.'

But in (31) we see that it is allowable to copy only one of two or more conjoined indices:

(31) nits-íksstat-a-wa noxkówa (ki niistówa) n-áxk-a'po'tak-ss-innaani
    1-want-SH-3   my-son-3 & I   1-might-work-conj.-1pl.
    'I want my son and myself to work.'

In (31) the complement subject is 'my son and I', yet only 'my son' is copied into the matrix as evidence by the 'third person object' affixes on the matrix verb.[11] (32) is an interesting example, for it shows that the second person component of 'inclusive we' can be copied separately, for in (32) second person is inflectional object of the matrix verb:

(32) kits-íksstak-k-a noxkówa áxk-a'po'taki-o'si
     2-want-SL-3   my-son-3 might-work-12(conj.)
     'My son wants us12 to work.'

While subject copying with the verb glossed 'want' is usually of no semantic effect, in cases such as (31) and (32) where a further option is available it stands to reason that the choice functions as a type of focus device. Thus (32) would most likely appear in the Blackfoot counterparts of contexts for which (33) would be appropriate in English:

(33) As for you, my son wants you and me to work together.

(34)-(38) are included to show that apparently any of two or more conjoined NPs may be copied, subject only to the coreferentiality constraint discussed in 3.

(34) kits-íksstat-o   k-oxkówa k-áxk-a'po'tak-ss-oaawa
     2-want(trans.)-SH(1) your-son 2-might-work-conj.-2pl.
     'I want you and your son to work.'
(35) nits-íksstat-a-wa koxkówa káxka'po'takssoaawa
     1-want(trans.)-SH-3

(34) and (35) differ only in that different members of the complex complement subject have been copied. The same is true of (36) and (37):

(36) nits-íksstat-a-wa omá noxkówa ki omí otákkaayi
     1-want(trans.)-SH-3 my-son-3 &   his-friend-4
     m-áxk-a'po'tak-ss-awa.
     3-might-work-conj.-3pl.
     'I want my son and his friend to work.'
(37) nits-íksstat-a-yini omá noxkówa ki omí otákkaayi
     1-want-SH-4
     máxka'po'takssawa.
(38)   { íksstaawa
                       want-3
                       nitsíksstakka
       noxkówa   1-want(trans.)-SL-3   omí otákkaayi
       my son-3   kitsíksstakka   his friend
                       2-want(trans.)-SL-3
                       íksstatsiiwa
                       want(trans.)-SH(3-4) }

áxk-oxkan-a'po'taki-o's-si
might-all-work-12-conj.
'My son wants you and me and his friend to all work.'

(38) shows all the possibilities with a tripartite complement subject consisting of fourth person, speaker, and addressee; the four alternative matrix verbs exhibit no copying, copying of speaker, copying of addressee, and copying of fourth person, respectively.

For those who accept arguments from universal grammar, these data make very important the claim that we are dealing with copying rather than raising here, otherwise the derivations for Blackfoot examples (31)-(38) would involve clear violations of the Coordinate Structure Constraint (Ross 1967), which forbids movement of one of conjoined NPs.

6. COPYING AND RECIPROCALIZATION

(40), which is equivalent to the conjunction of (2) [repeated here as (38)] and (39), indicates that copying from complements must precede a putative rule of reciprocalization (Frantz 1968); i.e. (38) and (39) meet the structural description of reciprocalization only because complement subjects have been copied into the matrices.

(38) nitsíksstatawa noxkówa máxka'po'takssi
      'I want my son to work.'
(39) nitsíksstakka noxkówa náxka'po'takssi
      'My son wants me to work.'
(40) noxkówa (ki niistówa) nits-íksstat-tsiiyi-xpinnaani
      my-son-3 & I   I-want-recipr-1pl.
      n-áxk-a'po'tak-ss-innaan
      1-might-work-conj.-1pl.
      'My son and I want each other to work.'

(Note that in addition to conjoining the two referential indices which were arguments of the matrix verbs and adding the reciprocal element to the common matrix verb stem, reciprocalization must collapse the two complement verbs into one with a complex subject.)

7. COPYING OF NON-SUBJECTS

7.1 *Object Copying*
(41) kit-aíksim'sstat-o k'áxk-oxk-awaayáki-ook-oo-xsi
      2-think-SH(1)   2-might-just-hit-SL-x-conj.
      'I'm thinking you might get hit.'[12]

(42) nít-ssksino-ok-a kínna   kit-akomímm-ok-ssi
     1-know-SL-3   your-father-3 2-love-SL-1-conj.
     'Your father knows you love me.'

In (41) the matrix verb has addressee as object, a copy of the object of the complement verb. In this case the copying of an object is not too surprising, for no subject of the complement verb is specified (Frantz 1971:40-41). In (42), the object rather than the subject of the complement has been copied. My impression is that this choice of object rather than subject serves to highlight the object: if this impression is correct, then a closer English equivalent for (42) might be 'your father knows I am loved by you'.

7.2 Instrument Copying

Instrument or 'means', which unlike instrument in English does not become subject even when no agent is involved (Frantz 1971:41, 84), can also be copied from a complement, though only rarely. We give but one example:

(43) nit-aíksim'sstat-ooxpi   omíistsi miistsí-istsi
     1-think(trans.)-inan.pl. those stick-pl.
     k-áxk-oxt-awaayáki-ook-oo-xsi
     2- might-means-hit-SL-x-conj.
     'I expect the sticks to hit you.'

Note that in (43) the matrix verb is inflected for a plural inanimate gender object, a copy of the complement means *miistsíistsi* 'sticks'. Compare (43) with its uncopied counterpart (44):

(44) nitaíksim'sstaa omíistsi miistsíistsi káxkoxtawaayákiookooxsi

7.3 Directional Copying

By 'directional' is meant the NP given as a reference point for one of a small set of 'directional preverbs' (Frantz 1971:107):

(45) íksstaa-wa omá noxkówa m-áxk-itáp-aapiksist-a-xsi
     want-3   my-son-3 3-might-toward-throw-SH-conj.
     kiistóyi omí pokón-i
     you   ball-4
     'My son wants to throw the ball to/at you.'
(46) kits-íksstak-k-a omá noxkówa máxkitápaapiksistaxsi (kiistóyi)
     2-want(trans.)-SL-3
     omí pokóni

The stem of the complement verb in (45) and (46) is complex, containing preverb *itap* 'toward' and *aapiksist* 'throw'. In both (45) and (46) this complement verb has 'ball' as its object. In (45) the matrix verb is intransitive, while the matrix verb of (46) has second person as object, a copy of the directional index in the complement. Consistent with Blackfoot's general treatment of independent person nouns for 'you' and 'I', the marking for second person on the matrix verb makes *kiistóyi* superfluous in (46), though its presence there does not make the sentence completely unacceptable.

The permissible retention of *kiistóyi* in (46) is a happy circumstance for the analyst, for its position supports the earlier claim that the process dealt with in this paper is copying rather than raising. If the process were raising, it would be most unlikely that the person noun could still be positioned in the middle of the complement out of which it was raised.

The next example of copying is the clearest evidence I have discovered that copying applies before lexical insertion; compare (47) with (48):

(47) íksstaa-wa n-oxkó-wa m-áxks-ipooxsáp-aapiksist-a-xsi omí pokon-i
      want-3   my-son-3   3-might-Iward-throw-SH-conj.   ball-4
      'My son wants to throw the ball to/at me.'
48)   nits-íksstak-k-a noxkówa máxksipooxsápaapiksistaxsi omí pokóni
      1-want(trans.)-SL-3

Semantically, (47) and (48) are exactly parallel to (45) and (46), except that the one at whom the ball might be thrown is addressee in (45) and (46) but speaker in (47) and (48). However, in (45) and (46) the directional reference point in the complement is indicated by a separate noun phrase, while in (47) and (48) the reference point is part of the meaning of the directional preverb /Ipooxsap/ 'toward the location of the speaker (at either the time of the locutionary act or the time of the event being predicated)'. Within the generative semantics model, the logical structure of (47) and (48) will be exactly parallel to that for (45) and (46). However, in the derivation of (47) and (48) the directional reference point 'speaker' is incorporated into the verb, where subsequently the combination of this component and the predicate TOWARD (normally spelled /itap/ as in (45) and (46)) is replaced by the lexical item /Ipooxsap/.

Observe now that in (48) the matrix verb has first person as object, a copy of the speaker index from the complement. But there is no separate surface indication of the directional reference point to be copied in (47) as there was in (45). Thus for ANY model to account for the distribution of inflected verbs in (45)-(48), it is necessary to make reference to the MEANING of the preverb /Ipooxsap/. In the model we are assuming here, this means the copying must take place before lexical insertion. And in order to keep the rule of copying general, copying must take place before incorporation of the speaker component into the verb.[12a]

8. REFERENTIAL SPECIFICITY AND COPYING

Indices for which the speaker has no particular referent in mind (termed 'non-specific'[13] in Frantz 1971:22) do not participate in the person or number inflectional systems, so it is not unexpected that no evidence has been found that such indices are copied; indeed, unless new criteria can be found to distinguish a matrix NP from a complement NP, it would be impossible to tell if a non-specific index had been copied. Thus there can be no 'copied' counterpart of:

(49) nits-íksstaa n-áxk-sskonak-ssi áattsistaai
      1-want   1-might-shoot-conj. rabbit[-spec.]
      'I want to shoot rabbit(s).'

Indices with generic reference, on the other hand, can be copied.[14] Compare synonymous examples (50) and (51):

(50) nít-ssksiniixpa iinií-waa'   ot-áooy'ssi matóyixkoi
      1-know   buffalo-3 generic C-eat-conj. grass
(51) nít-ssksino-a-wa iiniíwaa' otácoy'ssi matóyixkoi
      1-know(TA)-SH-3
      'I know buffalo eat grass."

In (51), the subject of the complement has been copied into the matrix, so that the matrix verb is transitive animate.

9. COPYING FROM EMBEDDED 'QUESTIONS'

Blackfoot sentences which translate as so-called embedded ('indirect') questions generally do not contain any interrogative words. There are two types:

Embedded 'questions' which do not deal with referential identification of subject or animate object of the embedded verb have that verb in the 'conjunct nominal' form (Frantz 1971:27). With regard to copying they behave very much like other complements:

(52) issksiním-a n-aanist-áps-spi
      know-3   1-manner-theme-conj.nom.
      'She knows what I'm like.'

(53) nít-ssksino-ok-a naanistápsspi
1-know(TA)-SL-3

Sentence (53) is synonymous with (52), but only (53) exhibits copying of the underlying subject of the conjunct nominal.

In embedded questions which deal with identification of the subject or animate object of the embedded verb we generally find a kind of 'free' relative (sometimes referred to as 'headless relative clauses'); these are nominals based on the verb root plus one of two relators (Taylor 1969:183-4; Frantz 1974). Copying (if that is what is involved here) is obligatory with this type of embedded question:

(54) *nítssksiniixpa annáxka kitóxtoawaxka
1-know the-one-3 2-hear-SH-3
(55) nítssksinoawa annáxka kitóxtoawaxka
1-know(TA)-SH-3
'I know who/want(anim.) you heard.'

The obligatoriness of copying of the index for the entire nominal in this type of embedded question can explain the ambiguity of (55); in addition to the gloss I have given it above, it can also mean 'I know the one (animate) that you heard'; with the latter meaning we must assume (55) arises without any copying from a basically transitive structure containing a relative clause rather than a complement.

10. CYCLICAL COPYING

In the previous section on copying from embedded questions we discussed part of the derivation of sentences like (56) in which an embedded index was copied as object of the matrix verb:

(56) nít-ssksino-a-wa m-aníst-sskonata'ps-spi
1-know(TA)-SH-3 3-manner-strong-conj.nom.
'I know how strong he is.'

Now consider a sentence in which the structure underlying (56) is itself embedded as a complement:

(57) nits-íksstaa n-áxk-ssksino-a-xsi
1-want 1-might-know(TA)-SH-3-conj.
manístsskonata'psspi
3-manner-strong-conj.nom.
'I want to know how strong he is.'

The complement of (57) differs from (56) in that the main verb of the complement has the morpheme /áxk/ as well as inflectional affixes from the 'conjunct order'. But now compare (58):

(58) nits-íksstat-a-wa   náxkssksinoaxsi manístsskonata'psspi
1-want(trans.)-SH-3 1-might-know(TA)-SH-3-conj.

Example (58) is synonymous with (57) and differs from it only by copying, as object of 'want', the third person index which is object of 'know'. But recall that I claim this latter verb did not have a third person object in the logical structure, but rather the object index for 'know' was a copy of an index in the embedded question. Thus the copy as argument of the first verb of (58) is a copy of a copy. For a single rule of copying to account for sentences such as (58), it must apply cyclically; in this case first on the cycle with 'know' as main verb, and again, on the next cycle with 'want' as main verb.[15] (59) is a similar example, differing mainly in that second person is involved rather than third person:

(59) kits-íksstat-o k-áxk-ssksino-o-xsi
2-want-SH(1) 2-might-know-SH(1)-conj.
k-aaníst-sskonata'ps-spi
2-manner-strong-conj.nom.
'I want to know how strong you are.'

11. 'TOUGH' COPYING

Blackfoot exhibits something akin to English '*tough*-movement' (Postal 1971:27) but here again we find that the process is copying rather than raising:

(60) iiks-íyikoo-wa k-áxk-anist-akomímm-ok-i-xpi
very-difficult 2-might-manner-love-SL-1-conj.nom.
'It's very hard for you to love me.'
(61) nits-iíks-íyikoos káxkanistakomímmokixpi
1-very-difficult(anim.)
'I'm very hard for you to love.'

Notice that although first person has been copied as subject of the matrix verb in (61), first person is still also the object of the verb underlying the conjunct nominal as complement.

The next two examples demonstrate that if the process were raising, then it would constitute a clear violation of Postal's (1971) 'crossover constraint':

(62) iiksíyikoo-wa n-áxk-anist-akomímm-oxs-pi
very-difficult 1-might-manner-love-reflex-conj.nom.
'It's hard for me to love myself.'
(63) nits-iíks-íyikoos náxkanistakomímmoxsspi
1-very-difficult(anim.)

But (63) is completely acceptable and synonymous with (62). Contrast the situation in English. If we attempt to apply *tough*-movement in the derivation of the English equivalent of (62) it does not yield fully acceptable sentences:

*Myself is difficult for me to love.
?*I am difficult for myself to love.
?I am difficult for me to love.

Examples such as (63) also provide evidence that 'tough' copying must precede reflexivization, for otherwise the latter rule would delete the object index before it could be copied in the derivation of (63).

12. SUMMARY

This preliminary study has only begun to delve into the enormous body of facts that need to be considered in order to adequately describe the process of copying from complements in Blackfoot. Some of the preliminary observations and tentative hypotheses of this paper follow.

The process involved copies a complement argument (unless it is 'non-referring') as object of the matrix verb; to view it as raising would leave unexplained why the complement verb still agrees with the copied index and why in more complex complements (such as (46)) the NP for that index may appear in the middle of the complement; in addition, the process dealt with here would in certain cases clearly violate both the otherwise universal coordinate structure and cross-over constraints.

Copying is governed to some extent by the matrix verb. With certain governing verbs, the process will be triggered by a component of some kind of focus on the copied index, and possibly also by contextual contrast; this 'triggering' is apparently always extant when some index other than a complement subject (with specified referent) is copied.

An index which is coreferential with the matrix subject may not in general be copied; i.e. copying only rarely leads to a reflexive matrix verb.

It is possible to copy one index out of a coordinate NP.

Copying is cyclic (or at least iterative), and must precede reciprocalization, reflexivation (which itself may be cyclic), and lexical insertion.

13. COPYING AND SUBSTANTIVE UNIVERSALS

In what follows I accept as laudable and important the goal of establishing a set of universal rules (Bach 1971) and valuing a given grammar that makes use of a language-specific rule less highly than another which differs only in that it uses a rule from the universal set to account for the same data.

Two rules that are found to be needed in language after language are Equi-NP Deletion and Subject Raising. The former accounts in English for the lack of a surface subject for *fly* in (64), and the latter for the objective form of the third person pronoun in (65):

(64) Snoopy wants to fly a biplane.
(65) I want him to fly a kite.

But it takes little imagination to see that the rule of Subject Raising could be changed to a rule of Subject Copying with no change in the output of the grammar, for if Equi-NP Deletion is allowed to apply after the embedded subject is copied, it will delete the original subject:[16]

As we have seen, Blackfoot does not need Subject Raising but does need Subject Copying (as well as other copying rules). Thus, for the data we have discussed for English and Blackfoot, the simplest set of universal rules includes Copying and Equi-NP Deletion but not Raising. (We discuss below how we can still maintain the important distinction between copying and 'chopping' (Ross 1967).)

This choice for the inventory of universal rules permits a more satisfying statement of this difference between Blackfoot and English. Recall that the verb of a Blackfoot complement is always inflected for its subject even if that subject is coreferential with an argument of the matrix verb. We may explain this by saying that Equi-NP Deletion does not apply in these cases.

In fact, the only need for a rule such as Equi-NP Deletion in Blackfoot is in those cases where Predicate Raising forms a complex verb, consolidating a matrix proposition and its embedded proposition into one;[17] e.g.:

```
S — V — TRY                          S — V — TRY
     NP — i            DELETE             V — WORK
     S — V — WORK    V-RAISE        NP — i
         NP — i        PRUNE        nit-ssáak-a'pao'taki
                      ⇒              'I'm trying to work.'
```

But if Equi-NP Deletion is not made use of in Blackfoot other than in this special circumstance,[18] we need to say no more about the lack of NP raising in Blackfoot; Blackfoot has copying from complements but does not make use of Equi-NP Deletion. English, on the other hand, also has copying (on subjects, primarily) but additionally has Equi-NP Deletion.

A number of English raising and movement rules have their closest Blackfoot counterparts in copying rules. If, as we have proposed for Subject Raising above, we reinterpret all (or even many) such 'chopping' rules of English as copying plus deletion, how can we still apply the universal constraints which have been proposed by Ross and others? Recall that there were two Blackfoot cases described above which, had they been chopping rules rather than copying, would have violated two otherwise universal constraints. This, coupled with the proposal that (many?) movement rules are accomplished by copying and deletion, suggests that the universal constraints are either applicable to the DELETION portion of the rules,[19] but not to the copying, or they are global derivational constraints (Lakoff 1970) which may make reference to more than one point in a derivation and, in effect, continue to be constraints on movement. As a matter of fact, Ross (1969a:276-8) has already demonstrated that his movement constraints must make reference to more than one point in certain derivations.

NOTES

* Tom Many Guns and Mike Peacemaker, both of Gleichen, Alberta, provided most of the data for this paper, including some verbalization of their intuitions about various sentences.

I have benefited from comments (on an earlier draft of this paper) by Jonathan Kaye, Greg Thomson, Gillian Story, and Irvine Davis.

[1] Or any other Algonquian language for that matter, though Rich Rhodes and

Jonathan Kaye have told me that they have observed a similar phenomenon in Ojibwa.

[2] In this portion of the paper and where it seems helpful in later portions, morphemes will be represented in the morphophonemic transcription of Frantz 1971; such forms will be enclosed in slant lines. Otherwise, transcription will be in the practical orthography mentioned in Frantz 1971:3, with two exceptions: *x* and acute accent are retained here, whereas in the orthography *h* and underlining are used.

[3] First and second person are not indicated by separate words in Blackfoot surface structure unless either their involvement is to be highlighted or there is no other surface indication that they are involved.

Abbreviations used in glosses throughout this paper include: 1 = speaker, 2 = addressee, 3 = major(animate) topic, 4 = subordinate (animate) topic, 12 = 'we' inclusive, x = unspecified animate participant, conj. = affixes from 'conjunct order', trans. = transitive stem, anim. = animate gender, TA = transitive animate stem TI = transitive inanimate stem, inan. = inanimate gender, SH = subject 'higher' person than object (see below), SL = subject 'lower' person than object, pl. = plural, neg. = negative, fut. = future, bro. = brother, da. = daughter, reflex. = reflexive, spec. = specific in reference.

[4] Throughout the paper we use the terms 'subject' and 'object' for what traditionally have been called 'actor' and 'goal' in Algonquian studies.

[4a] A complement does not count as a 'clause' as I am using the term here.

[5] In (1′) and (2′), S symbolizes 'proposition', V symbolizes 'predicate', and NP symbolizes 'argument'. S as an argument is not here labeled as an NP unless it is nominalized. We ignore here the morpheme /áxk/, glossed above as 'might', which in examples such as (1) and (2) seems to add little or no content, whereas elsewhere it is clearly meaningful. I am currently considering the hypothesis that /áxk/ signals nonfactivity.

[6] There are speakers who find (1) a bit strange; for these speakers subject copying is virtually obligatory with WANT.

[7] Here and in the remainder of the paper, hyphens separate morphemes. However, the exact position of hyphens is somewhat arbitrary in certain cases due to either regular morphophonemic processes or portmanteau realizations of combinations of morphemes.

[8] Since this was written, Greg Thomson has pointed out to me that there are speakers who accept at least some sentences that do not meet this condition, but that the matrix object in such cases is considered (presupposed?) to be involved in bringing about the complement proposition. Tom Many Guns consistently and unequivocally rejects all such sentences (he responds with "A word is missing.", and will often correct such sentences so that they do meet the condition). Mike Peacemaker will accept (12), for example, in a context where the parent is known to have full authority over the son. So my argument goes through with full force only in the case of speakers such as Tom Many Guns.

[9] Perhaps 'predicating an individual or personal attribute' would more accurately characterize the class of complements referred to here.

[10] Unlike the root /wikixt/ 'want' (see 2.), /Ixkln/ 'know' does not have an intransitive form: its transitive inanimate (TI) stem is used with complements even if they are not nominalized (see e.g. (50), (52), and (15)).

[11] There can be no good English gloss of (31) or its copyless counterpart because English *want* requires subject raising and consequently produces a structure which violates the 'inclusion constraint' (Postal 1971:173) [see also Green 1973:124]. But even if English had no such constraint, I think the gloss for (31) would be anomalous because of an interesting tension between subject raising and Equi-NP deletion with a complex complement subject (Green 1973:135), only one member of which meets the coreference requirements of Equi-NP deletion.

[12] The meaning of the morpheme *oxk* (here glossed 'just') is difficult to determine. Here it seems to serve to indicate that the speaker does not relish the idea expressed in the complement.

12a While this volume was in press, it became clear that there is no 'speaker incorporation', but rather that *Ipooxsap* has deictic reference. So examples such as (48) show only that *niistoyi* 'I' is deleted after copy-rasing.

13 Perhaps equatable to Donnelan's (1966) 'attributive' (vs referential) use of NPs, especially as generalized by Partee (1972).

14 When Frantz 1971 was written, I was unaware that generics were treated syntactically the same as specifics; thus the diagram on p. 23 of that work is in error. As the following examples indicates, animate generics, unlike NPs with nonspecific reference, participate in the 3 vs 4 person system and require the transitive stem in the verb of which they are object:

> siksiká-waa'   áwawa'kimats-iiwa   iinií -yii'
> Blackfoot-3generic chase(trans)-SH(3-4) buffalo 4generic
> 'The Blackfoot(generic) chased the buffalo(generic).'
> 'The Blackfoot (generic) chased the buffalo (generic).'

15 It is conceivable that a post-cyclic, iterative rule could account for this copying of a copy.

16 Postal 1971:163 and Ross 1969a: footnote 19 indicates that there may be reason to make Subject Raising a copying rule even if we consider only English syntax.

Postal 1974, published after this manuscript was submitted to the editors, rejects the copying plus deletion alternative for English (p. 268, fn. 1), primarily because items without referential identity, such as transformationally inserted *there* and pieces of idioms, can be raised. Postal points out that if these were copied, the original and the copy would not meet the coreference conditions of the rule of Equi-NP deletion, necessitating the addition of an ad hoc deletion rule to the grammar. However, note that no additional deletion rule would be needed if the methatheory contained a global principle inputing coreference to any pair of entities, one of which is a copy of the other. Such a principle would also have going for it that it would permit coreference relations between indices to be stated only in logical structure; new indices created by copying, such as that relating English (i) and (ii), as well as the process relating Blackfoot (iii) and (iv), would be assigned reference values by the principle globally.

(i) Harry's leg broke when he fell.
(ii) Harry$_1$ broke his$_1$ leg when he fell.
(iii) nít-ssiksiixpa n-oxkó-wa o-tókssini
  1-break(TI) my-son-3$_1$ his$_1$-bed[inan]
  'I broke my son's bed.'
(iv) nít-ssiksísssto-a-wa n-oxkó-wa otókssini
  1-break(TA)-SH-3$_1$ my-son-3$_1$ his$_1$-bed
  'I broke my son's bed.'

17 See Frantz 1971, Chapter 4, where Predicate Raising was accomplished by a rule called 'Proposition Consolidation' and Equi-NP Deletion was called 'Embedded Role Deletion', for numerous examples and derivations.

18 Actually, the 'deletion' in such cases is more like a collapsing into one of two identical indices and should probably be part of the effect of V-raising, rather than application of Equi-NP deletion.

19 Perlmutter 1972 makes such a proposal.

OBSTRUENT VOICING IN GITKSAN: SOME IMPLICATIONS FOR DISTINCTIVE FEATURE THEORY

JAMES E. HOARD

1. Gitksan is a Tsimshian language spoken today by several thousand people in the Skeena River valley of British Columbia principally in the region between Kispiox and Kitwanga. In the winter of 1971-72 I worked with Mr. Lonnie Hindle, a native speaker of Gitksan from Hazelton, B.C., in conjunction with a class on field methods at the University of British Columbia. Mr. Hindle is in his early 20's and is bilingual in English and Gitksan. I do not know if his pronunciation differs significantly from that of other Gitksan speakers; but I have no reason to believe that it is aberrant in any way. Nor do I know how much the knowledge and everyday use of English may influence his pronunciation of Gitksan. However, the obstruent voicing rule of Gitksan that is discussed in this paper is quite unlike anything in English phonology so that any influence English might have on Mr. Hindle's Gitksan seems to me not to be a consideration here.

2. The systematic phonemic inventory of Gitksan includes at least the following thirty consonants:

plain stops and affricates	p	t	c		k	kʷ	q	
glottalic stops and affricates	ṗ	t'	c̓	ƛ̓	k̓	k̓ʷ	q̓	ʔ
fricatives			s	ł	x	xʷ	x̣	h
plain resonants	m	n	y	l		w		
glottalic resonants	ṁ	ṅ	ẏ	I̓		ẇ		

There are apparently three underlying vowels occurring both long and short:

　　　　　short vowels:　a, i, u
　　　　　long vowels:　aa, ii, uu

The range of pronunciation of the short vowels is large, but not exceptional among Northwest Indian languages. The low vowel *a* is generally pronounced as [æ], [a], or [ɛ̆] in the environment of a plain front velar. *a* also has the the variants [ʌ], [ɐ], and [ɑ]; the last two are especially favored in the neighborhood of uvulars. The short vowel *i* has variants [i, ɪ, ɛ] and *u* has variants [u, ʊ, ɔ]. The variants [ɛ] and [ɔ] occur obligatorily next to uvulars and occur optionally next to /ʔ/ and /h/.

The same basic inventory of consonants and vowels is reported also by Rigsby (1967), who has, in addition, two more long vowels: *ee* and *oo*. These two vowels are pronounced [ɛɛ] and [ɔɔ], respectively, and, hence, the symbols ɛɛ and ɔɔ would perhaps be more appropriate to indicate them from a linguistic standpoint. However, the distinctive status of ɛɛ (versus *ii*) and of ɔɔ (versus *uu*) is questionable.

The vowel ɔɔ occurs mostly in the environment of *m*, *ṁ*, *w*, *q*, *q̇*, and *x̣*. I have no examples of *uu* in these environments save for the recent loan word [mɪsmúus] 'cow'. Conversely, *uu* occurs mostly between alveolars, palatals, and/or velars. In these environments I have recorded only three examples of ɔɔ in what seem to be single morphemes: [nɪgʷɔ́ət] 'father', [dɔɔc] 'man's sister or man's daughter', and [gyɔɔc] 'yesterday'. The long vowels *uu* and ɔɔ are, then, very nearly in complementary distribution and there are no cases of contrast in the data.

The distribution of *ii* and ɛɛ is similar to that of *uu* and ɔɔ. I have recorded no examples of *ii* in the environment of a uvular, adjacent to *y* or *ẏ*, or in final position. Conversely, I have recorded only a few cases of ɛɛ in non-uvular or non-*y* environments and, as for *uu* and ɔɔ, there are apparently no cases of contrast with *ii* and ɛɛ. They are, then, essentially in complementary distribution.

It seems likely that further work on Gitksan phonology will show that there are only three underlying long vowels. The vowel variants which occur immediately before morpheme boundaries are most in need of careful analysis; some of the long vowels which occur here are the result of phonological processes. For example, the word [λ̂ɔɔtxʷ] 'mud-like' should be compared with [λ̂ɔqʰ] 'mud'; ([λ̂] is a voiced implosive lateral affricate). The underlying form of [λ̂ɔɔtxʷ] is apparently /ƛuq+txʷ/. First, /u/ is lowered to [ɔ] before the uvular /q/; then intermediate [ɔq] becomes [ɔɔ] before the consonant cluster *txʷ*. The two rules result in the opaque [ɔɔ] in an alveolar environment.

Among the consonants, the pronunciation of /h/ is subject to much variation and tends both toward voicing and pharyngealization. I have recorded the voiceless pharyngeal [ħ] in [ħʊn] ~ [ħɔn] 'fish', [ħɔɔx] 'to use', [ħacʰ] 'to bite', [ħaatʰ] 'intestines' and [ħa] 'sky'. Voiced [ɦ] and/or the voiced pharyngeal [ʕ] is recorded in [ʕəpx] 'forehead', [ʕɔəbɪx] 'spoon', [ʕap] 'to trap', and [ʕʊxʷs] 'backbone strips of salmon flesh'. I have recorded [h] in such words as [hɐnáʔq̇] 'woman', [huutʰ] 'to flee' and [hʊcʰ] 'fingerling'. So far as I can tell, [h, ħ, ʕ, ʕ] are not really in contrast and are simply phonetic representatives of systematic phonemic /h/. There is the possibility, however, that Gitksan has more than one 'h', and, as for the long vowels, further study is needed to resolve the matter.

There is also some fluctuation between [h] and [ʔ] in the initial position; [ʔ] can be substituted for [h] in, for example, *hanaq̇* 'woman' and *hagʷali* 'I ran a little'. On the other hand, [h] cannot be substituted for [ʔ] in such items as ʔ*am* 'good', ʔ*ap* 'bee', ʔ*axʷ* 'night', ʔ*un* 'hand' nor, apparently, for any other instance of phonemic /ʔ/. Thus, [ʔ] is among the phonetic representatives of /h/, but [h] is not a variant of /ʔ/.

3. One of the most striking rules of Gitksan phonology, especially from an English speaker's point of view, is the rule of obstruent voicing. Consider first the examples in I. These words are representative of a large number which contain plain stops and affricates. The symbol [j] represents the voiced alveolar affricate.

I		II
[xbiʔI]	'ten'	/xpi/I
[bɐx]	'to run'	/pax/
[bɑn]	'belly'	/pan/
[dɐw]	'ice'	/taw/
[xdii]	'tea'	/xtii/
[duus]	'cat'	/tuus/
[jɐkʰʷ]	'kill'	/cakʷ/
[jágʷɐsxʷ]	'animal'	/cákʷasxʷ/
[gʸɛˇtʰ]	'man'	/kat/
[gupʰ]	'to eat (transitive)'	/kupʰ/
[gɪʔƛ]	'vermillion, (color of sockeye salmon)'	/kiƛ/
[tʰgʷantxʷ]	'to trip, stumble'	/tkʷantxʷ/
[ɢɑn]	'tree, wood'	/qan/
[ɢəətʰ]	'heart'	/quut/
[ɢɑcʰ]	'spill'	/qac/
[nɪgʷɔ́ətʰ]	'father'	/nikʷuut/
[nɪgʷɔ́ədi]	'my father'	/nikʷuut+i/
wɛkʸ]	'brother'	/wak/
[wɛˇgʸm̩] ~ [wɛˇgʸɪm]	'our brother'	/wak+m/
[pʰsɑ]	'clay'	/psa/

The distribution of the plain stops and affricates is clear. Before any voiced sonorant, plain stops and affricates are voiced; elsewhere they are voiceless. The alternation between voiceless and voiced stops in uninflected and inflected forms of such words as [nɪgʷɔ́ɔtʰ] 'father' and [wɛˇkʸ] 'brother' are typical. A rule of obstruent voicing for plain stops and affricates can be quite easily formulated.

Obstruent Voicing
[−cont] → [+voiced] / ___ [+sonor]

The obstruent voicing rule is formulated by Rigsby (1967:9) so that non-continuants are voiced before voiced segments. This formulation requires, however, the stipulation that the rule be non-iterative (to prevent voicing the initial *t* of [tʰgʷantxʷ], for example). No such complication is needed if voicing is stated as occurring only before [+sonor] segments.

The phonemicizations given in column II imply several consonant rules in addition to obstruent voicing: (1) Before a non-continuant obstruent or finally, plain stops and affricates are aspirated. (2) The plain velar stop is palatalized adjacent to /a/. (3) Final glottalized segments are pre-glottalized. (4) Final post-consonantal nasals are syllabic (or an epenthetic vowel is inserted to avoid the consonant cluster).

Consider now the examples in column III. [ĵ] represents the voiced alveolar implosive affricate. It is worth pointing out that the downward larynx movement of the affricative implosives is less pronounced than for the stop implosives. This is probably because of inherent phonetic difficulty in producing affricative implosives.

III		IV
[ɓdal]	'rib'	/pt'al/
[Gɔyβéx]	'bright (light)'	/quypáx/
[ɗaa]	'to sit'	/t'aa/
[t'ɗaa]	'to sit a lot, to sit a long time'	/t't'aa/
[wɪʔt']	'collar bone'	/wit'/
[ɗɑx̣]	'lake'	/t'ax̣/
[ɗɪs]	'to punch, slug'	/t'is/
[t'gʸa]	'skin'	/t'ka/
[ɗa]	'louse'	/t'a/
[t'ɗa]	'lice'	/t't'a/
[ĵɔɔqʰ]	'to adhere to'	/ćuuq/
[ĵuucʰ]	'bird'	/ćuuc/

[j͡aʔq̇]	'clam'	/c̓aq̇/
[j͡e̜ɬ]	'to laugh'	/c̓aɬ/
[λ͡ɔqʰ]	'mud'	/ƛuq/
[ġaqʰ]	'to open'	/k̃aq/
[ġʷatxʷ]	'be lost'	/k̃ʷatxʷ/
[G͡ɛlt]	'top (of hill)'	/q̇ilt/
[ẇɔʔq̇]	'to dig'	/ẇuq̇/
[G͡ʊs] ~ [G͡ɔs]	'to jump'	/q̇us/
[hɐnáʔq̇]	'woman'	/hanáq̇/
[hɐnáG͡ʊm]	'our woman'	/hanáq̇+m/

Final glottalized stops, as in [wɪʔt̓], [ʃaʔq̇], [wɔʔq̇], and [hɐnáʔq̇] are only weakly ejective (i.e. there is little or no larynx movement), although glottal closure is clearly audible before the onset of a glottalized stop or affricate and glottalic closure extends through the articulation of these stops and affricates.

The implosive glottalized segments of Gitksan sound quite unlike the corresponding ejective glottalized noncontinuants of other Northwest Indian languages (I am most familiar with Quileute and Puget Salish). The implosives sound so different from ordinary ejectives that when on occasion I failed to note on first hearing that a stop or affricate was glottalized, voiced stops were recorded rather than voiceless glottalized stops.

In reduplicated forms like [t̓ɗaa] and [t̓ɗa] the larynx movement is upward, in typical ejective fashion, on the first segment, then the larynx movement is rapidly downward on the second segment. An upward, then downward movement of the larynx is also quite apparent in forms like [ṗɗal] and [t̓g͡a]. However, in words like [ɗaa] and [j͡ɔɔqʰ] the larynx movement on the first segment is simply downward.

The distribution of voiceless and voiced glottalized stops and affricates is precisely the same as that for plain stops and affricates: voicing occurs before sonorant segments. Phonetic alternations for glottalized consonants as in [hɐnáʔq̇] versus [hɐnáG͡ʊm], are also precisely parallel to those for plain stops and affricates. The rule of obstruent voicing formulated above ought, then, to include in its domain both the plain and glottalized noncontinuants.

4. In attempting to write a simple rule for Gitksan obstruent voicing, we are immediately confronted with the problem, however, that separate 'ejective' and 'implosive' features, as in Chomsky and Halle (1968:322ff.), do not readily admit a phonetic alternation of ejective and implosive

sounds. To maintain 'ejection' and 'implosion' as separate features requires an unsatisfactory if-then formulation of Gitksan obstruent voicing:

$$\begin{bmatrix} -\text{cont} \\ \langle +\text{eject}\rangle \end{bmatrix} \rightarrow \begin{bmatrix} +\text{voice} \\ \langle +\text{impl}\rangle \end{bmatrix} / \underline{\quad} [+\text{sonor}]$$

Such a formulation misses the point that an ejective-implosive alternation ought to be quite natural here since ejective non-continuants are always voiceless and implosive non-continuants are usually voiced. Since it is impossible to voice an ejective (the upward movement of the larynx precluding sufficient airflow), the only way to have simultaneous voicing and glottalization is to move the larynx downward. Moreover, ejectives and implosives are similar in a crucial respect; larynx movement (upward or downward) effects an abrupt pressure gradient. There is also a pressure gradient for aspirated segments due to subglottal action and there is a pressure gradient with some velaric sounds. Let us, then, subsume the features 'velaric suction', 'implosion', 'ejection', and 'heightened subglottal pressure' of Chomsky and Halle (1968:299) under a single feature 'pressure' which encompasses velaric, glottalic, and pulmonic sounds whose production involves an abrupt pressure gradient. Greenberg (1970) notes that "injection and ejection need not be accepted as autonomous for general phonetic theory (126)." Greenberg is concerned in this article only with glottalic consonants and does not discuss the possibility that velaric clicks and aspirated consonants may share an essential characteristic with ejective and implosive glottalic sounds. In addition to the feature 'pressure', we need further revisions to the set of airstream mechanism and larynx features.

Since the 'suction' part of 'velaric suction' is now part of the feature 'pressure', a feature 'veleric' will distinguish plain clicks (which are [+pressure]) and co-articulated stops (some of which are [−pressure]) from ordinary pulmonic and glottalized sounds.

To characterize sounds which involve a narrowing of the glottal aperture, following Chomsky and Halle (1968:315), we postulate a feature of 'glottal constriction'. Although not recognized by Chomsky and Halle, the feature 'glottal constriction', as they define it, includes the voiced sounds. That is, sounds which are [+voiced] are necessarily [+glottal]. This is fortuitous since there is good evidence from Makah (Jacobsen, 1971) that voiced consonants and (voiceless) glottalized consonants are in a class (that does not include voiceless consonants) in several important rules of the language. It is quite clear that without 'glottal constriction' there can be no voicing. It is, thus, to be expected that there will be rules such as those in Makah where voiced and ejective consonants must be in a class. The feature 'checked', as defined in the Jakobsonian feature framework, corresponds in large measure to Chomsky and Halle's feature 'glottal constriction'; but 'checked' has, I think, also been considered to be quite independent of voicing instead of a necessary concomitant to voicing as is suggested here for 'glottal constriction'.

To complete the set of airstream mechanism and larynx features, we need also a larynx feature 'breathy' that characterizes sounds which have friction in the larynx. Breathy sounds do not necessarily involve a glottal constriction.

The feature 'tense' can be employed if it is ever necessary to distinguish [+tense] implosive [ɓ] from [−tense] creaky voice [b'] or if it is necessary to distinguish [+tense] ejective [ṗ] from [−tense] implosive [p̂].

A feature system which can distinguish the sound types which differ in airstream and/or larynx features that are known to contrast in language and which also permits a reasonable statement of a variety of quite natural phonological processes seems to me to include the features and feature specifications given below.

	p	pʰ	ṗ	p̂	b	bʰ	ɓ	b'	m	m̊	C	gᵇ
voiced	−	−	−	−	+	+	+	+	+	+	−	+
glottal constriction	−	−	+	+	+	+	+	+	+	+	−	+
pressure	−	+	±	+	−	+	+	+	−	+	+	−
breathy	−	+	−	−	−	+	−	−	−	−	−	−
tense	±	+	+	−	±	+	+	−	−	+	+	+
velaric	−	−	−	−	−	−	−	−	−	−	+	+

Chomsky and Halle (1968) state that: "The feature 'tenseness' specifies the manner in which the entire articulatory gesture of a given sound is executed by the supraglottal musculature. Tense sounds are produced with a deliberate, accurate, maximally distinct gesture that involves considerable muscular effort; nontense sounds are produced rapidly and somewhat indistinctly (324)". There would seem to be no conflict between the definition of tense and that for voiced. Chomsky and Halle nevertheless appear to claim that there are no tense voiced stops because the vocal tract must expand to permit voicing during the closure and "If the walls of the tract are rigid as a result of muscular tension, this expansion of the cavity volume cannot take place, and, therefore, tense stops will not show any voicing during the closure phase (325)." However, nothing in the definition of 'tenseness' implies rigidity of the vocal tract. Whatever expansion of the vocal tract is required for voiced stops could just as well be the result of a "deliberate, accurate, maximally distinct gesture" as the result of a sound "produced rapidly and somewhat indistinctly." If the rate of expansion is controlled, one would expect a tense/lax difference between voiced stops to be reflected in the timing of voicing onset. If expansion is "deliberate, accurate," etc. one would expect a tense voiced stop to show voicing commencing toward the end of the stop closure. If expansion is not impeded by "considerable muscular effort", then one would expect that voicing in a lax voiced stop should begin well before release of oral closure. Since both of these types of voiced stops are well attested, it seems to me that voiced stops can be either tense or lax, and I have so indicated in the above feature matrix. On the other hand, aspiration of a voiced stop should only be possible by a tense "deliberate" gesture since the overpressure necessary for aspiration will not arise if the vocal tract simply expands during the period of oral closure while air flows past the glottis. For this reason, I have taken [b^h] to be [+tense]. Chomsky and Halle take precisely the opposite position (326) because, as already noted, it seems to me they mistakenly equate rigidity with muscular tension. Incidentally, using their logic, one would be quite unable to chin oneself since the "considerable muscular effort" necessary for the task would result only in a rigid statue-like pose and an utter absence of motion.

There are a number of co-occurrence restrictions. Leaving aside velaric sounds, there are only eleven sound classes defined by the five features voiced, glottal constriction, pressure, breathy, and tense. The restrictions are: (1) [+voice] ⇒ [+glottal]; (2) [+breathy] ⇒ [+pressure +tense]; (3) [+pressure −glottal] ⇒ [+tense +breathy]; (4) [−voice +glottal] ⇒ [−breathy]; (5) [−voice +glottal −press] ⇒ [+tense]. Examples of all eleven of the possible sound types are given in the first eight columns of the chart. The [±tense] specification under *p* and *b* allow for tense and lax plain stops. The specification [±pressure] under the symbol *p̓* allows for ejective versus non-ejective voiceless glottalized sounds. The latter occur finally in Gitksan and also in such English words as *hit* [hɪt̓] and *stop* [stɑp̓]. I do not know if ejective and non-ejective voiceless glottalized sounds ever contrast. However, Greenberg (1970:127) notes that such a contrast is reported by Trubetskoy for the Northwest Caucasian language Andi. If so, then the now old-fashioned notation C! might be employed for true ejectives to distinguish them from sounds, like the final segments of *hit* and *stop*, which are merely glottalized.

Despite the co-occurrence restrictions which have just been noted, it should nevertheless be possible to employ this limited set of six distinctive features to form sound classes which will correspond quite well to the classes that are actually needed to describe synchronic and diachronic process. The success of any distinctive feature theory depends on its utility in characterizing just the classes of sounds which enter into phonological rules, sound changes, distributional classes, and so forth. Only to the extent that a distinctive feature theory provides the right parameters are we afforded a true understanding of phonological processes. Not only should processes be easily stated, but, in addition, if $x \rightarrow y$ is a commonly found phonologically process, then, all things being equal, we expect x and y to be relatively close phonetically. This should be reflected in the number of distinctive feature differences between x and y. For the feature system given above, the number of distinctive feature differences between sound types seems to correspond to the relative distance sound types actually exhibit in terms of phonological processes.

5. For the glottalized consonants of Gitksan, I take the underlying segments /ṗ, t̓, c̓, ƛ̓, k̓, k̓ʷ, q̇/, as given in the underlying forms in column IV above, to have the feature specifications [−voice, +glottal, +pressure, −breathy, +tense]. The glottalized segments differ in feature composition from the corresponding voiced implosives given in column III only with respect to voicing.

With the revised feature set presented in §4 it is unnecessary to state that the ejectives which are affected by the Gitksan obstruent voicing rule become implosives since this is automatically accounted for by phonetic theory. It is also unnecessary to say explicitly in the rule that [−glottal] becomes [+glottal] when [−voice] becomes [+voice]. By a co-occurrence restriction [+voice] ⇒ [+glottal]. The obstruent voicing rule of Gitksan can, thus, be stated simply and naturally just as it was given in §3: [−cont] → [+voice] / ___ [+sonor].

EQUATIONAL SENTENCE STRUCTURE IN ESKIMO

TH. R. HOFMANN

Up to the present, the theory of syntax has been concerned almost exclusively with what we may call *nuclear* sentence structures. In the functional structure of a nuclear sentence,[1a] the verb is the head or nucleus of the sentence. Noun phrases & prepositional phrases are arranged functionally around it as satellite phrases.[1b] Negation & many adverbials are likewise linked to the nucleus in several ways: semantically, through dependencies & in collocation selection. The linearization of such nuclear structures gives rise to the 2 fundamental types of deep structure, Vb+NP+NP+NP & NP+NP+NP+Vb as in Arabic & Japanese, respectively, from which other structures such as Subject-Predicate, e.g. NP+Vb+NP or Sj+Vb+Oj, appear to be derived.[2]

While some Eskimo sentences allow analysis into subject & predicate parts, & other sentences appear nuclear in structure, neither pattern suffices but for a fraction of sentences. Indeed, the largest portion of running text cannot be readily analysed as either of these types of structure. And because the primary constituents of these problematic sentences, taken individually or in pairs, can function as independent sentences & can then be analysed in nuclear or subject-predicate terms, one must conclude that the traditional structures exemplified by these constituents are special or trivial cases of a here-to-fore undescribed structure.

On the most intuitive level, these problems in analysis arise because one cannot reliably identify the nuclear verb or predicate of even a simple sentence like:

una pisuktuq iglaktuq.
   una   ≡ that, that one
pisuktuq ≡ he walks, the one who walks (OR is walking)
iglaktuq ≡ he laughs, the one who laughs (OR is laughing)

Such a sentence may be translated equally well as 'that one walks &

laughs', 'that one which is walking laughs', 'that walker laughs', or even with the right intonation, 'that one which laughs/is laughing walks/is walking'. This problem becomes more serious if more words are added. At first glance, it seems to be a purely semantic problem, but it has important syntactic implications as I will try to show.

Here I want to explore this other type of functional structure,[3] which I call *equational* because of its similarity to the structure of complex equations in algebra. To my knowledge,[4] equational sentences are not well represented in English or any other language on the Eurasian continent. In fact, the only language I know of which makes systematic use of this equational organization is Eskimo. This organization of expression does not affect what can be expressed, only how it is expressed. Moreover, this organization is exhibited only at the highest level of syntactic constituents. The constituents which are equationally related are themselves organized in a nuclear structure resembling that of sentences in English or other languages. These facts have given rise to seemingly contradictory statements like, "Each word in Eskimo is a sentence", & "Each word is a nominal"[5] & even (attributable to me) "The notion of sentence does not make sense for Eskimo". I have come to believe that each of these statements expresses some truth, but as seen from different viewpoints. The whole truth, it seems to me, is alien enough to the usual conception of syntax that I can not hope to convince any one who has not already studied Eskimo, or other equational language, if such exists. Accordingly this paper has limited goals:

1. to show that this equational type of analysis is possible, & meets the facts in Eskimo at least as well as any nuclear type of analysis;

2. to implant these ideas in the minds of both Eskimos & linguists, to flower at some later date if they are true; &

3. to provide an alternate model for the beginning student of Eskimo to integrate his experience. If, as I believe, this model is right the younger generation will be attracted to it in increasing numbers.

A theory of equational structures cannot be proposed at this time because it would be ill-motivated indeed, if it were based on a single language. There is however, a need for such a theory & its integration into a general theory of syntax & semantics, which I will speculate a bit on later. Prerequisite for that endeavor, however, is the identification of other languages of this or similar nature. I would hope then that the equational structures motivated here for Eskimo will be recognized as a minor type of functional sentence organization & similar languages, if there are any, will be analysed in comparable terms.

First, we shall build up some principles for the identification of equational structures, using the complex equational notation of elementary algebra as a model (1). Then (2) we shall turn to Eskimo to see that its several types of sentences do exhibit the characteristics of equational structures. Then after (3) reanalysing 1 of the problematic syntactic contrasts of Eskimo, we will return (4) to some equational structures in languages closer to home. Finally (5), I shall draw together the major observations & speculate on their relevance to modern syntactic theory.

1. *Equational Sentences.* The organization & properties of equational sentences are well illustrated in the notations which have evolved in arithmetic, algebra & calculus. There, a simple equation is the usual form for stating a proposition.

$$4xy = 6 + x$$

Such an equation can be asserted, denied, doubted, or questioned, although the standard notation does not include such performatives.[6] These performative notions are expressed in natural language accompanying the equation. Because "=" is symmetric, there is another equation, $6 + x = 4xy$, which is identical in meaning to the above. Following common usage, I will consider them to be "the same equation".

Not infrequently several equations are combined to make a "complex equation" which equates 3 or more terms.

$$3xy = 5y + x/r = r(x + y)$$

or

$$A = B = C$$

Such a complex equation can be decomposed into 3 underlying equations;

$$A = B$$
$$B = C$$
$$C = A$$

Only 2 of these underlying equations are independent; 1 of them adds nothing which was not in the others. It does not matter which 2 are considered to be the basic ones, the 3rd can always be derived from the other 2. If there are 4 terms equated, there are 6 underlying equations of which any 3 are independent, providing that all the terms occur in at least 1 of the 3 equations.

A complex equation of 4 terms,

$$A = B = C = D$$

is decomposed into 6 underlying equations,

$$A = B \quad A = C$$
$$A = D \quad B = C$$
$$C = D \quad B = D$$

With 5 terms there are 10 underlying equations. If 10 terms are equated, there are 45 underlying equations, & so on. In general, a complex equation of N terms can be decomposed into $N(N - 1)/2$ underlying equations. Complex equations provide a compact & efficient notation if a number of things are equated.

Decomposition into underlying equations is commonly used in mathematics to specify the meaning of a complex equation. Once the meaning of each simple equation is specified, the meaning of a complex equation is defined as the conjunction of its underlying simple equations. As we noted however, not all of the underlying equations are independent; some add nothing to the meaning of the others. So long as we do not consider different performatives, it is semantically irrelevant which of the underlying equations are chosen to be the base structures. It is somewhat unsettling for the theory of transformational grammar, however, to find propositions like these complex equations. They are derived from the conjunction of a number of structures, but it does not matter which of a set of structures are included in that conjunction, providing that a certain minimum number of independent ones are included. If syntactic theory requires identical deep structures for synonymous sentences like the above & its reflection $D = C = B = A$, then their deep structure must be this set of underlying equations. Consequently both complex equations must be syntactically ambiguous in a number of ways without any accompanying semantic ambiguity. Such annoying facts may be rejected from theoretical consideration on the basis that they concern an artificial mathematical notation, & are not facts about a natural human language. If however I can show that Eskimo has structures of this nature, these problems must be considered.

When a complex equation is denied (or questioned), it is possible that every equation in its decomposition is denied (or questioned). Invariably in usage, however, not every underlying proposition is denied (or questioned), but only some of them. It is of course impossible to deny only 1 of the underlying equations, as that will lead to contradiction. In the example above, to deny $A = B$ while leaving $B = C$ & $C = A$ is contradictory as $A = B$ can be derived from the latter 2. Two of the underlying equations must be denied together. In denying larger complex equations, 3 or more underlying equations must be denied together, the matter of which ones being rather important if contradictions are to be avoided.

In complex equational structures, propositional attitudes (doubt, assertion, imperative, interrogative, &c) logically apply to the *terms* of the equation, & not to the equal marks, nor to the underlying equations. If there are 7 terms equated, then there are 21 underlying propositions. If 1 of these terms is doubted, 6 terms remain equated without doubt applying to them. The equation of these 6 terms derives from 15 underlying equations which are not affected by doubt. That leaves 6 of the underlying equations which the doubt affected. It is clear why this is so. The minimal denial in a complex equation is to pull 1 term out of the group of terms which are equated. Since that term would otherwise be equated (in a group of 7) to 6 other terms, 6 underlying equations are denied. Denial or questioning of part of a complex equation is really a denial or questioning of a term, i.e. of its inclusion in a group of equated terms. The same logic & comments apply to negation. Thus in complex equational structures, performatives, & negation are associated semantically with the terms & not with the "=".

Based on these observations, it seems rather artificial to decompose a complex equation into simple equations. The underlying equations are numerous, & they flick into & out of existence in flocks when some term is negated, asserted, questioned, &c. If these complex equations are not derived from conjunctions of underlying simple equations, then the problems with syntactic ambiguity disappear, negation no longer applies to flocks of underlying equations, & negation (& performatives) may be expanded optionally in each term. But this decomposition is necessary if "=" is treated as a verb or predicating element of which there is only 1 in a sentence. Suspicions are aroused about treating equality as a verb, however, by Frege's semantic treatment of copular identification,[7] & by recent demonstrations that copular verbs do not exist in deep structure.[8]

Because the *equals* sign does not contrast with any symbol in a complex equation, it carries no semantic content. No other relation can replace an "=" without splitting a complex equation into 2 smaller equations. Moreover, except in a 2-term equation, it does not even contrast with its negation; negation, like the performatives, is associated with the terms. Thus, "=" can carry no information about descriptive semantic content, i.e. the meaning in the narrow sense. In a limited sense, however, "=" does contrast with other symbols. To equate a group of terms in the syntax of this notation, each term must be separated from the other terms by "=". If some other symbol occurs, then the term is not finished. Thus "=" carries syntactic information; it marks the boundaries of the terms.

Summing up the traits that characterize equational sentence structures, we have found the following. (1) An equational sentence has no syntactic end; it can be continued indefinitely. (2) There is no syntactic structure between the terms except perhaps for a single node dominating them. (3) The order of the terms is not significant. Any arrangement of the equated terms is equivalent.[9] (4) Negation applies to terms; each term may or may not be negated. (5) Performatives like question, assertion, &c likewise apply to terms. (6) The boundaries of terms must be detectable, & may be marked by an object like "=". Because it has these properties, an equational structure is formally equivalent to an unordered list of terms, where negation & performatives are optionally applied to each term.

2. *Equational structures in Eskimo*. An Eskimo sentence like

⟨man walk^{T}s   black^{T}s   laugh^{P}s⟩[10]
inuk pisuktuq qirniqtuq iglaqpuq.[11]
'The walking black man is laughing.'

appears to be equational in nature. It has no syntactic end; it can be continued indefinitely by adding more words. Any arrangement of these words makes a paraphrastic sentence, & any combination of them is also a sentence. Hence there is no structure between these words. Moreover, each of the words has the same distribution in the syntactic possibilities of the language, except for small variations. They are all noun-like, & ⟨man⟩ *inuk* is an unanalysable noun. Because all of these words except for ⟨man⟩ can be uttered in isolation as a complete sentence, let us call them "clause words". The 2nd ⟨walk^{T}s⟩, for example, can be translated either as a sentence "he walks", or as a nominal whose descriptive content is all in a relative clause, "he who walks". These clause words can embed negation ⟨-Neg-⟩ – *ŋŋit-*, as in ⟨walkNeg^{T}s⟩ *pisuŋŋittuq* "he (who) doesn't walk", & any of the performatives, e.g. binary question *-aa* ⟨-s?⟩ in ⟨walk^{P}s?⟩ *pisukpaa* "does he walk?" Moreover, any arrangement of the words is possible, the arrangements differing in the theme (topic) & focus.

⟨man walk^{T}s   laugh^{P}s   black^{T}s.⟩
inuk pisuktuq iglaqpuq qirniqtuq.
'The BLACK walking man is laughing.'

This matches quite closely what we expect for an equational sentence structure. There are indefinitely long sentences (1) with no structure between the constituents (2). Rearrangement makes no difference in descriptive content (3). Each word is syntactically the same sort of object, a "term" in the mathematical jargon. Lastly, negation (4) & performatives (5) apply to terms. The syntactic characteristics of equations & Eskimo sentences match perfectly, except that the " = " is not expressed in Eskimo: the term boundaries are phonological word boundaries (6), marked by the lack of assimilation & the possibility of pausing.

While this simple type of sentence is not exceptional, it is uncommon for a sentence to be composed of only this type of term. Quite common is an other type of structure, which appears to have a nuclear organization. These are traditionally called "intransitive" constructions. To say "the man walked (around) in Iqalluit (the town of Frobisher)" one can say,

⟨man walk^{T}s Iqalluit-at.⟩
inuk pisuktuq iqaluŋni.

The equational structure can still be found between ⟨man⟩ & the rest. Although any arrangement is still possible, to place ⟨man⟩ between ⟨walk^{T}s⟩ & ⟨Iqalluit-at⟩ is definitely emphatic. The obvious conclusion is that ⟨walk^{T}s⟩ & ⟨Iqalluit-at⟩ together form a constituent. This constituent is functionally equivalent to a term in an equational structure because it can be placed anywhere into the 1st type of sentence, & because other terms can be added to this type of sentence.

This type of behavior is exhibited by other "adverbs" of direction, manner or route. They are dependent on a clause word, which they modify semantically.

iqaluŋni	in/at Iqalluit
iqaluŋnit	from Iqalluit
iqaluŋnut	to Iqalluit
iqaluktigut	via Iqalluit
iqaluktitut	like Iqalluit

Even an indefinite direct object is expressed in this "intransitive" structure, with a postposition -nik ⟨^{3}ly⟩ (^{3} for plurals).

⟨bear man^{3}ly see^{P}s.⟩
nanuq inuŋnik takujuq.
'the bear sees some men.'

What is for us a verbal notion with satellite phrases (noun & prepositional phrases) around it is expressed in Eskimo as a single term which has a nuclear structure. Except for some grammatical objects incorporated into the clause word, the satellite phrases are separate words which we can call "adjuncts". Every adjunct is syntactically optional & is marked by a postposition indicating its relationship to the verbal notion. This nuclear verbal notion is expressed as an ordinary clause word, & marked with ⟨-s⟩ or 1 of the other endings[12] for clause words. Together with whatever adjuncts it has, the clause word forms a term like the ones above. It can stand alone, or it can be combined with as many other terms as is desired, always forming a complete sentence. Like a single clause word, the complex term composed of clause word plus adjuncts may be translated either as a complete & independent sentence, or as a relative clause.

At this point, I would like to underline the distinction between "word" & "term". A term is any word or group of words which can function as a single term in a sentence such as the one we began with. We have identified 3 types of phonological words; an unanalyzable noun, a clause word & an adjunct. A noun or a clause word is a term by itself, but both may combine with dependent adjuncts to form complex terms. The adjuncts we have seen must combine with a clause word to form a term, & a noun plus ⟨-Pos⟩ combines with a possessive adjunct marked by ⟨-'s⟩ to form a complex term (see below). Thus every term boundary is a word boundary, but the word boundary between an adjunct & its clause word is not a term boundary. However, as every adjunct is marked by a postposition & every clause word has a special ending, the term boundaries are easily identified as word boundaries across which there are no syntactic dependencies. The term is a constituent except that its unity can be destroyed by moving an adjunct away from the unit. The word is a lower level constituent which is composed of morphs arranged according to strict syntactic rules, but which cannot be split up or rearranged.

There is a 3rd type of term to be discussed, the so-called "transitive verb" & its adjuncts. Again it can be analyzed as a term of an equational structure. An utterance like

⟨man bear's see^{T}ThgPos.⟩
inuk nanuup takujaa.
'The man is seen by the polar[13] bear.'

can be analyzed as an equation between between ⟨man⟩ & the rest. The word ⟨bear's⟩ is the "relative" or "possessive" case[14] of ⟨bear⟩, & the ⟨see^{T}ThgPos⟩ can be analysed into ⟨see^{T}Thg⟩ *takujaq* "thing which is seen" marked for possession ⟨-Pos⟩ (-*a*) by a singular possessor. The relative case ⟨-'s⟩ (-*up*) is used to mark possessors, & the 2 together ⟨bear's see^TThgPos⟩ can be interpreted as 'a bear's seen-thing', i.e. 'thing which the bear sees'. Constituents such as this can enter into equational structures, so they must be terms as well.

>⟨bear's see^TThgPos walk^Ts   laugh^Ps.⟩
>nanuup takujaa   pisuktuq iglaqpuq.
>'The walking one which the bear sees is laughing.'

The apparently nuclear structure ⟨man bear's see^TThgPos⟩ is no more than a simple equational sentence with 2 terms.

There is 1 last type of support for the equational analysis of Eskimo. Nominal terms like ⟨that⟩ & ⟨bear⟩ can be put together to make a "nominal" sentence like the following. However, either term by itself does not form a sentence, & can be uttered only with a supporting context, for example, if preceded by a question.

>⟨that bear.⟩
>una   nanuq.
>'That's a (polar) bear.'
>*⟨that.⟩
>*una.
>*⟨bear.⟩
>*nanuq.

This is exactly what is expected if a sentence is a series of terms equated. The 1st sentence is unavoidable in this analysis because nouns are terms. But the 2nd & 3rd sentences are impossible because an equation must have at least 2 terms.

Many languages, e.g. Russian, have a copular sentence structure which looks superficially similar to these equational structures;

>Russian
>⟨I person.⟩
>ja čelovek.
>'I am a person.'
>⟨person good.⟩
>čelovek xoroš.
>'The person is good.'

I do not believe that these can be considered examples of equational sentences, except perhaps on a very superficial level. For them, there is no possibility of continuing as there is in Eskimo;

> Russian
> $*\langle$I person good.$\rangle$
> *ja čelovek xoroš.
> Eskimo
> $\langle$that person good^{T}s.$\rangle$
> una inuk   piujuq.
> 'That person is good./That is a good person.'

Further, rearrangement of these constituents is strongly limited, *čelovek etot, & negation is nuclear & applies to the whole sentence, "*etot net čelovek*" rather than being associated with a particular term.

In equational structures, performatives & negation apply to terms. A sentence of purely nominal terms is clearly equational, but there is no obvious way to negate these terms. However, there is a way to make a clause word out of a noun: to add -*u*- $\langle$Be$\rangle$ 'to be' & an ending like $\langle^P$s$\rangle$. Thus the following are effectively synonymous.

> $\langle$that bear.$\rangle$
> una   nanuq.
> $\langle$that bearBe^{P}s.$\rangle$ 'That is a bear.'
> una   nanuuvuq.

The latter, however, can be negated as it contains a clause word.

> $\langle$that bearBeNeg^{T}s.$\rangle$
> una nanuuŋŋittuq.
> 'That is not a bear.'

Similarly it can be questioned, or put under the action of any performative. In this way, the nominal terms are also susceptible to negation & performatives.

Perhaps the strongest demonstration of the equational nature of Eskimo is the possibility of negating the various terms individually. All of the possibilities in the following schema can occur.

$$\begin{bmatrix} \text{inuk} \\ \text{inuŋŋittuq} \\ 1 \qquad\qquad 1 \end{bmatrix} \begin{bmatrix} \text{pisuktuq} \\ \text{pisuŋŋittuq} \\ 2 \qquad\qquad 2 \end{bmatrix} \text{nanuup} \begin{bmatrix} \text{takujaa} \\ \text{takuŋŋittaa} \\ 3 \qquad\qquad 3 \end{bmatrix}.$$

$$\begin{bmatrix} \text{the person} \\ \text{the non-human} \\ 1 \quad\quad\quad 1 \end{bmatrix} \begin{bmatrix} \text{who} \\ \emptyset \\ 4 \quad 4 \end{bmatrix} \begin{bmatrix} \text{walks} \\ \text{doesn't walk} \\ 2 \quad\quad\quad 2 \end{bmatrix} \begin{bmatrix} \emptyset \\ \& \\ 4 \end{bmatrix} \text{is} \begin{bmatrix} \emptyset \\ \text{not} \\ 3 \quad 3 \end{bmatrix}$$

'seen by the bear.'

Thus negation applies to terms, as can doubt or question, except that it is not easy to find a context for much questioning. Rearrangement of these terms is generally possible, except that a pure noun not at the beginning is likely to have a *-uvuq* ⟨Be^{P}s⟩ attached.

The 4 types of structure discussed exhaust the possibilities of translation of independent & relative clauses of a western language. From the sorts of evidence noted, I conclude that Eskimo sentences are organized on an equational structure.[15] A sentence is a series of terms which are understood to be descriptive of the same object in the universe of interpretation. One type of term is a simple noun or demonstrative, the other type is a clause-word optionally accompanied by dependent adjuncts. These clause words can be negative, interrogative, assertive &c, as are the terms in an ideal equational structure.

3. *The p:t distinction.* I have avoided an important problem up to now, the contrast between 2 classes of clause-word suffixes; p-forms like ⟨^{P}s⟩ *-puq* & t-forms like ⟨^{T}s⟩ *-tuq*, & their allo-forms after vowels, *-vuq* & *-juq* respectively. The usage of p-forms & t-forms has been investigated under the guidance of J-P. Paillet by M. Devine, M. Uviluq, & J-M. Massenet. Their tentative conclusion (unpublished) is that once a p-form is used of some fact in the description of a particular situation, a p-form cannot be further used for that fact in that situation, either by the person who used it before, or by someone else. While this is an accurate description, it is not complete & it could be at best observationally adequate: it needs an explanation. It was speculated in the above investigation that using the p-form is somehow like claiming to be the discoverer of the fact. Once a fact has been discovered, no one else can claim it. Alternatively, it might be that the p-form marks the entrance of a new fact into the discussion. I would argue for an other interpretation: the p-form marks a predication, while the t-form marks an attributively used term. An other speaker can not predicate what someone else has recently predicated, just as in English. This explanation receives support from the interpretation of sentences such as the 1st several examples in the section above. There the p-form is translated as the predicate of the sentence, regardless of where it is located in the sentence. The t-forms are translated as attributive adjectives or relative clauses.

A perceptive native speaker, Abe Okpik,[16] has offered 2 different explanations of the p:t contrast. One is that t-forms are used for observed facts & p-forms for reported facts. This observation matches tolerably well with our hypothesis, as only observed or known facts can be used attributively. Reported facts, on the other hand, are those which are predicated or asserted. His other observation is that t-forms are for visible facts, while p-forms are for invisible facts. A literal interpretation of this is not possible, so I take "visible" to mean "known to the participants of the conversation", the facts one uses attributively, & "invisible" to mean "not already known", i.e. those facts that are predicated. Thus both of these generalizations support the analysis of the p:t distinction as a contrast between predication & attribution.

Syntactic support for this hypothesis is found in embedded clauses, which are invariably terms in t-forms. The p-forms are not possible in embedded position. For example, 'he sees someone walking',

⟨walk^{T}mik see^{T}s.⟩   pisuktumik takujuq.
*⟨walk^{P}mik see^{T}s.⟩   *pisukpumik takujuq.

The interpretation this hypothesis gives to this fact is that predications are not allowed in embedded clauses. Such a principle seems reasonable enough in the light of similar restrictions in other languages.

Moreover, p-forms are obligatory in questions. This fact also follows from our explanation. Because interrogation cannot be made about attributions used for reference, they are by nature restricted to predicative forms. This is a logical necessity for any language.

If the difference between the p- & t-forms is a difference between predication & attribution, it can explain the tendency in Québec dialects to avoid the p-forms, which are felt to be "vulgar" or "low class". Predication & assertion are not dissimilar. But to use an assertion is not very different from being assertive, a characteristic which is disapproved of by most Eskimo culture. If the p-forms are understood in Québec to express assertions, it is to be expected that their use would be avoided.

I hypothesize then that p-forms are predications or assertions, while t-forms are attributions (attributive forms used in further specifying a referent). However, a t-form can also be used predicatively, not only in Québec, but also west of Hudson's Bay. The motivating factor for this may be what I have proposed above. Nevertheless it is not immediately apparent how an attributive t-form can be used at all for predication. In other languages, however, a substantive (noun or adjective) may be used predicatively without other mark, although the resulting expression may not be grammatically acceptable. In English there is for example the following use of attributive forms, *big chief* & *smart*, as predicates.

>me, big chief.
>man coming, smart.

This "elementary" use of English is usually restricted to conversations with children or foreigners, i.e. with people we do not expect to be able to use the language well. Nevertheless it does demonstrate that there is a limited sub-code of English which uses attributive forms for predication.

In fact, the use of non-predicative forms for statements is not at all strange. Paillet discovered a class of examples in English where a similar type of usage is found. In the captions of pictures where the depicted object is known, non-predicating gerundive forms are common.

>PICTURE -I-
>Driving across the border with a load of hash.

>PICTURE -II-
>Explaining to the officials

A grammatical subject may be added to identify the depicted object, & in some cases, a 2nd comment can be added.

>PICTURE -III-
>André showing them how to smoke it.

>PICTURE -IV-
>All of us together enjoying the hash,
>the spirit of revolutionary solidarity.

Here there is a group of equated things: the picture, the description or comment(s), & optionally the "subject". Eskimo is similar to this type of English usage, so much so that Eskimo might conceivably be called a "picture caption language". I conclude from these usages of English & Eskimo that the use of non-predicative forms for predications is not unusual in language. It is thus a plausible hypothesis that the t-form is attributive, while the p-form indicates predication.

This hypothesis explains why in our 1st sentence the p-form was always translated as the predicate. That observation might seem to provide an easy way out of admitting equational structures in Eskimo, to take independent t-terms as relative clauses on the subject. However, this tack will not solve the problem, as several p-terms may occur in the same sentence, leaving us back where we started from.

⟨person walk^{P}s   laugh^{P}s bear^{3}ly   see^{P}s⟩
inuk   pisukpuq iglakpuq nanuŋnik takuvuq.
'The person walks & laughs & sees some bears.'

4. *Equational structures in English.* Because it is not enough, I believe, for a science of language to discover & attribute strange things to languages well removed from the direct experience of most researchers, I will indulge here in bringing these observations about Eskimo home to English speakers. I hope thereby that they will be able to "feel" to some degree a syntactic device which finds considerable use in Eskimo. At the same time, the theoretical problems raised by Eskimo are mapped into problems about a language which has been studied far more extensively.

English syntax is based on the nuclear structure where satellite phrases are arranged around, dependent on, & interpreted with respect to the nuclear verb. Notwithstanding, there are a few places where the equational type of sentence appears even in ordinary prose structures. I assume that both patterns are available to all languages, though 1 pattern may be much more frequent in 1 language than the other.

One crack in the general nuclear façade of English is the expression, "a rose is a rose is a rose". One is tempted to account for such as an emphatic form of "a rose is a rose", but similar emphatic forms do not occur for "a dog is an animal"; there is no *"a dog is an animal is an animal" or *"a dog is a dog is an animal". Nor is it an idiom restricted to the word *rose*; "a dog is a dog is a dog" is just as satisfactory. There appears to be no half-reasonable way to generate such sentences, without accepting that we have some competence in equational sentences which is restricted to equating obviously equal things.

An other sentence type which does not find a place in nuclear or subject-predicate models is the "parallel comparative";

the bigger he is, the harder he falls.

the bigger he is, the harder he falls, & the more he gets bruised.

There is an optional marker *then* to separate them. This suggests an *if...then...* source[17], but I cannot find such a source. There seems to be no reason to take the *then* as anything other than an explicit term-delimiter & a marker of the place in an equational structure after which are found the predicated elements. The intonation of these sentences is exactly that of a series of 2 or 3 nominals like:

the type it is & the strength of its surface.

the type they are, the colour they are, & the shape they might have.

However, the parallel comparatives cannot be conjunctions like these latter. The elements which are conjoined to make a compound sentence must themselves be sentences, but "the bigger he is" & "the harder he falls" are not sentences.

These examples cannot be explained in English grammar. At best, they can be handled as idioms which contain general NP slots, sort of "sentence-patterns" as it were. The alternative is to accept that equational structures are possible, but extremely restricted in English.

These equational sentences are anomalous by every nuclear model of syntax, from Tesnière to Fillmore, & they do not fare much better in the subject-predicate models (see note 1). Accordingly, these structures tend to be either ignored, or to be relegated to a secondary status. Because linguistic models of syntax have all been nuclear or subject-predicate, & because every linguistician tends to think in these terms, these examples can hardly be convincing. They are anomalous facts which are known of, but not worried about. I present them here to remind the nuclear-minded linguistician that the nuclear model cannot account naturally for systematic parts of even his own language. To be sure, he can stretch his model to account for them, but that stretching is needed only to counteract the assumption built into his model, that nuclear sentences exhaust the possibilities of sentence types.

For those who grew up with mathematics in their blood & got used to equational structures early in life, these examples demonstrate that one does not need to go to the North Pole to find equational sentences. For those who assume that there is a human competence for language, they must accept that we have this competence for equational sentences if Eskimos have it. Clearly, if we have this competence & our language does not encourage its use, it is fair to expect it to appear in the cracks & corners of our language. If such did not appear, I think it could be considered as evidence against an hypothesis of a competence for equational sentences. Since it does appear, we can only say that we should expect it with the present hypothesis. But since it is contrary to the general patterns of English, & cannot be explicated in those terms, I take it to be supporting evidence.

Although structures such as

>   John is our butcher.

may have an equational semantic effect, I would argue that it does not have an equational functional structure. Of the 6 characteristics isolated for equational structures, only the 3rd (that order is not significant) is clearly met. Others are not met: neither negation nor performatives are associated with the terms, & it can not be indefinitely continued.

> *he is John is our butcher is nice is a guy.
> OK: he is John, our butcher, & is a nice guy.

Thus unlike Eskimo structures, copular sentences of English do not exhibit a functional structure similar to that of equations.

5. *Summary.* We have observed the characteristics of complex equations & of the major type of constituent in Eskimo, & found them to be identical. We conclude that Eskimo is an "equational language" when analysed into these constituents (called 'terms'), a language wherein the equational structure plays a major role. If half of the arguments I have presented about Eskimo stand, then syntactic theory as it presently stands is seriously inadequate, & needs revision to account for equational languages.

The sentence constituents or 'terms' in Eskimo comprise 1 or more phonological words. Terms may be either nouns plus optional possessors, or clause words plus optional adjuncts. Every term of the latter type has exactly 1 clause word which has an inflection for person & number. To the clause word may be joined any number of adjuncts marked by postpositions which show their functional relations to the nuclear clause word. Thus the functional structure of a term is nuclear. Analysis of the clause words shows them to allow VP embedding, while adjuncts may embed terms.

The existence of 1 natural language with an equational nature poses a problem to linguistic theory: how can equational structures be described within a generative framework such as transformational grammar? All well-known transformational grammars have had a categorial component which expanded the axiom S either in a nuclear fashion $S \rightarrow Vb + NP + (NP) + (NP)$, or as a subject followed by a predicate, $S \rightarrow NP + VP$. Both types of expansion are totally inappropriate to complex equations, & by extension to equational structures in Eskimo. The only plausible explanation is to derive equational structures from a conjunction scheme, $S \rightarrow$ (and S)*, where each S is a term & * indicates the coordination of any number of the parenthesized constituent. For mathematical equations, this would be $S \rightarrow (= S)^*$, & for Eskimo it is $S \rightarrow S^*$.

This explanation naturally accounts for indefinitely long sentence structures in terms of a well-established expansion rule schema. It also accounts for the lack of structure above the terms & for their possibilities of rearrangement. Moreover it accounts for negation & performatives applying to terms, as the terms are sentential objects by this explanation.

This explanation poses serious questions about conjunction & about what *S* stands for. Either it is possible for the conjunction of 1 type of constituent to form a different type of constituent, or else *S* & *S* are constituents of the same type. Taking the latter alternative, i.e. not modifying our understanding of conjunction, we will have problems in blocking syntactically sentences that consist of only a single noun, like *⟨this⟩.

It also requires that attributive modifiers be treated as sentences which have been conjoined[19] with the subject & the predicated property. As we usually understand sentence conjunction, it is a conjunction of assertions with assertions, or questions with questions, or the like. Here however, we shall have to allow not only conjunction of assertions, questions, &c, but attributions as well. This explanation also requires treating words that are obviously nouns (e.g. *inuk* 'man') as constituents of this same type: sentence-like. However, if we adopt a generative semantic standpoint, these requirements are not undesired. Nouns, adjectives & verbs have been argued independently[20] to be all of the same nature, predicators. Thus, because the structure of Eskimo is inconsistent with the general notions of sentence-structure in which transformational grammar developed, Eskimo may turn out to be invaluable for further development of generative semantics, if it indeed expresses much more directly some aspects of the deep structures proposed in that theory.

Although the point of this paper is simply that there is this other type of structure, & that linguistics must deal with it, some deeper explanation may be proposed. The difference between nuclear & equational sentence structures may be explicated in terms of an adequate semantic representation, such as C-net theory.[21] In semantic representation, there must be non-verbal elements (points, indices or variables) which can refer, all lexical items must be represented as predicates which take referential elements or other predicates as arguments, & conjunction must be the unmarked relation between 2 predicates. In such a representation, nuclear sentence structure is an expression of some semantic network by means of choosing some particular predicate as the nucleus. The elements it predicates upon are expressed as its subject, object, indirect object, &c. Where the element predicated on is a referential element, a description composed of other predicates dominating it is given. Thus a nuclear structure expresses a portion of a semantic network by assigning some predicate a central or nuclear role, & attributing descriptive lexical elements to its actants.

The equational structure, as seen from this semantic viewpoint, is the "dual" of the nuclear structure. Instead of organizing expression around a particular predicate (the nucleus) & its actants, expression is organized around a particular referential element. A "sentence" is then a series of descriptions about a single individual. In algebraic equations, the referential element is a single number (constant or variable), of which there are several (at least 2) descriptions (our "terms"). In Eskimo, this element may be a person, thing or whatever. Each term expresses a predicate which describes it, & may relate it with other referential elements. It follows naturally that these sentences include indefinitely many terms. And since conjunction is the unmarked semantic relation between predicates, this equational structure may be analysed as a conjunction. And because negation & performatives apply to predicates, they must occur with terms. In short, the characteristics of equational sentence structures follow from a principle which organizes expression around a referential element, instead of around a predicate.

NOTES

[1a] Most recent models of language structure have been nuclear. See for example Tesnière, Pike, &, more recently, Fillmore. An other type of structure, subject-predicate or topic-comment, derives from Aristotle & has often been proposed as the basis of sentence organization (e.g. Chomsky before 1968). However, it is not a *functional* organization because it does not express the functional roles of the various nominal satellites in a sentence.

A more complete explanation of these notions is contained in my "Nuclear model of sentence organization" (1973, unpublished). That also contains the derivation of a number of syntactic facts from these basic assumptions.

[1b] At the author's request, we have retained his orthographic usage (numerals, ampersands & *an other* as 2 words). He argues that there is no advantage for an international publication language to follow all the idiosyncracies of a spoken idiom, & that written English is more useful as an international language with the adoption of these pasigraphic symbols.

[2] McCawley, "English as a VSO [Vb+Sj+Oj] language" (1970), *Language* 46:286-99.

[3] Discussions with J-P. Paillet have been invaluable in formulating a number of the observations made here. The translations into definite & indefinite articles derives from his paper "Elementary sentence structures in Eskimo" (1972) to the Canadian Linguistic Assn (Newfoundland). Other contributions of his are noted in discussion.

[4] Excluding (for lack of knowledge) languages of the Finno-Ugric, Uralic, & Dravidian groups. See A. Sauvageot, "Charactère oularoïde du eskimo" (1953), *BSocLing* 49:107-24.

[5] See A. Schmitt, "Der nominale Charakter des sogenannten Verbums der Eskimo-Sprache" (1955), *Zeitschrifte für Vergleichende Sprachforschung* 73:27-45.

[6] A question mark can be placed above the "=" for questioned equations, & a slash is often superimposed on the "=" for denied equations, but these are not standard & they do not contrast with a mark for assertion &c.

[7] G. Frege, "Über Sinn und Bedeutung" (1892), *Zeitschrift für Philosophie und für Philosophische Kritik* 100.

[8] E. Bach, "*Have* and *be* in English Syntax" (1967), *Language* 43:462-85.
[9] In natural language, we might expect that terms might be arranged in order of their information content, their specificity, their interest, or most likely, topic 1st & focus last.
[10] The angle brackets ⟨⟩ enclose a "pidgin translation" or morpheme-by-morpheme equivalent. The use of pidgin is intended to make the argumentation meaningful to the non-eskimologist without committing Eskimo forms to memory & learning the details of Eskimo morphophonemics. Moreover, the details of forms & morphophonemics differ from dialect to dialect, & people who know other dialects tend to be distracted by these differences. Lastly, as I intend my remarks to apply to all the dialects, regardless of their phonological details, the quoted phonologic forms are intended only to aid those who know this or a similar dialect. For the definition & motivations of a pidgin translation, see Hofmann & Harris, "Pidgin translation", in *Meta* 15:11-26 (1970).

Because there is a 1-to-1 correspondence between the formatives of the language & its pidgin, the argument is more easily followed in the pidgin unless one already knows Eskimo. However, this same correspondence requires that the p-forms & t-forms be kept distinct since we shall look at them more closely below. I have used ^{T} to indicate a t-form & ^{P} to indicate a p-form.

[11] The examples used here are from Eastern Eskimo, including the dialects of the Keewatin, Baffin Island & Québec. There are 3 distinctive vowels, i, u, & a, with lax I.P.A. values except when next to a uvular consonant. There they are lowered & backed (as possible), & pick up some r-colour. The consonants are as follows.

	MANNER		
nasal	(−)	−	+
voicing	−	+	(+)
POSITION			
labial	p	v	m
apical	t	j	n
dorsal	k	g	ŋ
uvular	q	r	
special	s	l	

( ) indicates redundancy

The voiceless consonants are usually stops, but single q is fricative in Québec, & single s is always fricative (pronounced [h] to the west of Keewatin). Doubled, s & q are either affricates or (long) stops, depending on the dialect.

The voiced non-nasal consonants are usually fricative, but are affricates when doubled. However, single j is a glide & single l is a liquid.

A word is a sequence of syllables, each of which begins optionally with 1 of the consonants above followed by a vowel, & is optionally closed by a consonant in which manner distinctions are neutralized. The special s or l cannot close a syllable, but any other cluster of 2 consonants is possible. However, manner features assimilate regressively in a cluster unless there is a boundary, & there is a strong tendency for them to assimilate in position as well (stronger to the east). The "special" position is not a phonetic position other than apical. It is a *position* only on the phonological level, where several phonological processes & the phonetic mapping require it to be a position.

This is an extremely concise statement of a system of phonological contrasts, yet it appears to be accurate & complete, excluding minor dialectal phonetic variations. In essence, this description defines segmental contrasts & gives their significant (& some major non-significant) phonetic realizations. In addition, it rules out all impossible phonotactic combinations & many morphemic possibilities which do not occur. Moreover, this description appears to be adequate for every dialect between northern Greenland & the MacKenzie River.

[12] ⟨-s⟩ -*uq* designates a singular referent. There are other endings for referents composed of 2 objects & for referents of more than 2 objects. Where the referent is the speaker or the addressee, there are special endings to designate that. All this is obvious & unquestioned by eskimologists, though there are serious questions as to the system of realizations for these endings, & there is considerable dialectal variation in the rarer combinations (e.g. Question + 1st person dual). Because I will use only obvious endings, & because one can get entangled in morphological detail which is irrelevant to the present purpose, I will not provide support for these endings. Indeed, that would bore the eskimologist, & be confusing or unnecessary for anyone else. If the reader desires to be convinced of this point, he should consult any good elementary grammar of Eskimo, such as L. Schneider's *Grammaire esquimaude du sous-dialect de l'Unqava* (1967) Direction générale du Nouveau-Québec (Québec, Qué.).

[13] *nanuq* means 'polar bear', but for the sake of a concise pidgin, & since *nanuq* is an unanalysable morph, I have used ⟨bear⟩ as its pidgin equivalent.

[14] Use of the relative case ⟨'s⟩ (-*up* singular) to mark a noun as a possessor is similarly elementary morphology. As with -*uq*, it is complicated by other factors which are suppressed here. See grammars mentioned in note 12 for details. The possessive case ⟨Pos⟩ marks the possessed (i.e. determined) N in N-N constructions, but its underlying morphophonemic shape is not certain. Both ⟨'s⟩ & ⟨Pos⟩ occur in N-N constructions, marking the possessor & the possessed, respectively. Because neither appears in any other construction, the use of ⟨'s⟩ marking the "logical subject" of these so-called transitive verbs provides additional support for the analysis of -*taa* as -*taq* + *a* ⟨Thg^{T}Pos⟩.

[15] In "On the notion *to be* in Eskimo" (in Verhaar (ed.), *The Verb* be *and Its Synonyms*, 2 (1968) Reidel), J. Mey discusses the ⟨-Be-⟩ which makes a bare nominal into a verbal, allowing inflection for negation, mood, person & number. His framework assumes that sentences have verbal heads, & he accordingly downplays the "nominal sentences" like ⟨that bear⟩. He realizes that something is missing in his description, as he says that Eskimo is "a language that (for all I know) is very unlike anything that so far has been described in a modern (e.g. generative) framework." The point of the present discussion is that Eskimo can be, & should be, analysed as having an unexpressed copula, & that this equational structure (with an unexpressed copula) is the most basic structure in Eskimo.

[16] Reported by S. T. Mallon, Inuktitut Education, Yellowknife.

[17] The superficial structure of *if* ... *then* ... sentences is neither nuclear nor subject-predicate. There is no superficial reason why either of these words or their associated clauses should be singled out as the nucleus or the subject. Their nuclear deep structure rests on the supposition that the functional structure of all sentences is nuclear. It is this supposition that we call into question on the basis of Eskimo.

These "parallel comparatives" differ from our algebraic equational model by not having the freedom of rearrangement. But this restriction applies only at the point which is optionally marked by *then*. On either side of that point, the phrases may be rearranged freely. The semantic interpretation of this point (whether explicitly marked or not) appears to be pure "causality". Increases described before that point "cause" the increases described after it. Thus "the more he practices, the better he gets & the more he likes it" = "the more he practices, the more he likes it & the better he gets", ≠ "The better he gets, the more he practices & the more he likes it".

This semantic observation can motivate a nuclear deep structure, but the surface structure is clearly *not* nuclear. Indeed there appears to be no motivation for a nuclear deep structure except for the assumption that all deep structures are nuclear. That assumption is unmotivated & obfuscating for 1 non-natural language, algebraic notation, & 1 natural language, Eskimo, is better analysed without it.

[19] One is reminded at this point of Kuroda's derivation of relative clauses from conjoined sentences. See his article in *Language* (1965).

[20] See G. Lakoff, "Linguistics & natural logic", pp. 545-665 in Davidson & Harman (ed.), *The Semantics of Natural Language* (1972), Dordrecht, or J. McCawley, *Grammar and Meaning* (1973), Tokyo.

[21] See my "Descriptions in natural language" (1974), *Language Sciences* 30:13-19. The semantic representation proposed with generative semantics is not far from this, but because it is motivated from within transformational grammar, it also represents facts about the syntax of expression & conjunction which is far from being unmarked. See the last part of my "Integrative semantics" (1972), *Cahiers de Linguistiuqe* 2:19-38, for a closer criticism.

RULE MITOSIS: THE HISTORICAL DEVELOPMENT OF ALGONQUIAN PALATALIZATION*

JONATHAN KAYE

Paul Kiparsky in his celebrated article characterized linguistic change as a "window on the form of linguistic competence that is not obscured by factors like performance..." (1968a:174). Specifically, he argues that data concerning linguistic change can be used to support or refute the linguistic reality of such devices as the brace notation. For example, "... we should predict that rules collapsed by braces should participate in reordering as blocks" (1968a:181). Further, Kiparsky states that if, say, braces are legitimate abbreviatory devices, it should be the case that no "... rule could be inserted between two rules collapsed by braces in such a way that they could subsequently no longer be so collapsed" (1968a:181).

In this paper I will deal not with brace notation, but with the abbreviatory device most basic to phonology: the natural class.[1] I will show that a single rule containing two subparts collapsed together as a natural class has undergone what I call rule mitosis, i.e. has split into two rules. The notion of natural class is so basic to phonology and so well supported that we cannot draw the conclusion from such an example that Kiparsky would suggest (substituting *natural classes* for *brace notation*) to wit "if such changes could be found they would be clear counter-evidence against the brace notation and would suggest that the generalization effected by means of braces are spurious ones." (1968a:181). Rather we will attempt to offer an explanation of the rule mitosis while preserving the notion of natural class.

The example to be considered here concerns the development of Algonquian palatalization [2] specifically as it has developed in Ojibwa. Bloomfield (1946) posits the sound system for Proto-Algonquian (PA) shown below in (1).

(1) p   t (č) k
     θ   s   š (x)
     w   y   h ʔ
     m   n
         l
     ī i   ō o
     ē e   ā a

The segment *x* is enclosed in parentheses because it is reconstructed only in clusters (*xp xk*). Its exact status is highly controversial. As for *č* by all accounts it did not form part of the inventory of underlying phonemes of PA. Rather it was an automatic alternant of *t* in a palatalizing environment.[3] Bloomfield (1946:92) set up the alternations t ∼ č and θ ∼ š before ī i, y which may be expressed informally by the following rule:

(2) $\begin{bmatrix} t \\ \theta \end{bmatrix} \rightarrow \begin{bmatrix} č \\ š \end{bmatrix} / \underline{\quad}$ ī, i, y

These alternations are exhibited by such forms as *pemāčihēwa[4] 'he makes him live' (verb root *pemāt-, plus causative *ih, plus inflectional endings), cf. *pemātesiwa 'he lives'; *mīkāši 'fight thou him' (verb root *mīkāθ- plus imperative *i), cf. *mīkāθēwa 'he fights him'.

Given the system of features proposed by Chomsky and Halle (1968), rule (2) can be reformulated as follows:

(3) [−son, +cor, −dist] → [+high] / ____ [−cons, +high, −back]

Inspection of the phonemic inventory of PA given in (1) will show that the natural class [−son, +cor, −dist] has just θ and *t* as its members. Rule (3) is hardly remarkable. The alternation of *t* ∼ *č* is of course quite familiar. The θ ∼ š alternation, while not so common (one might expect rather *s* ∼ *š*), is certainly not unheard of. In classical phonemic theory the alternation of *t* ∼ *č* would be termed allophonic, while that of θ ∼ š is morphophonemic (since š existed as a phoneme in PA). This is certainly no cause for suspicion with respect to rule (3). Indeed, one of the early contributions of generative phonology (Halle 1959) was the discovery that a level of autonomous phonemics makes a generalization as expressed by rule (3) impossible. At this point in time, the fact that a rule involves both "phonemic" and "morphophonemic" alternations seems hardly an appropriate argument against it.

In the course of this paper I will attempt to demonstrate that rule (3) split into two rules in Ojibwa. It is naturally important then that we begin the discussion with the confidence that rule (3) represented a single process in PA. The similarity of the alternations ($t \sim č$, $\theta \sim š$) and the identity of the conditioning environments is self-evident. All the evidence that indicates that the Ojibwa reflexes of this rule now involve two processes can be shown to have developed in the post-PA period. It must be borne in mind that in PA we are dealing with a reconstructed language. There is always the possibility that there was some process, now lost to us, that indicated that the $t \sim č$ and $\theta \sim š$ alternations were the result of two different rules. To use this as an argument against my premise that rule mitosis is possible, and in fact has occurred, would be to deprive Kiparsky's interesting hypothesis of any empirical content.[5] Alternations triggered by PA palatalization were quite common. They existed in both the inflectional and derivational morphology. In the inflectional morphology of verbs, $\theta \sim š$ occurred frequently (an example with the verb *mīkāθ- 'to fight with someone' was given above). It is important to note that $t \sim č$ alternations did not exist in the inflectional morphology of verbs. This is due to the fact that no verb stem ended in t in paradigms where a suffix began with a high front vowel or glide.

In nouns both types of alternations existed freely. PA had a set of suffixes to mark both singular and plural forms of animate and inanimate nouns. The animate forms, which do not concern us here, were *a (singular) and *aki (plural). The inanimate singular marker was *i, the plural *ali. Given rule (3), it is evident that nouns ending in -t or -θ will display alternations of the sort that interest us here: *ne+sič+i 'my foot', *ne+sit+ali 'my feet'; *wāš+i 'cave, hole', *wāθ+ali 'caves, holes'. The inanimate singular suffix appears to be the only *i- initial suffix in the inflectional morphology of the noun. This point will ultimately prove important.

In its development from PA to Ojibwa the palatalization rule became more and more opaque. A series of sound changes took place which had the effect of producing surface sequences of ti and θi (which became li and finally ni), and also having $č$ and $š$ appear in other than palatalizing environments. Before we pursue these sound changes, I would like to digress a moment and review the development of *θ and *l.

PA *θ is reconstructed on the basis of a set of correspondences which show Ojibwa, Fox, Menomini n and Cree t:[6] PA *aθemwa 'dog' O *animw*, F *anemoha*, M *anēm*, C *atim*: PA *aθoxkyē 'to work') O *anokkī*, F *anohkyē*, M *anohkī*, C *atoskē*. At some early stage *θ and *l merged in many languages, e.g. Ojibwa, Fox, Menomini, Micmac, Delaware, Abenaki. In Ojibwa *θ and *l merged as r or l, depending on the dialect. This stage is well documented with MSS dating back to the 17th century. It was sometime during this stage that palatalization was extended to *l*'s (or *r*'s) from **l*. Thus, the merger of **θ* and **l* became absolute. There was no longer any synchronic basis for distinguishing reflexes of these proto-phonemes. The palatalization rule would have to be reformulated to reflect the *l* ~ *š* alternation.

(4) [+cor, −nasal, −dist] → [+high] / ____ [−cons, +high, −back]

Rule (4) is unspecific with respect to *r* and *l*. It will apply to either liquid.

Finally, around the beginning of the 19th century, the Ojibwa liquid merged with *n* (< **n*) as *n*. Palatalization was not extended to reflexes of **n and accordingly, there is a synchronic basis for distinguishing reflexes of **θ, **l from those of **n. This may be done by either positing an abstract phoneme (e.g. *l*) or by the use of exception features. Thus, *mīn* (< **mīl) 'to give' *nimīnā* 'I give him', *kimīš* (< /ki+mīn+i/) 'you give me' vs. *wēwēpin* (< **wewepin) 'to swing' *niwēwēpinā* 'I swing him', *kiwēwēpin* 'you swing me'.

From a completely automatic set of alternations PA palatalization began to become more and more opaque as a result of a series of sound changes which effected several Algonquian languages. The first change[7] merged **i and **e as *i*. Fox, which did not undergo this change, remains our primary source for distinguishing **i from **e. The result of this merger was to make the palatalization rule opaque, i.e. a large number of surface sequences of the type *ti* and *li* (< **θe or **le) were created. It seems likely that at this point, *č* entered the inventory of underlying segments, at least morpheme-internally. Put another way, palatalization was restricted to applying at morpheme boundaries.[8] Thus, forms like **tīmāni 'canoe' would be analyzed as *čīmāni*, at this stage. A form like **temi 'deep' undergoing the change **e > i would now be analyzed as *timi*.[9] (Of course many *č*'s are still derived from *t*'s but always at morpheme boundaries.)

A second sound change which also affected many Algonquian languages (but again, not Fox) was the addition of a rule which deletes final lax vowels. It is important to understand the effect of this rule on the inflectional morphology of Ojibwa nouns. Recall that PA had singular markers which consisted of single lax vowels: **a for animate nouns and **i for inanimate nouns. If the distribution of these singular markers was parallel to the distribution of the plural suffixes (**aki animate, **ali inanimate), then it would appear that these suffixes occurred only in final position. If a rule is added to the phonology which deletes final lax vowels, then it is evident that these singular markers will never be realized phonetically.[10] I believe that with the emergence of this rule, Ojibwa ceased to have a set of singular suffixes. Up to this point assume that Ojibwa had the singular-plural pairs: *ni+sič+i/ni+sit+ali* 'my foot/feet', *wāš+i/wāl+ali* 'cave(s)'.[11] Now with the addition of this final lax vowel deletion rule the forms would come out: *ni+sič/ni+sit+al, wāš/wāl+al*. In fact, it is not clear if such a stage ever existed in Ojibwa. What appears to have happened is that the nouns were reanalyzed with no underlying singular suffixes. Inanimate noun stems ending in *-t* are no longer palatalized, thus *nisiči > nisit* 'my foot', *nikkāči > nikkāt* 'my leg', *nīpiči > nīpit* 'my tooth'. This data may be seen to reflect a reordering whereby palatalization applies after final lax vowel deletion. It will be obvious, when we examine what happened to the θ ∼ š alternations, that if this proposal is accepted, then final lax vowel deletion insinuated itself between the subparts of the PA palatalization rule. My position is that the singular suffixes simply no longer formed part of the inflectional morphology of nouns.

It is not the case that every instance of word-final historical *-či has gone to *-t* in Ojibwa. The reverse dictionary of Odawa (a south-eastern dialect of Ojibwa) in Piggott and Kaye (1973:214-317) lists twenty-four forms ending in *-č*. All twenty-four are not major category items (i.e. not nouns or verbs), which is to say that they are not inflected.[12] We have then what appears to be a textbook example of the situation described in Kiparsky (1968b). Only *č*'s which alternated with *t* go to *t*, while non-alternating *č*'s remain as *č*. These data also indicate that *č* was a phoneme at the time when final lax-vowel deletion entered the language. They provide some evidence that the merger of *i and *e preceded this rule, since that merger was the only other change which would have made the palatalization rule opaque enough for *č to have become an underlying phoneme. The assumption here is that all non-alternating *č*'s were underlying rather than derived from *t*.

There is one form with final *-č* which raises an interesting problem: *kīmōč* 'stealthily'. This form is obviously related to the verb *kīmōtisi* 'to sneak around'. These forms illustrate the fact that it is not just any kind of *t* ∼ *č* alternation that leads to final *č* going to *t*. Rather only those forms which alternate *within a paradigm* "regularize" the paradigm by eliminating *t* ∼ *č* alternations. Only alternations within the inflectional morphology bring about this change. The *t* ∼ *č* alternation is tolerated only in the derivational morphology.[13]

The problem is how to represent [kīmōč]. There appear to be two possibilities: *kīmōt+i* or *kīmōč*. In the first alternative, palatalization would apply before final lax vowel deletion to yield *kīmōč+i* as an intermediate stage. Final lax vowel deletion would then apply yielding *kīmōč*.

There are a number of difficulties with this solution. In modern Ojibwa, final lax vowel deletion can be shown only to apply to nouns and verbs. Examples of non-major category morphemes ending in a lax vowel abound: *mānta* 'this' (inanim.), *ānawi* 'although' *išiwi* 'there', *owati* 'over there', *ānti* (Western Ojibwa) 'where', *šāši* 'already', *nanko* 'now', *ēntako* 'isn't it so?', etc.

In the second place, to derive *kīmōč* from *kīmōt + i* requires palatalization to apply *before* final lax vowel deletion. Kaye and Piggott (1973) present evidence that the opposite ordering is required for Ojibwa.

Finally, a serious question arises when it comes to the interpretation of the events discussed. Consider a parallel example discussed by Kiparsky (1968b) regarding certain Eastern Yiddish dialects. As is well known, German has a rule which devoices obstruents in final position. When a given form may take a suffix (as can nouns, verbs or adjectives), it is possible to establish a final obstruent in the underlying representation of the form as either voiced or voiceless, depending on its value when a suffix follows. In the case of many non-major category items, no suffixes are added and accordingly a final obstruent will always be voiceless. Kiparsky argues that in such cases these forms should be represented as ending in underlying voiceless obstruents. Strong corroboration for this view is provided by Eastern Yiddish dialects which have lost the final devoicing rule (cf. Weinreich 1963:342). The effect of this loss is an "outcropping" of the underlying representation. Final voiceless obstruents which are voiced when followed by a suffix now show up as voiced obstruents in these dialects. Non-alternating voiceless obstruents remain voiceless, regardless of their historical source. Thus, in these dialects *und* is realized as [unt], which must be assumed to be its underlying representation.

Returning to the Ojibwa situation, there is no doubt that forms such as **nesiči* were derived from underlying **ne + sit + i*. After final lax vowels were lost, this form was restructured as *ni + sit*. Since there is no longer any conditioning vowel for palatalization, the underlying *t* now breaks through to the surface.

But now consider *kīmōč*. If this form were indeed derived from *kīmōt + i* at the point at which final lax vowels were deleted, why don't we now get **kīmōt*? If the ultimate development of final *či* sequences reflects the status of the underlying representations of these forms, we can only conclude that the underlying representation of [kīmōč] was *kīmōč* after final lax vowel deletion entered the phonology, the form *kīmōtisi* notwithstanding.[14] We are left with an analysis which has two allomorphs: *kīmōt* and *kīmōč* for the root meaning 'sneak', or else one which marks the adverb which would have the underlying representation *kīmōt* as undergoing palatalization. Presumably this latter solution would involve an abstract morpheme, say, ADVERB which triggers palatalization and then disappears. According to this "solution" the underlying representation of *kīmōč* 'stealthily' would be *kīmōt+ADVERB*, thus avoiding any allomorphy for the verb root.

Whatever synchronic analysis is chosen to account for kīmōč, the diachronic facts are clear: after the loss of final lax vowels, it is not simply the case that č's that alternated with *t*'s go to *t*. Rather, only those č's which alternate with *t*'s *within a paradigm* exhibit this behaviour.

Let us turn now to inanimate nouns ending in *θ. Given a noun like *wāθ+i 'cave, hole', we would expect the resulting noun to appear as *wāl* and ultimately *wān* in Ojibwa (recall that *θ > l > n in Ojibwa). Thus, just as *nesiči (pl. *nesitali) goes to *nisit*, so *wāši (< *wāl+i, at this stage; pl. *wāl+ali) would be expected to go to *wāl*. There is no evidence that such a form ever existed. Rather, the modern Ojibwa form is *wānš*.[15] Typically the plural form appears as *wānšan*. The locative is either *wānšink* or *wānink*. The latter form appears in place names such as Manitoulin Island and Manitowaning.[16] Similarly, PA *ne+tyāθ+i 'my nose' has *ničānš* (again with intrusive *n*) as its reflex, rather than *ničān. The non-palatalized version of this morpheme appears in incorporated verb forms such as *kākīčičānē* 'to have a sore nose' (*kākīt* 'sore'). Unfortunately, the locative and plural forms of this noun are unavailable, so it is not clear if an inflectional *n* ~ *š* alternation exists here.

One noun exists in Ojibwa which reflects a PA *θ ~ š alternation in its inflection. PA *mehθ+i 'a piece of firewood' shows up in Ojibwa as *miššī*. The plural is *missan*[17] (< *mehθ+ali). The final *i* of *miššī* is a vestige of the PA inanimate singular marker. Its presence in this form is due to the fact that final lax vowels are not deleted following short monosyllabic stems (cf. note 10). Although this pair of forms may indicate a synchronic basis for positing singular markers, I prefer to treat these forms as suppletive allomorphs which must be learned individually.

In any event, at this stage we see the first indications that the palatalization of *θ and *t are behaving differently. Nouns with *t* ~ *č* alternations have their singular forms in *t* in Ojibwa, e.g. *nesiči > Ojibwa *nisit*. Nouns with θ ~ š alternations retain š, e.g. *w̄aši > Ojibwa *wānš*.

We return now to the opacating of Algonquian palatalization. I would like to make one further claim concerning the proto-period. Recall that *y as well as *i and *ī triggered PA palatalization. It so happens that *y*'s are never found following alveopalatals in the daughter languages. That is, there are no attested sequences of *čy* or *šy*.[18] I assume that PA had a rule which deleted *y*'s following alveopalatals.

(5) PA y-drop y → ∅ / [č, š] ___

(6) *nenītyānehsa 'my child'
    nenīčyānehsa palatalization
    nenīčānehsa   y-drop

We consider now another sound change which affected post-consonantal *y. In PA *y freely occurred after consonants: *pyet- 'bring', *-tyāθ- (*-čāθ-) 'nose', *kyā- 'hide', *myēxkanāwi 'road', *nyēwi 'four'.[19] In Ojibwa (as well as several other central Algonquian languages) *y was lost post-consonantally.[20] Thus, for the above examples we obtain *pīt*, *-čānš*, *kā-*, *mīkkan* and *nīwin*, respectively. It is most revealing when we compare the situation in Fox. Recall that Fox underwent neither the merger of *i and *e nor the loss of final lax vowels. As a result there is every reason to suppose that *č* remains a variant of *t* even morpheme-internally in this language. Now Fox did not lose post-consonantal *y*. For the examples given above Fox shows *pyē-*, *kyā-*,[21] *myēwi*. I do not believe that it is a coincidence that the one language that did not merge *e and *i and did not lose final lax vowels is also the one language that retains post-consonantal *y*.

I claim that sequences of $C + y$ are relatively marked and unstable. While such sequences exist or have existed in many languages, there is a tendency for *y* to be lost in such positions, particularly if there are other forces at work which undermine the support for these sequences. If we consider the series of stops in both PA and Fox, we see the following situation obtains:

(7) p t   k STOP
    py ty ⟨= č⟩ ky STOP + Y

It can be seen that sequences of *stop + y* are present at all the points of articulation of the stop series. Now contrast (7) with the Ojibwa situation reconstructed prior to the loss of post-consonantal *y*.

(8) p t č k STOP
    py   ky STOP + Y

Once *č* has achieved phonemic status in Ojibwa, it no longer has *ty* as a possible source. All such clusters were morpheme-internal and though some *č*'s can still be derived from *t*, this is possible only at a morpheme boundary. It has already been argued that y was dropped following alveopalatals in the proto period. Accordingly, no čy clusters could exist. The system posited in (8) shows that post-consonantal y now has a distributional gap, viz. it does not appear following coronals. It is my contention that the inherent instability[22] of such sequences when combined with this distributional gap, led to the loss of all postconsonantal y's in Ojibwa.

This brings us now to the situation in modern Ojibwa. In this section I will argue that there are now two palatalization rules in Ojibwa: t-palatalization (involving $t \sim č$ alternations) and l-palatalization (involving $n \sim š$ alternations). The strongest kind of evidence for demonstrating that there are two palatalization rules would be to show that a third rule must be ordered between them. Piggott (1971:29f.) has demonstrated that l-palatalization must be ordered *before* final lax vowel deletion. The following forms (taken from Piggott's article) demonstrate the nature of the relationship:

(9)a. ki+mīn+i   [kimīš]   'you give me'
   b. ki+mīn+i+min [kimīšimin] 'you give us'
   c. ki+nān+i   [kināš]   'you fetch me'
   d. ki+nān+i+min [kinašimin] 'you fetch us'

From these examples it is clear that l-palatalization must precede final lax vowel deletion in order to avoid deriving the incorrect (9a) *[kimīn] and (9c) *[kinān]. In Kaye and Piggott (1973) the derivation of forms like *pēmātisit* 'he who lives' and *pēmātisičik* 'they who live' received a considerable amount of discussion. Our conclusion was that the singular form must have as its underlying representation, *pēmātisit+i* (irrelevant details omitted). The only way to derive [pēmātisit] from *pēmātisit+i* is to have final lax vowel deletion apply *before* t-palatalization. These rules applied in the opposite order would produce the incorrect *[pēmātisič].[23] The key to this argument is the acceptance of *pēmātisit+i* as the underlying representation of this form. Readers are urged to refer to Kaye and Piggott (1973) in order to draw their own conclusions as to the validity of the arguments presented there.

Piggott (1971:25ff.) presents another argument for the separate status of Ojibwa t- and l-palatalization. As was discussed above *i and *e merged as *i* in Ojibwa. These vowels are kept morphophonemically distinct with respect to a number of rules. Specifically, i < *i but not i < *e triggers l-palatalization, cf. ki+mīn+i [kimīš] 'you give me', but *ki+mīn+ikw* (< *-ekw) [kimīnik] 'he gives you'. There is another rule, vowel coalescence, which converts sequences of *aw+i* into *ā* before *k* and *ō* before *n* (< **θ*). This rule only applies when the *i* is etymological **e*, never when it is etymological **i*: *ki+nōntaw+ikw* (< **-ekw*) [kinōntāk] 'he hears you', but *nōntaw+i+kon* [nōntawikon] '(you pl.) hear him!'; cf. *mīn+i+kon* [mīšikon] (Bloomfield 1957:59) '(you pl.) give it to him!'. In short, coalescence and l-palatalization never apply before the same suffix. In the abstract solution suggested by Piggott [i]'s which trigger coalescence and not l-palatalization would be derived from underlying *e*'s. The remaining [i]'s are derived from *i*.

Now if l-palatalization and t-palatalization are really but manifestations of the same rule, we should expect the same sensitivity to reflexes of **i* and **e*. That is, the same suffix should not trigger both coalescence and t-palatalization. But this is exactly what happens. The suffix [ikē] 'action on an unspecified object' triggers both t-palatalization and coalescence. This suffix can be added to either a transitive-animate (TA) or transitive-inanimate (TI) stem to form an intransitive verb. Thus, from the verb *wēppit-* 'hit' one can form the verbs *wēppit+ikē* (based on the TI stem) and *wēppitaw+ikē* (based on the TA stem) both meaning 'to hit an unspecified object'. These forms show up phonetically as [wēppičikē] and [wēppitākē], respectively. On the other hand, this suffix does not cause l-palatalization; cf. *sīnin* 'to milk someone', [nisīninā] 'I milk her', [sīniš] (< *sīnin+i*) 'milk her!', but *sīninikē* 'to milk'.

The analysis adopted by Piggott and me to handle these data is to assume that the suffix [ikē] has as its underlying representation: *ekē*. The initial short *e* accounts for the coalescence of *wēppitākē*. Since l-palatalization occurs only before *i*, we get *sīninikē* and not **sīnišikē*. If we assume that t-palatalization has been generalized to apply before any short front vowel (*i, e*), then we can account for forms like *wēppičikē*. Other suffixes behave like -*ekē*, for example the passive suffix – *ekāso*: *mīnikāso* 'he is given' (cf. *kimīš* 'you give me'), *wēppitākāso*, *wēppičikāso* 'he is hit'. We see then that the environments for t-palatalization and l-palatalization are different. The former applies before any front vowel, the latter, only before *i*. Even if a less abstract approach is taken, say, one involving exception features, it is evident that these data point to two palatalization rules.

A further bit of evidence for the distinctness of t- and l-palatalization involves what was called "the sibilant effect" in Kaye and Piggott (1973). We demonstrated that t-palatalization is (optionally, in some cases) blocked if a sibilant appears following the conditioning vowel: *kākīčinikkē* 'have a sore arm', *kākīčikātē* 'have a sore leg' but *kākītisitē* 'have a sore foot', *kākītisi* 'be sore'. There is evidence that indicates that the sibilant effect is restricted to t-palatalization. It does not block l-palatalization. The following examples involve the animate-intransitive final -iššin having to do with 'falling' or 'lying':

(10) a.   pakki*t*iššin 'lean over'   pakkičipin 'pull someone up while leaning over'

      āšiki*t*iššin 'be turned over'   āšikičipin 'flip someone over'
      ači*t*iššin 'lie face down'   ačičikkīkāpawi 'stand on one's head'

   b.   tašiššin 'lie buried in a certain place'   ta*n*ēnim 'expect someone to be there'

      išiššin 'lie thus'   i*n*ēnim 'think that someone. .'

Inspection of the left-hand column of (10) shows that while t does not palatalize before -iššin (10a), n ($<$ *θ or *l) does. The right-hand column shows each verb root in its palatalized or non-palatalized form, respectively. These data indicate clearly that *tan-* and *in-* have been palatalized in *tašiššin* and *išiššin* while *pakkit-*, *āšikit-* and *ačit-* have resisted palatalization before the very same suffix. That a following sibilant influences t-palatalization but not l-palatalization is further evidence that these are distinct rules in modern Ojibwa.

The last piece of evidence for two Ojibwa palatalization rules that I wish to discuss is the role that each plays in the morphology. Ojibwa l-palatalization is well established in the verbal inflectional morphology (*nimīnā*, *kimīš*) and to a lesser extent in nouns (*wānš*, *wānink*). What is important is that stems show $n \sim š$ alternations within an inflectional paradigm.

The role of t-palatalization is almost entirely restricted to the derivational morphology.[24] The one exception is the $t \sim č$ alternation displayed by the participles, e.g. *pēmātisit* 'he who lives' *pēmātisičik* 'they who live'. Even in this case, however, t-palatalization effects only the suffix *-t*, not the verb stem (the verb stem is *pimātisi* with mutation of the initial vowel; *-t* is the third person suffix). In fact, no Ojibwa stems show $t \sim č$ alternations within an inflectional paradigm.

Having (hopefully) established that the PA palatalization rule underwent mitosis in its Ojibwa incarnation, an explanation for this phenomenon is worth pursuing. I will discuss two hypotheses.

The first hypothesis is quite appealing in its elegance and simplicity.[25] Recall that the PA palatalization rule involved the alternations $*t \sim č$, $θ \sim š$. As was noted above these are quite natural alternations. When *θ became *l*, however, the alternations were then $t \sim č$, $l \sim š$. The former is, of course, quite natural, but the latter alternation $l \sim š$ is rather bizarre.

This melding of a natural alternation with an unnatural one within one rule ultimately may have led to the mitosis. This hypothesis is particularly attractive in that it shows that rules do not simply come and go like strangers in the night, but rather can have a far reaching impact on the language. It illustrates the internal and formal nature of the causes of some linguistic change.

There is one difficulty with this hypothesis. The $l \sim š$ (now $n \sim š$) alternation is the one that is most common in Ojibwa. The fact remains that old alternations like *nesiči – *nesitali have ceased to exist. The rule of l-palatalization remains as a regular, productive rule of synchronic Ojibwa phonology. This hypothesis could be pursued by investigating another Algonquian language which did not undergo the change *θ > l. Cree is such a language. The Cree reflex of PA palatalization is $t\,(<\,*t) \sim č$ and $t\,(<\,θ) \sim š$.[26] Since $t \sim š$ (or s) is nowhere nearly as odd as l (or n) $\sim š$, one would expect that the PA palatalization rule did not split in Cree. Unfortunately, at present no definitive statement on the Cree situation can be made.[27]

An alternative or additional hypothesis would treat the mitosis of PA palatalization largely as an historical accident. Recall that l-palatalization is well established in the inflectional morphology, particularly in the verbal morphology. This is due to the fact that many TA verb stems ended in *θ and *l. Within the TA paradigm there are several suffixes which began with *i. So it is here that the alternations show up. On the other hand, no TA verb stem ended in *t, and as a result, no $t \sim č$ alternations appear within verbal paradigms. Perhaps it was because of this lack of support that all noun alternations involving $t \sim č$ came to be lost.

With the lack of any inflectional support Ojibwa t-palatalization developed in ways which differ significantly from l-palatalization. Once the $t \sim č$ alternation was lost in nouns, Ojibwa stems either never or always underwent t-palatalization within a paradigm.[28]

These morphological facts may underlie the mitosis of PA palatalization. The phonological facts cited in the first hypothesis may play a role. Both hypotheses could be correct and work in concert to achieve this result. There may, of course, be some other explanation which I have missed completely.

The point of this paper has been to show that rule mitosis has taken place. I cannot accept Kiparsky's conclusion that this constitutes evidence that the abbreviatory device involved in the rule, in this case a natural class, is suspect as a legitimate linguistic concept. It is my belief that the profitable line of investigation is to determine what the circumstances were that led to one palatalization rule in PA becoming two palatalization rules in Ojibwa.

NOTES

* Research for this paper was supported in part by Canada Council Research Grant S71-0596. Earlier versions of this paper were given at the University of Illinois and the annual CLA meeting in Kingston, Ontario May, 1973.
  I am grateful to John Hewson for providing me with a preliminary version of his computer-generated Fox dictionary. The Algonquian etymological dictionary compiled by Aubin and Lee (1968) also proved very useful. David Pentland has also provided helpful comments on earlier versions of this paper.
[1] Indeed the natural class is so basic it has not typically been referred to as an abbreviatory device.
[2] The possibility of the Proto-Algonquian palatalization rule undergoing mitosis was first raised in Piggott (1971). The present work represents a continuation of research begun there and followed up in Kaye and Piggott (1973).
[3] This point seems quite uncontroversial. The view expressed here regarding č (and later š) is similar to that expressed by Hockett (1956). The only problem area is two clusters, *čp and *čk, reconstructed by Bloomfield based on the Menomini reflexes. It is not at all clear that the reconstructions are correct and in any event, as Hockett points out, *t never occurs before *k or *p.
[4] I have altered Bloomfield's transcription only in indicating a tense vowel, V as $\bar{V}$, rather than VV.
[5] Piggott (1971:33) has argued that palatalization cannot be considered to be a single process in PA since to do so would entail the description of the process in Ojibwa. It strikes me as a more interesting enterprise to assume (as the facts suggest) that palatalization was a single process in PA which split in Ojibwa. One can then investigate the cause of the split.
[6] In certain environments PA *θ is retained as θ in Arapaho: Ar héθ 'dog', hóθoʔ 'star'.
[7] The order of changes presented here is speculative. There is no direct evidence as to their relative chronology.
[8] Some authors, e.g. Harms (1973:440) consider a rule which applies within and across morphemes to be simpler or more general than a rule which applies only across morphemes. It is not at all clear that this claim is correct. Certainly, a change that has a rule which starts out applying freely, being restricted to application at a boundary, appears to be quite common.
[9] I leave aside the question as to whether an abstract phoneme, e, should be set up for Ojibwa in suffix initial position to handle cases like nimīnik 'he gives me' (cf. kimīš 'you give me') where the suffix -ik(w) is historically *-ekw. I only claim there is no basis for such an analysis morpheme-internally.
[10] Actually this rule is restricted to forms which consist of more than two morae (with the singular suffix itself counting as one; a tense vowel counts as two morae). Thus, *maθkw+a 'bear', *nexk+a "Canada goose" *mehθ+i 'fire wood' become Ojibwa makkwa, nikka, and mišši, respectively. They do not lose their final vowel.
[11] The $t \sim č$ alternations persist in Fox to this day: ohkāči, 'his foot', ohkātani 'his feet'.
[12] Examples include ēkāčč 'slowly', ānč 'all over again', aškwāč 'the last time', etc.
[13] In a recent article Halle (1973:6) denies a significant difference between inflectional and derivational morphology. The example just cited appears to contradict this position. I believe this is not an isolated instance, but rather just one of a substantial number of cases where it is crucial to separate inflectional from derivational morphology; but this is a subject of another paper.

[14] Another possible explanation of the appearance of *kīmōč* rather than **kīmōt* is the apparent lack of non-major category items ending in *-t*. This may reflect some sort of constraint on the possible shape of these morphemes.

[15] The *n* is intrusive rather than etymological. It typically appears in monosyllables of the type $CVC(W)$, cf. *čānš* 'nose', *mōnsw* 'moose', *nōnss* 'my father'.

[16] These two names are actually doublets, being the same word taken from two different periods of Ojibwa. They are compounds meaning literally 'spirit cave' (*manitō* 'spirit'). Manitoulin is a misspelling. Long (1791) has *Manitoualin* for the island, presumably based on [manitōwāliŋ]. The town *Manitowaning* is the same word at a time after *l* had gone to *n*. The locative suffix is from PA *-enki. The initial short vowel of this suffix does not trigger palatalization.

[17] PA *hθ regularly becomes *ss* in Ojibwa. PA *mehθ+i was, of course, palatalized yielding *mehš+i. PA *hš becomes Ojibwa *šš*. Ojibwa geminates represent phonetically fortis (aspirated and voiceless) consonants. I agree with Hockett's analysis stated in the introduction to Bloomfield (1957) which treats fortis consonants as underlying clusters.

[18] An exception would appear to be Ojibwa *-ninčy* 'hand'. The sequence *čy* is never pronounced, however. In Ojibwa *y* is deleted postconsonantally in final position in polysyllabic words. Thus, *ni+ninčy* [nininč] 'my hand'. In monosyllables, *y* is vocalized to *i* in final position: *akky* [akki] 'land'. When followed by a vowel, *y* is converted to *ī*: *ni+nincy+an* [nininčīn] 'my hands'.

[19] I have been unable to find unequivocal examples of *θy (> *šy), *sy or *ly.

[20] This remark must be qualified in ways that do not concern us here. Cf. Kaye (1973: ftn. 10).

[21] There appears to be no Fox cognate for *-tyāθ- 'nose'. For the Fox reflex of *ty, cf. *nenītyānehsa 'my child', Fox *neničānesa*, Ojibwa *niničāniss*.

[22] Obviously a cross-linguistic study of the behaviour of $C+y$ sequences is necessary to substantiate my claim. Doug Woods has pointed out that a similar change involving the loss of post-consonantal *y* (spelled *j* in the examples) in the development of the Germanic languages. Thus, Gothic *nasjan*, OHG *neren* 'to save'; Gothic *waljan*, OHG *wellen* 'to choose'; Gothic *satjan*, OE *settan* 'to set'. Eung Do Cook (personal communication) has also noted that post-consonantal *y*'s are lost at some point between middle and modern Korean. MidK *kyečip* 'woman' > kečip, MidK *pyeči* 'abolition' > peči, MidK *lnhye* 'favours' > *inhe*.

[23] In fact, this form does exist in Algonkin (cf. Cuoq 1891, 1892) and Severn Ojibwa (cf. Todd 1970). It can be shown that the existence of this form has nothing to do with rule ordering but rather appears as one example of a general process whereby all final *-t*'s in conjunct, changed conjunct and participles, show up as *č*'s.

[24] The effects of l-palatalization are also seen in the derivational morphology as the examples in (10b) show.

[25] This hypothesis was suggested to me by C. Kisseberth, M. Kenstowicz and M. O'Bryan, all of whom arrived at it independently.

[26] In some Cree dialects the alternations are $t \sim ts$ and $t \sim s$, respectively.

[27] For some discussion of this point, see Piggott (1971:22f.).

[28] *akači* 'be shy' < *akat+i* is an example of a stem which undergoes t-palatalization throughout its paradigm. Derivationally related stems like *akatēntam* 'be ashamed' never undergo palatalization.

SURFACE STRUCTURE CONSTRAINTS AND NITINAHT ENCLITICS

TERRY J. KLOKEID

1. INTRODUCTION

In the present study,[1] I evaluate the hypothesis, advanced by Perlmutter (1971), that the theory of universal grammar must include a certain mechanism called a SURFACE STRUCTURE CONSTRAINT on the relative order of enclitics. I draw on facts about Nitinaht,[2] a language that is rich in enclitics.

A surface structure constraint (SSC) is displayed as a chart of the various enclitics in a language: it specifies both relative ordering and co-occurrence restrictions; it may make reference to the enclitic categories or to their phonological form. For example, in Nitinaht, the past tense enclitic *obt/ibt* precedes pronominal enclitics, such as *s* 'I, me', *id/ad* 'we, us', as in (1a, b) below.[3]

(1)a. X̱abop obt s.   'I know (him/her).'
       know past I
   b. X̱abop obt id. 'We know (him/her).'
              we

The SSC for Nitinaht looks in part like this chart:

| obt | s |
| | id |

The SSC is interpreted as specifying that the past tense morpheme *obt* must precede a first person pronominal enclitic, *s* or *id*. Moreover, *s* and *id* are mutually exclusive. Hence, this SSC rules out sentence *(2a) because *id* precedes *obt*; and it rules out *(2b) because *s* and *id* co-occur.

(2)a. *X̱abop id obt.
   b. *X̱abop s id.

Perlmutter's claim that SSCs 'are to be stated in ... chart notation ... in all natural languages' (1971:46) that have enclitics[4] is based on an extensive study of several languages including Spanish, French, Walbiri, and others. The general force of his argumentation is that the SSC permits generalizations to be captured that are otherwise lost, and moreover, the SSC allows the elimination of ad hoc constraints and conditions.

Perlmutter's studies dealt only with pronominal enclitics. Besides extending the study of SSCs to a different language family, the present study broadens the investigation of this mechanism to categories as tense (e.g. *obt* above) and mood, which are enclitics in Nitinaht.

In section 2, I introduce the enclitic categories of Nitinaht, and in section 3, the relevant surface structure constraint is fully displayed.

Sections 4, 5, and 6 examine areas of syntax where the SSC plays a role. In each instance, an alternative mechanism is examined. The conclusion (section 7) is that, if the SSC is included in Nitinaht, then the entire range of facts examined in the previous sections will be accommodated. Without the surface structure constraint, it is necessary to incorporate a wide range of mechanisms. In section 8, I examine briefly some facts that are not handled directly by the SSC, and which therefore require an additional condition on enclitics. But any other analysis requires a special statement for the same facts, and so there is no argument here against SSCs.

2. ENCLITIC CATEGORIES AND THEIR PLACEMENT

The above examples of Nitinaht were verb-initial, and in fact the typical word order (disregarding enclitics for a moment) is verb-subject-other nominals, as the sentences in (3) show.[5]

(3)a. P'osāk ʔa xādaʔak ʔaq.
    V   1   the
   'The girl (is) tired.'
        1   V

b. Dātcīl ʔa xādaʔak ʔaq ʔōyoqw bowatc ʔaq.
    V   1   ACC   2
   'The girl is watching the deer.'
        1   V   2

c. Aptā ʔa xādaʔak ʔaq ʔiyax̣ tc'apats ʔaq.
    V   1   LOC canoe
   'The girl is hiding in the canoe.'
        1   V

The declarative enclitic ʔa is in second position in these examples. If we add the past tense enclitic *obt, ibt* to the above sentences, then it immediately precedes the declarative enclitic ʔa:

(4)a. P'osāk ibt ʔa xāda ʔak ʔaq.
      V   1   the
     'The girl was tired.'
         1   V

b. Dātcīl ibt ʔa xādaʔak ʔaq ʔōyoqw bowatc ʔaq.
    V   1   ACC   2
   'The girl watched the deer.'
       1   V   2

c. Aptā bt ʔa xādaʔak ʔiyax̣ tc'apats ʔaq.
    V   1   LOC   canoe
   'The girl was hiding in the canoe.'

The position of the various enclitics in the sentence so far can be expressed in two different ways:

> HYPOTHESIS A
> Enclitics such as *obt/ibt* and ʔa follow the verb.
>
> HYPOTHESIS B
> The above enclitics follow the first word of the clause sentence (whatever it may happen to be).

We have no way of choosing between Hypothesis A and Hypothesis B on the basis of the examples so far, because it so happens that the verb is the first word in all of these. But an empirical difference arises in sentences where the verb is not initial, as when some nominal is made the topic of the sentence. A topic nominal, together with its preposition, must precede the verb. I show some sentences with topics (marked TOP) in (5) and (6). In *(5a) and *(6a), the enclitics *ibt*[6] and ʔa are placed according to Hypothesis A, i.e. right after the verb: the sentences are definitely ungrammatical, although sentences like them are heard occasionally as slips of the tongue. The first word of these sentences happens to be a preposition, ʔōyoqw or ʔiyax̣. If we place the enclitics according to Hypothesis B, i.e. attaching them to the sentence-initial preposition, then the results are fully grammatical: (5b), (6b).

(5)a. *Ōyoqw bowatc ʔaq dātcīl ibt ʔa xādaʔak ʔaq. (cf. (4b))
     ACC   TOP/2 the V   1

b. Ōyoqw obt ʔa bowatc ʔaq dātcīl xādaʔak ʔaq.
      ACC   TOP/2   V   1
      'The deer, the girl was watching (it).'
      TOP/2   1   V
(6)a. *Iyax̱ tc'apats ʔaq ʔaptā ʔa xādaʔak ʔaq. (cf. (4c))
      LOC TOP/canoe V   1
   b. Iyax̱ ʔa tc'apats ʔaq ʔaptā xādaʔak ʔaq.
      LOC   TOP/canoe V   1
      'The canoe, the girl hid in (it).'
         TOP   1   V

Thus, we must reject Hypothesis A and accept Hypothesis B.

There are various other ways in which the verb can come to stand in non-initial position. For example, if the negative word *wik* 'not' is present, it precedes the verb, and then the enclitics attach to *wik*, as in (7).

(7) Wik ibt ʔa p'osāk xādaʔak ʔaq.
    not   V   1
    'The girl wasn't tired.' (cf. (4a))
         1   V

There are a great many enclitic categories, of which we have so far examined only tense, person, and mood. The mood enclitics, such as the declarative ʔ*a*, belong to a rather large set of formatives that I call the specifiers (SPC). In a subordinate clause, the declarative ʔ*a* is replaced by another specifier, ʔ*aq*. Hence, corresponding to the simple sentence (8a) is the subordinate clause of (8b). Hypothesis B is still valid here, since the enclitics of the subordinate clause of (8b) come in second position in that clause. (The alternation between the verb prefixes ʔ*o-* and *yaq-* has to do with the differences between main and subordinate clauses.)

(8)a. O-kwaqil ʔa   yā John.
      V   SPC 1
      'He is named John'
      1   V
   b. Kab'at'p s yaq-kwaqil ʔaq yā.
      know   I V   SPC 1.
      'I know what he is called'
                 1   V

The specifier ʔ*aq* also appears with nominals, where it is equivalent to the determiner 'the': cf. (3), (4), and many other sentences above. When functioning as a nominal determiner, the specifier ʔ*aq* obviously does not come in second position in the containing clause: in all the examples so far, it has followed the noun with which it is associated. But this is again just an instance of the second-position principle expressed by Hypothesis B. Given that a nominal and any modifiers such as quantifiers, adjectives, etc. (but excluding the preposition), form a constituent, Noun Phrase, then it can be seen that the specifier *ʔaq* follows the first word of the Noun Phrase:

(9) Dātcīl ibt ʔa xādaʔak ʔaq ʔōyoqw ʔix ʔaq bowatc.
    V   1   ACC   big SPC 2
    'The girl watched the big deer'. (cf. (4b))
         1   V   2

So only a slight modification of Hypothesis B is required:

    HYPOTHESIS B
        Clitics such as tense, person, and specifiers follow the first word of the clause or of the Noun Phrase.

3. THE SURFACE STRUCTURE CONSTRAINT

There are over thirty enclitic categories in Nitinaht. For the purposes of this paper, we need to examine only a selected number of these.

Past tense *ibt* has already been illustrated (cf. (1), (4)). The future tense can be represented by *ʔītl* (FUT), as in example (10a). The future and past formatives are combined, in that order, in the result clause of a counterfactual conditional, e.g. (10b).

(10)a. Oyē ʔitl   s itsx̱ bōll.
        V   FUT 1 2   ball.
        'I'll give you a ball'
        1   V   2

   b. Oyi wik it   qō   sokw tlawaxa tc'apats ʔaq, ʔoyē ʔitl
        if not PAST SPC you approach canoe   V   FUT
        ibt   s itsx̱ bōll.
        PAST 1 2   ball.
        'If you hadn't approached the canoe, I would have given you a ball'
                                                1   V   2

A portion of the SSC must therefore be:

ʔītl	ibt

Among the dozen specifiers, only the declarative ʔ*a* and the determiner ʔ*aq* need concern us immediately. (Later, additional specifier morphs will be introduced.) Sentences (11a, b) show that the specifiers follow tenses.

(11)a. Sokwitl ibt   ʔa   yad'aqak ʔaq ʔōyoqw bōll.
      V   PAST SPC 1   ACC   2
      'The child grabbed the ball'
        1   V   2

   b. Daqcitl ʔitl   ʔa   yad'aqak ʔaq tc'aʔak.
      V   FUT SPC 1   2
      'The child will drink water
       1   V   2

The SSC can accordingly be expanded:

ʔitl	ibt	ʔa ʔaq

Subject, direct object, and possessive pronouns encliticize. Three persons and two numbers are distinguished, resulting in a not unfamiliar six position pattern, including the unmarked third person singular. There is some allomorphy of pronominal enclitics and adjacent specifier. Thus, the declarative specifier ʔ*a* is absent with the first person pronoun clitics *s* 'I, me' (12a) and (*i*)*d*/*ad* 'we, us' (12b), but present with the second and third persons: hence the sequences ʔ*a s* 'SPC you' (12c), ʔ*a l* 'SPC they' (12d). Third person singular is unmarked, as in (12e); I ignore second person plural in this study. Combinations with the determiner specifier ʔ*aq* are transparent for first and third persons: ʔ*aq s*; ʔ*aq ad*; ʔ*aq al* (13a, b, c). The combination of this specifier with the second person singular requires the suppletive form (*q*)*īk* 'determiner/you' (13d).[7] As always, third person singular is unmarked, (13e).

(12)a. Tl'ixwā s.   'I'm laughing'
      laugh
   b. Tl'ixwā d.   'We're laughing'
   c. Tl'ixwā ʔa s.   'You're laughing'
   d. Tl'ixwā ʔa l.   'They're laughing'
   e. Tl'ixwā ʔa.   'He/she is laughing'
(13)a. Kab'at'p ʔa xādaʔak ʔaq yaq-kwaqil ʔaq s.
      know   girl   V   SPC 1
      'The girl knows what I am called'
                  1   V

b. Kab'at'p ʔa xādaʔak ʔaq yaq-kwaqil ʔaq ad.
                            V   SPC 1
   'The girl knows what we are called'
                        1   V

c. Kab'at'p ʔa xādaʔak ʔaq yaq-kwaqil ʔaq al.
                            V   SPC 1
   'The girl knows what they are called'
                        1   V

d. Kab'at'p ʔa xādaʔak ʔaq yaq-kwaqil ik.
                          V   SPC/1
   'The girl knows what you are called'
                    1   V

e. Kab'at'p s yaq-kwaqil ʔaq.
            V   SPC
   'I know what (he/she) is called'
                     V

Possessive pronouns have the same form as subject pronouns. Direct object pronouns, however, are distinct in the second person: the singular is *itsx̱*.

(14) a. Ts'oqwcitl ibt   s itsx̱.
      V   PAST 1 2
      'I speared you'
      1   2

b. Ts'oqwcitl ibt id itsx̱.
               1 2
    'We speared you'
    1

First person and third person plural have the same form for direct object as for subject, as shown in (15a, b, c). The ordering of pronominal clitics is according to person: first-second-third. Third person singular is unmarked, (15d).

(15) a. Ts'oqwcitl ibt   s is.
      V   PAST 2 1
     'You speared me'
     1   V   2

b. Ts'oqwcitl ibt id is.
               2 1
    'You speared us'
    1   2

c. Ts'oqwcitl ibt ʔa s al.
          SPC 1 2
    'You speared them'
      1   2
d. Ts'oqwcitl ibt ʔa s.
          SPC 1
    'You speared (him/her)'
      1   2

Thus the SSC must be expanded as follows:

(16) Surface Structure Constraint

ʔitl	ibt	ʔa ʔaq/qīk	s id	is itsx̱	al

This is not the fullest SSC that can be established for Nitinaht enclitics, but it is sufficiently elaborated for an evaluation of its role in the syntax.

4. THIRD PERSON PLURAL ENCLITIC

There are six person-number categories in Nitinaht. Setting aside reflexives and reciprocals,[8] there are twenty-six logical combinations of subject and direct object pronoun enclitics. However, not all these possibilities are grammatical surface structures. One factor reducing the surface combinations is a restriction reflecting hierarchical conditions associated with the passive, i.e. the rule which advances direct object to subject. The portion of the restriction that is relevant here can be stated briefly as follows:[9]

(17) Chain of being hierarchy constraint
    The surface direct object may not outrank the surface subject on the following hierarchy:
    1. First or second person
    2. Third person.

When the subject and direct object are of equal rank as in (18), where they are both third person, then the active and passive are optional variants. (When the passive applies as in (18b), then the former subject is marked with the preposition ʔox̱wīt and the verb with the suffix -ʔīt.) But when the direct object outranks the subject, as in (19), where the initial subject is third person and the direct object first person, then the constraint is violated in the active (19a), but not in the passive (19b), which doesn't even have a surface direct object.

(18)a. Ts'oqwcitl ibt ʔa Bill ʔōyoqw John.
      V   PAST SPC 1   ACC   2
    'Bill speared John'
    1   V   2
  b. Ts'oqwcitlʔit ibt ʔa John ʔoxฺwīt Bill.
     V   1
    'John was speared by Bill
    1   V

(19)a. *Ts'oqwcitl ibt ʔa Bill ʔōyoqw s(iy'a).
     V   1   ACC   2
    (lit. 'Bill speared me')
    1   V   2
  b. Ts'oqwcitlʔit ibt s ʔoxฺwīt Bill.
     V   1
    'Bill speared me', lit. 'I was speared by Bill'

The net effect of the chain-of-being hierarchy constraint, then, is to make the passive obligatory whenever the initial subject is third person and the initial direct object is first or second person. This eliminates six logical possibilities for combining subject and direct object pronoun clitics, reducing the number of expected surface combinations to twenty:

> First person (singular or plural) subject and second or third person (singular or plural) direct object (eight combinations).
>
> Second person (singular or plural) subject and first or third person (singular or plural) direct object (eight combinations).
>
> Third person (singular) subject and third person (singular or plural) direct object (two combinations).
>
> Third person (plural) subject and third person (singular or plural) direct object (two combinations).

Of these twenty possible combinations, in fact only nineteen are grammatical. The combination of third person plural subject enclitic and third person plural direct object enclitic is ungrammatical:

(20) *Dātcīl ibt ʔa l al.
    watch PAST SPC they they
    (lit. 'They watched them')

Yet there is no general restriction against the co-occurrence of third person plural subject and direct object. In (21), the subject is *yayad'aqiy* 'children', and the direct object is *xatxādatciy* 'women'.

(21)   Dātcīl ibt   ʔa   yayad'aqiy ʔōyoqw xatxādatciy ʔaq.
       V   PAST SPC 1   ACC   2   SPC
       'Some children watched the women'
                1   V   2

Moreover, there is a well-formed sentence that expresses the meaning intended for *(20). That sentence is (22).

(22)   Dātcīl ibt   ʔa   l.
       watch PAST SPC they
       'They watched them', 'he/she watched them', 'they watched him/her'

Sentence (22) is three ways ambiguous, as to whether the subject, the direct object, or both of these, will be plural.[10] The SSC (16) can be used to account for these facts. That surface structure constraint permits just one occurrence of the pronominal clitic *(a)l*, representing either subject or direct object.[11] Suppose that we now add the statement (23) to the grammar of Nitinaht:

(23)   The third person plural pronominal clitic *(a)l* can be deleted (i.e. without affecting meaning).

Now, when both subject and direct object are third person plural, (23) can apply, eliminating the potential sequence *(a)l al*. Thus the SSC (16), combined with (23), accounts both for the ungrammaticality of *(20) and the ambiguity of (22). (Call this Solution 1.)

An alternative analysis, Solution 2, can be constructed that avoids any reference to the SSC (16). Instead it employs an allomorphy rule that says:

(24)   Third person plural subject + third person plural direct object →
       (a)l.

Rule (24) correctly predicts the illformedness of *(20) and the ambiguity of (22). However, Solution 2 will still need some mechanism for ordering the enclitics properly, something automatically handled by the SSC (16) of Solution 1.

A crucial factor in the choice between the SSC (16) and the allomorphy rule (24) must be the statement (23). On the face of it, it looks as though the SSC (16) requires extra machinery, i.e. (23), while the allomorphy rule (24) dispenses with it. But this is not really so, because statement (23) is necessary in any case. Sentence (25) shows this: here, there is no overt third person plural pronoun enclitic, and yet this sentence has three distinct readings involving third person plural subject, direct object, or both.

(25) Dātcīl ibt ʔa.
watch PAST SPC
'She/he watched her/him'
'They watched her/him'
'She/he watched them'
'They watched them'

These three readings are shared with sentence (22). The most direct way to express this relationship is with statement (23). This is valid quite independently of any other considerations, in particular the choice between (16) and (24).

Thus, when we use (23) together with the SSC (16) to account for sentences like *(20) and (22), we are relying on something that must be stated anyway. On the other hand, we can now see that the proposed allomorphy rule (24) would be doing part of the work of (23). This would introduce a duplication in the grammar.

In this section, we have seen that the surface structure constraint (16) accounts for the ungrammatical sequence consisting of two third person plural pronominal enclitics. An alternative analysis, involving the allomorphy rule (24), introduces an undesirable loss of generality by virtue of duplicating an already necessary statement of third person plural pronoun deletion, (23).

A third analysis, Solution 3, both avoids reference to SSCs, and the objection raised against Solution 2. For both Solutions 1 and 2, I tacitly assumed that the initial syntactic representation of a sentence has some direct connection with the semantic representation, i.e. that if a sentence is understood as having, say, a third person plural pronominal subject, then the initial syntactic representation will manifest that pronoun, even if it is deleted, as, say, in sentence (25). Solution 3 rejects this set of assumptions, in favour of an 'interpretive' account of semantics along the lines suggested by Jackendoff (1972) and others.

In constructing a sentence in Solution 3, we generate nominals and pronominal enclitics freely, and establish meaning on the basis of material present in the surface structure. The relative order of clitics, and the restriction to one occurrence of each (e.g. (*a*)*l*) is established by a rule something like (26), for the initial syntactic structure. (S → means 'sentence consists of').

(26) $S \rightarrow \ldots (\text{?ītl})(\text{ibt}) \left(\begin{Bmatrix} \text{?a} \\ \text{?aq/qīk} \end{Bmatrix}\right) \left(\begin{Bmatrix} s \\ id \end{Bmatrix}\right) \left(\begin{Bmatrix} is \\ its\underline{x} \end{Bmatrix}\right) (al) \ldots$

Now, we have interpretive principles of the following kind: *id* is 'we' (subject) if it precedes *itsx*, but is 'us' (direct object) if it precedes *is*. That is, the meaning and grammatical relation of these clitics are established on the basis of their arrangements in particular sentences. It is obvious that the statements required in Solution 3 are rather different from those assumed in Solutions 1 and 2. However, the only aspect of Solution 3 of crucial relevance is the interpretation provided for sentences like (22) and (25). The interpretive principles are essentially as in (27).

(27)a. Interpret (*a*)*l* as either 'they' (subject or 'them' (direct object).
 b. If no clitic has been interpreted as subject, as direct object, or both, then these grammatical relations can be interpreted as being borne by either third person singular or third person plural pronouns.

Applied to sentence (22), principle (27a) will interpret *al* as either subject or direct object. Then, the remaining grammatical relation will be assigned either a singular or a plural meaning by (27b). This correctly produces the three-way ambiguity of (22). Similarly, (27b) creates a four-way ambiguity for sentence (25).

By adopting a radically different view of semantics, the 'interpretive' approach, it is thus possible to avoid the mechanism of SSCs for the facts described in this section.

5. TENSE-SUBJECT COPY AND TOPICS

In the previous section, I focused on restrictions involving pronominal enclitics. In this section, I will describe a restriction that extends to other enclitics, such as specifiers, as well.

A topic nominal precedes the verb, as in the (28a), (29a). The corresponding sentences (28b), (29b) lack topics. In general, a topic nominal must have its preposition, e.g. the benefactive preposition *ʔōtsaxad* 'for' accompanies the benefactive nominal *John* in (28), but a small number of expressions, such as *ʔābay* 'yesterday' (29) do not require a preposition.

(28)a. Ōtsxad s John tc'āpats-īl.
 BEN 1   2/V
 'For John, I am building a canoe'
 BEN TOP 1   V   2

   b. Tc'āpats-īl s ʔōtsaxad John
       2/V   1 BEN
       'I'm building a canoe for John'

(29)a. Ābay ibt   s ʔowiy ʔiyax Matolli.
       TOP PAST 1 V   LOC
       'Yesterday, I went to Victoria'
       TOP   1   LOC
   b. Owiy ibt   s ʔiyax Matolli ʔābay.
       V   PAST 1
       'I went to Victoria yesterday'

As we have already seen previously, the enclitics of the clause attach to the first word of the sentence, which most often is the verb (28b), (29b), but which could be a topic nominal (29a) or a preposition (28a).

The relevance of topics to the issue of SSCs lies partly in the fact that there is an optional copying of the tense and subject of the sentence onto prepositions. For example, (28b) has the optional variant (30), in which the subject enclitic *s* has been copied onto the benefactive preposition *ʔōtsaxad*.

(30) Tc'āpats-īl s ʔōtsaxad s John.
      2/V   1 BEN
      'I'm building a canoe for John'
      1   V   2   BEN (paraphrases (28b))

Tense can also be copied along with the subject, as in (31b). (Tense-Subject Copy has not applied in (31a).) Alternatively, the tense alone may be copied, (31c).

(31)a. Ts'axwcitl ʔitl   s ʔōyoqw bowatc ʔaq.
       V   FUT 1 ACC   2
   b. Ts'axwcitl ʔitl   s ʔōyoqw ʔitl s bowatc ʔaq.
       V   FUT 1 ACC   2
   c. Ts'axwcitl ʔitl   s ʔōyoqw ʔitl bowatc ʔaq.
       V   FUT 1 ACC   2
       'I will spear the deer'
       1   V   2

We can of course make the direct object of (31a) the topic, (32a). A sentence in which Tense-Subject Copying applies cannot have a topic nominal, as we can see if we try to make topics out of the direct objects in (31b, c). No matter what ordering we try between the sentence enclitics and those copied onto the preposition, ungrammatical sentences result.

(32)a. Ōyoqw ʔitl   s bowatc ʔaq ts'axwcitl. (cf. (31a))
    ACC   FUT 1 2   V
  b. *Oyoqw ʔitl s ʔitl s bowatc ʔaq ts'axwcitl.
    ACC   2   V
    *Ōyoqw ʔitl ʔitl s s bowatc ʔaq ts'axwcitl. (cf. (31b))
    ACC   2   V
  c. *Ōyoqw ʔitl ʔitl s bowatc ʔaq ts'axwcitl.
    ACC   2   V
    *Ōyoqw ʔitl s ʔitl bowatc ʔaq ts'axwcitl.
    ACC   2   V

The SSC (16) accounts for the illformedness of *(32b, c) in a direct fashion: it permits only one occurrence per enclitic sequence of the future *ʔitl* or the first person singular *s*. Therefore, (32a) conforms to the SSC, but none of the sentences in *(32b, c) do. (Call this Solution 1.)

An alternative analysis Solution 2, can be formulated that does not require the SSC (16). In Solution 2, the placement of the topic, and Tense Subject Copying are ordered rules, as in (33), and a condition is added to Tense-Subject Copying. (I will also put the enclitics in the surface position prior to Tense-Subject Copying, but nothing hinges on this.)

(33)   { Topic Placement
       { Tense-Subject Copying

We can see what the necessary condition on Tense-Subject Copying must be, if we contrast the construction of (32a) and the first illformed sentence of *(32b), with the construction of sentence (31b), which lacks a topic.

With both the topic and the enclitics in place, we have the representation (34) (ultimately to yield (32a), and potentially *(32b)).

(34) Ōyoqw ʔitl   s bowatc ʔaq ts'axwcitl.
    ACC   FUT 1 TOP/2   V

With the enclitics in place, but with no topic, we have the representation (35) (ultimately yielding (31b)):

(35) Ts'axwcitl ʔitl   s ʔōyoqw bowatc ʔaq.
    V   FUT 1 ACC   2

Now, we are ready for Tense-Subject Copying. Applying this rule to (35) yields (31b). But we must block the rule from applying to (34), in order to have (32a) but not *(32b). The condition evidently must be of this form:

(36) Condition on Tense-Subject Copy (needed in Solution 2)[12]
This rule must not apply to a topic nominal.

Given condition (36), the formation of *(32b) is prevented; and only the well-formed (32a) results. Thus, Solution 2 works as well as Solution 1 for this data, and dispenses with the need for any SSC. However, this does not make Solution 2 superior, because there is actually a trade-off: instead of the SSC (16) of Solution 1, we have to have extrinsic ordering in Solution 2, in order to state (33), plus the condition (36) on Tense-Subject Copying.

Moreover, while the SSC (16) handles the facts of both the previous section and the present one, there is no overlap in the theoretical apparatus of either Solution 2 or Solution 3 of the previous section with that of Solution 2 in the present section.

6. TOPICS AND PHONOLOGICALLY ABSENT ENCLITICS

It was mentioned in passing in the previous section that some nominals, e.g. time expressions like ʔābay 'yesterday', do not require a preposition when functioning as topic, as in (37a) (there is no topic in (37b)).

(37)a. Ābay ibt   ʔa   ʔowiy ʔiyax̱ Tlōʔōs.
        TOP PAST SPC V   LOC
        'Yesterday, he went to Clo-oose'
        TOP   V
    b. Owiy ibt   ʔa   ʔiyax̱ Tlōʔōs ʔābay.
        V   PAST SPC LOC
        'He went to Clo-oose yesterday'

Time expressions like ʔabay can optionally take the determiner specifier, ʔaq; it usually then also takes a further enclitic ʔatl 'them' (which precedes all other enclitics): ʔābay ʔatl ʔaq 'yesterday', lit. 'the yesterday then'. With these enclitics, the time expression cannot be topic, no matter how the various enclitics are ordered, as in *(38a); cf the well formed (38b) which lacks a topic.

(38)a. *Ābay ʔatl ʔaq ibt ʔa ʔowiy ʔiyax̱ Tlōʔōs.
        TOP   V   LOC
        *Ābay ʔatl ibt ʔaq ʔa ʔowiy ʔiyax̱ Tlōʔōs.
        TOP   V   LOC
    b. Owiy ibt ʔa ʔiyax̱ Tlōʔōs ʔābay ʔatl ʔaq.
        V   LOC

The SSC (16) handles this automatically, for the illformed sentences in *(38a) contain violations of (16,) in that the specifiers ʔaq and ʔa can not co-occur. (Again, I refer to the analysis with SSC (16) as Solution 1.)

An alternative, Solution 2, imposes a condition on topic nominals:

(39) Condition on Topics (Solution 2)
      No nominal that has its own enclitics (e.g. ʔatl, specifier ʔaq) can function as topic.

Solution 2 handles the facts of (38) perfectly, and without reference to an SSC. Moreover, there is some promise here that (39) might be extended to handle the facts of Section 5, thereby eliminating the special condition (36) and the extrinsic rule ordering apparatus needed for (33).

Unfortunately for Solution 2, the condition (39) is not the correct one for prepositionless topics like ʔābay.

While clauses with the overt declarative specifier ʔa are characteristic in conversation, narrative style typically has no clause specifier (the 'absolutive' of Haas and Swadesh 1933) and often no tense. Sentence (40) is in the narrative style.

(40) Owiy ʔiyax̣ Tlōʔōs.
      V   LOC
      'He went to Clo-oose'

If we now add the time expression ʔābay as topic, it may take its own enclitics:

(41) Ābay ʔatl ʔaq ʔowiy ʔiyax̣ Tlōʔōs.
      TOP   LOC
      'Yesterday, he went to Clo-oose'

Clearly, condition (39) makes an incorrect prediction. According to (39) sentence (41) should be illformed, and yet it is clearly grammatical. So (39) has to be replaced by the more complex condition (42):

(42) No nominal that has its own enclitics can function as topic, unless the sentence is in narrative style.

Yet no modification of Solution 1 is needed to handle sentences like (41); such sentences are grammatical under Solution 1 because they contain no violation of the SSC (16).

We have seen, then, that the SSC (16) accounts for the grammaticality and ungrammaticality of the sentences considered in this section. An alternative to the SSC requires a complex condition on topics, (41).

7. CONCLUSIONS

The SSC automatically accounts for a wide range of facts:

(43) i. There is a fixed relative ordering of enclitics.
   ii. If both subject and direct object are third person plural pronouns, then at least one of them must be deleted (Section 4).
   iii. A topic may not undergo Tense-Subject Copying (Section 5).
   iv. A nominal that lacks a preposition may not function as topic if it has associated enclitics, except when there are no sentence enclitics, as in the narrative style (Section 6).

Alternative analyses which make no use of SSCs require the following additional theoretical apparatus, rules or conditions:

(44) i. There must be a device for ordering enclitics relative to each other.
   ii. (a) There is a special allomorphy rule for third person plural subject plus direct object.
       or
       (b) The semantic representation is constructed (at least in part) interpretively; the initial syntactic representation contains an ordered sequence of enclitics lacking (at least in part) meaning and grammatical relations.
   iii. (a) Extrinsic rule ordering is necessary in syntax.
        and
        (b) Tense-Subject Copying may not apply to a topic nominal.
   iv. The statement of (43iv) must be added as a condition on topics.

8. TENSE-SUBJECT COPYING AND ENCLITICIZATION TO PREPOSITIONS

The interaction of Tense-Subject Copying and a further phenomenon, Encliticization to Preposition, reveals a condition on enclitics that cannot be stated in terms of the SSC (16) without an additional statement. This cannot be used as an argument against the notion of SSC, however, because any alternative analysis that has been examined above also requires an additional statement.

Sentence (45a) contains the benefactive nominal *John*; its preposition is ʾōtsaxad 'for'. In (45b), Tense-Subject Copying has applied, copying the subject enclitic *s* onto ʾōtsaxad.

(45)a. Tc'āpats-il s ʾōtsaxad John.
        2/V   1 BEN

b. Tc'āpats-īls s ʔōtsaxad s John.
   2/V   1 BEN
   'I'm building a canoe for John'
   1 V   2   BEN

If we now replace the benefactive nominal *John* by a pronoun, say the second person singular, then we find that that pronoun typically encliticizes, in the same form as the direct object *itsx̣* 'you', to its preposition, as in (46). In *(46a), Tense-Subject Copying has not applied; in (46b) it has.

(46)a. *Tc'āpats-īl s ʔōtsaxad itsx̣.
       2/V   1 BEN
   b. Tc'āpats-īls s ʔōtsaxad s itsx̣.
      2/V   1   BEN
      'I made a canoe for you'
      1 V   2   BEN

We can see that there is a condition on Encliticization to Preposition. It is required that Tense-Subject Copying also apply, to get a well-formed sentence, (46b). This is true only for the pronouns which have distinct subject and non-subject forms, however. So (47a) is as grammatical as (47b), even though Tense-Subject Copying has applied in the latter only.

(47)a. Tc'āpats-īl ʔa   s ʔōtsaxad s.
       2/V   SPC 1 BEN
   b. Tc'āpats-īl ʔa   s ʔōtsaxad s is.
      2/V   SPC 1 BEN
      'You are building a canoe for me'

Thus, the following condition is needed:

(48) Encliticization to Preposition can apply to the second person pronoun (*itsx̣*) only if Tense-Subject Copying also applies.

This condition on Encliticization to Preposition is not a restriction that is expressed directly by the SSC (16), and therefore must be added to the grammar as the separate statement (48). On the other hand, any of the alternatives to SSCs that we have considered in this study would also require (48).

So, while the SSC (16) is not an exhaustive statement of the restrictions one nclitics in Nitinaht, the additional statement that is needed, (48), is necessary in any analysis.

NOTES

[1] This paper has gone through at least three rewritings, the most recent earlier draft being Klokeid (1974). In each of the previous versions, I assumed some more or less specific version of transformational-generative grammar as the framework of investigation. At the risk of being somewhat vague at times, I have made the present version less committed to such a framework. My purpose is not so much to argue for one framework over another, as to explore the work that surface structure constraints can do in Nitinaht, and to see what alternative formal apparatus would be needed.

I acknowledge perceptive commentary on my earlier ideas about the subject matter of this paper offered by Avery Andrews, Jack Chambers, Kenneth Hale, G. Hubert Matthews, David M. Perlmutter. I haven't always acted on their insights however, nor have any of them had a chance to see the present version. Thanks also to Eung-Do Cook for useful comments. The research for this paper has been supported in part by Canada Council, the U.S. National Institutes of Mental Health (Grant no. MH13390-03), and the Phillips Fund of the American Philosophical Society.

[2] Nitinaht is a language of the Southern branch of the Wakashan family, of the West Coast of Vancouver Island. I am grateful to members of the Nitinaht community, especially Frances and Joe Edgar, and the late Mary Chipps, for their hospitality and assistance in my study of their language.

The Nitinaht orthography used in this paper is based on the transcription practice of Alexander Thomas for Tseshaht and owes much to discussions with Ron Hamilton. I have described the Nitinaht orthography in Klokeid (1975). In the present paper, I suppress a sentence-initial glottal stop to avoid confusion with a question mark. Thus, *Aptā* at the beginning of a sentence is the word *ʔaptā* 'hide', and so on for all sentence-initial words that are written here beginning with a vowel.

[3] Haas and Swadesh (1933:198) use the term 'word suffix' for a set of morphemes that is nearly, but not completely, a coterminous with the set of enclitics. Sapir and Swadesh (1939:236-41), in dealing with the more northerly West Coast languages, especially Tseshaht (which they erroneously refer to as 'Nootka'), called the corresponding set 'incremental suffixes'. These scholars based their distinction on purely phonological criteria, while the present study is concerned with syntax as well. In addition to the enclitics, the 'incremental' or 'word suffixes' include certain true suffixes such as the passive *ʔit*.

An essentially complete listing of Nitinaht enclitics is contained in Klokeid (1976).

[4] Actually, Perlmutter's claims are more general, since he extends the function of SSCs to account for all clitics, i.e. both enclitics and proclitics. As Nitinaht has enclitics but not proclitics, I drop the more general term clitic here.

[5] I use the following abbreviations: V, Verb; 1, subject; 2, direct object. The Accusative preposition *ʔōyoqw* is glossed as ACC, and the Locative *ʔiyax* 'in, to' as LOC.

The morpheme *ʔa* is the Declarative enclitic. It will receive more attention directly.

While the enclitics are always written as separate units, it has to be kept in mind that they always coalesce phonetically with the immediately preceding lexical item to form a single phonetic word.

One consequence of this is that phonological rules that are otherwise word-internal apply across enclitic boundaries. I limit examples here to the following two. A glottal stop coalesces with a preceding non-fricative consonant and deletes after a fricative. Hence *p'osāk ʔa* (3a) is phonetically [p'osāk'a] and *dātcīl ʔa* (3b), [dātcīla]. A vowel deletes after another vowel. Hence the sequence of *ʔaptā* plus *ibt* is phonetically [ʔaptäbt] (4c).

The status of the enclitics in the West Coast languages of Vancouver Island was recognized long ago, e.g. by Brabant (MSa, MSb) for Hesquiaht, and significantly, it was also reflected in the manuscripts prepared by Alexander Thomas (Thomas and Sapir 1910—; cf. also Klokeid 1971). However, in the published versions of Thomas' material (Sapir and Swadesh 1939, 1955; Thomas and Arima 1970), enclitics are written solid with the preceding word.

⁶ The past tense is abstractly /ibt/ (possibly from /ibit/ by syncope); the alternant /obt/ is derived by assimilation of the vowel to an immediately preceding consonant or to a preceding labial vowel.
  Hereafter, I refer to this morpheme enclitic only in the more abstract representation, *ibt*.
⁷ The initial consonant of *qīk* is deleted by a regular rule (which applies when at least two vowels precede), when the preceding morpheme ends in a consonant. Furthermore, there is a rule which shortens long vowels past the second syllable. Both these rules have applied in (13d), hence *qīk* is reduced there to *ik*.
⁸ Reflexives are marked by the reflexive prefix *-k-* on verb or preposition, while reciprocals are marked by the suffix *-sp'at'al* on the verb. In neither instance does a direct object enclitic appear.
⁹ The full hierarchy makes reference to non-person categories such an animacy. Also, the constraint extends to indirect objects. Furthermore, the notion 'surface subject' is inaccurate: in the theory of Relational Grammar being developed by David M. Perlmutter and Paul M. Postal (forthcoming), the correct notion is *canonical subject*. In a derivational framework, this is essentially equivalent to cycle-final subject.
¹⁰ There is, however, a marked preference for the third person plural enclitic *al* to be understood as referring to the subject (if no first or second person pronominal enclitic is present). Thus the preferred reading for (22) is 'they watched him/her'. It may be that Makah, a southern relative of Nitinaht, has the same preference; this account for some of the remarks in Jacobsen (1973) concerning the interpretation of the Makah cognate of Nitinaht *al*.
¹¹ Jacobsen (1973) observes that the restrictions for Makah pronominal enclitic sequences are much more severe than for Nitinaht. For example, not only is the Makah cognate of the sequence **al al* 'illformed', but also those which combine second person (singular or plural) with third person plural, e.g. the wellformed Nitinaht enclitic sequences *qō sokw al* (SPC you them) and *qō sow'itc al* (SPC you/plural them) find no grammatical cognate sequences in Makah.
¹² This condition could be formulated in a variety of ways. For example, if we assumed that the initial representation of a sentence consists of an ordered string, then we could say that Tense-Subject Copying may only apply to nominals to the right of the original enclitics. This exploits the fact that Topics are to the extreme left of the sentence, while other nominals are to the left of the verb. One of two formal mechanisms is then needed:

  (i) Extrinsic rule ordering:
  $\begin{cases} \text{Clitic Placement} \\ \text{Tense-Subject Copying} \end{cases}$
  (ii) Abstract ordering of clitics, e.g. after the verb.

In approach (i), Tense-Subject Copying must duplicate in its structural description the formative ordering accomplished by Clitic Placement. This is an undesirable repetition in the grammar. Approach (ii) demands an ad hoc, otherwise unmotivated abstract ordering of enclitics with respect to other elements such as the verb.

UNE 'CONSPIRATION' EN ESKIMO

J. M. MASSENET

Cet article traite d'un exemple de 'conspiration' en phonologie, notion qui tend à dégager de la variété structurale des règles formelles l'unité fonctionnelle de certains processus phonologiques.

Dans le dialecte Eskimo de l'Ungava,[1] au moins deux règles de nature structurale très différente (insertion d'une consonne et effacement d'une voyelle) sont nécessaires pour expliquer certains faits. Il est clair cependant que ces deux règles, impossibles à unifier par la théorie normale actuelle, 'conspirent' pour remplir la même fonction: empêcher la formation de séquences de plus de deux voyelles.

Bien qu'aucune réponse satisfaisante ne soit donnée quant aux facteurs qui déterminent le choix entre ces deux règles, certains faits cependant portent à croire qu'ils sont d'ordre morpholoqique. En ce qui concerne la règle d'insertion d'une consonne, les conditions déterminant la nature de cette dernière se laissent difficilement prédire. Donc, il va sans dire que les règles proposées ici n'expriment que certaines tendances sujettes à révision.

Considérons les données suivantes:

(A) 1 nuna 'pays' nunaaluk 'grand pays'
    2 inuk 'Eskimo' inualuk 'grand Eskimo'
    3 tupiq 'tente' tupialuk 'grande tente'
    4 nasaq 'chapeau' nasaaluk 'grand chapeau'
(B) 1 kikiak 'clou' kikiaraaluk 'grand clou'
    2 kuuk 'rivière' kuuraaluk 'grande rivière'
    3 umiaq 'bateau' umiaraaluk 'grand bateau'
    4 qaaq 'matelas' qaaraaluk 'grand matelas'
    5 saa 'table' saaraaluk 'grande table'
    6 ui 'mari' uiraaluk 'grand mari'

En (A) le morphème qui signifie 'grand' apparaît comme -*aluk*, après l'effacement de la consonne finale, s'il y en a une en (B) comme -*raaluk*. La distribution est claire: nous avons -*raaluk* avec les radicaux VV(C), -*aluk* avec les radicaux en V(C). Dans les deux cas l'affixe semble effacer la consonne finale du radical. Quelle est la forme sous-jacente de cet affixe et quelles sont les règles qui expliquent les deux représentations phonétiques? Si nous posons -*aluk* comme forme sous-jacente, il faut expliquer:

1. l'effacement de la consonne en (A)2-4;
2. l'insertion de -*ra*- en (B)5-6;
3. l'effacement de la consonne plus l'insertion de -*ra*-, ou l'insertion de -*a*- plus l'abaissement et/ou le voisement de la consonne (/k, q/ → /r/) en (B)1-4.

Il serait bien difficile de motiver des règles rendant compte de 2 et 3.

Si par ailleurs nous posons -*raaluk* comme forme sousjacente, nous devons expliquer:

1. l'effacement de la consonne en (B)1-5;
2. l'effacement de -*ra*- en (A) plus l'effacement de la consonne en (A)2-4.

De nouveau, cette solution serait complètement ad-hoc en ce qui concerne 2.

Une autre solution s'impose. En effet, remarquons que jamais, dans les données ci-dessus, nous n'avons une séquence de plus de deux voyelles. En fait une telle séquence est interdite en Eskimo de l'Ungava. Or il existe deux processus communs pour empêcher la formation d'une séquence de plus de deux voyelles: l'effacement d'une voyelle ou l'insertion d'un segment consonantique. Dès lors si nous posons -*aaluk* comme forme sous-jacente, il suffit d'expliquer:

1. l'effacement de la consonne en (A)2-4 et (B)1-4;
2. l'effacement de la voyelle en (A);
3. l'insertion de la consonne en (B).

L'effacement de la consonne est largement motivé:

(C) ipuligaq 'manche de pipe'
ipuligaartuq 'dont le manche se brise'

uddjuk 'phoque'
uddjuayuq 'il en a tué plusieurs'

tasiq 'lac'
tasiarpâ 'il le traverse'

qanik 'neige qui tombe'
qanialârtuq 'il neigeotte'

iksivik 'caisse, cercueil'
iksiviiyuq 'il l'a mis en bière"

komak 'poux'
komairpâ 'il lui a enlevé ses poux'

inuk 'Eskimo'
inuilaq 'qui est sans homme'

kiinaq 'visage'
kiinailitaq 'protection pour le visage'

kukik 'ongle'
kukiuyaq 'coquillage'

uqaq 'langue'
uqaut(i) 'mot, parole'

tupiq 'tente'
tupiup 'de la tente'

Il est clair que pour rendre compte de ces données nous avons besoin d'une règle comme:[2]

(1) effacement de la consonne

$C \to \emptyset / \underline{} + V$ (où "+" marque une frontière de morphèmes)

En ce qui concerne l'insertion de la consonne et l'effacement de la voyelle, quelques problèmes surgissent.

D'abord nous avons ici un bon exemple de 'conspiration': deux règles de nature formelle très différente remplissent la même fonction (empêcher la formation d'une séquence de plus de deux voyelles):[3]

– la règle d'effacement de la voyelle explique (A):

    nuna+aaluk   inuk+aaluk
(1)   inu+aaluk
    nunaaluk   inualuk

– la règle d'insertion explique (B):

    kikiak+aaluk ui+aaluk
(1)kikia+aaluk
    kikiaraaluk   uiraaluk

Ces deux règles sont nécessaires. Il est facile de les motiver.

(D)   nuna 'pays'   nunaup 'du pays'   nunait '(les)pays'
       umiaq 'bateau'   umiap 'du bateau' umiat 'bateaux'
       kikiak 'clou'   kikiap 'du clou'   kikiat 'clous'
       saa 'table'   saap 'de la table'   saat 'tables'

Ces exemples montrent également que c'est la troisième voyelle qui est effacée. La règle d'effacement de la voyelle se présente donc comme suit :

(2)   Règle des trois voyelles [4]
      V → ∅ / VV ___

L'insertion d'une consonne empêchant la formation d'une séquence de plus de deux voyelles est également facile à motiver :

(E)   anaana 'mère'   anaanauvuq 'c'est (une)mère'
      inuk 'Eskimo'   inuuvuq 'c'est (un) Eskimo'
      kikiak 'clou'   kikianguvuq 'c'est (un)clou'
      qaaq 'matelas'   qaanguvuq 'c'est (un)matelas'
      ui 'mari'   uinguvuq 'c'est (un) mari'
      aiq 'manches'   aingittuq 'sans manches'
      ui 'mari'   uingittuq 'sans mari'
      auk 'sang'   auqaaluk 'beaucoup de sang'

Que le mophème soit *-uvuq* et non *-nguvuq* est suggéré par le fait que /ng/ initial d'affixe ne tombe jamais ailleures : *kangi-ngerpâ* 'il l'a porté à terre', *siuti-ngujuq* 'il a mal aux oreilles'

Malheureusement ces exemples introduisent un deuxième problème : comment déterminer la nature de la consonne insérée ? Pourquoi avons-nous tantôt /ng/ ou même /g/ (dernier exemple en (E)), tantôt /r/ ?

Concernant le choix entre la règle des trois voyelles (2) et la règle d'insertion, remarquons que (2) ne s'applique pas dans le contexte VV+ VV. Si (2) s'appliquait dans ce contexte, une première application de cette règle fournirait la séquence VV+V qui est encore interdite et qui devrait de nouveau subir (2) ou la règle d' insertion.

Ex : kikiak+aaluk 'grand clou'
   (1) kikia+aaluk
   (2) kikia+aluk
   *{ kikia+luk (par une deuxième application de (2))
      kikia+raluk (par insertion)

(Notons que *kikialuk* existe, mais il s'agit alors d'un affixe signifiant 'sale petit').

Dans les contextes VV+V ou V+VV on peut appliquer la règle d'insertion ou la règle d'effacement, comme le montrent les exemples suivants :

(F)   V+VV
      qamuti+aaluk → qamutialuk 'grand traîneau'
      qamuti+uijuq → qamutinguijuq 'il travaille à son ...'

VV+V
kikiak+it → kikiat 'clous'
kikiak+uvuq → kikianguvuq 'c'est (un) clou'

Que ce ne soit pas des facteurs phonologiques mais plutôt la nature de l'affixe qui détermine le choix entre la règle d'insertion et la règle d'effacement est suggéré par ces exemples. Malheureusement ceci ne résoud pas le problème car les propriétés sémantiques et/ou syntaxiques des affixes de l'Eskimo sont loin d'être connues.

Une solution à tendance fonctionnelle expliquerait que l'application de la règle d'insertion a lieu afin d'empêcher la 'mutilation' de l'affixe entraînée par (2).

Ex: kikiak+uvuq → *kikiavuq

où le morphème -u- signifiant (grossièrement) 'être' disparaît complètement. Il est difficile cependant de formaliser cette notion de "mutilation". Le plus souvent l'application de (2) entraînerait des changements d'ordre sémantique. Ainsi *qamuti+uijuq* 'il travaille à son traîneau' deviendrait par application de (2) *qamutiujuq* qui signifie 'c'est (un) traîneau'.

Une explication plus plausible, que nous proposons ici, fait appel à la distinction encore vague entre affixes dominants vs affixes non-dominants. Les affixes dominants constituent la tête d'une construction dont ils déterminent le comportement syntaxique. Autrement dit, ils imposent à la construction la classe syntaxique à laquelle ils appartiennent. Les affixes non-dominants par contre sont 'récessifs' en ce sens qu'ils subissent les propriétés syntaxiques de la construction dont ils font partie. Ainsi, dans *qamuti+uijuq*, *uijuq* peut être considéré comme le centre (ou la tête) de la phrase tant du point de vue sémantique que du point de vue syntaxique (+*uijuq* impose sa nature 'verbale' à l'ensemble de la construction). Dans *umiaq−up* 'du bateau', −*up* évidemment n'est pas un affixe dominant. Notons que cette distinction ne recouvre pas celle entre affixes dérivationnels et affixes inflectionnels: bien que ces derniers soient sans doute toujours non-dominants, les premiers peuvent être dominants ou non. Or selon nous, le choix entre la règle d'insertion et la règle d'effacement serait précisément déterminé par cette distinction: la règle d'insertion s'appliquant aux affixes dominants, la règle d'effacement aux affixes non-dominants. Dès lors *qamuti+uijuq* devient par dérivation *qamutinguijuq*, tandis que *umiaq−up* devient *umiap*.

Il est important de remarquer que cette distinction entre affixes dominants et affixes non-dominants s'impose ailleurs.

(G) 1 ataniq−vik   'un grand roi'   atanivik
    imaq−vik   'une grande eau, un océan' imavik

2	sinik+vik	'place pour dormir'	sinigvik
	niuviq+vik	'magasin de vente'	niuvirvik

La différence entre $-vik$ en (G)1 et $+vik$ en (G)2 n'est pas phonologique. En (G)1 $-vik$ est un affixe non-dominant et il efface la consonne du radical; en (G)2 au contraire il est dominant et n'efface pas la consonne du radical.

Les faits qui précèdent semblent prouver que cette distinction joue un rôle important en Eskimo. Dans le lexique il faudra donc spécifier pour chaque affixe s'il est dominant ou non. Une solution simple serait de convenir que tous les affixes sont sujets à la règle d'insertion, sauf ceux qui sont explicitement marqués comme devant subir la règle d'effacement (c'est-à-dire les non-dominants). Dans la suite, nous ferons précéder de '−' tous les affixes nondominants, les autres étant précédés de l'ordinaire '+'.

Le deuxième problème soulevé par la règle d'insertion concerne la nature de la consonne insérée. A notre connaissance, cette consonne peut être /r/, /ng/ et /g/. Bien qu'il ne s'agisse que d'une tendance, il semble que:

1. /r/ apparaît devant /a/

   /r/ est en variation libre avec /g/ lorsque le radical se termine par une vélaire:

   ex: kikiaraaluk *ou* kikiagaaluk 'grand clou'
   kuuraaluk *ou* kuugaaluk 'grande rivière'

2. /ng/ apparaît devant /i/ et /u/

   /ng/ est souvent en variation libre avec /g/

   ex: kuungudzaq *ou* kuugudzaq 'pris par la rivière'
   gusukpuq *ou* ngusukpuq 'il est heureux'

Compte tenu du fait qu'il semble y avoir variation libre entre /g/ et /ng/ on pourrait supposer que la consonne insérée sousjacente soit une vélaire continue qui par suite d'un abaissement devant une voyelle basse (/a/) devient l'uvulaire /r/. La règle d'insertion ressemblerait donc à:

(3) Epenthèse

$$\emptyset \rightarrow \begin{bmatrix} +\text{cons} \\ -\text{voc} \\ +\text{post} \\ +\text{cont} \\ +\text{haut} \end{bmatrix} / \begin{Bmatrix} \text{VV} \underline{\quad} \begin{Bmatrix} + \\ - \end{Bmatrix} \text{VV} \\ \text{VV} \underline{\quad} + \text{V} \\ \text{V} \underline{\quad} + \text{VV} \end{Bmatrix}$$

Cette règle serait suivie de:

(4) Abaissement

$$\begin{bmatrix} +\text{cons} \\ -\text{voc} \\ +\text{post} \\ +\text{haut} \\ +\text{cont} \\ -\text{nasal} \end{bmatrix} \to [-\text{haut}] \Bigg/ \begin{matrix} VV \underline{} \left\{ \begin{matrix} + \\ - \end{matrix} \right\} \begin{matrix} V \\ [+\text{bas}]\,V \\ V \end{matrix} \\ \\ VV \underline{} + [+\text{bas}] \\ V \underline{} + [+\text{bas}]\,V \end{matrix}$$

(4) cependant est difficile à motiver. D'autant plus qu'il y a un cas particulier où devant /i/ nous n'avons ni /ng/ ni /g/ mais toujours /r/:

(H)	anguvâ	anguiyuq	'rattraper un voyageur'
	aggamikpâ	aggamiivuq	'il le touche de la main'
	nipippâ	nipiiyuq	'il l'a collé à quelque chose'
	ameiyarpâ	ameiyaiyuq	'il lui enlève sa peau'
	ilaorpâ	ilaorivuq	'il lui a ajouté des morceaux'
	kiktoraavâ	kiktoraagivuq	'il le casse plusieurs fois'
	aukpâ	augivuq	'il le saigne'
	kiakpâ	kiagivuq	'il l'a cloué'
	kiglaupâ	kiglaugivuq	'il en longe le bord'

Dans la deuxième colonne nous avons affaire à l'affixe dit 'semi-transitif' dont la forme sous-jacente est -*i*- (nous donnons la même glose pour le transitif – première colonne – et le 'semi-transitif'). Cet affixe semble effacer la consonne finale du radical. Dans le contexte VV-u, /g/ est insérée (ex: *kiktoraa-ivuq* vs *angu-iyuq*) sauf si le radical se termine en /q/.

Ceci suggère que dans les contextes VVk et VVq il n'y a sans doute pas effacement de la consonne mais plutôt spirantisation. A l'ouest de la Baie Hudson la règle de spirantisation semble obligatoire. Dans l'Ungava ce n'est pas très clair. Dans les exemples (H) il semble qu'elle soit appliquée. Par ailleurs avec les affixes commençant par /u/ il y a, semble-t-il, toujours effacement (cfr. (E)): la consonne insérée n'est jamais /r/. Si nous posons une règle de spirantisation:

(5)   C → [+cont] / comme (3)

nous devrons reviser la règle de l'effacement de la consonne afin qu'elle n'efface pas les consonnes continues:

(1) revue

$$\begin{bmatrix} +\text{cons} \\ -\text{cont} \end{bmatrix} \to \emptyset \,/\, \underline{} - V$$

Si nous ne tenons pas compte des quelques cas en *ri* (cfr. (H)), nous aurons besoin d'une règle qui change /r/ en /g,ng/ devant /u/ et /i/. Sinon nous obtiendrions *umia-ruvuq au lieu de *umianguvuq* 'c'est (un) bateau', *umiarir-pâ au lieu de *umiangirpâ* 'il brise le bateau', etc. La règle d'abaissement (4) changeait /g,ng/ en /r/ devant /a/. Maintenant nous avons besoin d'une règle qui change /r/ en /g,ng/ devant /u/ ou /i/. Nous pouvons combiner ces deux règles:

(4) revue

$$\begin{bmatrix} +\text{cons} \\ -\text{voc} \\ +\text{post} \\ \alpha\ \text{haut} \end{bmatrix} \rightarrow [-\alpha\text{haut}] / \underline{\quad} + \begin{bmatrix} -\text{cons} \\ +\text{voc} \\ -\alpha\text{haut} \end{bmatrix}$$

Dans le dernier exemple de (H) *kiglaupâ*, on pourrait penser que le radical se termine en VV. Il n'en est rien. En effet, comme le montrent les autres exemples, la terminaison transitive est $-p\hat{a}$ lorsque le radical se termine par une consonne, $-v\hat{a}$ lorsqu'il se termine par une voyelle. Pourquoi la consonne finale disparait-elle dans *kiglaupâ*? Considérons les exemples suivants:

(I)
1. annekit̄-   annekiksatuq   'il trouve que c'est peu'
2. ômmaluk-   ômmaluksatuq   'il le trouve peu actif'
3. inurqit-   inurqisartuq   'il le trouve chic'
4. opinnait-   opinnaisartuq   'il le trouve normal'
5. annetu-   annetuksatuq   'il trouve que c'est grand'
6. angi-   angiksatuq   'il le trouve trop grand'
7. mamaq-   mamarsatuq   'il le trouve bon'
8. ishuaq-   ishuarsatuq   'il le trouve bon'

Ces exemples soulèvent plusieurs problèmes. Ils sont rapportés ici uniquement pour illustrer la règle des doubles consonnes et la règle des trois consonnes. La forme sous-jacente de l'affixe signifiant 'il le trouve...' est *-ksaq*. Cependant cet affixe n'apparaît jamais sous cette forme. C'est que l'Eskimo de l'Ungava n'admet pas la succession de deux groupes de deux consonnes et les séquences de plus de deux consonnes. Si dans une dérivation deux, trois... groupes de deux consonnes se succèdent, la première consonne du deuxième (quatrième, sixième, etc) groupe est effacée. Si nous avons un groupe de trois consonnes, généralement la première est effacée. Ainsi en (I)1-2, 5-6-7-8 il y a effacement du /q/ de *-ksaq* parce que d'une part l'affixe commence par deux consonnes et que d'autre part il est suivi d'une terminaison commençant par une consonne.

Ex: annekit+ksaq+tuq
   anneki+ksaq+tuq (règle des 3 consonnes)
   anneki+ksa+tuq (règle des doubles consonnes)

En I)3-4, c'est le /k/ de -*ksaq* qui tombe:
   inurqit+ksaq+tuq
   inurqi+ksaq+tuq (règle des 3 consonnes)
   inurqi+saq+tuq (règle des doubles consonnes)

Il serait intéressant d'étudier plus en détail la relation qui existe sans doute entre les restrictions imposées sur les séquences de voyelles et les séquences de consonnes. Le lien qui unit les règles concernant ces restrictions apparaît difficilement si l'on adopte une analyse purement formelle. N'est-il pas évident cependant que d'un point de vue fonctionnel ces règles sont étroitement apparentées: elles forment une 'conspiration' tendant à préserver certaines propriétés rythmiques de l'Eskimo de l'Ungava (propriétés dont malheureusement nous ignorons quasi tout).

Cet article laisse intacts bien des problèmes. Pour les résoudre il faudrait entre autres mener une étude intensive de l'affixation en Eskimo. Pourquoi certains affixes effacent-ils la consonne du radical, alors que d'autres ne l'effacent pas? Par ailleurs le rôle de l'accent pourrait se révéler crucial dans certains problèmes que nous n'avons qu'effleurés ici. Ainsi il semble que la loi des doubles consonnes et la formation des groupes de consonnes (ou tension) ait un rapport avec l'accentuation. En est-il de même au niveau des restrictions imposées sur les groupes de voyelles?[5]

NOTES

[1] La plupart des exemples sont tirés du *Dictionnaire Esquimau-Français du Parler de l'Ungava*, Schneider, Presses de l'Université de Laval, 1970, et de la thèse de Maîtrise d'A.-M. Willis, *Some Phonological Problems of an Eskimo Dialect of the Ungava Region*, Ottawa, Juin 1971, où les problèmes traités ici sont déjà abordés. D'autres exemples sont tirés de ma thèse (dirigée par J.-P. Paillet et T. Pavel), *Morphologie Absolue et Sémantique Transitive en Eskimo* (*Ungava*), Université d'Ottawa, Juin 1972. La transcription adoptée ici suit celle de Schneider. Voir aussi en annexe la matrice des traits.
[2] Cette règle devrait tenir compte aussi de certains affixes commençant par une consonne. Mais ceci demanderait une étude intensive de l'affixation en Eskimo.
[3] Y at-il une relation entre ces règles et la règle des doubles consonnes (voir plus loin)?
[4] En réalité le contexte gauche n'est pas limité à VV. Il devrait inclure V: (voyelles tendues). Mais la distinction entre voyelles doubles, tendues et longues n'est pas claire dans les données.
[5] On trouvera une version revue de cet article dans ma thèse de doctorat, *La quantité phonologique en Eskimo*, Université de Toronto, 1977.

REGLES

Les règles que nous avons proposées devraient s'appliquer dans l'ordre suivant:

1. *Spirantisation*

$$C \rightarrow [+\text{cont}] / \begin{cases} VV \underline{} \begin{Bmatrix} + \\ - \end{Bmatrix} VV \\ VV \underline{} + V \\ V \underline{} + VV \end{cases}$$

2. *Effacement de la consonne*

$$\begin{matrix} C \\ [-\text{cont}] \end{matrix} \rightarrow \emptyset / \underline{} -V$$

3. *Epenthèse*

$$\emptyset \rightarrow \begin{bmatrix} +\text{cons} \\ +\text{post} \\ +\text{cont} \\ +\text{haut} \\ -\text{nasal} \end{bmatrix} / \text{ comme en 1.}$$

4. *Ajustement*

$$\begin{bmatrix} +\text{cons} \\ -\text{voc} \\ +\text{post} \\ \alpha\text{haut} \end{bmatrix} \rightarrow [-\alpha\text{haut}] / \underline{} + \begin{bmatrix} -\text{cons} \\ +\text{voc} \\ -\alpha\text{haut} \end{bmatrix}$$

5. *Trois voyelles*

$$V \rightarrow \emptyset / VV \underline{}$$

6. *Trois consonnes*

$$C \rightarrow \emptyset / \ldots \underline{} CC \ldots$$

7. *Doubles consonnes*

$$C \rightarrow \emptyset / \# \ldots CCV(V) \underline{} C \ldots \#$$

Matrice des traits

	p	v	m	t	n	s	k	g	ng	q	r	N	l	j	a	i	u
voc	−	−	−	−	−	−	−	−	−	−	−	−	+	−	+	+	+
cons	+	+	+	+	+	+	+	+	+	+	+	+	+	−	−	−	−
ant	+	+	+	+	+	−	−	−	−	−	−	−	+	−			
coro	−	−	−	+	+	+	−	−	−	−	−	−	+	−			
cont	−	+	−	−	−	+	−	+	+	−	+	+	+	+	+	+	+
nas	−	−	+	−	+	−	−	−	+	−	−	+	−	−	−	−	−
haut	−	−	−	−	−	+	+	+	+	−	−	−	−	+	−	+	+
post	−	−	−	−	−	−	+	+	+	+	+	+	−	−	−	−	+
bas	−	−	−	−	−	−	−	−	−	−	−	−	−	−	+	−	−
lat													+				
sono	−	−	+	−	+	−	−	−	+	−	−	+	+	+	+	+	+

PROTO-ALGONQUIAN *sk IN WOODS CREE

DAVID H. PENTLAND

There are more than thirty consonant clusters reconstructed in Proto-Algonquian. Most are well represented, making their existence as distinct entities relatively easy to prove. However, there are a number of minor clusters which occur in only one or two reconstructions. This group includes *šp (two stems, *ešp- 'high' and *kyi·špene 'if'), *št (only in *-štekwa·ni 'head'), *čp (only in *no·čp- 'pursue'), *čk (three stems), *θp (perhaps two stems), and Hockett's *nh (only *-e·nh- 'diminutive') and *Xp ("θp"; two stems, *keXp- 'thick' and *koXp- 'inland').[1] A few other clusters are also individually rare, but they belong to well established sets – *hl, for example, is found only in two words, but there are about one hundred stems with consonant clusters beginning with *h-. In Bloomfield's first attempt at a reconstruction of Proto-Algonquian (1925:152) he also set up a cluster *çk (now usually written *sk) on the basis of a single correspondence, the stem *meskw- 'red, blood'. He later obtained additional evidence for the existence of *sk as a separate consonant cluster when he found that it appeared as htk in the Swampy Cree dialect of The Pas, Manitoba (Bloomfield 1928a:100). Finally he discovered that the Ojibwa sources he had used in 1925 did not note that the language distinguishes sk (< *sk) from šk (< *šk). By the time this information was published (Bloomfield 1946:88), however, other Algonquianists, especially James Geary (1941), had discovered more than a dozen stems with the *sk cluster, showing beyond any doubt that it was a genuine correspondence.

The 1925 reconstruction of *sk was cited many times in later years, most notably by Sapir (1931), as one of the most striking demonstrations that the comparative method, as developed by the Neogrammarians in the nineteenth century, applied not only to Indo-European but also the so-called "primitive" languages of the rest of the world. Although the forms in each of the daughter languages (as they were available to Bloomfield) could derive from any one of a number of Proto-Algonquian consonant clusters, the correspondence as a set was unique and justified the reconstruction of a separate cluster.

The first hint that there might be a special reflex of *sk in another Cree dialect appeared in Michelson's *Linguistic classification of Cree and Montagnais-Naskapi dialects* (1939:76) where he wrote: "According to some published and unpublished sources in the *th*-dialect *miθku* "blood" occurs in place of *mihku*." This apparently was the only recognition or mention of this fact until Ives Goddard and I independently noticed the θk reflex in Edward Chappell's *Voyage to Hudson's Bay* (1817). Chappell's vocabulary was not collected by him – he received it from "a Trader who had resided Thirty Years in that Country", perhaps the Mr. Swaine who supplied Thomas M'Keevor with a similar vocabulary in 1812. The θk cluster first appears in Henry Kelsey's journal of 1690-91. It is also found in James Isham's *Observations* (1743), Andrew Graham's *Observations* (1767-91) and Alexander Mackenzie's *Voyages* (1801). The last mention of it in a primary source is in Watkins's *Dictionary* (1865).

As Michelson recognized, the θk reflex of *sk occurs only in the *edh* dialect or Woods Cree. This dialect appears to have been much more important, at least to the fur traders, than it is today. Woods Cree is now spoken by about five per cent of the total number of Cree speakers. However, almost all the early explorers' and fur traders' journals give only Woods Cree forms. Besides the sources listed above, Samuel Hearne (1795), Edward Umfreville (1790), Howse (1844), and all the early maps drawn by Englishmen (see Warkentin and Ruggles 1970 for a representative sample) give only Woods dialect words. Harmon (1820), Henry (1897), and John McLean (1849) are the only three early sources of any importance known to me in another dialect (Plains Cree). John Oldmixon (1708) gives a short vocabulary in an *r* dialect collected by Thomas Gorst at Rupert House, Quebec, in 1670-71.[2]

The reason for the predominance of Woods Cree in the eighteenth century is not hard to find – until about 1775 the Hudson's Bay Company remained resolutely on the coast, expecting the Indians to come to them with their furs. Only a few Englishmen had been any distance from the bay – Kelsey had been sent in 1690 and 1691 to encourage the inland Indians to come down to trade, Hearne made his way to the Arctic Ocean (more in search of copper than of furs), and a very few others had traveled up the rivers under the orders of individual Factors. Not until the marked success of the Montreal traders made a serious dent in the HBC trade did the Company undertake inland expeditions and posts.[3] Around the forts on the bay were settled small bands of "Home" Indians, hired to provide meat for the traders. These people were "Southern" Indians, i.e. Cree, and from the linguistic evidence, Woods Cree. There was even some intermarriage, although the Hudson's Bay Company strongly discouraged it – Richard Norton's half-breed son Moses was the Factor at Fort Prince of Wales (Churchill) from 1763 to 1773.[4] When the English finally got around to exploring inland it was Woods Crees that they used as guides, as these were the only Indians they knew well. Henry Kelsey even tried to teach the HBC employees to speak Woods Cree and the Company printed up a dictionary he had written.[5] The epidemics of smallpox which accompanied the fur traders struck the Woods Cree harder and more frequently than most other tribes, reducing them to a number of small bands along the Churchill River. York Factory itself became part of the Swampy Cree territory, and today is a ghost town, the population having moved to Churchill and elsewhere in 1957.

In all the words found in early Woods Cree sources that can be traced to a Proto-Algonquian stem with *sk, the Woods form has θk (written variously as *thk*, *thc*, etc.), e.g. *mith-coo* 'blood' *C*.262 (*meskwi), *athkeek* 'seal' *G*. 117 (*a·skikwa), *ithkinum* 'he drains it' (Watkins 1865:209) (*eskenamwa). There are no exceptions: in all the vocabularies of the dialect that I have seen there is not one occurrence of any of these words *without* θk. This exceptionlessness is what we would expect in the case of a regular sound change. On the other hand, there are only two[6] stems without *sk that ever appear with θk, and neither occurs with this cluster with any regularity. The usual representation of pre-aspiration in the early records is zero: *mo co mon* 'knife' (*mo·hkoma·ni), *coo coosh* 'pig' (Moose Cree ko·hko·š), *e'qua* 'louse' (*ehkwa), *at tick* 'deer' (*atehkwa), *shar qua she wuck* 'minks' (*ša·nkwe·hšiwaki), *u'spim mick* 'above' (*ešpemenki) (examples from Isham 1743). Thus there is normally no confusion between *sk and the other two clusters which give hk in modern Cree, *hk and *nk. With equal regularity, clusters which appear as sk in modern Cree (*xk, *θk, *šk, *čk) also have *sk* in the early sources, e.g. *es' qua 'u* 'woman' *I*.8 (*eθkwe·wa).

The two variable stems are *kaθk- 'black' and *penkwi 'dust, ashes'. The reconstruction of *kaθk- with *θk is based solely on the Plains Cree form kask- (kaskite·wa·w 'it is black', etc.); Swampy and modern Woods Cree have kahk-, while Moose Cree has mahkate·-, apparently a loan from Ojibwa. The early records have examples of both kask-, e.g. *kur ske ta'u* 'it is black' *I*.28, and kaθk-, e.g. *cuthcatue* 'black' *G*.208, *cathcatew whewe* 'blue goose' *G*.44 (compare *kurs ka ta wa we wuck* 'blue geese' *I*.23;

Plains Cree kaskite·we·hwe·w). Each writer was consistent in his choice of cluster: Isham always has kask-, Graham (his successor as chief at York Factory) has kaθk-. Chappell, who may have received his vocabulary from Graham, agrees with him in having kaθk-, but Umfreville (1790), who definitely shared other vocabularies (of Atsina and Blackfoot) with Graham and was employed by him, has kask-. Since the reconstruction is uncertain, we cannot be sure of the reason for this variation. It appears that *kaθk- has a doublet which reconstructs as *kaHk- (where H = *n, *h, *s) – it may be *kahk-, due to the influence of the apparently synonymous *mahkate·-, or, as the Woods Cree forms suggest, *kask-.

The reconstruction of *penkwi 'dust, powder, ashes' (post-contact also 'gunpowder') is certain. Both Isham and Graham give the expected Cree form pihko: *pe co I*.38, *pecu G*.207 but they also both give forms with θk: *pethco I*.55, *pethko G*.323. In his phrase book, Isham gives the sentence "who serves powder out[?] – *awunna cutta mattinaway peco* (or *pethco*)", showing that he knew the two forms as acceptable variants, not as mere alternate spellings. This suggests that there were two dialects in use around York Factory, as would be expected at the largest trading centre in the area. For at least part of the year Woods Cree speakers would be exposed to the speech of other Crees who did not have the θk cluster. Pihko happens to be one of a very small set of Cree words: it is one of three nouns which are disyllabic and end in -o. The others are wi·ko 'kidney fat'[7] and mihko 'blood'. Since mihko (*meskwi) appears in Woods Cree as miθko, we have the classic situation for analogical change:[8] in dialect X (presumably Swampy Cree), the two words are mihko and pihko; in Woods Cree, they are miθko and pihko. The root miθkw- 'red' occurs in innumerable derivatives, while pihko stands alone – at least until it changes to piθko, It is noteworthy that the two cases of "irregular" θk, piθko and kaθkite·-, while structurally dissimilar, are very close semantically: both piθko and kaθkite·w usually mean 'gunpowder', especially in fur trade circles.

The following list gives all the forms I have found with θk corresponding to *sk, as well as the two "irregular" cases discussed above.

1. *meskw- 'red, blood'.
1.1. *meskwi 'blood' (Bloomfield 1925:141): F meškwi, Cp mihko, Mt mihk^w, mohk, M mɛhki·h, O miskwi, Sh mškwi, Dm mohk, Du mhukw, Nt *musquéheonk*, Nr *misqué*, Ar bé?, At bó?ooc (with *-a·pyi 'liquid' and vowel harmony); Cw miθko (*mith-coo C*.262, *mirth co*[9] *I*.ll, *mith coo M*.112,[10] *Mithco* 'Blood Indian' *G*.207 and Cocking 1908:110).
1.2. *meskwesiwa 'he is red' (Bloomfield 1925:152): F meškosiwa, Cp

mihkosiw, Cs (The Pas) mihtkosiw, Mt mɨhkošiw, mohkwišiw, O miskosi, Dm máxksəw, Du máxkso, cf. M mɛhko·n, Pe mkʷìko; Cw miθkosiw (*mith-coo-sue* C.262).

1.3. *meskwe·wi* 'it is red' (Bloomfield 1925:152): F meškwa·wi, Cp mihkwa·w, Cs(The Pas) mihtkwa·w, M mɛhki·w, O miskwa·, D máxke·w Mc megweg (historically the changed conjunct form), Nt *musqui, mishque*, Nr *msqùi*, cf. Cm mihkwan (also mihkwa·w); Cw miθkwa·w (*mith-gwow* C.262). Fox, Cree, and Ojibwa have reshaped this and some other verbs which originally had *e· (in third person forms) alternating with *a· (elsewhere).

Isham has *mis quock* I.28 and I.50, the second time in a sentence; this is the Ojibwa conjunct (miskwa·k). Other miskw-forms appear in his vocabulary, which is otherwise entirely Woods Cree. The atrocious grammar of some of his sentences (for some examples, see **15** below) show that Isham did not use an informant when he compiled his phrase book, but relied upon his own memory.

1.4. *meskwa·piwa* 'he has red eyes': *meskw- + *-a·piwa 'see'; Cw miθkwa·pit (conjunct) (mith-quah-pit "red eyes" C.264).

1.5. *meskw- + *-a·pyi ~ *-epyi ~ *-e·ya·pyi 'vein, artery' Cp mihkwe·-ya·piy, O miskwe·ya·p (both *-e·ya·pyi), Ar béʔib (*-epyi); the Cw form seems to be a reshaped miθkwiya·piy (*mirth co ap pee* I.11).

1.6. *meskwa·kamyiwi* 'it is red liquid' (Bloomfield 1946:#373): Cp mihkwa·kamiw, M mɛhkuakamiw, O miskwa·kami, Sh mškwa·kami, Pe mkʷākame 'red lake'; Cw miθkwa·kamiw (*Mithquagomow* G.206). Graham's form is given as the name of an Ojibwa (*Nakawewuck*) band which traded at Fort Albany; it must refer to the Red River of Manitoba, which also appears as a place name in its Ojibwa form, *musquagamy* and *musquagamaw* G.261. In his journal for August 6, 1691, Henry Kelsey described "another River wᶜʰ runneth down to yᵉ southward of us and is called *Mith* * * * *. Now yᵉ water wᶜʰ runneth down this River is of a Blood red Colour by yᵉ description of those Indians wᶜʰ hath seen it . . ." (Kelsey 1929:10). Although the Cree word has been crossed out and was unreadable by the editors, it is obviously the same word for 'Red River', and as such is the earliest record we have of the θk reflex in Woods Cree.

1.7. *mesko·hkoma·ni* 'red knife': *meskw- + *-o·hkoma·ni (from *mo·hkoma·ni 'knife'); *m- is regularly lost in compounds of this type, and *w drops before *o·. The posterior part is based on C mo·hkoma·n, 0 mo·kkoma·n. Cw miθko·hkoma·n (*Mithcocoman* G.205). Graham's word is the unglossed name of an Athapaskan (*Wechepowuck*) band trading at Churchill, no doubt the Yellowknives.

1.8. *meskwa·pye·makwi 'red willow': Cᴘ mihkwa·pe·mak, Cs(The Pas) mihtkwa·pe·mak, M mɛhku·pi·mak, cf. O miskwa·pi·miš and miskwa·pi·minako·ns; Cw miθkwa·pe·mak (*mith-qua-pim-mook* C.262).
1.9. *meskwe·kenwi 'red cloth': F meškwe·kenwi, Cᴘ mihkwe·kin, Cs (The Pas) mihtkwe·kin, O miskwe·kin, cf. M mɛhki·kan; the Cw form may be miθkoke·kan (*mithco-kegan* G.209), but Graham's form is more likely due to his own *ad hoc* combination of two wrongly segmented elements, miθkw- and -e·kin. Isham gives the Ojibwa form *mis qua ig gan I.*39 – he, too, has misanalyzed the suffix (compare his *kur ska ta ig gan* 'blue cloth' *I.*39, **6.5** below).
1.10. *meskwixpwa·kana 'catlinite pipe': F meškohpwa·kana, Cᴘ mihkospwa·kan, Cs(The Pas) mihtkospwa·kan. Apparently *aʔsenya 'stone' may be suffixed, though *-a·peθk- would be more usual: Cw miθkospwa·kan-asiniy (may be two words) (*mithco-aspoken-assinee* 'red pipestone' G.139). Ojibwa puts the elements together in a different order, miskwassin oppwa·kan 'catlinite pipe', miskwassin 'red (pipe)stone'.
1.11. *meskominehsi 'red berry (diminutive)': *meskw- + *-min- (Bloomfield 1946:107) + *-ehs-; Cw miθkominis (with misprinted *c* for *h*, *mitcko-minish* G.208).
1.12. *meskwame·pila 'red sucker': Cs mihkome·pin, M mɛhkuamɛ·pen, cf. O miskwane·pin. The word for 'sucker' is *name·pila (Bloomfield 1946:#178); Cree also has a looser formation with *meskw-, mihkoname·pin. Graham gives a form which is definitely incorrect as it stands (*mithnamepith* G.122), but which may belong to either source: miθkoname·pið, if a syllable has been dropped, or miθkome·pið, if the *n* is an error for *ko*.
1.13. *meskowi·pitehsehsa 'red-toothed fish' has the appearance of a late formation, probably within Cree itself, due to the double diminutive and the neglect of sandhi rules (which should give *meskwi·pit-, or better *meskwa·pit-). Cocking's *mithcowepitesish* (1908:103) seems to be Cw miθkowi·pitisis.
1.14. *meskwatehsa·waya·ni 'red dye plant': *meskw- + *atehsa·wiya·ni, Cᴘ atisa·wiya·n, O atissa·waya·n, cf. Canadian French tisavoyanne (Graham 1969:136). Graham gives Woods Cree *sawayan* 'northern bedstraw, *Galium* sp.' and the prefixed form *mithco sawyan* or *sawayan* G.135, pseudo-Cw miθko-(ati)sa·waya·n.
1.15. *pekweskwe·šiwa 'he lets blood': cf. Cᴘ pikohkwe·swe·w 'he bleeds him'; Cw pikoθkwe·siw (*puck-queth-qua-sue* C.272). Note that Chappell has medial *wi* where *o* is expected. This appears to be a fairly common occurrence in Woods Cree, e.g. apoy 'paddle, propellor' alternating with apwiy (especially with plural or obviative ending: apwiyak); the locative

apo·hk shows that the underlying form has o. Many words (mostly nouns) lose an initial *m-, *n-, or *w- when medial, e.g. *mo·hkoma·ni 'knife' (**1.7**), *wexpwa·kana 'pipe' (**1.10**), *name·pila 'sucker' (**1.12**), and *meskwi 'blood' here.

1.16. *wesa·weskwesiwa 'he is bloody': *wesa·w- 'yellow' + *(m)eskw-. The first part is based on CP osa·w-, O osa·w-, cf. Sh we·θa·wa·ki 'yellow thing', Ar nííhooyóóʔ, At nííhooyoo (last three all changed conjunct). CP osa·wiskowiw 'he is bloody' provides the connecting link semantically (the -isk- suffix is common with colour terms, and is not connected with *(m)eskw-). Cw osa·wiθkosiw (*sow-with-coo-sue* C.273).
2. *a·skikwa 'seal' (Siebert 1967a:19): CP a·hkik, Mt a·hčikʷ, a·hčok, O a·skik, Pe àhkikʷ, Ab akik8; Cw a·θkik (*ath keek* I.22, *athkeek* G.117).
3. *wi·skwayi 'bladder, pouch, swelling' (Geary 1941:305): CP wi·hkway, M wi·hko·s (diminutive) 'crop (of goose)', O wi·skway; Cw wi·θkway (*wirth qui* 'bladder' I.11).
4. *esk- 'dry up': Geary (1941:306) reconstructs *eska·ʔte·wi 'it dries up' based on F aška·hte·-, CP ihkaste·w, M ihka·ʔte-, O iskatte·. He quotes Watkins's Cree dictionary as giving the form *ithkustāo*. What Watkins actually writes is the following:

> ikepuyew, *v.imp.* It sinks, it abates, it assuages. NOTE. Those Indians who make use of the letters *th*, insert them in the first syllable of this and most of the following words commencing with *ik*; thus, *ithkepuyew, ithkinum,* &c. (Watkins 1865:209)

The complete list of words in Watkins beginning with *ik* is given below; a systematic phonetic transcription is followed by his spelling in parentheses:

> ihkipayiw (*ikepuyew*) 'it sinks, abates, assuages'
> ihkinam (*ikinum*) 'he drains it, sponges it up'
> ihkipa·cikan (*ikipachikun*) NA 'sponge'
> ihkacike·payiw (*ikuchikāpuyew*), ihkacike·payin (*ikuchikāpuyin*) 'it absorbs, soaks up'
> ihkahipa·n (*ikuhipan*) NA 'sponge'
> ihkahipe·w (*ikuhipāo*) 'he bails, sponges (it)'
> ihkahipayiw (*ikuhipuyew*) 'it absorbs, sucks up'
> ihkaham (*ikuhum*) 'he sucks it (as with a sponge)'
> ihkasow (*ikusoo*) 'he is left dry'
> ihkaste·w (*ikustāo*) 'it is left dry, is abated'

The second edition of Watkins's dictionary (ed. Faries 1938:258) gives two more forms, ihka·pa·cikan (*îkapa'chikun*) NI 'sponge' and ihkahipa·tam (*îkuhipatum*) 'he bails, pumps it out'.

Several problems are evident: Watkins is only being careless when he gives the form *ithkepuyew* (iθkipayiw). The correct Woods Cree form of this and the other words cited with *-puyew* is -paðiw, but the Plains form is always used in both editions of the dictionary even with words explicitly marked as from other dialects. More important is that none of his Plains Cree forms shows an h in the first syllable: of all the stems mentioned in this paper, this is the only one in which Watkins consistently omits the expected aspirate. However, both Lacombe (1874:340–341) and Faries (1938:258) give forms with ihk-. Geary's reconstruction also poses a problem: the Cree form corresponding to *eska·ʔte·wi definitely has a short vowel in the second syllable – in fact, only Fox provides any evidence for the long a·.

5. *meskam- 'insult' (Geary 1941:306): Cp mihkame·w; Geary gives this and *nesk- as alternants of *nemeskam-, based on Cp nimihkame·w and O nimiskama·. The Woods Cree form represented by *mathky* "curse an Englishman" *G*.208 is not known, but it appears to be cognate. This set has more than its fair share of problems: there are three variants offered for Proto-Algonquian; the Woods Cree form is not traceable; and Graham's *mathky* has an anomalous first vowel (if it is more than a simple error in transcription). Although Geary argues that the correct gloss is 'make an insulting gesture to someone's face', the forms given all have *-am- 'by mouth', suggesting that the meaning (originally, at least) is simply 'insult (by words)'.

6. *kaθk- 'black' (Hockett 1957:#24): F kahk-, Cp kask-, O kakk-. Fox and Ojibwa apparently have this stem only in the word for 'ashes, charcoal', *kaθkeše·wi: F kahkeše·wi and reshaped kehkeše·wi, Cp kaskase·w and reduplicated kaskaskase·w, kaskaskisiw, all 'ember', O kakkiše·, cf. Pt kəkš·e. Woods Cree has the variant *kaHk- mentioned above.

6.1. *kaθkite·wi 'black', (prenoun), 'ashes, gunpowder': Cw kaskite·w and kaθkite·w (*cuthcatue G*.208, *cuthcatue athinue* 'Negro' *G*.207 (iðiniw 'person'), *kur ske ta'u* 'black, grey, blue' *I*.28, *kur ske tau* 'gunpowder' *I*.38, *kur ska tau che stem mo* 'black tobacco' *I*.39 (ciste·ma·w 'tobacco'), *cur ska tau me ke shue* 'black fox' *I*.20 (mahke·siw 'fox').

6.2. *ka·kite·wa·piwa 'he has black eyes': cf. **1.4**; Cw kaθkite·wa·pit (conjunct) (*kuth-ke-tai-wap-pit* "black eyes" *C*.260).

6.3. *kaθkite·mina 'black berry, bead': cf. **1.11**; Cw kaskite·min (*kur ske ta me nuck* "blue beads" *I*.38).

6.4. *kaθkite·we·hwe·wa 'blue goose': *kaθkite·- + *we·hwe·wa 'blue goose': CP we·hwe·w, O we·ʔwe· (*wêwe* Baraga 1878:410); Cw kaskite·- we·hwe·w and kaθkite·we·hwe·w (*cathcatew whewe* G.44, *kurs ka ta wa we wuck* (plural) *I*.23).

6.5. *kaθkite·kenwi 'black cloth': cf. **1.9**; Cw kaθkite·kin and kaskite·kin (*cuthcatue-kegan* G.208, *kur ska ta ig gan* *I*.39). Neither Graham nor Isham has segmented the form correctly – these are their own *ad hoc* formations.

7. *penkwi 'powder, dust, ashes' (Geary 1941:306): F pekwi, CP pihko, O pinkwi, Nt *pukquee*, Ar čeʔiθee, At čʔitee (both with added element); Cw piθko and pihko (*pethco* 'gunpowder' *I*.55, *pethko* G.323, *peco* *I*.38, *pecu* G.207).

Another phenomenon of wider distribution than the occurrence of θk seems to be connected to it in some way. In the same early Woods Cree sources there appear a number of words with θt (usually written *th-t*), usually corresponding to a modern Cree ht cluster. The solution of this problem is far more difficult than the distribution of θk, and I offer no answers here. While it is unlikely that an English speaker would hear pre-aspirated k as [θk], Cree ht often sounds (to an English-speaking person) like [θt], and this is an acceptable pronunciation in at least some dialects.[11] Usually, ht appears in the early sources as plain *t*, e.g. *me tar tut* 'ten' *I*.34 (**meta·tahθ-), *no taw* 'my father' *I*.8 (**no·hθ-), *wur sqi ar tick* 'birch tree' *I*.26 (final *-a·htekwa). There are also some examples of θt which must be misprints – words with a single consonant, not an ht cluster, such as Chappell's *muthch-e-puthue* 'it moves badly, slowly' *C*.263 (for macipaðiw), *n'ne-mith-too-too-lakk* "he uses me well" *C*.262 (for nimiðotota·k), and *pis-seth-che-hin* 'listen to me' *C*.269 (for pisicihin). We are left, however, with a residue of θt forms which do not have such an easy explanation. Two stems, 'half' and 'smoke', occur five times each, always with θt. One word, *ap peth* 'steel' *I*.39, seems to be a misprint (or rather, mistranscription) of a·piθt (Plains Cree a·piht); since it occurs twice, in differing environments, it seems more likely that Isham's *th* represents an unreleased θt rather than a misprint of (h)t.

The occurrence of θt is not a simple case of sound change, as *sk > θk is. The Proto-Algonquian reconstructions have almost every possible cluster: *ht, *hθ, *nt, and *ʔt (or *ʔθ). The first three become ht in all modern Cree dialects, but the last becomes st. The situation seems to reflect "sporadic sound change" – a concept rejected since at least 1925 in North American linguistic theory – carried to the point of absurdity: any Proto-Algonquian consonant cluster ending in *t or *θ *may* become θt in early Woods Cree.

There does not appear to be any special environment which might condition a change, nor do the words involved fall into any obvious semantic category. The following list gives all the words I have found with apparent θt in Woods Cree.

8. *mehši (plural *mehθali) 'firewood' (Michelson 1935:141): Cp mihti, O mišši (plural missan), Ar bés, At bís (i unoriginal, otherwise At should have *bʸís). Hewson (1973:194) points out that early Montagnais has *michi* (i.e. miši) which *may* be the original C-Mt form,[12] but also *mitai* "bois de haute futaie", and suggests there may have been some confusion between the two words. Isham gives a Woods Cree form which seems to derive from an otherwise unrecorded *mehθa·wi, Cw miθta·w (*meth ta'u* I.25).

9. *pi·nt- 'inside'.

9.1. *pi·ntwike·wa 'he enters a dwelling' (Bloomfield 1946:#14): F pi·tike·wa, Cp pi·htoke·w, M pi·htikɛw, O pi·ntike·, Nt *pētukau*; Cw pi·θtoke·w (*peth ta ku* "to come in" I.32). The anomalous second vowel in Isham's form is probably due to a misreading of the manuscript. His final -u occasionally represents -e·w instead of -iw: cf. *me stick a nap pu* (mistikona·pe·w) 'carpenter' I.16 with the same two errors. H. C. Wolfart (personal communication) reports pi·θtoke·w in the Swampy Cree dialect of Norway House, Manitoba.

9.2. The word for 'smoke (tobacco)' seems to have the same root: Cp pi·htwa·w 'he smokes', O pi·nta·kke· (Bloomfield 1957; most dialects have the unrelated sakasswa·); Cw pi·θtwa·w (*wepethtwan* "I Long to smoak" I.48, *pethtahommawin* "Let me smoak with you" I.48, *kullapethtwan* (misprint – see next) I.49, *kuttapethtwan* I.54, *cuttapethtwan* I.64 "to smoak").

10. *šenta·po·wi 'spruce beer':[13] *šenta 'evergreen' (Siebert 1967a:27) + *-a·po·wi 'liquid' (Bloomfield 1946:107). The first part is based on Cp sihta, Dm šə̀nt 'hemlock', Pe sə̀ti, cf. M sɛhta·k 'bough, needle of evergreen', Dakota šĭtá. Cw siθta·po·w (*sheth taw po* I.16).

11. *a·peht- 'half, middle'.

11.1. *a·pehtawi 'half, middle': Cm a·pihtaw, O a·pitta. In this and the following derivative, Woods Cree appears to have a form a·piθtaha·w or a·piθte·ha·w; it is not possible to determine which is correct, but the first form is more likely (*ap peth ta hau* "the midle" I.7, *ap peth ta ha'w* "half" I.31).

11.2. *a·pehtaki·šek- 'midday': *a·peht- + *ki·šek- 'day' (Hockett 1957:#91); Cw a·piθtaha·ki·sika·w (*ap peth ta ha ke shic kaw* "the afternoon or middle of the day" I.7).

11.3. Cree pi·sim 'sun' apparently does not have a cognate in any other Algonquian language, and the modern Woods Cree word for 'clock' is pi·simohka·n, but the following is perfectly well formed: Cw a·piθtapi·-sim (*ap peth ta be sum* 'clock, watch' *I*.17).

11.4. *a·pehtakahikani(?) 'key': Cp a·pihtakahikan (this is also the form in modern Woods Cree), cf. O apa·pikaʔikan with the same final, but Cw a·piθtakitahikan(?) (*ap peth ta kit a hi gan I*.17). The reconstruction is uncertain, but the root does appear to be *a·peht-.

12. I do not know of a reconstruction that will fit Cp a·piht 'fire steel', but it is unlikely to be the same as **11**. This may not be a genuine case of θt, since only Isham gives a form with *th* (discussed above): Cw a·piθt, a·piht (*ap peth I*.39, *apit G*.209). Isham also gives *be sum ap peth* 'burning glass' *I*.40, which may belong here (Cw pi·sima·piθt?) or may (more likely) be a misprint for pi·sima·pisk, with *-a·peθk- 'stone, metal, glass'.

13. *kehtemiwa 'he is lazy' (Hockett 1957:#42): Cp kihtimiw, O kittimi; Cw kiθtimiw(?) (*kethtamau I*.54). The Woods Cree form may be kiθtima·w; note, however, that Graham gives *citimi G*.209 without the θt cluster.

14. *kwanta·kani 'throat' (Hockett 1957:#96): F kota·kani, Cp ko·hta·-kan, M ko·htakan, O konta·kan, Sh nikota·ka 'my throat', Nt ukquttunk 'his throat', Nr *qúttuck*, Ar béitóo (with *me- 'someone's'); At bʸiitóoo; Cw ko·θta·kan (*koth to gan I*.10).

15. *pe·Htamwaʔ 'he hears it' (H = *n or *h): Cp pe·htam; Cw pe·θtam (*path tum* "the hearing or to hear" *I*.12). We also find a couple of ungrammatical forms with this root: *kepathtum* "you hear" *I*.55 (the expected form is kipe·θte·n), (nitha) *pethtuin* "I hear" *G*.209 (the expected form is nipe·θte·n).

16. *Se·ʔta·kwiʔ 'thread' (S = *s or *š; the cluster may be *ʔθ or even the otherwise unique *št): Cp se·sta·k, se·sta·kos (diminutive); Cw se·θta·kos (*sheth ta kush* "thread" *I*.39, *sheth ta cush* "twine" *I*.41).

17. *okeškemani·ʔsiwa 'kingfisher' (Siebert 1967a:16): Cp okiskimanisiw, M okɛ·skemani·ʔ, O okiškimani·ssi, Pe kaskamanəsso. Graham gives *kiskeman, ethtecoo* "belted kingfisher" *G*.96, which cannot be reconciled to the reconstruction. It appears to be a compound of *okeškeman- and *-i·nteko·wa (from *wi·nteko·wa 'cannibal monster'). The semantic problem is not all that great – Fox wi·teko·wa means 'owl'.

A number of different phenomena seem to be involved in the creation of θ- consonant clusters in early Woods Cree. There is the problem of misprints, which has created a number of apparent clusters beginning with *th* – this, of course, happens only after the manuscript has left the hands of the original writer. A related problem is mistranscription, that is, writing the word incorrectly in the first place. It is difficult in some cases to decide which of the above was responsible for the occurrence of a *th* cluster. As mentioned above, Isham compiled his word-and phrase-list without the aid of an informant. It is noteworthy that all but two of the θt clusters occur in his work, suggesting that *th-t* was in most cases his own invention, not an accurate recording of the local dialect. Only the stem for 'hear', pe·θt-, occurs in two sources, and here we are hampered by the lack of cognates outside Cree. Most likely, θt represents the occasional recording of an allophone of ht, and the apparent consistency of Isham is illusory. As already noted, some Plains Cree dialects have this pronunciation – Michelson (1939:76) wrote "The Cree dialect at Turtle Mountain (North Dakota) is a *y*-dialect; in my vocabulary of over 25 years ago [1911–12] I recorded θt in place of *ht* (*wāpaθtam* for *wāpahtam* "he sees it")."[14]

The unique occurrence of a θp consonant cluster is found in Bloomfield's MS Cree lexicon, where he gives name·θpin 'wild ginger' in The Pas dialect.[15] It, too, corresponds to an h cluster elsewhere: Swampy Cree hp (< *hp). This is the only θp recorded in Bloomfield's lexicon or anywhere else – I leave it to someone else to explain.

On the other hand, the θk reflex in early Woods Cree seems clear enough – it is the regular reflex of Proto-Algonquian *sk. The strange htk reflex in The Pas Swampy dialect (Bloomfield 1928) suggests that *sk was kept distinct from all other Proto-Algonquian consonant clusters in some western dialects of Cree for a considerable time, just as *sk is still kept separate in Ojibwa. Bloomfield's recording can hardly be challenged – he was aware of the significance of his find and must have taken care in eliciting it, as the number of derivatives he lists attests. The relative rarity of *sk eventually led to its merger with Cree hk in all but this one dialect, but the Hudson's Bay Company traders have preserved for us the earlier stage.

NOTES

[1] Reconstructed Proto-Algonquian forms are preceded by an asterisk; forms quoted from early journals, etc., are italicized; phonemicized transcriptions are unmarked. Glosses from the early sources are given in double quotation marks: other glosses are in the usual single quotation marks. Language abbreviations: Ab Abenaki, Ar Arapaho, At Atsina (Gros Ventre), Cм Moose Cree, Cp Plains Cree, Cs Swampy Cree, Cw Woods Cree (phonemicized from early sources; modern Woods Cree is specifically marked), D Delaware (Dм Munsee dialect, Du Unami dialect), F Fox, M Menomini, Mc Micmac, Mt Montagnais, Nr Narragansett, Nt Natick, O Ojibwa, Pe Penobscot, Pt Potawatomi, Sh Shawnee. Sources (followed by page number): *C.* Chappell 1817, *G.* Graham 1767(-91), *I.* Isham 1743, *M.* Mackenzie 1801.

Modern Woods Cree forms are from my own field notes, collected during the summer of 1971 at South Indian Lake under a grant from the Manitoba Museum of Man and Nature. This dialect differs from the early Woods Cree records in having the usual Cree reflex of hk for *sk and in having the sound change *e· → [i·]. Further field work and research (1972-) has been under a Canada Council doctoral fellowship.

The present state of this paper owes much to critical readings of an earlier draft by H. C. Wolfart and J. D. Kaye. Remaining errors are my typist's.

[2] Hewson (1973:193) suggests that this is really early Montagnais, since one word has *st* where Cree has sk. However, there are so many obvious typographical errors, e.g. *spog.m* 'pipe' for ospwa·kan, and one form which may be Woods Cree, *soth.im.m* "red lead" (PA *walamana), that little can be decided on the basis of this vocabulary. The survival of a Cree (not Montagnais) *r* dialect in the Kesagami Lake area of Ontario into the twentieth century (Cooper 1945:40-41) seems to settle the matter in favor of Cree.

There are occasional traces elsewhere of an *r* dialect: Isham gives *ha ra ca naw* 'bread' (compare the place name Harricanaw River, but Graham's *hethekanaw*). Some of the forms with *r* are, however, probable misprints, such as Isham's *Ra mars* 'fish' and Hearne's *Arathapescow* 'Athabaska', which he later corrected to *Athapuscow*. Most of the early HBC men were posted to "the bottom of the Bay" before going to York Factory, so occasional *r* dialect words slip into a number of the Woods Cree records.

[3] See Innis 1956, chapter III, especially pp. 152-158, and Graham 1969:343-48.

[4] Isham and Graham were two others who had half-breed children: see Graham 1969:145*n*. Isham's instructions in 1751 included the order "do not harbour or Entertain any Indian Woman or Women in our Factory or permit others under you so to do" (Isham 1949:322); his half-breed son later worked for the HBC.

[5] There is some dispute over when this book was published. Hall (1970:41) says Kelsey's dictionary was begun in 1698 and was printed and sent out from London in 1702. Johnson (in Davies and Johnson, eds., 1965:389) quotes a letter from the Committee in London in 1710: "wee have sent you your dixonary Printed that you may the Better Instruct the young Ladds with you, in ye Indian Language."

[6] Chappell's *peth-coo-wow* "to penetrate" *C*.272 is excluded from discussion, since I know of no reconstruction or cognate corresponding to it.

[7] I am indebted to H. C. Wolfart for this product of his computerized Cree dictionary.

[8] If, that is, analogical change exists. I invite other explanations (besides the trivial h → θ /Ci ___ ko).

[9] Isham was from London: *ir* stands for a vowel like [i].

[10] Gallatin (1836:320) cites *mithcoo* from Harmon 1820, but this must be an error for Mackenzie 1801, Gallatin's other Cree source, since Harmon's vocabulary is Plains Cree and does not give a word for 'blood'.

[11] Michelson 1912:227 notes that "'*t* is apt to be heard as θt" in the Fort Totten (Plains) dialect.

[12] Modern Cree and Montagnais have reformed the singular of this word on the model of the plural; similar are most other (inanimate) nouns with final *t ($\sim$ *c) and *θ ($\sim$ *š): wa·ti 'hole' < *wa·θ-, -i·pit 'tooth' < *-i·pit-, etc. A few nouns still maintain the alternations (in some dialects), as do all verbal forms: Plains Cree has o·si 'canoe' but oto·t 'his canoe'.

[13] Hosie 1969:70 notes "A cure for scurvy was made by boiling young spruce twigs, adding molasses, honey or maple sugar and allowing the liquid to ferment."

[14] The one Cree speaker I found at Turtle Mountain in the summer of 1972 had the normal Plains Cree reflex of all consonant clusters. I heard no θ's whatsoever.

[15] The complete entry in Bloomfield is:

    namähpin, wild ginger E   (namäθpin ? N)

ä = e·, E is Swampy Cree, and N is The Pas (Swampy) dialect. For the full reference I am indebted to H. C. Wolfart, who informs me that the question mark may have been a later addition. In his *Menomini language* (1962:259), Bloomfield suggests that the Menomini cognate, nami·hpen, may be a derivative of 'potato', Proto-Algonquian *wexpenya, but the Cree forms will not fit.

SOME IMPLICATIONS OF ALGONQUIAN PALATALIZATION*

GLYNE L. PIGGOTT

1. INTRODUCTION. In this paper we intend to examine in some detail some cases of consonant-alternation in Algonquian languages, which are clearly the result of a process of palatalization. We will consider, in the course of our presentation, data drawn primarily from the so-called Central group of languages, the core of which are Ojibwa, Fox, Cree and Menomini.[1] These languages are the chief sources of the evidence used by Bloomfield (1925 and 1946) in his reconstruction of Proto-Algonquian (PA). It has subsequently been argued quite convincingly by Goddard (1967) that the reconstruction based on the Central languages is perfectly valid. We therefore assume that, until proven otherwise, any conclusions we reach here will be valid outside the scope of the four principal languages cited above. It will be noticed, however, that, of these languages, the data from Ojibwa (specifically the Odawa dialect of Ojibwa)[2] provide valuable insights into Algonquian palatalization and are most crucial to our analysis.

In addition to the material provided by the four languages mentioned above, we take as a point of departure Bloomfield's illuminating reconstruction of Proto-Algonquian phonological system, as outlined in the (1946) article. For the purpose of citation, we will also adopt, with few minor modifications, Bloomfield's method of transcription,[3] which is now generally familiar to Algonquianists and which should therefore facilitate the reading of the examples cited.

To some extent we are interested here in a diachronic analysis of a phonological process, but, as the title of this paper indicates, an important part of our presentation will be devoted to a discussion of the relevance of the facts to phonological theory in general. For example, this study examines the question of the validity of setting up, in a synchronic description of a language, underlying segments which are never realized in the surface phonetic representation. This issue has recently been the subject of much controversy among phonologists.[4] We will attempt to formulate at least one condition which must be met in order to justify positing such instances of *absolute neutralization*.⁵ In addition we will discuss certain constraints on phonological rules, which have become entrenched in generative phonology. To these issues we will return later.

2. The facts, synchronic and diachronic, of Algonquian palatalization are now well known to researchers in the area. In the paragraphs to follow, these facts will be briefly reviewed. Proto-Algonquian is presumed to have distinguished eight vowels, four long and four short, and two glides */y/ and */w/. A description of these is presented, with all the relevant information, in the following chart:

(1)

	i.	i	e.	e	o.	o	a.	a	y	w
High	+	+	−	−	+	+	−	−	+	+
Back	−	−	−	−	+	+	+	+	−	+
Tense	+	−	+	−	+	−	+	−	−	−

Of the PA-consonants reconstructed by Bloomfield,⁶ it appears that only */θ/ and and */t/ were subject to palatalization, the conditioning factor being the presence of a morpheme-initial, high, non-back, non-consonantal segment (*i, i., y*). I will now examine the comparative evidence for the preceding hypothesis, most of which is well-documented and is quite convincing.

The languages of the Central group have a number of cognate forms which show a segment [t] alternating with an affricate. For example, there is, in each language, a suffixed morpheme *-t* which marks 3rd person in the indicative mode of the conjunct order.⁷ This suffix is always subject to palatalization, when the structural conditions are met. Consider the following:

(2)a. Cree: nipa.-t   '(that) he is asleep'
               nipa.-c-ik   '(that) they are asleep'
    b. Ojib: nipa.-t   '(that) he is asleep'
               ne.pa.-č-ik   'those who are asleep'
    c. Men: pia-t   '(if) he comes'
               pia-c-en   'whenever he comes (iterative)'

Other Central languages such as Potawatomi and Fox show the same change (*t* → *č*) as does Ojibwa. That this alternation is clearly not to be considered innovative within these languages is suggested by the occurrence of a similar change in the Eastern languages. For example:

(3) Delaware:[8] ne.lto.nhe.-t   'as he was talking'
    ne.lto.nhe.-č-i.1   'as the other was talking'

The evidence supporting the hypothesis that PA */θ/ was subject to palatalization is less clear-cut, but no less convincing. As we did above, we draw attention to the fact that there are certain cognate verb forms in these languages which show alternation of a stem-final segment. Consider the verb stems in the following languages:

(4)a. Cree: *na.t-*
        ki-na.t-itin   'I fetch you'
        ki-na.s-in   'you fetch me'
   b. Ojib: *na.n-*
        ki-na.n-in   'I fetch you'
        ki-na.š-(i)   'you fetch me'
   c. Men: *na.n-*
        ke-na.n-en   'I fetch you'
        ke-na.s-em   'you fetch me'

(The parenthesized segment in the second Ojibwa example above is deleted by a general rule of final lax vowel deletion, to be discussed later.) Noticeable is the fact that in the above forms the segment [t] of Cree corresponds to [n] in Ojibwa and Menomini.

There is, however, another set of cognates which shows a different kind of correspondence. In these cases a stem-final [n] of Ojibwa, Fox and Menomini corresponds, not to Cree [t], but to [l] (at least in some dialects of this language).[9] However, in the forms in which the above correspondence holds, the Cree [l] is not palatalized, but the [n] of the other Central languages shows the same alternation exhibited in (4) above. This is readily observable in the following examples:

(5)a. Cree: *mi.l-*
        ki-mi.l-itin   'I give you'
        ki-mi.l-in   'you give me'
   b. Ojib: *mi.n-*
        ki-mi.n-in   'I give you'
        ki-mi.š-(i)   'you give me'
   c. Fox: *mi.n-*
        ke-mi.n-en   'I give you'
        ke-mi.š-(i)   'you give me'

d. Men: *me.n-*
   ke-me.n-en 'I give you'
   ke-me.s-em 'you give me'

Examples such as those cited in (4) and (5) above would suggest that the segment [n] of Ojibwa, Fox and Menomini which corresponds to Cree [t] is the reflex of a different PA-segment from that which gives rise to the [n]-[l] correspondence. Furthermore, from the evidence presented in (2), it is unlikely that either of the two PA-segments involved could be */t/. It also seems unlikely that either of the correspondences can be derived from PA */n/, for all the languages show a segment [n] which does not alternate when it occurs in environments similar to those indicated in (4) and (5). Consider the following data from Cree and Ojibwa:

(6)a. Cree: ki-we.pin-itin 'I am leaving you'
           ki-we.pin-in 'you are leaving me'
   b. Ojib: ki-we.pin-in 'I am leaving you'
           ki-we.pin-(i) 'you are leaving me'

Similarly the stem-final [n] of the Menomini form *ke-ke.ten-em* 'you are hurting my sore spot' is not palatalized, though it occurs before the morpheme-*em* which causes palatalization in the examples cited in (4) and (5).

All the available evidence would therefore suggest that there are three sources of [n] in Ojibwa, Fox and Menomini. On the basis of the correspondences illustrated in (4), (5) and (6), Bloomfield (1946) concludes (and we concur) that one source is PA */n/, realized as [n] in all Central languages, and this segment was not subject to palatalization. The PA-segment which is realized as [l] in Cree and [n] in the other languages is generally regarded as */l/, and this segment too did not seem to alternate. Finally, the third source of [n], in all Central languages except Cree, is reconstructed, on evidence from Arapaho, as */θ/.[10] Reflexes of this segment appear in all the forms cited in (4), and it may be recalled that palatalization takes place even when the reflex is Cree [t]. It therefore seems reasonable to assume that PA */θ/ was subject to palatalization.

But if */l/ did not undergo palatalization, it is necessary to account for the fact that the reflex of this segment is palatalized in some languages, all of which show a merger of */θ/ and */l/ (see (5) above). In such cases it seems likely that, with the merger of these two segments, the palatalization of the reflex of */θ/ has been generalized to the reflex of */l/. However, in at least one related language exactly the opposite situation obtains. That is, */θ/ and */l/ also merged and the non-alternation of the reflex of */l/

has been generalized to the reflex of */θ/. This seems to be the situation in the Eastern language, Delaware, in which both PA-segments are realized as [l]. Consider the Delaware forms cognate with those in (4) and (5):

(7)a. na.l-
      kə-na.l-əl 'I went after you'
      kə-na.l-i 'you went after me'
  b. mi.l-
      kə-mi.l-əl 'I give you'
      kə-mi.l-i 'you give me'

Both the palatalization of the reflex of */l/ in some Central languages and the non-palatalization of the reflex of */θ/ in Delaware are thus considered innovations. The loss of the palatalization rule in Delaware and the extension of this rule in Ojibwa and certain other Central languages can both be considered instances of simplification (Kiparsky 1968a). An obvious question which may be posed is: What explanation is there for these different changes? At present, we can offer none. Further investigation may lead to an understanding of the factors causing these apparently contrary innovations. Cree, then, is the only Central language, and more generally, one of the few Algonquian languages, which preserves the historical distinction between */θ/ and */l/ with respect to palatalization.

We may now take a brief look at another instance of palatalization. This involves the segment [s] (or [ss]) in some Central languages. In Fox, Potawatomi and Ojibwa, certain verb stems which on the surface, at least, end in such a segment show alternation:

(8)a. Fox: ke-nes-en 'I am killing you'
          ke-neš-i 'you are killing me'
  b. Pot: ki-niss-in 'I am killing you'
         ki-nišš-i 'you are killing me'
  c. Ojib: ki-niss-in 'I am killing you'
         ki-nišš-(i) 'you are killing me'

It is significant that the Menomini forms cognate with those of (8) above show stem-final [-ʔn] alternating with [-ʔs]:

(9) Men: ke-nɛ.ʔn-en 'I am killing you'
         ke-nɛʔs-em 'you are killing me'

In Cree, on the other hand, cognates of the above examples show stem-final [hy], which does not alternate. Furthermore, there are other instances in which Ojibwa, Fox and Potawatomi stem-final [-s] or [-ss] and Menomini [-ʔn] correspond, not to Cree [-hy], but to [-st], and this [-st] seems to alternate in the palatalizing environment with -s.[11] Consider the following examples from two languages:

(10)a. Cree: kost-e.w 'he fears him'
             ki-kos-in 'you fear me'
    b. Ojib: o-koss-a.n 'he fears him'
             ki-košš-(i) 'you fear me'

Recall, now, that one source of the segment [t] in Cree is PA */θ/ and that this segment was subject to palatalization. It therefore seems likely that Bloomfield (1946) and others are well-motivated in reconstructing the source of Cree [-st] and Ojibwa [-ss], in forms such as those occurring in (10), as */ʔθ/, the glottal stop still being present in Menomini [-ʔn]. On the other hand, for the cognates cited in (8), in which the correspondences are: Cree [-hy], Menomini [-ʔn], and [-ss] or [-s] in other Central languages, there is good reason to consider these as reflexes of PA-stem-final */-ʔl/. This suggests that we are dealing with another instance in which alternation of the reflex of */θ/ has been generalized to the reflex of */l/ in those languages in which */θ and */l/ merged.

However, in Ojibwa, Menomini, and Fox */θ/, */l/ and */n/ are all realized as [n]. Yet the palatalization of [n] < */θ/ has only been generalized to [n] < */l/ and not to [n] < */n/. A possible explanation for this state of affairs lies in the history of the merger of these three PA-consonants, and the different morphophonemic processes in which they were involved. There were two stages to the merger. First */θ/ and */l/ merged, and, at a later stage, the resulting segment merged with [n] < */n/. The first stage was one of absolute merger. In other words, the segments became phonetically and morphophonemically identical. This means that it is at this stage that the palatalization rule was generalized. At the second stage, the merger was only partial, the resulting segments being only phonetically identical.

The proposal that the merger was a two-stage process is well supported. Attention has already been drawn to the fact that in Eastern languages, notably Delaware, Abnaki, Penobscot and Passamaquoddy-Malecite, there was a merger of */θ/ and */l/, but the resulting consonant remains phonetically and morphophonemically distinct from the reflex of */n/. In these languages, the result of the merger is [l]. Given the situation in some of the Central languages (i.e. Fox, Menomini and Ojibwa) in which the reflexes of */θ/ and */l/ are still morphophonemically distinct from the reflex of */n/, one might therefore suspect that these languages passed through a phase in which the segment resulting from the merger of */θ/ and */l/ was phonetically distinct from [n] < */n/.

In fact, this is exactly the situation that did occur. Hanzeli (1969) cites sources that document such a stage for the Ojibwa-Odawa-Algonquin group of dialects. The manuscript evidence of the mid-18th century indicates that the result of the first stage of the merger was [l], and this segment was subject to palatalization.[12] We summarize the history of the merger in the following diagram:

Let us now examine briefly some differences that characterize the consonants involved in the merger. All the comparative evidence would indicate that palatalization was the only morphophonemic rule which */θ/ underwent and which */l/ did not undergo. The absolute merger of these segments would therefore involve the non-application or the generalization of just one rule. But at the second stage of the merger, [n] < */n/ not only did not undergo palatalization, but was also not involved in at least one other morphophonemic process in which [l] (the result of the merger of */θ/ and */l/) was involved. For example, in Ojibwa it appears that when [n] < [l] (< */θ/, *l) is followed by a lenis consonant it is involved in a process which is characterized as dissimilation. The result of the combination of the two segments is a phonetically fortis segment:[13] e.g. *wa.pam-in-k-wa.* > [wa.pamikkwa.] '(if) they see you (sg.)'. On the other hand, [n] < */n/ is not subject to the change in a similar environment: e.g. *wanissin-k* > [wanissiŋ] '(if) it gets lost'. The derivation of the form [wanissiŋ] clearly involves the general processes of nasal assimilation and final velar dropping. The absolute merger of these consonants at the second stage would require the non-application or the generalization of more than one rule.

It may very well be the case that the process of absolute merger is blocked (or at least impeded) when any of the segments involved is subject to more than one rule which the other does not undergo. Another condition which favours blocking of absolute merger would be the case in which the segments involved in the merger are each subject to different phonological rules. These assumptions do not imply that merger will always be absolute if the situation requires the generalization (or non-application) of just one rule. We wish to suggest, rather, that such a situation is more likely to produce absolute merger than one in which a greater number of rules is involved. We do not wish to carry our speculations on merger any further, as the issues involved are not crucial to the discussion at this stage, and, in any case, a greater number of clear cases would have to be investigated before a principle could be firmly established. These assumptions are, however, certainly worth consideration in investigating phonological change.

In our review so far we have devoted our attention almost entirely to discussion of the consonants which undergo palatalization. We may now consider the environment in which the change takes place. Earlier the assumption was made that PA-palatalization occurred only before morpheme-initial high front vowels or the glide */y/. Notice, however, that in all the examples cited above only the Fox forms consistently show palatalization before [i] (and not before any other vowel). In Cree and Ojibwa the consonants alternate before some instances of [i] but not others, and in Menomini before some occurrences of [e] and not others. It is clear, however, that across languages the suffixed elements which seem to trigger palatalization are semantically related. For example, Fox [-i], Ojibwa [-i], Cree [-in] and Menomini [-em] all occur in forms involving second person subject and first person object (see (4) and (5) above). Similarly, in the same sets of examples, the non-palatalizing suffixes are semantically related.

It is now generally accepted that the initial vowels of those suffixes which, as indicated above, trigger palatalization are reflexes of PA */i/. The seemingly complex situation in the respective languages with regard to the palatalizing environment is a consequence of the various historical changes which characterize the development of their respective vowel systems. Various splits and mergers determine the realization of the vowels in all these Central languages except Fox, which is assumed to have preserved the PA eight-vowel system illustrated in (1). The vowels of Ojibwa, Cree and Menomini reflect at least the following changes:

In Cree and Ojibwa there is no generalization of the environment in which palatalization occurred in Proto-Algonquian to include [i] < */e/. Similarly, in Menomini [e] < */e/ does not cause palatalization. These cases are thus examples of what we have referred to as partial merger and it will later be seen that they are in accord with our previous assumptions about merger.

Given the situation as outlined above, it should therefore not be surprising to discover that there are several instances in which the occurrence of Cree and Ojibwa [i], and Menomini [e] does not cause palatalization. Some of these are already illustrated in (4), (5), (8) and (9) above. One further illustration of the results of the splits and mergers may be cited here. In the imperative, forms indicating second person singular as subject and third person as object show palatalization, but forms for second person plural as subject and third as object do not. Consider the following examples:

(13)a. Ojib: na.š-(i)
      Cree: na.s-(i) '(you sg.) fetch him (them)'
      Men: na.s-en

b. Ojib: na.n-ikk
   Cree: na.t-ihk '(you pl.) fetch him (them)'
   Men: na.n-hkon

In (13a) the suffix is reconstructed as PA */i/, but in (13b) the endings in all three forms are consistent with the development of the PA suffix */-ehko/.

3. The preceding observations seem to support the hypothesis that in Proto-Algonquian only */θ/ and */t/ were subject to palatalization and only before */i., i, y/. We may now formulate a rule which will account for the alternation of */θ/ with */š/ and of */t/ with */č/:[14]

(14) $*\begin{bmatrix} -\text{son} \\ +\text{cor} \\ -\text{dist} \end{bmatrix} \rightarrow [+\text{high}] / \underline{\quad} + \begin{bmatrix} -\text{cons} \\ +\text{high} \\ -\text{back} \end{bmatrix}$

It is important to note that, since there are apparently no intervening rules that would force one to regard the two instances of alternation as independent of each other, one is constrained, in generative phonology, to represent the palatalization of these two segments as a single process.

On the assumption that the proposed rule (14) effectively captures a single phonological process in Proto-Algonquian, let us now consider how this rule is reflected in some of the languages. (We will give no further consideration to the situation in Menomini, since the available data is not crucial to future discussion.) In Fox, it may be recalled, the alternations are as follows:

(15) $t \rightarrow č$
$n \rightarrow š$ / ___ + $\begin{Bmatrix} i \\ i. \\ y \end{Bmatrix}$
$s \rightarrow š$

Accepting these segments in their 'autonomous' phonemic shape (see Kiparsky (1968b)), the following rule may be proposed:

(16) $\quad$ C

$\begin{bmatrix} +\text{cor} \\ \langle +\text{nasal} \rangle \end{bmatrix} \rightarrow \begin{bmatrix} +\text{high} \\ \langle +\text{cont} \rangle \end{bmatrix}$ / ___ + $\begin{bmatrix} -\text{cons} \\ +\text{high} \\ -\text{back} \end{bmatrix}$

The situation in Fox differs from that in Ojibwa only in the fact that [s] rather than [ss] alternates. But if we regard Ojibwa [ss] as an underlying cluster in which the second member is *s*, then the above rule (16) is also adequate to account for palatalization in this language. One need only postulate a later rule to account for the fact that the cluster is reduced to a phonetically fortis segment. (The exact status of this rule is irrelevant to the issues involved here.) However, in Ojibwa the palatalization rule as formulated above would be considerably restricted in application, both with regard to the segments that undergo change and the environment in which the change takes place, since there are 'autonomous' *n*'s that do not alternate as well as 'autonomous' *i*'s that do not trigger palatalization (see preceding discussion).

In Cree the situation is somewhat different. There was a partial merger of */θ/ and */t/ as [t], but, as was noted above, [t] < */θ/ alternates with [s] and [t] < */t/ becomes /c/ under palatalization. Since, in the dialect of Cree which concerns us here, there seems to be no phonetic distinction between [s] and [š], we assume that the segment [s] is palatalized. This accords with the various descriptions of this segment which has been characterized somewhat imprecisely as phonetically intermediate between [s] and [š]. We thus have, in Cree, a somewhat unique situation.

(17) $\quad$ *t > t $\rightarrow$ c / ___ + $\begin{Bmatrix} i \\ y \end{Bmatrix}$ [15]
$\quad\quad$ *θ > t $\rightarrow$ s

Again, accepting the segments in their 'autonomous' phonemic shape, and rejecting any analysis which would allow for setting up underlying phonological segments which are never realized phonetically, it would appear that in Cree no single palatalization rule can account for the alternations. We obviously would have to posit two rules, and the various forms with the segment [t] would have to be specified in some way for the rule that is applicable (or inapplicable). For the present, the two rules are as follows:

(18) $\begin{bmatrix} -\text{son} \\ +\text{cor} \end{bmatrix} \rightarrow \begin{bmatrix} +\text{ant} \\ +\text{high} \\ +\text{del rel} \end{bmatrix} / \underline{} + \begin{bmatrix} -\text{cons} \\ +\text{high} \\ -\text{back} \end{bmatrix}$

(19) $\begin{bmatrix} -\text{son} \\ +\text{cor} \end{bmatrix} \rightarrow \begin{bmatrix} +\text{ant} \\ +\text{high} \\ +\text{cont} \end{bmatrix} / \underline{} + \begin{bmatrix} -\text{cons} \\ +\text{high} \\ -\text{back} \end{bmatrix}$

Rule (18) applies in all cases in which [t] changes to [c] and (19) in the other instances (where [t] changes to palatalized [s]).

If Cree palatalization must be expressed in the form of two independent rules, this would represent a very interesting development of the rule (14) proposed for Proto-Algonquian. Such a situation would suggest that a single rule of PA has split in Cree into two rules. This would be of considerable significance, since this type of phonological change has not been attested, as far as we are aware, in the history of any language. Indeed, it has been proposed that the various kinds of phonological changes can be characterized in the following terms: (a) addition of rules at the end of the grammar, (b) insertion of new rules,[16] and (c) simplification of existing rules. According to Kiparsky (1968a), simplification includes loss of parts of rules, loss of entire rules, and change in the order of rules. But rule splitting can hardly be subsumed under any of these. The fact is that the possibility of a single rule splitting is apparently rejected by generative grammar, since the theory claims that a rule reflects a single process. If, therefore, we can show a genuine case of rule splitting, then we have discovered a serious flaw in the theory, and some modification would be necessary to allow for such cases.

But before the possibility that Cree palatalization is a case of a single rule splitting can seriously be entertained, one should first examine the basis on which such a position would be taken. It would depend partly on the rejection of abstract underlying phonological representations. The issue here is whether or not all underlying segments should be overtly manifested in the phonetic output of a set of partially ordered rules. But the case for rule splitting is also dependent on the assumption that the proposed rule (14) does in fact give an accurate characterization of palatalization in Proto-Algonquian. If either of these positions is shown to be untenable, then it can be argued that the example under discussion is not necessarily a case of rule splitting. More specifically, if it can be shown that phonological theory should allow for instances of absolute neutralization in which underlying segments are not overtly manifested on the surface, then, instead of rules (18) and (19) palatalization in Cree could be formulated as a single rule, the two *t*'s being represented as different underlying segments. The Cree rule would then be considered a natural development of rule (14) for Proto-Algonquian. On the other hand if, independent of the Cree situation, it can be shown that palatalization in Proto-Algonquian should be considered as separate processes, then one may be able to accept rules (18) and (19) as possible developments of two PA palatalization rules, but this would seem to require that rule (14) be rejected. We will therefore turn next to a consideration of these two issues.

4. As we mentioned in our introductory remarks, much of the recent discussion in phonology is concerned with the issue of abstractness of phonological representation. Generative phonologists have generally taken the position that quite abstract representations of underlying segments are to be permitted. If we were to adopt this approach in a description of Ojibwa phonology, the final consonants of verb-stems such as *na.n-* (see (4) above) and *we.pin-* (6) would differ in their underlying representation. The palatalization rule would be formulated in such a way that the final segment of *we.pin-* would not meet its structural conditions. Implicit in an analysis along such lines would be a purported explanation for the fact that, on the surface, final [n] of *na.n-* alternates with [š], but final [n] of *we.pin-* does not. It would only be necessary to include a later rule, the effect of which would be the neutralization of the underlying differences between these consonants in the phonetic representation.

Such abstract solutions are challenged by Kiparsky (1968b). He argues that the resort to abstract representations leads ultimately to arbitrary and non-unique solutions, a criticism which generative phonologists have also made, with justification, of traditional morphophonemics. He proposes, therefore, that phonological theory should include an *alternation condition*, which in effect would disallow setting up underlying differences which are absolutely neutralized in the phonetic output. As an alternative to such abstract solution, Kiparsky proposes that exceptions to a rule should be recognized as such and be entered in the lexicon in what he calls their 'autonomous phonemic shape' and be marked by a rule exception feature. E.g.

(20) X [−rule n]

(In the formula *X* represents any form which meets the conditions for the input to *rule n*, but does not undergo the rule.) This proposal, if adopted, would seem to avoid arbitrary and non-unique solutions.

In formulating the rules given above we have more or less been constrained by Kiparsky's *alternation condition* in its strong form. Consequently, in a description of any of the languages, some forms would have to be marked as exceptions to palatalization. For example, in Ojibwa the stem *we.pin-* will be marked as an exception in contrast with *mi.n-* or *na.n-* both of which are sensitive to the rule. In addition, a suffix such as *-in* (see (5) and (6)) would also have to be marked as an exception to the palatalization rule, and this will be true of several suffixes in Ojibwa. In a description of Cree the situation would be complicated somewhat by the fact that there seem to be two palatalization rules, both of which are applicable to the segment [t]. Some forms would therefore be entered in the lexicon as exceptions to one palatalization rule or the other. Notice, however, that suffixes such as *-itin* and *-ihk* do not serve as environments to either palatalization rule.

But it seems to be significant that in Ojibwa the majority of exceptional suffixes (i.e. those with initial [i] that do not cause palatalization) are involved in another unrelated rule. Except for a few cases which we will discuss later, this rule does not apply to the suffixes which seem to trigger palatalization. In order to make this point clear we will now cite some Ojibwa forms based on the stems *mi.n-* 'give' and *no.ntaw-* 'hear', roughly indicating the phonetic realizations in square backets:

(21)a. ki-mi.n-i   'you give me'
      [kimi.š]
   b. ki-mi.n-in   'I give you'
      [kimi.nin]
   c. ki-mi.n-ikw   'he gives you'
      [kimi.nik]
(22)a. ki-no.ntaw-i   'you hear me'
      [kino.ntaw]
   b. ki-no.ntaw-in   'I hear you'
      [kino.nto.n]
   c. ki-no.ntaw-ikw   'he hears you'
      [kino.nta.k]

It is clear from (21) above that the suffix *-i* causes palatalization, but the suffixes *-in* and *-ikw* do not. On the other hand, examples in (22) suggest that the suffix *-i* is not involved in the process which produces [o.] in (22b) and [a.] in (22c). In fact, our own research has confirmed the findings of others that the environment of palatalization is, in a large number of clear cases, different from that of what is referred to as *coalescence*.[17] Therefore, unless one wishes to regard this fact as nothing but coincidence, it would seem that one should attempt to capture in a description of the language what is the fundamental difference between the two environments of these two rules. It also seems unlikely that this can be achieved unless one allows some degree of abstractness in phonological representation. Consequently, we part company with Kiparsky at this point, and set up the initial vowel of the suffixes which participate in the coalescence rule as *e*. Informally the rule may be formulated roughly as follows:[18]

(23) $\text{aw} + \text{e} \rightarrow \begin{cases} \text{a. } / \underline{\quad} \begin{Bmatrix} k \\ t \end{Bmatrix} \\ \text{o. } / \underline{\quad} n \end{cases}$

It is also necessary to include in the grammar the following rule which is ordered after both coalescence and palatalization, and serves to neutralize phonetically the distinction between *i* and *e*:

(24) e → [i]

It is interesting that in Fox cognates of all the forms in which we would set up an underlying [e] show such a phonetic segment. But even if one ignores the comparative evidence, we believe that evidence internal to Ojibwa could provide motivation for setting up the initial segment of suffixes which serve as the environment for coalescence as [e]. A look at the surface realization of Ojibwa vowels reveals that there are only seven, and six of these must be specified as [+tense], but corresponding to [ē.] which is [−high] and [+tense] there is no segment which must be specified as [−high] and [−tense], features which would be appropriate to [e].

However, in spite of our proposed solution to the Ojibwa palatalization and coalescence phenomena, we do not disagree entirely with Kiparsky (1968b). The cases described by him as evidence for his position are not identical with that outlined above. His cases involve the non-application of a single rule to forms which meet the input conditions of this rule, but these exceptional forms are not themselves subject to independent rules. We would propose that the *alternation condition* be relaxed in cases where phonetically identical segments undergo separate rules (A or B), and, furthermore, those cases to which rule *A* applies are just the cases to which rule *B* does not apply. Such a situation may be illustrated in the following chart, where X and X' jointly exhaust the occurrences of a segment to which either rule *A* or *B* applies:

(25)

	A	B
X	+	−
X'	−	+

What we reject, therefore, is Kiparsky's strongest position.[19]

Returning now to the Cree situation, if it can be demonstrated that the application of the above condition requires that those [t]'s that alternate with [s] be set up in underlying representation as dfferent from those [t]'s that alternate [c] (see (18) and (19) above), then one may postulate a single palatalization rule for Cree. However, we will now attempt to show that, even if one fails to provide justification for setting different underlying representations for the different [t]'s in Cree, the independence of the two palatalization rules proposed for this language can, in fact, be considered to reflect a natural (rather than weird) development of PA-palatalization, and one is not necessarily dealing with an instance of rule splitting. To show this we will provide evidence to support the claim that palatalization of */θ/ and */t/ in Proto-Algonquian were separate rules, and that rule (14) formulated above does seem to make an inappropriate generalization. This would then be one instance in which what seems to be a well-formed rule within the theory turns out to be unsubstantiated by subsequent changes. The crucial data is provided by Ojibwa.

5. In our earlier examination of Ojibwa we proposed what seems to be a procedure for determining whether suffixes with initial phonetic [i] should be set up with underlying *e* or *i*. From the examples cited (see (21) and (22) above) we suggested that, if a suffix does not trigger palatalization of (alternating) [n] but is involved in coalescence, such a suffix would be presumed to have underlying *e*. Applying this criterion to the forms cited below, we would posit the underlying form of the suffix involved as -*eka.so* Consider the examples, in which the verb stems are *mi.n-* 'give' and *wi.ntamaw-* 'tell to someone':

(26)a. [mi.nika.so]   'he is given'
   b. [wi.ntama.ka.so] 'he is told'

However, this suffix consistently causes palatalization of [t]. For example, when the Transitive Inanimate (TI)[20] stem *we.ppit-* 'hit' combines with this suffix the phonetic output is [we.ppičika.so] 'he is hit'. Notice that the same suffix may also occur with the stem *we.ppitaw-*, the Transitive Animate

(TA) counterpart of *we.ppit-*, and the coalescence rule clearly applies. The resulting form [we.ppita.ka.so] is apparently identical in meaning to [we.ppičika.so]. Indeed there are several suffixes in Ojibwa which both cause palatalization of [t] and are involved in the coalescence process. Among these is the frequently occurring suffix *-eke.* [ike.] which marks indefinite object and combines freely with TI-stems. None of the suffixes which are involved both in palatalization of [t] and in coalescence ever causes palatalization of alternating [n].

It now seems clear that rule (16) as formulated earlier for Ojibwa and Fox, cannot account for the palatalization of [t] and [n] in Ojibwa. Even if we assume that the neutralization rule (e → i) is ordered before the palatalization rule (16) we still could not account for the non-palatalization of [n] before certain suffixes. If the neutralization rule occurs after palatalization, the rule (16) as formulated would not allow for those instances of the palatalization of [t] just noted. The problem can clearly not be solved by ordering of rules. But given only the information presented so far, we can still persist in the assumption that Ojibwa palatalization is a single process, and rule (16) can be modified to allow for the fact that [t] palatalizes before [e] and [i], but [n] only before [i]. This rule may be formulated as follows:

(27) $\begin{bmatrix} +\text{cor} \\ \langle +\text{nasal} \rangle \end{bmatrix} \rightarrow \begin{bmatrix} +\text{high} \\ \langle +\text{cont} \rangle \end{bmatrix} / \underline{} \begin{bmatrix} -\text{cons} \\ \langle +\text{high} \rangle \\ -\text{back} \end{bmatrix}$

It should be noted that the above re-formulation is possible only through the use of the 'angled parentheses' convention. Without the use of such a convention, we would have been forced to posit two palatalization rules, independent of each other, to account for the alternation of [t] and [n] in Ojibwa. Indeed, it will turn out that the generalization captured above is a spurious one, for other evidence to be presented below indicates that there are two independent palatalization rules.

Before we present the crucial data, we must first discuss briefly another rule which will figure in our analysis of the problem. This rule accounts for deletion of lax vowels and glides when these are in word-final position. Consider the following forms based on the intransitive verb-stem *kittimi* 'be lazy'. An indication of the phonetic realizations is given in square brackets:

(28)a. ni-kittimi 'I am lazy'
    [nkittim]

b. ki-kittimi 'you are lazy'
   [kkittim]
c. kittimi-w 'he is lazy'
   [kittimi]

In (28a) and (28b) stem-final [i] is never realized on the surface, but appears in (28c) when protected from dropping by the suffix -*w* which marks third person. This suffix -*w* appears in other 3rd person forms such as the plural [kittimiwak] 'they are lazy'. This phenomenon of lax vowel and glide deletion is noted by Bloomfield (1957) and several others who have worked on Ojibwa. We therefore propose the following rule to account for this process:

(29) $\begin{bmatrix} -\text{cons} \\ -\text{tense} \end{bmatrix} \rightarrow \emptyset \,/\, \underline{} \, \#\#$

(The word boundary is indicated by ## simply because it is necessary to distinguish three kinds of boundaries in Ojibwa.)

Let us now reconsider in relation to this rule, some of the Ojibwa forms cited earlier in this paper. The verb stems involved are again *mi.n-* 'give' and *na.n-* 'fetch'. Here are the examples:

(30)a. ki-mi.n-i   'you give me'
       [kimi.š]
    b. ki-mi.n-i-min 'you give us'
       [kimi.šimi]
(31)a. ki-na.n-i   'you fetch me'
       [kina.š]
    b. ki-na.n-i-min 'you fetch us'
       [kina.šimi]

Notice that the phonetic realization of the forms (30a) and (31a) show quite clearly that the suffix -*i* has been deleted. But the deletion of this vowel must occur after the palatalization of final [n]. If the deletion rule (29) occurred before palatalization, then the environment for palatalization would be lost. Hence the ordering of the two rules is crucial here.

Consider now some participial forms of Ojibwa based on the stem *nipa.-* 'sleep' cited earlier under (2), and, in addition, some forms based on the stem *kittimi-*. Only approximate phonetic realizations of these forms will be given, since the underlying representations will be the subject of further discussion. The forms are:

(32)a. ne.pa.t   'he who is asleep'
    b. ne.pa.čik 'they who are asleep'

(33) a. ke.ttimit 'he who is lazy'
     b. ke.ttimičik 'they who are lazy'

(We will not be concerned with the mutation of the initial vowel in these forms, a phenomenon referred to in various descriptions as *initial change*.)

It is obvious that, in addition to the two stems involved here, one of the other morphemes present is *-t*, a suffix that consistently serves to mark 3rd person in the indicative mode of the conjunct order. We have mentioned this suffix before under (2). That this suffix is a general 3rd person marker, rather than a marker for singular only, is also well established. We note that it occurs after the suffix which marks plurality in the conjunct indicative form *nipa.-wa.-t* [nipa.wa.t] '(if) they are asleep'. The problem, then, is to account for the palatalization of this segment *-t* in forms (32b) and (33b).

It may be recalled that [t] was shown to be subject to palatalization before underlying [e] and [i], but we have found no evidence in the language for a suffix with initial [i] or [e] which marks plurality of 3rd person. There is, however, a suffix *-ak* which marks plurality of (syntactically) animate nouns, e.g. *ota.pa.n* 'a car', *ota.panak* 'cars'. This suffix also occurs frequently in verb forms of the independent order, one of which, cited above, was *kittimiwak* 'they are lazy'. Assuming then that the underlying representations of forms (32b) and (33b) are respectively *nipa.-t-ak* and *kittimi-t-ak*, we could speculate on what triggers palatalization of the [t]. One possible position could be that the vowel of the plural suffix changes to a front vowel in this environment. However, we can find no independent motivation for such a rule in Ojibwa, nor as far as we are aware, is there any such alternation in any of the related languages.

An alternative explanation, now offered, seems more plausible. We propose that there is present in the forms under discussion an underlying front vowel which we represent as [i] on the basis of its phonetic realization (Recall that [e] would also cause palatalization of [t].) This vowel seems to mark participial forms.[21] It is attested not only in the plural participial forms of Animate Intransitive (AI) verbs such as those cited above, but also in participial forms of other kinds of verbs. The vowel appears on the surface whenever there is a following suffix. The following suffix may also be *-an*, which marks obviation,[22] e.g. [ne.pa.ničin] 'the other who is asleep'.

It is worth noting that in Fox, the conjunct order shows a distinction between two modes. These two modes are described by Bloomfield (1946) as (a) the *subjunctive*, ending in [e] and used in subordinate clauses of events which have not yet occurred, e.g. *ki.šinepa.te* 'when he goes to sleep' (stem: *nepa.-*), and (b) the *indicative*, ending in [i] and used in other subordinate clauses, e.g. *pema.tesiči* 'that he lives' (stem: *pema.tesi-*). If one assumes that Fox is conservative in this respect as it seems to be in many other cases, then it seems quite likely the two modes merged in the other Central languages. The attested participial and conjunct indicative forms in Ojibwa can be the development of either of these modes. The important point, however, is that Fox shows a front vowel in just the cases in which we are interested.[23] Data from other languages also point to the existence of such a vowel. Michelson (1912) cites for Algonkin what he calls a third person singular suffix -*či*, and furthermore he records a similar suffix for the Cree spoken at Fort Totten and for Peoria.

In any event, we feel there is sufficient internal justification for setting up the underlying representation of those forms cited in (32) and (33) as outlined in (34) and (35) below:

(34)a. nipa.-t-i
  b. nipa.-t-i-ak
(35)a. kittimi-t-i
  b. kittimi-t-i-ak

From such underlying representations we can now account for the phonetic realizations given in (32) and (33) by the application of various phonological rules the operations of which are well motivated in the language. The processes involved are (a) the deletion of final lax vowels, (b) the palatalization of [t], and finally (c) the deletion of a short vowel which immediately follows another vowel. This last rule (vowel truncation) we have not discussed before but it is clearly well established. A single illustration will suffice here. When the plural suffix -*ak* occurs after a noun stem ending in a vowel, the initial vowel of this suffix is always deleted, e.g. [manito.] 'spirit, monster', [manito.k] (plural).[24]

Now when we consider the underlying forms cited in (34) and (35) in relation to the phonetic realizations illustrated in (32) and (33), the order in which the various rules must be applied becomes quite clear. The deletion of final short vowels must precede palatalization if we are to account for the fact that in the singular forms (32a) and (33a) the segment [t] does not undergo palatalization. If palatalization of [t] preceded final short vowel deletion we would expect the phonetic output to be *[ne.pa.č] and *[kittimič] respectively.

This observation raises a problem. We have previously established that the palatalization of (alternating) [n] must occur before the dropping of the final lax vowel (see examples (30) and (31) above). If therefore the palatalization of [t] and [n] is a single process as we had assumed in our reformulated rule (27) above, an impossible situation presents itself. In one instance we require the rule (27) to be ordered before final lax vowel deletion (29), and in other instances the reversal of the ordering is necessary. Clearly, then, the alternation of [t] and [n] cannot be captured in a single rule. There must be two rules involved. We therefore propose for Ojibwa the following order for those rules which are crucial to our position:

(36)(1) Coalescence (23)
    (2) *n*-palatalization
    (3) Final lax vowel/glide deletion (29)
    (4) Neutralization (e → i) (24)
    (5) *t*-palatalization

The coalescence and *n*-palatalization rules are not crucially ordered with respect to each other, nor are the neutralization and final lax vowel/glide deletion rules. In addition it is now irrelevant whether neutralization occurs before or after *t*-palatalization, but it seems historically accurate to assume that the environment of *t*-palatalization was extended to include [i] < e.

6. PA-PALATALIZATION RECONSIDERED. We may now re-examine some of our earlier hypotheses concerning palatalization in the Central Algonquian Languages. Now that we have demonstrated that in Ojibwa the palatalization of various consonants must be considered to be independent of each other, involving at least two rules, the two rules (18) and (19) proposed for Cree no longer seem to be such a strange and unique development. Jointly, then, the Cree and Ojibwa situations suggest that we erred in proposing a single rule (14) to account for the alternation of the Proto-Algonquian consonants */θ/ and */t/, for, unless we wish to assume that a single rule can possibly split, we must recognize the independence of the two processes for Proto-Algonquian as well.

However, it should be noticed that none of our observations so far has any direct bearing on Fox. The palatalization rule (16) which we had previously assumed to be appropriate both to the Fox and Ojibwa situations now seems to be applicable only to Fox. We are forced to treat palatalization in terms of two rules in the Cree and Ojibwa situations, but the motivations for doing so are closely related to certain historical changes peculiar to each language. In the case of Cree, the important development seems to be the merger of PA */θ/ and */t/ as phonetic [t]. In Ojibwa, the crucial facts seem to involve the extension of the environment of *t*-palatalization to occurrences of [e], and the development of final short vowel/glide deletion rule. In Fox, on the other hand, [t] does not palatalize before [e] and, as far as we are aware, the final short vowel is preserved in all the forms cognate with those which turn out to be crucial in Ojibwa. Fox, therefore, apparently does not provide internal motivation for setting up two palatalization rules. However, if we regard rule (16) as well-formed and appropriate to the Fox situation, we may assume that two PA-rules have merged in this language. At least this does not appear to be as unlikely an occurrence as rule splitting. But we should observe that palatalization is represented in rule (16) as a single process only by resorting to the use of the 'angled parentheses' convention. One should bear in mind that the use of this device leads to an apparent spurious generalization in the case of Ojibwa palatalization. As long as we allow the possibility of rules merging as a historical process, the Fox situation admittedly does not represent a case against the 'angled parentheses' notational convention. However, ultimately this device may have to be constrained in some ways.

One further issue concerns us here. It is noticeable that, given the Proto-Algonquian situation with regard to palatalization, one is constrained by the theory of generative phonology to formulate a single rule to account for the alternations of */θ/ and */t/. Recall that the evidence supporting the independence of the alternation of [t] from the alternation of other segments can be correlated with various attested historical changes. Unlike the Ojibwa situation we have no evidence for a PA-rule which could possibly be considered to have separated *θ-palatalization from *t-palatalization. (N.B. that the crucial rule in Ojibwa involves the dropping of a final short vowel – a change that post-dates the proto-language.) Here, then, is a potential situation in which the theory constrains one to a position which tends to contradict a fundamental claim of the theory itself. If one posits a single PA-palatalization rule, then one must allow for rule splitting, and this contradicts the notion inherent in the theory that a rule (not a schema) is an indivisible unit. Notice we said a 'potential situation', for in dealing with the undocumented history of a language one can never be absolutely certain of the facts.

7. CONCLUSION. In reviewing our discussion, it seems quite likely that we have succeeded in raising more questions than we have answered. However, we believe that we have succeeded in showing why in Proto-Algonquian the palatalization of */θ/ and */t/ ought to be regarded as independent processes. In addition, we have questioned the validity of the strong form

of the *alternation condition* proposed by Kiparsky (1968b), and have proposed instead a circumstance under which the *alternation condition* should be relaxed. Finally we have drawn attention to a potential situation in which the constraints on rule formulation could result in making false claims and contradictions. Many of the issues raised, both in relation to Algonquian linguistics and to phonological theory, must await further investigation.

NOTES

* This paper is a slightly revised version of one that appeared in *The Odawa Language Project First Report*, Anthropological Series 9, Department of Anthropology, University of Toronto (1971). The revisions are restricted to minor clarifications of some points and to a few references to works that have appeared since then.
[1] Sources of data for the languages referred to here and elsewhere are as follows: *Ojibwa* – Baraga (1878), Bloomfield (1957), Rogers (1963), Odawa Language Project; *Cree* – Lacombe (1874), Ellis (1962); *Menomini* – Bloomfield (1962); *Potawatomi* – Hockett (1948); *Fox* – Bloomfield (1946), Michelson (1912, 1913 and 1914).
The above are the principal sources, but information has also been obtained from other sources mentioned in the bibliography.
[2] Odawa (Ottawa in much of the literature) is remarkably similar to the Walpole Island dialect of Ojibwa described in Bloomfield (1957). However, the citations given for Ojibwa are largely from field notes on the Odawa dialect.
[3] The transcription referred to is that used in Bloomfield (1957). A single symbol represents a lenis consonant. A sequence of two identical symbols represents a phonetically fortis consonant, but it can be argued that these are really underlying clusters. We use slant lines (/ /) only when citing reconstructions of the proto-language.
[4] E.g. Kiparsky (1968b), Hyman (1970).
[5] The term is taken from Kiparsky (1968b).
[6] Bloomfield (1946) reconstructs the simple consonants */p, t, č, k, θ, s, š, l, m, n, h/. Other segments such as /ʔ, x, ç/ were reconstructed only in consonant clusters. Siebert (1967b) argues that the segment which Bloomfield reconstructed as */ç/ may actually be considered */s/.
[7] Verb forms of the conjunct order occur in subordinate clauses. The terms are in accordance with Michelson, Bloomfield and other Algonquianists.
[8] The source for Delaware is Goddard (1969).
[9] Other dialects of Cree show [r], [y] or [n].
[10] Cf. Bloomfield (1946:87).
[11] If one assumes that the final [t] of *st* changes to *s*, then the resulting sequence *ss* would normally be realized as *s* in Cree. Cree shows no phonetic contrast between [s] and [ss] (lenis vs fortis).
[12] The relevant manuscript referred to in Hanzeli (1969) is Du Jaunay's French-Ottawa dictionary, available on microfilm from the library of McGill University.
[13] In a recent paper (Piggott 1973) this process of dissimilation is discussed in some detail. According to the analysis proposed there, the first of the two segments became [h], so that the underlying form *wa.pam-in-k-wa.* first became *wa.pam-ih-k-wa.*, and subsequently [wa.pamikkwa.].
[14] In formulating this and all subsequent rules, we have followed suggestions in Chomsky and Halle (1968). Rules are therefore linked to the relevant conventions. One of these (not mentioned in Chomsky and Halle), assigning the correct value to the feature "distributed", appears in Harris (1969).
[15] Some dialects of Cree such as the one described by Ellis (1962) apparently distinguish [s] and [š]. The alternations in such dialects seem to be [t] → [č] and [t] → [š].

¹⁶ For a discussion of the question whether or not 'rule insertion' does occur, see King (1970, 1973).
¹⁷ Cf. Michelson (1919, 1920), and Bloomfield (1957).
¹⁸ For further discussion of the operation of this rule, see J. D. Kaye's "A Case of Local Ordering in Ojibwa".
¹⁹ Apparently it will still be necessary to mark a suffix such as *-ikk* (see example (13)) with a rule exception feature, since it neither triggers palatalization nor is involved in coalescence, e.g.

(a) mi.n-ikk   'you (pl.) give him/them'
     [mi.nikk]
(b) we.ppitaw-ikk   'you (pl.) hit him/them'
     [we.ppitawikk]

²⁰ TI-stems occur with (syntactically) inanimate objects.
²¹ For further argument in support of this position, see Kaye and Piggott (1973).
²² For further discussion of 'obviation', see Bloomfield (1957:32).
²³ One may argue that the Fox participial forms show no front vowel in the singular: e.g. *pe.ma.tesita* 'he who is asleep', *pe.ma.tesičik* 'they who are asleep'. We propose that the underlying forms are: *pe.ma.tesi-t-i-a* and *pe.ma.tesi-t-i-aki* and this would require that the following rule be operative before palatalization of [t] occurs:

$$\begin{bmatrix} V \\ -\text{tense} \end{bmatrix} \rightarrow \emptyset \Big/ \begin{matrix} \underline{} V \# \# & \text{(a)} \\ V \underline{} C & \text{(b)} \end{matrix}$$

Even if it is shown that this analysis of the Fox data is inappropriate, it would not affect our argument.
²⁴ For further discussion of this rule, see Kaye and Piggott (1973).

ON RESTRICTING THE POWER OF GLOBAL RULES IN PHONOLOGY: A CASE FROM DAKOTA

PATRICIA A. SHAW

Within the recent literature, a number of cases from various languages[1] have been adduced which are incompatible with the hypothesis that phonological derivations are strictly Markovian in character and which argue for the necessity of global rules in phonology. Rather than weakening the theory of phonology to allow global rules that are characterizeable only on a language specific basis, Kiparsky (1973) proposes that the theory may instead be strengthened through the specification of certain universal conditions under which a phonological rule may utilize information from an earlier stage of a derivation. Specifically, Kiparsky hypothesizes that:

(i) Rules cannot look back at any arbitrary stage of a derivation. They need only distinguish between derived and non-derived representations and the constraint is always that the rule applies to the former only.
(ii) Not any arbitrary rule can look back, but only a certain type of rule, namely a neutralization rule.
(iii) Application to derived forms only can be required generally of non-automatic obligatory neutralization rules. It can be made obligatory for all neutralization rules only if absolute neutralization can be eliminated completely. (Kiparsky 1973, p.25)

The present paper investigates each of these three tenets with respect to k-palatalization, a putative global rule in Dakota, and concludes that although (ii) and (iii) are basically sustained, (i) does not provide an adequate specification of which derived forms the palatalization rule may correctly apply to. In particular, it is seen that k-palatalization does not apply to all derived forms, but only to a particular subclass of derived forms, specifically those which are "actively" derived through the operation of some phonological rule rather than those which are "passively" derived through the simple juxtaposition of morphemes. Moreover, a re-examination of the Klamath data which Kisseberth (1973) argues requires analysis in terms of a global rule of Vowel Shortening reveals that Kiparsky's proposal fails in the very same way to adequately characterize the application of the Klamath global rule to only certain derived forms.

1. THE GLOBAL NATURE OF DAKOTA k-PALATALIZATION

There is a fairly widespread phenomenon in Dakota whereby velar stops palatalize after a front vowel. Very generally, this rule may be represented as:

(1) $\begin{bmatrix} k \\ k^h \\ k^? \end{bmatrix} \rightarrow \begin{bmatrix} c \\ c^h \\ c^? \end{bmatrix}^2 / \left\{ \begin{matrix} i \\ e \end{matrix} \right\} \underline{\quad} V$

This rule does not automatically apply to every input form which meets the phonetic specifications however. Various conditions must be specified in order to correctly characterize both (a) which velars will be subject to palatalization given the appropriate environment and (b) which front vowels will in fact function to trigger palatalization.

For example, with respect to conditions of type (a), it seems to be generally the case that transitive verb stems with an initial velar will undergo palatalization in the appropriate environment, whereas intransitive verb stems in the same environment will not.[3]

(2) *transitive stems*:

ma + kʰúte	'he shoots at me' (∅[4] + me + shoot at)
wa + kʰúte	'I shoot at him' (∅ + I + shoot at)
ũ + kʰúte	'we shoot at him' (∅ + we + shoot at)
wicʰá + kʰute	'he shoots at them' (∅ + them + shoot at)
ma + yá + kʰute	'you shoot at me' (me + you s. + shoot at)
ni + cʰúte	'he shoots at you' (∅ + you s. + shoot at)
cʰi + cʰúte	'I shoot at you' (I-you[5] + shoot at)
ic?í + cʰute	'he shoots at himself' (reflex. + shoot at)
wa + k?á	'I dig it' (∅ + I + dig)
na + cʰí + c?a	'I dig it for you by foot' (instr. 'by foot' + I-you + dig)
ma + kóza	'he waves at me' (∅ + me + wave at)
ũ + ní + coza	'we wave at you' (we + you s. + wave at)

intransitive stems:

ma + kʰáta	'I am warm' (I + warm)
ni + kʰáta	'you are warm' (you + warm)
na + íc?i + kʰata	'he makes himself warm by walking' (instr. 'by foot' + reflex. + warm)
ma + kíza	'I squeak'
ni + kíza	'you squeak'
na + ní + kĭza	'he makes you squeak by kicking you' (instr. 'by foot' + you + squeak)

The above data serve to illustrate the application of rule (1) to each of the three series of velar stops in Dakota, and to exemplify one type of constraint which is necessary in order to determine which k's will palatalize given the appropriate environment. Whether this process always occurs across a morpheme boundary, as it does in all the above examples, will be investigated below. The informal representation of rule (1) specifies that there be some vowel as right context, for k will never palatalize if followed by a true consonant:[6]

(3) ni + kšú = pi[7]   'they pile on you' (∅ + you + pile on + pl)
    mi + kté = pi   'they are killing mine' (∅ + mine + kill + pl)
    mi + kpázo   'I show myself' (myself + to show oneself)

In fact, it is more probable that this constraint, rather than being an integral part of the palatalization rule, is instead an ancillary condition deriving from an MSC and surface constraint against any affricate occurring as the initial member of a consonant cluster.[8]

Of particular relevance to Kiparsky's hypothesis are the conditions of type (b) alluded to above: i.e., not all i's or e's function to trigger palatalization of a following velar, even if all other conditions are appropriate. The e's in particular are problematic for underlying e's will not cause palatalization, whereas an e which derives from an a will. Specifically, there are a large number of verb stems and a small subset of enclitics in Dakota which ordinarily appear with a final -a or -$ã$, but which change to a final -e when followed either by a dependent verb stem or by a member of a particular subclass of grammatical enclitics (5). A very general representation of this "changeable -a" rule would be:

(4) $\{a, ã\} \rightarrow e \,/\, \underline{\quad} \{\text{dependent verb stems}, \Sigma \text{ subclass of enclitics}\}$

(5) Σ subclass of enclitics (from Boas and Deloria, 1941, p. 29):
    ya   'adv. ending'   ka   'kind of, rather'

šni	'not'	la	'diminutive'
sʔa	'regularly'	lakʰa	'evidently ... for ...'
sʔe	'as though'	séca	'probably'
ca	(doubtful meaning)	ʔ	'terminal of declarative S'
kĩ	'the (det.)'	ló	'male speaker'
kʔũ	'the aforesaid'	lé	'female speaker'
kʔeš	'optative'	kĩhã	'when, future'
kʔéyaš	'but'	kʔũhã	'when, past'
xca	'very'	šã́	'but, nevertheless'
		so	'conversational interrogative'

Amongst the clitics which do *not* trigger a change of terminal -*a* to -*e* are the interrogative marker *hã* and the plural marker *pi*. Consequently, one may observe alternations such as the following, according to rule (4):

(6)   ma + cʰápʰa   'he stabbed me'
      ma + cʰápʰa = hã   'did he stab me?'
      ma + cʰápʰe = šni   'he didn't stab me'
      glihã́   'he lands on his feet'
      glihã́ = hã   'did he land on his feet?'
      glihé = ya   'perpendicular (adverb)'
      ũ + kʔá = pi   'we are digging' (we + dig + pl)
      wa + kʔá   'I am digging'
      wa + kʔé ló   'I am digging' (male speaker)

Unhappily, it appears that not only the Σ subclass of enclitics which triggers rule (4), but also the class of morphemes which are themselves subject to this change, must be morphologically defined.[9] For example, Dakota verb stems are clearly divisible, on the basis of both syntatic and phonological criteria,[10] into two classes: the first is consonant final of the form $C_0^2VC_1^1+a$ where the terminal C is underlyingly a single unaspirated stop or voiceless spirant (p t c k s š x) and the terminal -*a* is epenthetic;[11] and the second is vowel final, of the form C_0^2V or $C_0^2VC_1^2V$ where the last C is any consonant or consonant cluster, and where there are no restrictions on the terminal vowel. The stems which exemplify a changeable -*a* in (6) are all of this second type. However, the subset of roots in which terminal -*a* changes to -*e* by rule (4) cuts across the verb subcategorization. Consequently we may note that there are other Class II verb stems which also happen to end in -*a* or -*ã* and are otherwise phonologically similar to those of (6), but which do *not* change their final -a to -e in the appropriate environment:

(7) šúka ma + pʰá   'the dog barks at me' (dog me + bark)
šúka ma + pʰá = šni   'the dog didn't bark at me'
wicʰá + pʰa = sʔa   'it regularly barks at them'
šúka = wã yuhá   'he has a dog' (dog a ∅ + have)
wicʰá + yuha = šni   'he does not have them'
yuhá = kʔeš   'would that he had it' (optative)
ma + cíkʔa = la   'I am very small' (I + small + dimin.)
cíkʔa = pi = la   'they are very small' (small + pl. + dimin.)
cíkʔa = ye^{12} = la   'small, pent up in a small place' (adverb)

Similarly, there are some verbal stems of Class I which do manifest a changeable -a, such as those in (8) below, and some which do not, as shown in (9):

(8) aɣúyapi wa + káɣa   'I am making bread' (bread I + make)
aɣúyapi wa + káɣe = šni   'I am not making bread'
sáka   'it is dry, hard, raw'
sáke = xca   'it is really dry'
sápa = hã   'is it black?'
sápe = šni   'it is not black'
(9) wákpa cáɣa = hã   'is the river frozen?' (river frozen = Q)
cáɣa = šni   'it is not frozen'
tʰáka   'it is large'
tʰáka = xca   'it is really large'
ápa   'it is daytime'
ápa = šni   'it is not daytime'

Consequently, the set of morphemes which undergo the changeable -a rule (4) must be morphologically defined. As mentioned previously, this set includes not only verbal stems as shown in the examples above, but also a very small subset (again morphologically defined) of enclitics, including -ya in the last example of (7) and those of (10):

(10) kta   'future'   hã   'continuative'
     xca   'very'   ka   'kind of'
     škʰa   'it is said'   séca   'probably'
     eg: sápa   'it is black'
          sápe = xca   'it is very black'
          sápe = xce ló   'it is very black (man speaking)'

With regard to the global nature of velar palatalization in Dakota, it is essential to see that palatalization occurs after an -*e* which derives from -*a* by rule (4), but it does not occur after an underlying -*e*. Consider, for example, the data below, where enclitics such as *ka* 'kind of', *kĩ* 'the', *kʔũ* 'the aforesaid' remain unpalatalized after an underlying -*e* (examples (a)) and after a terminal -*a* not subject to rule (4) (examples (b)), but palatalize after an -*e* which derives from -*a* (examples (c)):

(11) *ka*:
    a. xʔé   'it is rough'
        xʔé = ka   'it is roughish, it is kind of rough'
    b. tʰáka   'it is large'
        tʰáka = ka   'it is largish'
    c. sápa   'it is black'
        sápe = ca   'it is blackish'

kĩ:
    a. wašté   'it is good'
        wašté = kĩ   'the good one'
        pté   'buffalo'
        pté = kĩ   'the buffalo'
    b. háska   'he is tall'
        háska = kĩ   'the tall one'
    c. sápa   'it is black'
        sápe = cĩ   'the black one'

kʔũ:
    a. é   'general demonstrative: here is'
        pté = kʔũ lé é   'this here is the aforesaid buffalo'
                        (buffalo the-aforesaid this here-is)
        lé é = kʔũ   'this is he, the aforesaid one'
    b. háska = kʔũ   'the aforesaid one is tall'
    c. iyáya   'he has gone'
        iyáye = cʔũ   'the aforesaid one has gone'

It is alternations such as these which force a global analysis for velar palatalization in Dakota. That is, if the rule is given an input form with an -*e* as left context (assuming all other requisite conditions are met), then it must know whether that -*e* is underlying or is derived from -*a*. Because global rules are such a powerful device to admit into phonological theory, it is desirable to attempt, as Kiparsky (1973) has done, to place restrictions on their use. Let us investigate, therefore, specifically how the Dakota data relate to each of the tenets of Kiparsky's hypothesis regarding how global rules may be constrained. I deal with parts (ii) and (iii) first, then part (i).

2. DAKOTA k-PALATALIZATION AS A NEUTRALIZATION RULE

Kiparsky's subhypothesis (ii) claims that only a "neutralization" rule may look back to a previous stage of a derivation. One must determine, therefore, if the velar palatalization rule is the only source of c, c^h, and $c^{\prime}$ in Dakota, or if these also occur as underlying segments. Although historical evidence suggests that there were no underlying palatal affricates in Proto-Siouan, synchronically one must posit an underlying series c, c^h, $c^{\prime}$ in Dakota. There are three types of data which argue for this. First, there are stems such as:

(12)a. wăca   'once'
        t^hăc^{h}ą́   'body'
        nacá   'chief of war party'

which invariably have an internal c or c^h in a non-palatalizing environment.[13] Secondly, there are stems which invariably have an affricate in initial position, as do the forms in (12b):

(12)b.
c^hap^{h}á	'to stab'	cík$^{\prime}$a	'small'
c^hą́	'wood'	cóna = la	'few + dimin.'
c^héya	'kettle'	céka	'to stagger'
c^hĭ	'to want'		
c^ho	'flesh'	ũ / c$^{\prime}$ónica	'to be prevented, penned up'
c^huwí	'torso'		

Thirdly, c occurs morpheme-internally as the second element of a consonant cluster, as in (12c):

(12)c. kca   'to hang loose (like hair)'
        xca   'indeed, very (adv.)'
        pcelyé = la   'briefly, for a little time' (Teton, from Riggs 1890)
        scepá́ + ku   'woman's sister-in-law + kin suffix' (Riggs 1890)
        šcíli   'the Pawnees, as called by the Teton' (Riggs 1890)

Although the distribution of k as the second element of a consonant cluster does not overlap entirely with that of c, both occur after s and $š$ in non-alternating forms, thus further arguing for the necessity of an underlying c.[14] On the basis of these three types of data, it is nesessary to postulate an underlying affricate series synchronically.

Given a rule of the form:

$$A \rightarrow B \ / \ C \_\_\_ D$$

it is a neutralization rule if there exists input of the form CBD. Thus, for the k-palatalization rule to be neutralizing, there must be input to the rule of the form *icV*, *ecV*, *ic^{h}V*, etc. Dakota indeed has numerous cases of an underlying affricate in such an environment, both morpheme-internally, as in (12d), and across a morpheme boundary as in (12e):

(12) d. wic^{h}a   'man, person'
      seca   'to be dry'
   e. ni + c^{h}apa 'he stabs you'
      ni + ceka   'you are staggering'

It follows that k-palatalization is therefore a neutralization rule and thus conforms to the second tenet of Kiparsky's hypothesis.

3. Derived input to k-palatalization

Having established that k-palatalization is neutralizing and noting that it is quite definitely non-automatic, it remains to determine whether it ever applies to non-derived forms or if instead it is consistent with Kiparsky's claim (part iii) that it may apply to derived forms only. Kiparsky defines a *derived* input to a phonological rule as an input which is created either (a) by juxtaposing morphemes, for example through derivation, inflection, compounding, etc., or (b) by applying a phonological rule, this latter giving either a derived context or a derived segment which itself will undergo further change. Therefore, the question is whether k-palatalization ever applies morpheme-internally where no part of the structural description of the rule is derived. Given the above arguments for underlying palatals, then there appear to be no cases where this kind of morpheme-internal application is necessary or justifiable. For example, given a monomorphemic form such as *wic^{h}á* 'man, person' the *c^h* is indeed in an environment appropriate to the palatalization rule, but considering that it never alternates with a *k^h* and that there are other, independent arguments for underlying *c^h*, it is not defensible to postulate an underlying form **wik^{h}a*, thereby extending the range of application of k-palatalization to non-derived forms.

There is a second class of stems, however, which show an alternation between *c* and *k*, and which initially might appear to require the palatalization rule to apply morpheme internally. These are reduplicated forms such as:

(13) t^{h}éca   t^{h}ekt^{h}éca   'to be new'
     šíca   šikšíca   'to be bad'

These forms (additional data in (14) below) all belong to the Class I type of verb stem defined above: that is, stems whose underlying structure is consonant final and which take an epenthetic stem-formative -*a* when functioning either as a verbal or derived nominal stem. On the basis of the *c* ~ *k* alternation in (13), one might postulate an underlying *k* which when reduplicated is prevented from palatalizing because of a following consonant, but when immediately followed by a vowel (in this case the epenthetic -*a*) appears in palatalized form. There are other forms, however, where the final consonant of these same stems shows a third alternation. Specifically, in adverbs which do not have the stem-formative -*a* and which, in some cases, may take an adverbial suffix *ya*, the *c* ~ *k* surfaces as *l*:

(14)

verb	redup. verb	adverb + ya	adverb	
tʰéca	tʰek + tʰéca	tʰel + ya		'be new'
šéca	šek + šéca	šel + ya		'be dry and dea'
šíca	šik + šíca	šil + yá	šil	'be bad'
zíca	zik + zica	zik + zil + ya	zil	'be elastic'
—	tik + tíca	tik + til + ya	tik + til	'be soft, sticky' (redup. only)
cʰéca	cʰek + cʰeca			'be similar'

Verb stems which in unreduplicated form have a final *t* show a similar pattern of alternation between *t* ~ *k* ~ *l*:

(15)

zṹta	zũk + zṹta	zũl + yá	'be upright'
sutá	suk + súta	sul + ya	'be hard, firm'
žáta	žak + žáta	žal + ya	'be forked'

It will be noted that the stems in both (14) and (15) all have an initial consonant which is [+coronal]. When verb stems with a final *c* or *t* have an initial [-coronal] segment, the *c* or *t* only shows an alternation with *l* and not with *k*:

(16)a. *stems with final c*:

wáca	wãl + wãca		'be once'
γica	γil + γíca	γil + γíca + hã	'be awakened' (hã is another adverbial suffix)
pʰicá	pʰil + pʰíca	pʰicá + ya	'be rather good'
kʰĩca	kʰĩl + kʰĩca	kʰĩl + kʰĩca + hã	'scrape off top layer'

b. *stems with final t*:

kʰáta	kʰal + kʰáta	kʰal + yá		'be hot'
kʰíta	kʰíl + kʰíta		kʰíl	'be wiped off'
γáta	γal + γata	γal + γál + ya	yu + γál	'be branched'
pʰáta	pʰál + pʰata			'to butcher'
yúta	yúl + yuta			'to eat'
óta	ol + óta			'be many'

In contrast, verb stems which have a final k in unreduplicated form never show any alternations in reduplicated or adverbial forms:

(17)
céka	cek + céka		pa+cék	'be staggering'
zúka	zuk + zúka	ka + zúk + zuk + ya		'hang in mucuous strings'
yŭká	yŭk + yŭka	yŭk + yŭka + hã		'be in reclining position'
tʰaka			tʰak	'blocked, held'

If one hypothesized that the forms of (14), for example $cʰéca$, $cʰek + cʰeca$, have an underlying k which palatalizes when between a front vowel and any following vowel, then a form such as $céka$, $cek + céka$ of (17) could only be accounted for as exceptional. Furthermore, this hypothesis would be dependent on the palatalization rule crucially specifying that there be some vowel as right context, and as indicated above this condition is probably ancillary rather than integral to the rule. Also, it would imply that palatalization may take place after an e which is underlying rather than derived from an a, whereas it has been shown above that there are no other cases in the language where an underlying e triggers palatalization. Finally, this analysis would have considerable difficulty accounting for the appearance of an l in the adverbial forms, since all other forms with an underlying k, i.e. those of (17), retain the k in adverbs.

Clearly, then, it seems to be the case that the forms of (17) have an underlying k whereas those of (14) do not. Moreover, one cannot choose an l as the underlying final consonant for the stems of (14) and (16a), since the data of (15) and (16b) show that t neutralizes to l in the very same contexts. Therefore, one most conclude that the stems of (14) and (16a) have an underlying c and those of (15) and (16b) have an underlying t. The alternations of both t and c with k and l may be accounted for as follows.

Consider first the environments where t and c neutralize as l. The reduplicated verb forms of (16a) and (16b) show that *t* or *c* becomes *l* if the following segment is [−coronal]. Additional examples are:

(18) γíca γíl + γĭca 'to snort'
 cʰuwíta cʰuwíl + wita 'to feel cold'

The adverbial forms of (14), (15), and (16b) which have an *l* before the suffix *ya* are consistent with this proposal, eg.:

(19) šíca šil + yá 'be bad'
 kʰáta kʰal + yá 'be hot'

However, there are environments other than [-coronal] where this same process occurs. First, we may note that the unsuffixed adverbs of (14) and (16b) indicate that *t* or *c* becomes *l* / ___ #. Additional forms exemplifying this alternation are:

(20) verb adverb
 škica škil 'there being liquid squeezed out'
 skica a + gla + skil 'be compressed'
 kóta pa + kól 'be probed into'
 žũta žũl 'reach into a cavity'
 škita škil 'be grooved, ridged'
 ptuta yu + ptul 'be sprinkled'
 hĭta hĭl 'clear off a surface'
 wĭta wĭl 'be stroked over, rubbed on'

Secondly, in syntactically derived compounds, which Chambers (1974) proposes are separated by a # boundary (because the stress rule will not apply across it), it is seen that *t* surfaces as *l* even before a [+coronal] consonant:

(21) škáta škál # tukel 'playing in a way'
 zúta ka + zúl # tukel 'in an upright manner'

Similarly, if there is a / boundary (proposed by Chambers (1974) for lexical compounds which do not block the regular application of accent to the second syllable from the left; cf. footnote 7), it is again the case that *t* becomes *l*, regardless of the following [+coronal] *n* of *nakpa*:

(22) pʰeta 'fire'
 pʰel / íle = ye 'kindling' (fire + to burn + causative)
 pʰel / nákpa + kpa 'fire crackles' (fire + to crackle)

Consequently, it seems that there is a general *lateralization rule* whereby *t* or *c* goes to *l* before any boundary, i.e.:

(23) $\begin{Bmatrix} t \\ c \end{Bmatrix} \rightarrow 1 \,/ \underline{\quad} \, [-\text{segmental}]$

Functionally, such a rule reflects a surface phonetic constraint in Dakota against a stem-final *t* or *c*. In fact, it may be readily seen that the stem-formation rule conspires with (23) towards this same end. For example, given a root #šic# 'bad' or #kʰat# 'hot', then either stem-formation will apply to derive a vowel-final surface form, i.e. #šíca# or #kʰáta#, or lateralization will apply to change the final *c* or *t* to an *l*, yielding #šil# and #kʰal#.[15]

The alternations of *t* and *c* with *k* in the reduplicated forms of (14) and (15) remain to be accounted for. Additional data exhibiting this same pattern of alternation include:

(24) níca   nik + níca   'to lack'
    žíca   žik + žíca   'to sniffle'
    títã   tik + títã   'to have force exerted'

As pointed out earlier, this alternation occurs consistently before stems with an initial [+coronal] segment. Furthermore, there is at least one instance of *n* alternating with *k* in this same environment:

(25) cóna = la   cok + cóna = la   'to be few = diminuative'

Given that the proposed lateralization rule (23) applies to change underlying *c* or *t* to *l* before any boundary, then the reduplicated forms of (14), (15), (24), and (25) can be accounted for by postulating a subsequent rule of *coronal dissimilation* which will change *l* or *n*, readily characterizeable as a natural class in terms of [+sonorant, +coronal], into *k* before another [+coronal] segment. That is:

(26) $\begin{Bmatrix} l \\ n \end{Bmatrix} \rightarrow k \,/ \underline{\quad} \, + [+\text{coronal}]$

Note that it is necessary to specify a + boundary in order to account for forms like (21) and (22), eg. *pʰel / nakpa + kpa*, where the *l* does not dissimilate before coronals.

Furthermore, it may be noted that an underlying *l* as well as an *l* derived from either *t* or *c* will undergo the coronal dissimilation rule (26), for a form such as *líla* 'very' reduplicates as *líg.lila*. Intermediary stages would be *lil + lila*, then *lik + lila* by rule (26); then *k* becomes voiced by a general rule which voices any stop before a liquid or nasal resonant.

To exemplify the application of the various rules proposed above, consider the derivation of the different surface forms of *zíca* (from (14)) from the underlying verb root #zic# 'to be elastic':

(27)	verb	redup. verb	adverb	adverb redup. + ya
	#zic#	#zic + REDUP#	#zic#	#zic + REDUP + ya#
Redup:	—	zic + zic	—	zic + zic + ya
Stem-form:	zica	zic + zica	—	—
Lateral(23):	—	zil + zica	zil	zil + zil + ya
Dissim(26):	—	zik + zica	—	zik + zil + ya
output:	zica	zikzica	zil	zikzilya

In summary, then, it has been argued that the $k \sim c$ alternation in forms such as *zik + zíca* or the other stems of (14) arises not from an underlying *k* undergoing the velar palatalization process of rule (1), but rather from an underlying *c* which is first subject to lateralization according to rule (23) and then coronal dissimilation as represented by rule (26). Amongst the consonant-final verb forms with an underlying *k* (eg. those cited in (17)), the only one which superficially appears to be in a palatalizing environment is *ceka* 'to stagger', but as pointed out earlier, the *e* here is underlying rather than derived and consequently would not serve to trigger palatalization anyway. In conclusion, there seem to be no forms in Dakota which require the palatalization rule to apply morpheme-internally and consequently Kiparsky's hypothesis that the rule may apply to derived forms only is substantiated.

4. THE INADEQUACY OF DERIVED FORMS AS INPUT

The final issue is whether or not it is sufficient for the correct application of *k*-palatalization that the rule know merely whether the input form is derived, which is what Kiparsky hypothesizes in part (i). It will undoubtedly have become evident in the course of the above discussion that this information alone is inadequate for the Dakota palatalization rule. Specifically, to return to the data of (11), we saw that in cases where all other conditions for palatalization were appropriate, *k* would not palatalize after an underlying -*e*, as in:

(28) x'é = ka   'it is roughish'
      wašté = kĩ   'the good one'
      pté = kĩ   'the buffalo'
      lé é = k'ũ   'this is he, the aforesaid one'

whereas *k* would palatalize in such situations if the preceding *-e* were derived from *-a*:

(29)   sápe = ca   'it is blackish'
       sápe = cĭ   'the black one'
       iyáye = cʔũ   'the aforesaid one has gone'

According to Kiparsky's definition, the forms in (28) are indeed "derived", since they result from the concatenation of morphemes. His hypothesis predicts, falsely, that they should be subject to palatalization.

The problem, then, is how to correctly identify palatalizeable input forms without merely weakening the theory to allow unconstrained global rules. A re-examination of the various types of derived forms which serve as input to *k*-palatalization reveals an interesting dichotomy. It has been shown that velar palatalization occurs after either *i* or *e*. The globalness of the rule, however, is relevant only to cases involving a preceding *e*, and not at all to those with a preceding *i*. Now, if one considers the instances where *i* triggers palatalization, it will be noted that they exclusively involve forms which are simply juxtaposed or concatenated by processes of inflection or derivation as in (30a) or lexical compounding as in (30b). This type of derived form may be termed "passively derived", in contrast to forms which are "actively derived" through the application of some phonological rule. Thus, examples of the passively derived input to *k*-palatalization after *i* include:

(30)a. *pronoun + verb stem*:
        wa + kʰúwa   'I pursue him'
        ichí + cʰuwa = pi   'they pursue each other'
        ma + yá + kaxniya   'you choose me'
        ni + cáxniya   'he chooses you'
        instrumental (or locative) prefix + verb stem:
        kahíta   'he sweeps'
        i + cáhita   'broom' (instr. + sweep)
        kʰúwa   'he hunts'
        i + cʰúwa   'something to hunt with'
        noun + kinship suffix:
        hãká + ku   'his sister-in-law'
        tʰošká + ku   'her brother's son'
        tʰũwí + cu   'father's sister' (3rd pers. poss.)
        tʰawí + cu   'wife' (3rd pers. poss.)

b. *lexical compounds*:
tʰi / kaya → tʰicáya   'to pitch a tent' (dwelling + make)
mni / kʔa = pi → mnicʔápi   'well' (water + dig + pl.)

If this distinction is applied to cases of palatalization after *e*, however, it is immediately evident that this "part" of the rule applies only to actively derived input forms – actively derived in that they have all undergone a change from *a* to *e* by rule (4). This in fact is integral to the definition of "global". What Kiparsky's hypothesis predicts, however, is that any rule which is global (and therefore applies to actively derived inputs) will necessarily also apply in non-global or Markovian fashion to passively derived inputs. As has been shown above, this prediction does not strictly hold in Dakota, for there are no instances of palatalization applying to a form with an underlying *e* which is juxtaposed through some morphological process to a form with an underlying initial velar. The prediction does, however, hold for that "part" of the rule which involves palatalization after *i*.

The problem therefore is this. Palatalization occurs in Dakota after either *i* or *e*. The notion of a natural class allows us to group these together as [+vocalic, −back], thereby assuming that a single rule such as that represented in (1) captures a linguistically significant generalization about the palatalizing behavior of velar stops after front vowels in Dakota. However, it has been noted that one "part" of the rule is Markovian, the other "part" global. Moreover, the global part must be constrained to apply to actively derived forms only, whereas the non-global part must be allowed to apply to passively derived forms. If a rule is clearly divisible into two subparts, each having significantly different constraints, then is conflation really justified?

There is, in fact, other evidence which supports the possibility of there being two separate rules. For example, forms which palatalize by one part do not by the other. That is, the velar in morphemes such as *kĩ* 'the' or *kʔũ* 'the aforesaid' palatalizes after a derived *e* (<*a*), but not after *i*:

(31) cʰą́ icú = kte = cĩ   'the one who was about to get wood'
               (wood + get + future (kta) + the (kĩ))
      cʰą̃ icú = pi = kĩ   'the act of getting wood'
               (wood + get + pl. + the)
      sápe = cĩ   'the black one'
      tʰí = pi = kĩ   'the house' (live + pl. + the)
      tʰáwa = ke = cʔũ   'the aforesaid one who was in a way hers'
               (posses. + rather + the aforesaid)

ú = pi = kʔũ   'the aforesaid one who had come'
                (come + pl. + the aforesaid)

Furthermore, there are examples where a given morpheme sometimes serves to trigger palatalization, and other times does not:

(32) mni = kĩ   'the water'
      mni / cʔa = pi 'well' (water + dig (kʔa) + pl)

What appears to be the significant factor in these cases is the boundary over which palatalization is applying. In fact, a brief survey of the data reveals that a derived *e* will trigger palatalization across a word boundary # and the enclitic boundary = , whereas an *i* will trigger palatalization across either a morpheme boundary + or the / boundary of lexically-derived compounds and bound main verbs (cf. Chambers in this volume; also see footnote 7). Forms exemplifying this complementarity are shown in (33). The only case I have not found an example of is a morpheme boundary between a derived *e* and a velar stop; this analysis however predicts that palatalization would not occur in such a form.

(33)a. *palatalization after derived e:*
        sápa = ka → sápe = ca   'rather black'
        sápa = kĩ → sápe = cĩ   'the black one'
        iyáya = kta # kʔéyaš →
              iyáyĩ[16] = kte # cʔéyaš... 'he was going to go on,
                                             but...'
   but: tʔa / kúza → tʔe / kúza   'he pretends to be dead'
        nũwa / kapĩ → nuwe / kapĩ   'he is too lazy to swim'
        ya / kʰíya → ye / kʰíya   'he makes him go'
   b.   *palatalization after i:*
        cʰi + kʰúte → cʰi + cʰúte   'I shoot you'
        ũ + ní + koza → ũ + ní + coza   'we wave at you'
        mni / kʔá = pi → mni / cʔá = pi 'well'
   but: mní = kĩ   'the water'
        ohíti = ka   'furious + rather'
        wicʰótʰita # g.lí # kʔéyaš...   'he came back to the camp,
                                          but...'

In short, then, the palatalization rule may be schematized as follows:

(34) $\begin{bmatrix} k \\ k^h \\ k^{\mathrm{?}} \end{bmatrix} \rightarrow \begin{bmatrix} c \\ c^h \\ c^{\mathrm{?}} \end{bmatrix} / \left\{ \begin{matrix} i \{ {+ \atop /} \} \underline{} \\ e \{ {\# \atop =} \} \underline{} \end{matrix} \right\} V$

Global condition: e < a, by rule (4)

Thus, not only do the two subparts have different conditions on the type of derived forms to which each will apply, but they also have different conditions on the type of boundary over which palatalization will occur.

With respect to the grammar of Dakota, this observation raises some interesting questions. Synchronically, should the subparts be considered independent with merely coincidental overlap, or as basically unary but with different conditions on each subpart? Diachronically, can velar palatalization be viewed as a once unary process now splitting apart (i.e. in a state of mitosis[17]), or alternatively as the merging together (i.e. zygosis?) of two once distinct processes?

Regardless of which synchronic analysis ultimately proves most viable, i.e. splitting (34) into two rules or retaining it as is, it is clearly the case that the global "part" must be constrained to apply to actively derived input forms only. Moreover, this revision of Kiparsky's proposed constraint is necessary not only for the Dakota global rule of velar palatalization, but also for a global rule of vowel shortening in Klamath, as postulated in Kisseberth (1973). A brief examination of the Klamath data will substantiate this.

5. A GLOBAL RULE OF VOWEL SHORTENING IN KLAMATH

Kisseberth (1973) observes in Klamath a process of vocalization of the glides w, $\dot{w}$ to $o(:)$ and y, $\dot{y}$ to $i(:)$ if preceded by a consonant and followed by either a C or #. The length of the resultant vowel alternates between $o:$, $i:$ and o, i in certain well-defined environments; specifically, the vocalized glide will be short if there is (a) a preceding long vowel or (b) a preceding consonant cluster and either a following consonant cluster or no following vowel. This yields three-way alternations such as (cf. Kisseberth 1973 for additional data and more detailed discussion of ancillary phonological processes):

(35)   -wk   'in order to, because of, as a result of'
      gi + wk   'because of being, doing'
      gmoč + o:k   'because of being tired'
      loyk̄ + ok   'because of picking berries'
  -(o)yki:n- 'to the edge; out of fire, water'
      sg + oyki:n + a   'canoes to the edge'
      kiw + i:ki:n + a   'pokes an object out of fire, water with a sharp instrument'
      wa:m + iki:n + a 'extends out of water in a line'

verb stems:
- mbotẏ + a   'wrinkles'
- mbodi: + tk   'wrinkled'
- mbompdi + tk   'distributive wrinkled'

Since the conditions which determine the length of the vocalized glide are not revelant to the actual vocalization process, Kisseberth argues that they should therefore be formalized as separate processes. Furthermore, he argues in favour of the output of the vocalization rule being long vowels, thus requiring a Vowel Shortening rule of the form (the rule number is according to Kisseberth's article):

(K-13) $V \atop [+\text{long}] \to [-\text{long}] \,/\, \begin{Bmatrix} V \\ [+\text{long}] \; C_0 \underline{\quad} \\ C_2 \underline{\quad} \begin{Bmatrix} C_0 \# \\ C_2 \end{Bmatrix} \end{Bmatrix}$

This shortening rule, however, must be constrained to apply only to those long vowels which derive from underlying glides, for no underlying long vowels will be subject to length alternation under these conditions. Amongst the examples of basic long vowels which fail to shorten in the environments characterized by (K-13) are forms such as:

(36) sčiwa:g + o:l + a   'takes off a skirt'
      peč + łaq + wi: + s   'foot print'
      pe:w + o:l + a   'finishes bathing'
      bonw + o:t + s   'cup'
      čawl + o:t + s   'chair'

Even if one chose to analyze vocalization as yielding short vowels as output, these then being subject to a lengthening rule, the same problem remains, for Kisseberth notes numerous examples demonstrating that underlying short vowels do not lengthen in the environments where vocalized glides appear as long vowels. Kisseberth further argues that in order to account for the above facts in a manner consistent with other strongly supported assumptions about how the grammar of Klamath works (in particular, a cyclical hypothesis, cf. Kisseberth (1972) and (1973)), it is necessary to consider the vowel shortening rule as global. That is, since only long vowels which derive from underlying glides are subject to shortening whereas underlying long vowels are not, the structural description of the rule must have access to the derivational history of the input form – either to the fact that the vowel undergoing the rule is one which is derived through the operation of vocalization or, more generally, that it is one which is underlyingly a glide (as Kisseberth points out, the two alternative conditions in this case define the same set of segments).

Assuming the correctness of Kisseberth's arguments for the requisite globalness of the rule governing vowel length alternation in Klamath, one may then ask whether this vowel shortening rule is subject to Kiparsky's proposed constraints on the utilization of information from earlier stages in a derivation. Examination of the above data reveals that it is not and, in fact, fails in the very same way as Dakota k-palatalization.[18] Specifically, part (i) of Kiparsky's hypothesis postulates that a global rule need only distinguish between derived and non-derived representations, and will apply to the former only. But given Kiparsky's definition of "derived" as including those forms which simply result from the juxtaposition of morphemes, all the forms detailed in (36) above should undergo the vowel shortening rule since in each case the underlying long vowel is adjacent to a morpheme boundary and therefore in a derived context. Consider, for example, how vowel shortening, constrained only to apply to any derived form, will affect the derivation of $loyk + ok$ 'because of picking berries' and $pe:w + o:l + a$ 'finishes bathing':

(37)   #loyk̃ + wk#   'berry picking + because of'
    vocal: loyk̃ + o:k
    V-short: loyk̃ + ok   (applicable envir. is / C_2 ___ $C\#$)
         #pe:w + o:l + a#   'bathe + finish + indicative'
    vocal: —
    V-short: *pe:w + ol + a   (envir. is / $V:C_0$ ___)

In the case of $loyk + ok$, the rule of vowel shortening may interpret the input form as "derived" both in terms of $o:$ coming from underlying w and in terms of the immediately preceding morpheme boundary. In the case of *$pe:w + ol + a$, the rule will interpret the input form as derived on the basis of the preceding boundary. But, as Kisseberth points out in data such as that of (36), underlying long vowels *never* shorten, even across a morpheme boundary. Only long vowels derived from underlying glides will, given the appropriate environments of the rule (K-13).[19]

The distinction proposed in Section 4 above to account for the applicability of the global part of k-palatalization in Dakota to "actively" derived forms and its inapplicability to "passively" derived forms provides an accurate characterization of the conditions under which the global rule of vowel shortening may apply in Klamath. Specifically, the data of (36) show an underlying long vowel in a passively derived context, i.e. a context resulting simply from the combination or juxtaposition of morphemes, and such passively derived forms are not subject to vowel shortening. In the data of (35), however, the long vowel is "actively" derived from an underlying glide through the phonological process of vocalization, and such an actively derived input form will undergo vowel shortening.

6. CONCLUSION

It is argued above that at least two languages, Dakota and Klamath, each have within their phonological component a global rule which cannot be adequately characterized by Kiparsky's proposed constraint that a global rule need only distinguish between derived and non-derived input forms, and that it will apply consistently to the derived ones. Instead, it is suggested that a further distinction between actively and passively derived forms is necessary, and that at least for Dakota and Klamath an even stronger constraint on global rules may be hypothesized:

Part (i)': Rules cannot look back at any arbitrary stage of a derivation. They need only distinguish amongst input representations which are (a) actively derived through the operation of some phonological process, (b) passively derived through the simple juxtaposition of morphemes, or (c) non-derived. A global rule will be constrained to apply to actively derived representations only.

Although this revised constraint seems clearly to capture the relevant facts of Dakota and Klamath, its applicability to other proposed cases of global rules should be further investigated.

NOTES

My sincerest thanks to both Jack Chambers and Jonathan Kaye, who have contributed greatly to the development of this paper.

[1] Kisseberth (1972, 1973), Kenstowicz and Kisseberth (1970), Hill (1970).

[2] c represents a $[-\text{anterior}, +\text{coronal}]$ affricate. The aspirate and glottalized consonants are interpreted as unit segments, although cf. note 6.

[3] Unless otherwise noted, the data in this paper are taken from the Teton dialect of Dakota as recorded in Boas and Deloria (1941).

[4] Third person subject forms have no overt representation.

[5] I-you s. is collapsed into the portmanteau c^hi.

[6] This analysis assumes $k^{\textquoteright}$ and k^h to be unit segments rather than clusters. If, as has been suggested by R. Carter (personal communication), these should in fact be analyzed as clusters, then the generalization that palatalization will not occur before true consonants will still be seen to hold, neither ʔ nor h being $[+\text{consonantal}]$.

The right context then would be specified simply as [−consonantal, +segmental], rather than [−consonantal, +vocalic].

[7] A note on the marking of boundaries. Chambers has argued that in addition to the morphological + boundary and the word # boundary, it is necessary to recognize two other boundaries in order to account for the placement of accent in Dakota. Briefly, he postulates a / boundary to be present before bound main verbs (eg. *ye* / *wá* + *ši* 'I order him to go' (to go / I + order)), and in lexically formed as opposed to syntactically derived compounds (eg. *cʰap* / *kʰúwa* 'beaver hunting'). The Dakota Accent Rule (DAR) applies freely across this boundary and, as exemplified above, regularly stresses the second syllable from the left of a stem. A fourth boundary = , over which the DAR will not apply, is postulated to exist between verb forms and certain enclitics such as *pi* 'plural', *la* 'diminutive', *šni* 'negation', which never receive stress (eg. *kʔú* = *pi* 'they give'). However, there are certain of these postverbal particles which do take stress: for example, the male and female particles *ló*, *lé*; *kʔũhá* 'when, past' (some other forms are included in (5)). These therefore must be assumed to be separated from the verb by a # boundary, so that each form will receive accent, e.g.:

  wicʰá + kʔu # ló 'to them I give' (male speaker)
  blé # ló 'I go' (male)

[8] The question then arises as to whether palatalization would occur / _____ #. Although there are adverbs with a terminal *k*, I have not yet found any forms which happen also to have a palatalizing vowel as left context; for example, *stak* 'listlessly', *šwok* 'in an overflowing manner', *wo*+*xtak* 'in forcible contact', *ya*+*zók* 'be tasted, licked'. There is one form *cek* 'staggeringly' which superficially appears to resolve the issue, but as will be shown shortly, the *e* here is underlying and thus not a "palatalizing" *e*. Consequently, regardless of the possible role of a right context, the palatalization rule is blocked in this particular form because the left context is not met. The question is clearly an empirical one, but in the absence of crucial data will not be pursued further here.

[9] No one has yet proposed any phonological, syntactic, or semantic criteria by which these classes may be adequately characterized.

[10] Cf. Chambers (in this volume) and Boas and Deloria (1941).

[11] Chambers (1974) and R. Carter (personal communication).

[12] The "adverbial" *ya* is one of the suffixes which itself changes *a* to *e*.

[13] Moreover, there are at least two stems which internally retain *k* in the environment of a preceding front vowel:

  céka 'to stagger'
  cíkʔa 'small'

[14] R. Carter has proposed (personal communication) that another possible source of *c* or *cʰ* may be from t-palatalization, presumably before a front vowel. This proposal still leaves a number of the above forms unaccounted for, but it is certainly suggestive. For example, the Sioux Valley dialect of Santee has alternating forms *cistina* and *tistina* for 'little', although it is interesting that it is the older people who use the palatalized form, whereas the younger have introduced *tistina*.

[15] The exact conditions under which stem-formation will apply are still not clear to me. Moreover, it is readily apparent that the two rules of stem-formation and lateralization (23) are mutually bleeding. Regardless of its conditions of application, it seems reasonable to assume that the stem-formative *a*, being inserted epenthetically, will not be separated from the stem by a formal boundary. Consequently the present analysis assumes that stem formation is crucially ordered before lateralization, and that the latter will obligatorily apply to any remaining forms with a stem-final *t* or *c*.

[16] Changeable *a* becomes *ĩ* before *kta* 'future' or *na* 'and'.

[17] Cf. Kaye (in this volume).

[18] My thanks to Jonathan Kaye, who first brought this to my attention.

[19] It may be significant that in all the data cited by Kisseberth, the vocalized glides which undergo shortening do have an adjacent morpheme boundary. In fact, the only forms which have a vocalized glide morpheme-internally are a subset of the

distributive forms which do *not* undergo vowel shortening in the environment
C _____ C. For example, (Kisseberth, 1971b, p.24):

(i)   sda*y*n + ḱa   'little heart'   sdasd*i:*n + ḱa   'distributive'
     njo*y*lg + a   'is numb'   njonj*i:*lg + a   'distributive'
     ste*w*L + as   'tule mat'   stest*o:*L + ḱa   'distributive'

This might lead one to hypothesize that in Klamath for a long vowel to be subject to vowel shortening it must be *both* actively and passively derived. However, since there are distributive forms with a morpheme-final vocalized glide which like the above data fails to shorten in the environment C _____ C (eg. (ii) below), it seems rather that the requisite constraint is one peculiar to distributive forms, rather than to a general condition on the rule of vowel shortening.

(ii)   pni*w* + pč + a   'blows out'   pnipn*o:* + pč + a   'distributive'
      ksi*w* + lg + a   'dances'   ksiks*o:* + lg + a   'distributive'

THE ORIGIN OF BLACKFOOT GEMINATE STOPS AND NASALS

GREGORY E. THOMSON

In this paper evidence will be presented for what I believe to be the major diachronic source of geminate stops and nasals in Blackfoot.[1]

In seeking a solution to the problem of the origin of the Blackfoot geminates, the comparativist working from published reconstructed proto-Algonquian material is hampered by the shortage of relevant Blackfoot data which are clearly cognate.[2]

The present proposal is based primarily on internal reconstruction, with a small amount of comparative data put forward in support of the results. The proposal is that Blackfoot once had a syncope rule (possibly more than one rule), the operation of which resulted in the formation of various consonant clusters. Heterorganic stop clusters, as well as clusters of a stop plus a nasal, were then converted into geminate clusters by (complete) regressive assimilation.

1. THE PROBLEM

For each of its three simple oral stops /p, t, k/ and two nasals /m, n/, Blackfoot has a corresponding geminate.[3] Now there are a few instances where a Blackfoot geminate seems to correspond to a PA simple consonant. Perhaps the best example is the first person exclusive plural suffix, PA *-ena·n, Blackfoot -enna·n.[4] In the absence of conditioning factors to explain the Blackfoot geminates, such examples might suggest that such geminates were present in the parent language, but are now preserved only in Blackfoot. However, there is evidence to the contrary in that a few PA items seem to have two Blackfoot reflexes, one with a geminate, and one with a simple consonant. A case of such doublets is mentioned by Taylor (1969:241). It is an instrumental suffix -t 'by cutting edge' (PA *-eš) which shows up as -tt in at least two themes.

2. INTERNAL EVIDENCE

2.1 SNAKE-STEMS. An even better indication that the geminates constitute a Blackfoot innovation is found in a small group of stems which appear to exhibit a synchronic process of gemination. These irregular stems discussed by Taylor (1969:140-41) begin with a sequence of the form

$$\begin{bmatrix} -\text{cont(inuant)} \\ \alpha\text{nas(al)} \\ \beta\text{ant(erior)} \\ \gamma\text{cor(onal)} \end{bmatrix} V \begin{bmatrix} -\text{cont} \\ \delta\text{nas} \\ \epsilon\text{ant} \\ \zeta\text{cor} \end{bmatrix}$$

when word initial, but a sequence of the form

$$i \begin{bmatrix} -\text{cont} \\ \delta\text{nas} \\ \epsilon\text{ant} \\ \zeta\text{cor} \end{bmatrix} \begin{bmatrix} -\text{cont} \\ \delta\text{nas} \\ \epsilon\text{ant} \\ \zeta\text{cor} \end{bmatrix}$$

otherwise. All known examples of such stems (henceforth SNAKE-stems) are given in Table 1.[5]

TABLE 1. *Snake-stems*

Initial stem	Medial stem	
1. petI·ki·na·	-ittI·ki·na·	'snake'
2. ponoka	-innoka	'elk'
3. ponopa·ni	-innopa·ni	'quiver'
4. kepeta	-ippeta	'elderly'
5. ke·po	-ippo	'ten'
6. pIna·p-	-inna·p-	'east, eastward'
7. nena·	-nna·	'man'

Expected medial stem	Expected medial stem after proposed syncope
*-i-petI·ki·na·	*-iptI·ki·na
*-i-ponoka	*-ipnoka
*-i-ponopa·ni	*-ipnopa·ni
*-i-kepeta	*-ikpeta
*-i-kepo	*-ikpo
*-i-pIna·p-	*-ipna·p-
*-nena·	-nna·

The 'expected medial stems' in the table are obtained by prefixing CONNECTIVE /i/ to the corresponding initial stem.[6] Note that in the 'expected medial stems after proposed syncope' regressive assimilation in the consonant clusters would give the actual medial stems. It should be pointed out that heterorganic stop clusters and clusters of a stop and a nasal would violate present day Blackfoot phonotactic restrictions.

Although the syncope plus assimilation proposal provides a reasonable explanation for the snake-stem alternation, certainly further evidence is needed. Fortunately, there is independent evidence for each of the two proposed phonological processes.

2.2 SCRATCH-STEMS. Evidence for the earlier existence of a syncope rule is provided by another small set of stems, also discussed by Taylor (1969:72). These stems (henceforth SCRATCH-stems) take part in an alternation which, from the point of view taken here, is similar to that of the snake-stems. They are given in Table 2.[7]

TABLE 2. *Scratch-stems*

Initial stem	Medial stem	
8. kistIk-	-ikstIk-	'scratch'
9. kistonimm-	-ikstonimm-	'cut bangs'
10. ki·skem-	-ikskem-	'hunt'
11. kiskan-	-ikskan-	'in morning'
12. pist-	-ipst-	'in, into'
13. pista·xk-	-ipsta·xk-	'get tobacco'

The medial stems, of course, have connective /i/ already added.

Clearly, we are dealing with syncope in the case of these stems. Here, however, the clusters which result from the syncope do not violate Blackfoot phonotactic restrictions.

2.3 SUFFIXES IN -0. The evidence which supports the claim that complete regressive assimilation took place, at least in stop clusters, is also due to Taylor (1969:153). The relevant phenomenon is discussed by Frantz (1971:5) as well. He uses an ad hoc symbol *O* for the first segment of a small group of suffixes having an irregular allomorphy which does not motivate a general phonological explanation. Two examples are the reciprocal suffix -*OtIIyI* (PA *-*etwi*) and the subjunctive inverse theme sign -*OtI*. The property of *O* which concerns us is that it is realized as ∅ following a stem final /t/. (This is, by the way, further evidence in support of the syncope proposal.) Thus a·nit + OtI + InIke → a·nisttsi·niki ('tell' + inverse theme sign + subjunctive suffix) 'if/when he tells me/you'.

A third suffix in -O is the independent indicative inverse theme sign -*Ok* (PA *-*eke* ∼ -*ek*). Taylor (1969:153) has the following to say about this suffix (his -[oːk]-): "The suffix -[oːk]- ... has the shape ‖k‖ in the environment of transitive stems which terminate in ‖t‖. The resulting sequence ‖tk‖ appears as /kk/ at the phonemic level...." For example, ne + aꞏnit + Ok + wa → nitaꞏnikka (first person + 'tell' + inverse theme sign + third person) 'He told me.' This is exactly the type of assimilation which was proposed in connection with the snake-stems.

2.4 DISTRIBUTIONAL EVIDENCE. There is clear distributional evidence that geminates other than those of the medial snake-stems (and of the suffixes in -*O*) originated in the same manner. Out of about one hundred etymologically distinct lexical items containing a geminate stop or nasal which were tabulated in connection with research for this paper, forty four begin with a vowel followed by the geminate. Of these forty four, three begin with /e/, three with /a/, and three with /o/. The remaining thirty five begin with /i/. This situation would be quite expectable given the assumption that most geminates in this environment developed in the manner proposed for the medial snake-stems.

3. AN EXAMPLE

The argument will be summarized at this point with an example. I will trace a part of the probable history of the preverbal root *inn*- 'down, downward'.

It will be recalled that the snake-stem meaning 'east, eastward' had the initial variant *pIna·p*- (see Table 1). Now directional preverbal stems are frequently formed by adding -*ap*- to the right of directional roots. Note however, that the form for 'east, eastward' ends in /a·p/ rather than /ap/. The reason for this becomes apparent upon examination of the medial variant of the stem -*inna·p*-, which should literally mean 'downward direction', from *inn* + *ap*. The root -*inn*- has the peculiar property that the vowel which follows it is always lengthened.

We are led to conclude tentatively then that the root -*inn*- was earlier -*pIn*-. Then a syncope rule was added to Blackfoot phonology which, together with connective /i/, resulted in the root having the medial variant *-*ipn*-. Either at the same time, or at a historically later point, a rule of regressive assimilation was also added, giving the medial variant -*inn*- from underlying /pIn/. Then at some point the medial form was generalized, replacing the initial form in the lexical representation of the root. The original *pIn* would have been lost permanently, had it not been fortuitously preserved in the now irregular initial variant of a former idiom *pIna·p*-, once literally 'downward direction', now simply 'east, eastward'.

4. COMPARATIVE EVIDENCE

I have used less than twenty lexical items and other formatives, together with a fact about phoneme distribution, in an attempt to induce the major diachronic source of Blackfoot geminate stops and nasals. Comparative evidence, though as yet not abundant, clearly supports my proposal. Consider the following reconstructed PA forms and their probable Blackfoot reflexes.

Proto-Algonquian		Blackfoot
14. *ketem	'poor'	kemm-
15. *temi	'deep'	immi-
16. *kenw	'long'	inno-
17. *ki·t	'sore'	ittI- ('ache')
18. *meketekwi	'knee'	mottokis
19. *kosekw	'heavy'	Issoko
20. *kesi·	'rub, wipe, wash'	Issi-

Items 17, 19, and 20 are offered with less confidence than the rest. The /o/ of the first syllable of Blackfoot 18 is the result of analogical leveling in Blackfoot body part terms (see Voegelin 1940:407). The same is probably true of the final /s/. The /o/ preceding the /k/ is a regular reflex of PA *e through distant assimilation to postconsonantal *w. For the final /I/ of Blackfoot 17 I have no explanation at present.

If Blackfoot 19 and 20 are in truth reflexes of the PA items, then we have evidence that some geminate /s/'s originated in this way also. (Actually, the first vowel of Blackfoot 19 and 20 is probably /e/, but this would get us into problems beyond the scope of our discussion. If it is /e/, however, this would be through a later development.)

5. THE SYNCOPE RULE

In the snake-stems, scratch-stems, and comparative data, excluding items 2, 3, and 19, the vowel which appears to have undergone syncope is a front vowel. Even 2 and 3 could have had /e/ at an earlier stage, since the following syllabic nucleus could be from PA *we or *wi, and an /e/ in the first syllable would in that case have changed to /o/.

In all of cases 1 through 20 the vowel which appears to have undergone syncope was preceded by a syllable containing a front vowel.[8]

Although these two facts are very suggestive, it cannot be claimed that the syncope rule took out the second of two front vowels in successive syllables (under certain unknown conditions) until some possibly serious problems are solved. For one thing, both /o/ and /a/ presently occur before geminates.

The distribution of the geminates themselves sheds a little light on the problem of determining the actual form of the syncope rule. The approximately one hundred examples of stems with geminates which I tabulated fall into three main groups. In the largest group the geminate is preceded by a morph initial vowel; in the second largest it is morph final; and in the third significant group it follows a morph initial consonant plus vowel. Less than ten have geminates in positions other than these three, and no doubt even some of those ten contain, or once contained, formative boundaries of which I am not aware, and which would put them into one of the three main groups.

Unfortunately, it must be conceded that these facts, however tantalizing, are insufficient to enable us to come to even an approximate formulation of the syncope rule (or rules), once synchronically operative in Blackfoot, which, together with regressive assimilation, provides us with a highly plausible explanation of the origin of Blackfoot geminate stops and nasals.

NOTES

[1] I would like to express my gratefulness to Donald G. Frantz, Allan R. Taylor, and Randall Speirs for their helpful comments.

[2] Proto-Algonquian reconstructed forms used are from Michelson 1935, Bloomfield 1946, and Hockett 1957.

[3] Little will be said about geminate /s/. Many examples of this may derive synchronically from /x/ and /xs/ (see Taylor 1969:104).

[4] Blackfoot /e/ and /i/ (Taylor's ‖i‖ and ‖I‖ respectively) undergo absolute neutralization after, among other things, ki → ksi and it → ist. In noncontrastive underlying environments, /I/ is used in this paper to represent the archi-segment, as this simplifies comparative-historical discussion.

[5] Stems 1 through 5 are from Taylor 1969:140-41. Blackfoot *nena·* 'man' has the regular medial form *-ena·* by a general rule. The form *-nna·* appears for certain in only one known construction, a denominal noun theme (Taylor 1969:181). Here *-nna·* is found following the third person prefix *o-*, and hence, though noninitial, it is not a true medial stem. The theme in question we would expect to be **onena·ʔsin*. Instead it is *onna·ʔsin* 'all the menfolk'.

[6] Connective /i/ in Blackfoot is usually prefixed to stop initial stems when they occur noninitially, regardless of whether a vowel or consonant precedes (see Taylor 1969:75).

[7] Stems 8 and 9 are from Taylor 1969:72. Stem 10 is from Frantz 1971:13. The /s/ of the medial clusters is for many speakers /ss/, pointing to an earlier (and underlying?) /x/.

[8] The noninitial form of snake-stem 7 occurs following the third person prefix *o-*. This, however, is from PA *we-.

HOW MANY OBVIATIVES: SENSE AND REFERENCE IN A CREE VERB PARADIGM

H. CHRISTOPH WOLFART

In his sketch of Algonquian (1946) which has become both a methodological classic and a substantive point of departure for Algonquian studies, Leonard Bloomfield uses a series of Plains Cree examples to introduce the grammatical category of *obviation*. Within any given stretch of discourse, if there are more third persons than just one, they are assigned to distinct categories whose function is particularly obvious in cross-reference.

Among Bloomfield's Cree examples is one which is intended to illustrate a further distinction between a *nearer* and a *farther* type of obviation. While this view of Cree structure seems to have gone unchallenged until now, and has in fact been elaborated in later works on Cree and Algonquian, it is the thesis of the present discussion that a distinction of two obviative categories is not warranted by the Plains Cree evidence.

In large part this evidence derives from a close examination of *transitive animate verbs*. In the course of this analysis, markedness and the distinction of sense and reference are found to throw new light on the structure of the central verb paradigm of Cree.[1]

OBVIATION

Whenever two third persons of animate gender interact within a stretch of discourse or *contextual span*, they are distinguished semantically, syntactically, and morphologically. One of them is *in focus*, the other *peripheral*, and while focus assignment is far from being fully understood, it clearly relates to such features as order of appearance, deliberate emphasis, and of course to the preceding part of the discourse.

The morphological distinction is most clearly discernible in nouns. In Bloomfield's first example (1946:94),

(1) *okimâw iskwêwa kitotêw*
    'the chief talks to the woman,'

okimâw 'chief' shows no readily identifiable suffix whereas *iskwêwa* 'woman' has an additional *-a*. The focal form *okimâw* is called PROXIMATE and the peripheral form *iskwêwa*, OBVIATIVE.

That this is definitely not a matter of subject and object cases, and that focus and subject vary independently, is shown by sentence (2) whose focus is opposite to that of sentence (1). The focus of (2) reflects a determining context or deliberate emphasis; the flavour of the latter might be approximated (and somewhat exaggerated) by the translational paraphrase, 'it is the woman the chief talks to.'

(2) *okimâwa iskwêw kitotik*
    'the chief talks to the woman'.

By virtue of its contrasting verb form, sentence (2) has exactly the same subject and object (and the same basic translation) as sentence (1). But now the subject *okimâwa* 'chief' is obviative and peripheral, and the object *iskwêw* 'woman' is proximate and in focus.

In isolated, unmarked sentences the proximate plays three syntactic rôles. In sentence (1) it functions as subject (or *actor*) of a transitive verb and in sentence (3), of an intransitive verb:

(3) *iskwêw nikamôw*
    'the woman sings.'

It also serves as the object (or *goal*) of transitive verbs if the subject is a first or second person (i.e., if the verb is a *one-place verb* in the sense of Lyons 1968:350), e.g.,

(4) *okimâw nikitotâw*
    'I speak to the chief.'

If the subject of the transitive verb is a third person, however, (and the verb a *two-place verb*) as in sentence (1), then the object is obviative.

Apart from characterizing subject and object in sentences with transitive verbs, the proximate-obviative distinction also contributes to the expression of concord and cross-reference. In sentence (5) the obviative suffixes indicate the concord of the subordinate verb *ê-nikamoyit* 'who sings' with the obviative noun *iskwêwa* 'woman' of the main clause:

(5) *okimâw iskwêwa kitotêw ê-nikamoyit*
    'the chief talks to the woman who sings.'

In possessive constructions where the possessor is a third person, the person being possessed (e.g., *otêma* 'his horse') is obligatorily obviative, e.g.,

(6) *okimâw otêma*
     'the chief's horse.'

Only the proximate shows a distinction of number, e.g., *okimâw* 'chief,' *okimâwak* 'chiefs.' The suffix of the obviative is number-indifferent; in nouns it has the underlying form /h/.[2] While the reflex of morphophonological /h/ in word-final position is not phonologically distinctive, it blocks the apocope of a vowel which would otherwise be word-final.

ONE OR TWO OBVIATIVES?

A possessive construction where the possessor is himself already obviative, provides Bloomfield's crucial example:[3]

(7) *okimâw okosisa otêmiyiwa*
     'the chief's son's horse.'

The same configuration of obviatives may be found in another, more common syntactic context:

(8) *okimâw wâpamêw okosisa otêmiyiwa ê-sakâpêkinât*
     'the chief saw his son leading his (the son's) horse.'

In both these examples *okimâw* 'chief' is proximate. *okosisa* 'his son' and *otêmiyiwa* 'his (obviative) horse' are both obviative; in Bloomfield's words (1946:94), "a few inflectional forms distinguish a nearer and farther obviative."

While Bloomfield merely lists and labels examples (6) and (7), a more detailed and explicit analysis is presented by Hockett (1966) and Ellis (1971) who treat the NEARER and FURTHER OBVIATIVE as distinct categories which are commensurate with one another and with the proximate.

The distinction was well known to the Latin-trained grammarians of the nineteenth century who variously used the terms *accusative* and *relative* for our obviative. Lacombe, for example, who has easily been the most influential author on Cree, describes the relevant aspects of noun inflection in a straightforward manner, e.g., "Quand un nom animé est l'objet ou le régime d'un verbe, à la 3me personne, alors ce nom prend une terminaison en *a*, pour le singulier et le pluriel, c'est l'accusatif latin, v.g., . . ., *nipahêw kinosêwa*, il tue des poissons;" (1874:12; Cree transcription standardized). His discussion of obviation in verbs (which also deals with other issues that he considered related) is much more problematic but certain fundamental positions are quite clear: "Je diviserai le *relatif* en deux classes, que j'appelle le *relatif direct* et le *relatif indirect*." (1874:49) "Il y a *relatif indirect*, quand l'adjectif ou le verbe est gouverné par un nom, exprimé, ou sous entendu, déjà au relatif..." (1874:50; emphases original). In short, the distinction of two obviatives has long been taken for granted, and continues to be taken for granted, in the analysis of Cree.[4] To cite some more recent examples, it is found in the standard pedagogical work on Cree (Ellis 1962) as well as in the most extensive set of paradigms (Ellis 1971) published since Hunter and Lacombe.

Whether or not Cree actually distinguishes two obviatives, may seem a minor issue. The assumption, however, which lie behind this distinction, deserve closer scrutiny.

Obviative morphemes

The simplest reason for positing two obviatives in Cree may be seen in the suffixal difference between the two obviative nouns in examples (7) and (8). *okosisa* consists of a third person personal prefix *o-* 'his' followed by the stem *-kosis-* 'son' and the inflectional suffixes /(w)a/ 'third person' and /h/ 'obviative.' *otêmiyiwa* which includes the stem *-têm-* 'dog, horse' has the same structure except for the additional morpheme /eyi/ between the stem and the inflectional suffixes.

Rather than attributing /eyi/ to a "further obviative" morpheme (which would be an implausible analysis in any case since it precedes the third person suffix /(w)a/), we can adduce several other noun forms which show it to be part of the possessive theme, thus expressing the obviative status, not of the noun itself, but of the noun's possessor.

The *locative*, for instance, stands outside the proximate-obviative dimension and never interacts with it in any way. The locative suffix /ehk/ is added directly to the stem, e.g., *kôn-*: *kôna* 'snow,' *kônihk* 'in the snow,' or to the possessed theme, e.g., *-têm-*: *nitêm* 'my horse,' *nitêmihk* 'on my horse;' *nitêminân* 'our horse,' *nitêminânihk* 'on our horse.'

If the noun is possessed by a proximate third person, the expected obviative suffix does not occur, e.g., *-têm-*: *otêma* 'his horse' but *otêmihk* 'on his horse.'

If the possessor is an obviative third person, his status is expressed by the personal prefix and the thematic obviative suffix /eyi/; in example (9) the possessor *okosisa* 'his son' is obviative and is marked as such in cross-reference by the /eyi/ of *otêmiyihk* 'on his (obviative) horse:'

(9) *okimâw okosisa otêmiyihk*
     'on the chief's son's horse.'

As a locative, *otêmiyihk* itself takes no part in obviation. Consequently the occurrence of /eyi/ does not argue for recognizing a second, further obviative in sentences such as (7) and (8).

A similar argument arises from the inflection of *inanimate nouns* which participate in obviation covertly but have no overt obviative suffix of their own. In sentences (10) and (11) the noun *cîmân* 'canoe' is shown to be covertly obviative by the subordinate verb *ê-misâyik* 'which is big (obviative)' with which it stands in concord:

(10) *okimâw ocîmân ê-misâyik*
     'the chief's big canoe'
(11) *okimâw wâpahtam cîmân ê-misâyik*
     'the chief sees a big canoe.'

Contrast the proximate form of the subordinate verb in
(12) *niwâpahtên cîmân ê-misâk*
     'I see a big canoe.'

Now if the possessor – in (10) and (13) – or the subject – in (11) and (14) – is already obviative, the subordinate verb remains the same but the noun *cîmân* takes the suffix /eyi/ which in turn lets the inflectional suffix /(w)i/ (whose vowel is subject to apocope) appear at the surface:

(13) *okimâw okosisa ocîmâniyiw ê-misâyik*
     'the chief's son's big canoe'
(14) *okimâw okosisa wâpahtamiyiwa cîmâniyiw ê-misâyik*[5]
     'the chief's son sees a big canoe.'

As with the locative, /eyi/ is shown to be a strictly thematic morpheme which constitutes part of the possessive theme.

While the inflectional system of nouns is fairly well understood, the same degree of comprehension cannot be claimed for all parts of the verbal system. *Transitive animate verb endings containing two obviative morphemes* may well have contributed to the positing of two obviative categories.

The objects of sentences (15) and (16) are traditionally taken as instances of nearer and further obviative, respectively:

(15) okimâw wâpamêw okosisa
      'the chief sees his son'
(16) okimâw okosisa wâpamêyiwa otêmiyiwa
      'the chief's son sees his (the son's) horse.'

The ending of *wâpamêyiwa* 'he (obviative) sees (him)' consists of the theme sign /ê/, the thematic obviative morpheme /eyi/, the third person suffix /(w)a/, and the obviative suffix /h/ which does not appear in the phonological representation. The presence of two obviative morphemes is puzzling but has no bearing on the number of obviatives to be recognized.

Without appealing to the paradigmatic argument which will be made in a later section of this paper, the irrelevance of these endings can be seen from the fact that they are not restricted to transitive, two-place verbs. One example has already been given, in sentence (14), of a transitive inanimate verb with the same two morphemes. Since the inanimate object of a transitive inanimate verb does not exhibit any obviative endings, no such endings – *quâ* object markers – should be expected in the verb itself.

That the same ending is found with clearcut one-place verbs, in the animate intransitive paradigm, is perhaps more convincing evidence:

(17) okimâw okosisa nikamoyiwa
      'the chief's son sings.'

Finally, while it is unnecessary in the main arguments of this paper to discuss verbs in modes other than the *independent order*, we find in this case that the corresponding endings of the subordinate *conjunct order* contain only *one* obviative morpheme:

(18) okimâw wâpamêw okosisa kinosêwa ê-nipahâyit
      'the chief sees his son killing a fish.'

The ending of *ê-nipahâyit* 'as he (obviative) kills (him)' consists of the theme sign /â/, the thematic obviative morpheme /eyi/, and the conjunct order third person suffix /t/.

Thus individual paradigmatic endings present no evidence for positing two obviative categories.

Syntactic aspects

In many contexts it is a rhetorical advantage, whilst discussing non-Western languages, to be able to point to situations where an ambiguity typically found in an Indoeuropean language is treated unambiguously in the supposedly "primitive" language. The cross-referential function of obviation is such a case: the ambiguity of the English sentence, 'the chief's son sees his horse,' simply does not exist in Cree.[6]

(19) okimâw okosisa otêma wâpamêyiwa
 'the chief's son sees his (the chief's) horse'
(20) okimâw okosisa otêmiyiwa wâpamêyiwa
 'the chief's son sees his (own, the son's) horse.'

Unfortunately, arguments of this sort soon break down, as does the ability of Cree to distinguish third persons beyond the proximate and the obviative.

The indexing of more than two third persons is most easily accomplished by beginning a new contextual span, with new focus assignment. If more than two third persons need to occur within the same contextual span – a need which arises primarily in the context of possessive constructions – all but the proximate are simply obviative. As in most other languages, they must be kept apart by the general context of the discourse, appositions, various demonstratives, emphatic volume, word order, and similar devices.

In a somewhat contrived example such as (21), one might in principle expect the object to be either 'his father's horse' or 'his horse's father:'

(21) okimâw okosisa ohtâwîyiwa otêmiyiwa wâpamêyiwa
 'the chief's son sees his father's horse',

in practice, the issue hardly ever arises.

The same inherent ambiguity is also found in more representative sentences such as (18) where either *okosisa* 'his son' or *kinosêwa* 'fish' could in principle function as the subject of *ê-nipahâyit*. It is in sentences of this type that a distinction of two obviatives would be most likely to surface. That the ambiguity is left unresolved (e.g., by distinct suffixes) is a negative argument, to be sure, but one that cannot be ignored.

As the absence of discrete endings for nearer and further obviative might lead one to expect, there are no examples of a syntactic distinction of two obviatives. The strongest evidence from the area of syntax is clearly the observation that the claimed further obviative occurs *in possessive constructions exclusively*, and never as a member of the subject-object relationship.

Sense and reference

It is a fundamental assumption of Cree grammarians that transitive verbs generally include morphemes for both subject and object. This assumption is made more or less explicitly in attempts at morphological analysis[7] but implicitly it pervades all writing on Cree. It is displayed visually in the traditional arrangement of the transitive animate paradigm (cf. Table 1).

In examining this assumption it is essential to distinguish between the syntagmatic and paradigmatic relationships typical for syntax and morphology. Even though paradigmatic form and syntactic function coincide in most of the affixes under study, their failure to coincide in a small set of crucial cases appears to have gone unnoticed.

Both subject and object are readily recognizable in those forms which include a prefix. In *nisâkihâw* 'I love him,' for instance, the first person subject is expressed by *ni-* and the third person object by the suffix /(w)a/ whose final vowel is apocopated in word-final position but surfaces before the third person plural suffix /k/, e.g., in *nisâkihâwak* 'I love them.'

The theme sign /â/ marks the *direction* of the subject-object relationship with respect to the fixed sequential order of affixes in the verb. In the DIRECT form *nisâkihâwak* 'I love them' the first-mentioned (or leftmost) person is the subject and the last-mentioned (or rightmost), the object. In the INVERSE form *nisâkihikwak* 'they love me' this order is reversed: the theme sign /ekw/ indicates that the first-mentioned person is the object and the last-mentioned, the subject.

The direct theme sign /â/ and the interaction of a third person with a non-third person define the MIXED subset of the transitive animate paradigm. The members of this set show full agreement of morphological make-up and syntactic function.[8]

The two nouns of sentence (22) are subject and object complement, respectively, of the verb *sâkihêw*.

(22)   *okimâw sâkihêw okosisa*
       'the chief loves his son.'

At first glance there seems to exist no reason why this verb form which clearly refers to both of them, should not also be taken to contain markers for both subject and object. Morphological analysis, however, thwarts this ready parallelism with the mixed set. The ending *-êw* and its plural pendant *-êwak* have the same basic structure as the suffixes (and the suffixes only) of the affix combinations *ni—âw* 'I—him' and *ni—âwak* 'I—them': they consist of the direct theme sign /ê/ and the third person suffix /(w)a/ which may be followed by the plural suffix /k/. As the first-mentioned (leftmost) person morpheme, /(w)a/ is the subject marker, and there is no evidence of an object marker.

TABLE 1. *The traditional arrangement, reflecting syntactic function and reference.*

SUBJECT	OBJECT proximate singular -3	proximate plural -3p	nearer obviative -3'	further obviative -3''
indefinite actor, indf-	sākihāw	sākihāwak	sākihimāwa	
first singular, 1-	nisākihāw	nisākihāwak	nisākihimāwa	
second singular, 2-	kisākihāw	kisākihāwak	kisākihimāwa	
first plural exclusive, 1p-	nisākihānān	nisākihānānak	nisākihimānāna	
first plural inclusive, 21-	kisākihānaw	kisākihānawak	kisākihimānawa	
second plural, 2p-	kisākihāwāw	kisākihāwāwak	kisākihimāwāwa	
proximate singular, 3-			sākihēw	sākihimēw
proximate plural, 3p-			sākihēwak	sākihimēwak
(nearer) obviative, 3'-				sākihēyiwa

The THIRD-PERSON subset of the transitive animate paradigm consists of forms whose reference is to two third persons. The members of this set have no prefix; they use the direct theme sign /ê/ rather than /â/.

Leaving -imêw and -imêwak aside for discussion in a later section, the remaining member of the third-person set, -êyiwa, shows the theme sign /ê/ followed by the thematic obviative morpheme /eyi/; next come the third person suffix /(w)a/ and the obviative suffix /h/ which blocks the apocope of -a. The presence of two obviative morphemes in linear sequence might tempt one to interpret this form as reflecting both subject and object. However, evidence has already been presented, along with examples such as (17), to show that the same complex ending occurs with one-place verbs and that the corresponding conjunct order ending contains only one obviative morpheme. Thus, while a two-person interpretation of this form cannot be ruled out *a priori*, it is not at all plausible. More important, the third-person forms themselves certainly do not require the recognition of both subject and object markers.

Table 1 represents the "traditional" arrangement of the partial paradigm under discussion,[9] which is most readily accessible in Ellis 1962 and 1971. It is made up of a number of individual forms arranged in a strictly two-dimensional diagram whose coordinates are subject and object. The rows and columns are simply reflections of the subject and object *references* of each individual form. Thus Table 1 displays nothing more than the syntactic and referential function of isolated forms; it does not reflect the structure of the paradigm.

Bloomfield's position in this matter seems strangely contradictory. He uses (and probably even created) what is here called the "traditional arrangement" in a set of handwritten paradigm tables (generously made available to me by Hockett) which he extracted from Hunter 1875. In *Language*, on the other hand, he only cites mixed forms which contain unambiguous subject and object morphemes to illustrate that "some languages ... include both actor and goal, as Cree: *nisâkihâw* 'I love him,' *nisâkihâwak* 'I love them,' ..." Then again, he closes the list of examples by appearing to subsume the entire set of endings, appropriate or not: ".... and so on, through a large paradigm" (1933:257).

The distribution of entries in Table 1 is skewed: only forms with third person subjects have the claimed further obviative objects, and the lower part of the diagram is distorted in accordance with the principle (much too powerful in its traditional form) that the same person may not function as both subject and object. A major asymmetry results from the fact that the further obviative functions only as object and not as subject as well.

TABLE 2. *Morpheme-by-morpheme analysis.*

	OBJECT			
SUBJECT	singular -3	proximate plural -3p	obviative -3'	
MIXED				
indefinite actor, indf-		/-â-wa-k/ -dir-3-p	/-em-â-wa-h/ -obv-dir-3-obv	
first singular, 1-	/ne—â-wa/ 1—dir-3	/ne—â-wa-k/ 1—dir-3-p	/ne—em-â-wa-h/ 1—obv-dir-3-obv	
second singular, 2-	/ke—â-wa/ 2—dir-3	/ke—â-wa-k/ 2—dir-3-p	/ke—em-â-wa-h/ 2—obv-dir-3-obv	
first plural exclusive, 1p-	/ne—â-enân-a/ 1—dir-1p-3	/ne—â-enân-a-k/ 1—dir-1p-3-p	/ne—em-â-enân-a-h/ 1—obv-dir-1p-3-obv	
first plural inclusive, 21-	/ke—â-enaw-a/ 2—dir-21-3	/ke—â-enaw-a-k/ 2—dir-21-3-p	/ke—em-â-enaw-a-h/ 2—obv-dir-21-3-obv	
second plural, 2p-	/ke—â-ewâw-a/ 2—dir-2p-3	/ke—â-ewâw-a-k/ 2—dir-2p-3-p	/ke—em-â-ewâw-a-h/ 2—obv-dir-2p-3-obv	
THIRD-PERSON				obviative -3'
proximate singular, 3-		/-ê-wa/ -dir-3		/-em-ê-wa/ -obv-dir-3
plural, 3p-		/-ê-wa-k/ -dir-3-p		/-em-ê-wa-k/ -obv-dir-3-p
obviative, 3'-		/-ê-eyi-wa-h/ -dir-obv-3-obv		

In order to discover the dimensions that define the paradigm (rather than merely the coordinates of a diagrammatic table) we need to consider the paradigmatic structure of the verbal forms and their *sense* (in Frege's use of these terms; cf., for example, Lyons 1968:424ff.) in addition to their syntactic function and *reference*.

Table 2 summarizes the morphological analysis of the partial paradigm under discussion; its arrangement is identical to that of Table 3, to be discussed below. In a form of the mixed set such as *nisâkihâw* 'I love him' there is no reason to suppose that sense and reference differ any more from one another than do syntactic function and morphological structure. The members of the third-person set, on the other hand, not only have a morphological structure which differs from their syntactic function; they also exhibit a clear discrepancy of sense and reference.

Referentially, the traditional gloss of *sâkihêw* 'he loves him' is an appropriate representation of the overt or covert referents of this form. Significationally, by contrast, *sâkihêw* is much less restricted than the referential gloss indicates. It means 'he loves an animate object (*sc.* neither first nor second person)' and nothing else is specified about that object. For practical reasons, a significational gloss shows the unspecific referent in parentheses, e.g., 'he loves (him).'

Thus the members of the third-person set contain only one morphologically expressed person marker, and only one person is significationally specific. In direct forms, the subject is morphologically expressed and significationally specific while the object is left completely unspecified, e.g., *sâkihêwak* 'they love an animate object.' In inverse forms, it is the object which is morphologically expressed and significationally specified; the subject is unspecific,[10] e.g., *sâkihikwak* 'an animate subject loves them'. In all cases, the unspecified referent is of course a third person, and its gender is animate by virtue of the meaning of the paradigm as a whole.

Table 3 illustrates a re-arrangement based on paradigmatic structure instead of syntactic function and on sense rather than reference. Thus its labels and alignments are more than mere aids for easier reading; they are intended to reflect the dimensions and the structure of the paradigm itself.

Only one obviative

Individual endings, syntactic constructions, and the structure of the transitive animate verb paradigm having been examined, the evidence up to this point unambiguously argues against the distinction of two obviatives in Cree.

The question of *-imêw* and *-imêwak* remains to be discussed.

TABLE 3. *The structure of the paradigm, reflecting morphological composition and sense.*

	OBJECT		
SUBJECT	proximate singular -3	plural -3p	obviative -3'
MIXED			
indefinite actor, indf-	sākihāw '(one) loves him'	sākihāwak '(one) loves them'	sākihimāwa '(one) loves him'
first singular, 1-	nisākihāw 'I love him'	nisākihāwak 'I love them'	nisākihimāwa 'I love him'
second singular, 2-	kisākihāw 'you love him'	kisākihāwak 'you love them'	kisākihimāwa 'you love him'
first plural exclusive, 1p-	nisākihānān 'we love him'	nisākihānānak 'we love them'	nisākihimānāna 'we love him'
first plural inclusive, 21-	kisākihānaw 'we love him'	kisākihānawak 'we love them'	kisākihimānawa 'we love him'
second plural, 2p-	kisākihāwāw 'you love him'	kisākihāwāwak 'you love them'	kisākihimāwāwa 'you love him'
THIRD-PERSON			
proximate singular, 3-	sākihēw 'he loves (him)'		obviative -3'
plural, 3p-	sākihēwak 'they love (him)'		sākihimēw 'he loves him'
obviative, 3'-	sākihēyiwa 'he loves (him)'		sākihimēwak 'they love him'

MARKED AND UNMARKED CATEGORIES

The existence of two pairs of parallel endings (*-êw*: *-imêw* and their plural pendants *-êwak*: *-imêwak*) within the third-person set of the transitive animate paradigm at first glance seems to vitiate the arguments which have so far been presented against the distinction of two obviatives. Even if *sâkihêw* can be shown to express and specify only one person, its normal referential complements are a proximate subject and an obviative object. *sâkihimêw* thus would seem to have a proximate subject interacting with yet another category – the further obviative?

The function of the additional morpheme /em/ is most clearly seen in the mixed set (cf. Table 3) where it occurs in all direct forms with an obviative object, and in no others; it is not found in any inverse forms. In (23), for instance, the verb *nisâkihimâwa* 'I love him (obviative)' indicates *okosisa* 'his son (obviative)' rather than *okimâw* 'chief (proximate)' as the object:

(23) *okimâw okosisa nisâkihimâwa*
 'I love the chief's son.'

In a sense, then, the obviative is doubly marked in these forms: by /em/ and by the final suffix /h/ which blocks the apocope of *-a*. In the conjunct order, on the other hand, /em/ is the only sign of the obviative.[11]

It is tempting to speculate on the relation of the obviative /em/ of transitive animate verbs to the /em/ which forms the possessive theme in some nouns, e.g., *sîsîp* 'duck,' *nisîsîpim* 'my duck.' But since the distribution of the nominal /em/ has proven a refractory problem, an attempt to link the two would be premature.

Wide and narrow meanings

In the forms of the third-person set, /em/ provides a constraint on the range of the unexpressed and unspecified referent. Thus the forms with /em/ are restricted to occurring with obviative objects while those without /em/ have two meanings: the *wide meaning* covers the entire range of third person objects (both proximate and obviative), i.e., the object is completely unspecific. The *narrow meaning* applies only to those objects which are not specifically marked as obviative. It must be emphasized that our concern in this section is no longer with reference (in terms of which the preceding statement might be problematic) but with sense exclusively.

The textual evidence for the present analysis is not as full as we would like it to be; complex obviative constructions are fairly rare even in literary texts and a tendency towards avoiding the more uncommon forms entirely has been observed among younger speakers. The instances which have been found are compatible with our hypothesis.

The forms with /em/ occur only with nominal objects which are already possessed by an obviative and thus highly marked as obviative. Using the restricted lexicon of our earlier examples, it is easy to see that in sentence (24) the noun *okosisiyiwa* 'his (obviative) son (obviative)' is most highly marked as obviative:

(24)   *iskwêw okimâwa okosisiyiwa sâkihimêw*
       'the woman loves the chief's son'

However, the observed distribution of the /em-/-forms is not consistent in this respect. Even with highly marked obviative objects such as *okosisiyiwa*, /em/-less forms have also been found.

The factors which contribute to the selection of the wide or narrow form are only incompletely understood. For example, while the mixed set contains /em/-forms exclusively, the textual frequency of third-person /em/-forms is extremely low.[12]

If the relation of the verbal /em/ to the thematic /em/ of nouns could be established, it might be reasonable to posit a special verb theme in /em/ whose meaning would include the specification of action upon an obviative object, e.g., *sâkihim-* (obviative theme) 'to love an obviative object.'

The marked status of the obviative

The hypothesis of wide and narrow meanings for /em/-less endings may be restated in terms of an opposition:

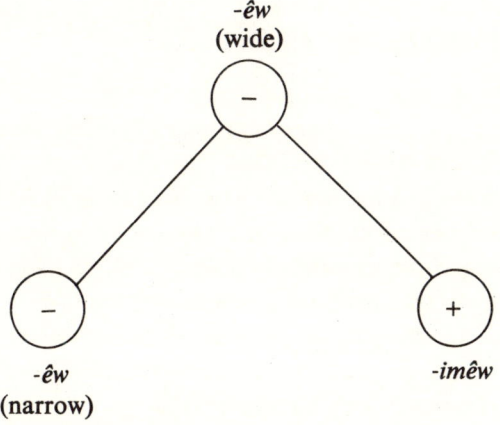

-êw as the unmarked member of the opposition is found in contexts of neutralization.

The marked status of the obviative in the opposition of proximate and obviative is established by independent evidence and thus constitutes strong support for our current hypothesis. Not only is the obviative always expressed by a morpheme – /em/, /eyi/, or /h/ – which is added to the non-obviative form. More important, it is the proximate member which occurs in contexts of neutralization. For example, the personal pronoun of the third person, *wiya* 'he', is used for both proximate and obviative referents; or, if the subject of a verb includes both a proximate and an obviative noun, the verb takes a proximate plural ending.

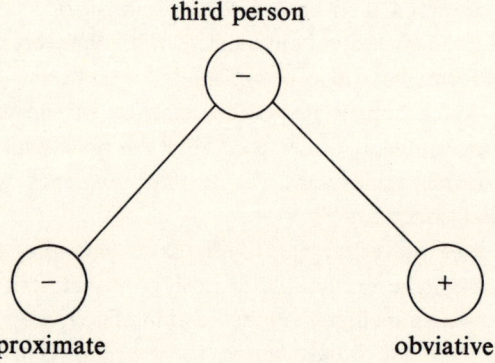

By labelling the top node of the second diagram *third person* (rather than merely *proximate*), we close the circle back to the analysis of the preceding section where the meaning of *-êw* was characterized as including an unspecified, unmarked third person object.

Accordingly, the proximate-obviative opposition exists within, rather than on a par with, the third person category.[13]

The paradigm

The troublesome question of *-imêw* and *-imêwak* appears capable of being solved within a framework which exploits the Prague concept of marked and unmarked members of an opposition. While some pieces of evidence may be short of convincing when considered by themselves, their combination seems to make possible a consistent account of the entire problem.

Only a practical problem remains: how best to portray marked and unmarked categories in a paradigmatic table.

CONCLUSION

The common-sense observation that even the most elaborate system of person indexing cannot entirely avoid referential ambiguity, casts doubt on the commonly-held assumption that Cree subjects and objects may never belong to the same person category.

Once this basic assumption is challenged, other questions arise: What is the evidence, from various areas of Cree structure, which justifies the distinction of two obviatives? If verbs of the transitive animate paradigm are syntactically transitive, does it follow that each verb form must include specific morphemes for both subject and object? And, finally, how can we account for third person endings like *-imêw* which occur only with obviative objects?

In dealing with semantic evidence primarily, the recognition of marked and unmarked members of an opposition, of wide and narrow senses, and the distinction of sense and reference prove to be useful conceptual tools. In conjunction with other arguments they show that the traditional interpretation of the Cree transitive animate verb paradigm is overly narrow in being based on syntactic and referential criteria to the exclusion of strictly morphological, i.e., *paradigmatic*, and significational considerations.

The view of the Cree transitive animate paradigm which results from our discussion, differs from the traditional one mainly in two points. First, there is only one obviative in Plains Cree which functions within the third person category. Second, the meaning of the third-person verb forms is much less restricted than their reference would indicate.

NOTES

[1] An earlier and much briefer version of this paper was presented to the Algonquian-Iroquoian Conference held at Trent University, Peterborough, Ontario, August 28-30, 1970. Many of its arguments were developed in discussions with Floyd G. Lounsbury, and of course I am also indebted to my Cree teachers in both Alberta and Manitoba.

The Cree studies on which this paper is based have over the years been supported by a variety of grants; most recent and most important has been the support of the Canada Council.

[2] Phonological representation is indicated by italics, and morphophonological representation by symbols enclosed in slashes. For further details cf. Wolfart 1973: Appendix A.

[3] The omission of Bloomfield's final *h* in *otêmiyiwah* does not affect the issue under discussion. We also deviate from his practice in a few other points (e.g., by using *subject* and *object* rather than *actor* and *goal*) where the specialist terminology of Algonquian studies might needlessly burden the non-specialist reader.

[4] A similar distinction is claimed for Ojibwa, e.g., by Piggott and Mossop 1973:52,

73, 77. An explicit second obviative is reported for Potawatomi (Hockett 1966:63) where the obviative suffix may be doubled.

[5] The transitive inanimate verb *wâpahtamiyiwa* 'he (obviative) sees (it)' includes the same suffix /eyi/ to mark the obviative subject.

[6] Lacombe and others have pointed out a parallel (in effect but of course not in means) to the Latin contrast of *suus* and *eius*, e.g.,

(19′) *filius ducis equum eius videt*
(20′) *filius ducis equum suum videt*.

[7] For instance, Gleason 1961:116-22, Pittman 1965, or Kelkar 1965. (We may note in passing that none of these attempts has been particularly successful. Gleason admits failure, Pittman's is obvious, and Kelkar's paper is too obfuscatory even to permit assessment.)

[8] The indefinite actor form *sâkihâw* 'one loves him, there is loving him' is the only member of this set (along with its plural and obviative pendants, of course) to lack a personal prefix. Since it is in all other respects perfectly parallel to the prefixial mixed forms, a zero prefix might be posited (for this form only) to satisfy the generalization that, in direct forms, the leftmost person morpheme marks the subject. (There are no inverse indefinite actor forms.)

[9] It is not necessary to consider the entire paradigm of transitive animate verbs many complexities of which do not bear on our discussion. The direct subset of the independent order paradigm is representative not only of its inverse counterpart but also of the other orders and modes; for further details cf. Wolfart 1973. One form, *-imêwak*, is not attested in the texts but is confirmed by the major missionary sources. The tables use Bloomfield's (and Lacombe's) example of the stem *sâkih-* 'love someone.'

[10] The apparent homonymy of the transitive animate inverse form *sâkihik* '(he) loves him' and the short variant of the inanimate actor form *sâkihik* '(it) loves him' (cf. Wolfart 1973:5.83) may well be only a superficial echo of a deep-seated relationship between the two forms: in both, only the object is expressed and specified, and the subject is completely open – to the extent even of gender being irrelevant. (In Ellis' James Bay paradigms, the longer variant *-ikōw*, which in Plains Cree is restricted to the inanimate actor form, is found in the inverse paradigm as well.)

[11] In Plains Cree – an interesting new model using both morphemes in sequence has emerged in the James Bay dialect described by Ellis; cf. Wolfart 1973:5.663.

[12] There is a great deal of dialect – and perhaps even temporal – variation in this matter: the early missionaries cite /em/-forms liberally but in current texts (including Bloomfield's) there is a clear preponderance of the wider, /em/-less forms. The James Bay dialect described by Ellis is the only one to have expanded the range of /em/.

[13]. An interesting discrepancy with respect to this issue exists between Hockett 1966 (which was part of a polemical exchange) and his *Course in modern linguistics*. In his general treatment of grammatical categories, the proximate *quâ* third person and the obviative are not portrayed as commensurate: "Algonquian has a *subsidiary* distinction *within* the third person, for animates, between a 'proximate' and an 'obviative' ..." (1958:234; emphasis added).

REFERENCES

Aubin, G. and Hong Bae Lee. 1968. An etymological word list of reconstructed Proto-Algonquian. MS. Brown University.
Bach, E. 1971. Questions. *Linguistic Inquiry* 2:153-66.
Bach, E. and R. Harms (eds.). 1968 *Universals in linguistic theory*. New York: Holt, Rinehart and Winston.
Baraga, Frederic. 1878. *A dictionary of the Otchipwe language, explained in English*. Montreal: Beauchemin & Valois.
Bierwisch, M. and K. Heidolph (eds.). 1970. *Progress in linguistics*. The Hague: Mouton.
Bloomfield, Leonard. 1925. On the sound-system of Central Algonquian. *Language* 1:130-56.
Bloomfield, Leonard. 1928a. A note on sound-change. *Language* 4:99-100.
Bloomfield, Leonard. 1928b. The Plains Cree language. International Congress of Americanists, *Proceedings* 22.2:427-31. Rome.
Bloomfield, Leonard. 1930. *Sacred stories of the Sweet Grass Cree*. National Museum of Canada, Bulletin 60. Ottawa.
Bloomfield, Leonard. 1933. *Language*. New York: Holt.
Bloomfield, Leonard. 1934. *Plains Cree texts*. American Ethnological Society, Publication 16. New York.
Bloomfield, Leonard. 1946. Algonquian. In H. Hoijer *et al.*, *Linguistic structures of native America*, 85-129. New York: Viking Fund Publications in Anthropology 6.
Bloomfield, Leonard. 1957. *Eastern Ojibwa*. Ann Arbor: University of Michigan Press.
Bloomfield, Leonard. 1962. *The Menomini language*. New Haven: Yale University Press.
Bloomfield, Leonard. MS. [Cree-English lexicon.] In the possession of C. F. Hockett.
Boas, Franz (ed.). 1911. *Handbook of American Indian languages*. Part I. BAE Bulletin 40. Washington, D. C.: Government Printing Office.
Boas, Franz and John R. Swanton. 1911. Siouan (Dakota). In Boas (ed.), 1911, 875-965.
Boas, Franz and Ella C. Deloria. 1932. Notes on the Dakota, Teton dialect. *IJAL* 7:97-121.
Boas, Franz and Ella C. Deloria. 1941. *Dakota grammar*. National Academy of Sciences Memoire 23. Washington.
Borkin, A. 1973a. *To be* or not *to be*. Papers from the Ninth Regional Meeting, Chicago Linguistic Society.
Borkin, A. 1973b. Some clausal remnants with *as*, and the equi vs. raising alternative. Paper read at the Annual Meeting of the Linguistic Society of America, San Diego.
Brabant, Augustus Joseph. MSa. (ca. 1910). A few remarks on the language of the Hesquiats. Archives of Roman Catholic Diocese, Victoria, B.C.
Brabant, Augustus Joseph. MSb. (ca. 1910). Hesquiat language or Nootka language of the West Coast of Vancouver Island. Archives of Roman Catholic Diocese, Victoria, B.C.

Chafe, W. L. 1970. *Meaning and structure of language*. Chicago: The University of Chicago Press.
Chappell, Edward. 1817. *Narrative of a voyage to Hudson's Bay in His Majesty's ship Rosamond*... London: J. Mawman. [Reprinted Toronto: Coles, 1970.]
Chomsky, N. 1964. *Current issues in linguistic theory*. The Hague: Mouton.
Chomsky, N. 1965. *Aspects of the theory of syntax*. Cambridge: The MIT Press.
Chomsky, N. and M. Halle. 1968. *The sound pattern of English*. New York: Harper and Row.
Cocking, Matthew. 1908. An adventurer from Hudson Bay: journal of Matthew Cocking, from York Factory to the Blackfoot country, 1772-1773 [ed. by Lawrence J. Burpee]. Royal Society of Canada, *Transactions*, series 3, **2**:89-121.
Cook, E.-D. 1971a. Vowels and tones in Sarcee. *Language* **47**:164-79.
Cook, E.-D. 1971b. Morphophonemics of two Sarcee classifiers. *IJAL* **37**:152-55.
Cook, E.-D. 1971c. Phonological constraint and syntactic rule. *Linguistic Inquiry* **2**:465-78.
Cook, E.-D. 1972. *Sarcee verb paradigms*. Mercury Series 2. National Museum of Man, Ethnology Division. Ottawa.
Cook, E.-D. 1974. Central Indian languages. MS.
Cooper, J. M. 1945. Tête-de-Boule Cree. *IJAL* **11**:36-44.
Coues, Elliott. 1897. *New light on the history of the greater northwest: the manuscript journals of Alexander Henry and of David Thompson, 1799-1814*. New York: Francis P. Harper.
Cuoq, L'Abbé. 1891, 1892. Grammaire de la langue algonquine. The Royal Society of Canada, *Transactions* **9**:85-114, **10**:41-119.
Davidson, D. and G. Harman (eds.) 1972. *Semantics of natural language*. Dordrecht: Reidel.
Davies, K. G. and A. M. Johnson (eds.) 1965. *Letters from Hudson Bay 1703-1740*. Hudson's Bay Record Society, Publication 25.
Davis, Philip W. and Ross Saunders. 1973. Lexical suffix copying in Bella Coola. *Glossa* **7**:231-52.
Deloria, Ella C. 1932. Dakota texts. *Publications of the American Ethnological Society* **14**:1-279.
Deloria, Ella C. 1954. Short Dakota texts including conversation. *IJAL* **20**:17-22.
Dingwall, W. O. (ed.). 1971. *A survey of linguistic science*. Linguistics Program, University of Maryland. College Park.
Donnellan, K. 1966. Reference and definite descriptions. *The Philosophical Review* **75**:281-304.
Dorian, Nancey C. 1973. Grammatical change in a dying dialect. *Language* **49**:413-38.
Ellis, C. Douglas. 1962. *Spoken Cree, West Coast of James Bay*. Part I. Toronto: The Anglican Church of Canada.
Ellis, C. Douglas. 1971. Cree verb paradigms. *IJAL* **37**:76-95.
Faries, Richard (ed.). 1938. *A dictionary of the Cree language* Toronto: Church of England in Canada.
Fidelholtz, James L. 1968. Micmac morphophonemics. Ph.D. dissertation. MIT.
Fidelholtz, James L. 1971. On the indeterminacy of the representation of vowel length. *Papers in Linguistics* **4**:577-94.
Fidelholtz, James L. 1973. The methodology and motivation of transformational grammar. In Shuy 1973, 82-94.
Frantz, Donald. 1968. The reciprocal in Blackfoot (and English). *Glossa* **2**:185-90.
Frantz, Donald. 1970. Toward a generative grammar of Blackfoot (with particular attention to selected stem formation processes). Ph.D. dissertation. University of Alberta.
Frantz, Donald. 1971. *Toward a generative grammar of Blackfoot*. Summer Institute of Linguistics publications in linguistics and related fields, 34. Santa Ana: Summer Institute of Linguistics.
Frantz, Donald. 1974. Blackfoot and Weggelaar's 'The Algonquian verb'. *IJAL* **40**:253-56.

REFERENCES

Gallatin, Albert. 1836. A synopsis of the Indian tribes within the United States east of the Rocky Mountains. American Antiquarian Society, *Transactions* 2:1-422.
Geary, J. A. 1941. Proto-Algonquian *çk, further examples. *Language* 17:304-10.
Gleason, Henry A., Jr. 1961. *An introduction to descriptive linguistics.* 2nd ed. New York: Holt Rinehart and Winston.
Goddard, Ives. 1967. Notes on the genetic classification of the Algonquian languages. In *Contributions to anthropology: Linguistics I (Algonquian).* National Museum of Canada Bulletin No. 214, 7-12. Ottawa.
Goddard, Ives. 1969. Delaware verbal morphology: a descriptive and comparative study. Ph.D. dissertation. Harvard University.
Golla, V. K. 1970. Hupa Grammar. Ph.D. dissertation, University of California, Berkeley.
Graham, Andrew. 1767/1967. *Andrew Graham's observations on Hudson's Bay. 1767-91.* Hudson's Bay Record Society Publication 27.
Green, Georgia. 1973. Some remarks on split controller phenomena. Papers from the Ninth Regional Meeting, Chicago Linguistic Society.
Greenberg, Joseph. 1970. Some generalizations concerning glottalic consonants, especially implosives. *IJAL* 36:123-45.
Haas (Swadesh), Mary and Morris Swadesh. 1933. A visit to the other world, a Nitinat text. *IJAL* 7:195-208.
Hall, Frank. 1970. A brief history of education in Manitoba. *Red River Valley Historian* 4:40-47.
Halle, Morris. 1959. *The sound pattern of Russian.* The Hague: Mouton.
Halle, Morris. 1973. Prolegomena to a theory of word formation. *Linguistic Inquiry* 4.1:3-16.
Hanzeli, V. E. 1969. *Missionary linguistics in New France: a study of seventeenth and eighteenth century descriptions of American Indian languages.* The Hague: Mouton.
Harmon, Daniel W. 1820. *A journal of voyages and travels in the interiour of North America....* Andover: Flagg and Gould.
Harris, James. 1969. Sound change in Spanish and the theory of markedness. *Language* 45:538-52.
Harms, R. 1973. How abstract is Nupe? *Language* 49:439-46.
Hearne, Samuel. 1795. *Journey from the Prince of Wales's fort in Hudson's Bay to the northern ocean, 1769-1772.* London: A. Strahan and T. Cadell.
Hewson, John. 1973. Review of Bonaventure Fabvre, Racines montagnaises. *IJAL* 39:191-94.
Hill, Jane. 1970. A peeking rule in Cupeño. *Linguistic Inquiry* 1:534.
Hockett, Charles F. 1948. Potawatomi 1: phonemics, morphophonemics, and morphological survey. *IJAL* 14:1-10.
Hockett, Charles F. 1956. Central Algonquian /t/ and /c/. *IJAL* 22:202-07.
Hockett, Charles F. 1957. Central Algonquian vocabulary: stems in /k-/. *IJAL* 23:247-69.
Hockett, Charles F. 1958. *A course in modern linguistics.* New York: Macmillan.
Hockett, Charles F. 1966. What Algonquian is really like. *IJAL* 32:59-73.
Hofer, E. D. 1974. Topics in Sarcee syntax. M.A. thesis, The University of Calgary.
Hoijer, H. 1963. The Athapaskan languages. In Hoijer *et al.* 1963, 1-29.
Hoijer, H. 1973. Galice noun and verb stems. *Linguistics* 104:50-73.
Hoijer, H. *et al.* 1946. *Linguistic structures of native America.* Viking Fund Publications in Anthropology 6. New York.
Hoijer, H. *et al.* 1963. *Studies in the Athapaskan languages.* University of California Publications in Linguistics, vol. 29. Berkeley and Los Angeles: the University of California Press.
Hosie, R. C. 1969. *Native trees of Canada.* 7th ed. Ottawa: Canadian Forest Service.

Howren, R. 1969. The phonology of Rae Dogrib. To appear in the *Bulletin of the National Museum of Canada.*
Howse, Joseph. 1844. *A grammar of the Cree language, with which is combined an analysis of the Chippeway dialect.* London: J. G. F. and J. Rivington.
Hunter, James. 1875. *A lecture on the grammatical construction of the Cree language.* London: Society for the Propagation of Christian Knowledge.
Hyman, Larry. 1970. How concrete is phonology? *Language* 46:58-76.
Innis, Harold Adams. 1956. *The fur trade in Canada: an introduction to Canadian economic history.* Revised ed., Toronto: University of Toronto Press.
Isham, James. 1743/1949. *James Isham's observations on Hudson's Bay, 1743, and notes and observations on a book entitled* A voyage to Hudsons Bay in the Dobbs Galley,*1749* [ed. by E. E. Rich and A. M. Johnson]. Champlain Society Publications (Hudson's Bay Company series), 12.
Jackendoff, Ray. 1972. *Semantic interpretation in generative grammar.* Cambridge: MIT Press.
Jacobs, R. and P. Rosenbaum (eds.) 1970. *Readings in English transformational grammar.* Boston: Ginn.
Jacobsen, William. 1971. Makah vowel insertion and loss. Paper presented to the VIth International Conference on Salish languages.
Jacobsen, William. 1973. The pattern of Makah pronouns. Paper read at the VIIIth International Conference on Salish Languages.
Jones, David. 1971. Odawa noun morphology, In Kaye, Piggott and Tokaichi, 1971, 39-79.
Jones, William. 1911. Algonquian (Fox). In Boas (ed.) 1911, 735-873.
Kaye, J. D. 1971. A case of local ordering in Ojibwa. In Kaye *et al.* 1971, 3-10.
Kaye, J. D. 1974. Opacity and recoverability in phonology. *Canadian Journal of Linguistics* 19:134-49.
Kaye, J. D. and G. L. Piggott. 1973. On the cyclical nature of Ojibwa T-palatalization. *Linguistic Inquiry* 4:345-62.
Kaye, J. D, G. L. Piggott and K. Tokaichi (eds.). 1971. Odawa Language Project, First Report, Anthropology series no. 9. Department of Anthropology. University of Toronto.
Kelkar, Ashok R. 1965. Participant placement in Algonquian and Georgian. *IJAL* 31:195-205.
Kelsey, Henry. 1929. *The Kelsey papers.* Ed. by A. C. Doughty and C. Martin. Ottawa: Public Archives of Canada and the Public Record Office of Northern Ireland.
Kenstowicz, M. and C. Kisseberth. 1970. Rule ordering and the assymetry hypothesis. Papers from the 6th Regional Meeting, Chicago Linguistic Society, 504-519.
Kentowicz, M. and C. Kisseberth (eds.). 1973. *Issues in phonological theory.* The Hague: Mouton.
King, R. D. 1970. Can rules be inserted in the middle of a grammar? MS.
King, R. D. 1973. Rule insertion. *Language* 49:551-78.
Kiparsky, Paul. 1968a. Linguistic universals and linguistic change. In Bach and Harms (eds.) 1968, 171-204.
Kiparsky, Paul. 1968b. How abstract is phonology? [Distributed by Indiana University Linguistic Club.]
Kiparsky, Paul. 1971. Historical linguistics. In Dingwall (ed.) 1971, 576-649.
Kiparsky, Paul. 1973. Abstractness, opacity, and global rules. [Distributed by Indiana University Linguistics Club.]
Kiparsky, Paul and Carol Kiparsky. 1970. Fact. In Bierwisch and Heidolph (eds.) 1970, 143-173.
Kisseberth, C. 1972. Cyclical rules in Klamath phonology. *Linguistic Inquiry* 3:3-34.
Kisseberth, C. 1973. On the alternation of vowel length in Klamath: a global rule. In Kenstowicz and Kisseberth (eds.) 1973,9-26.

REFERENCES

Klokeid, Terry. 1971. On the west coast (Nootka) text. Manuscripts of Edward Sapir and Alexander Thomas. Unpublished report to the National Museum of Man, Ottawa.
Klokeid, Terry. 1974. Output conditions, semantic interpretation, and Nitinaht auxiliaries. Papers for the IXth International Conference on Salish Languages, pp. 168-195. Vancouver: University of British Columbia.
Klokeid, Terry. 1975. The Nitinaht feature system: a reference paper. ERIC Clearinghouse on Language and Linguistics, Centre for Applied Linguistics, Washington, D.C.
Klokeid, Terry. 1976. Encliticization in Nitinaht. Working papers for the XIth International Conference on Salish Languages, 211-246. Seattle: University of Washington.
Krauss, M. E. 1964. Proto-Athapaskan-Eyak and the problems of Na-Dene; the phonology. *IJAL* **30**:118-31.
Lacombe, Albert. 1874. *Dictionnaire et grammaire de la langue des Cris*. Montreal: Beauchemin and Valois.
Lakoff, George. 1969. On derivational constraints. Papers from the Fifth Regional Meeting, Chicago Linguistic Society.
Lakoff, George. 1970. Global rules. *Language* **46**:627-39.
Li, F.-K. 1930. A study of Sarcee verb-stems. *IJAL* **6**:3-27.
Li, F.-K. 1933a. Chipewyan consonants. Studies presented to Ts'ai Yuan P'ei. (Supplementary volume 1, *Bulletin of the Institute of History and Philosophy*, Academia Sinica, Peiping, 429-469.)
Li, F.-K. 1933b. A list of Chipewyan stems. *IJAL* **7**:122-51.
Li, F.-K. 1946. Chipewyan. In Hoijer *et al*. 1946, 398-423.
Long, J. 1791. *Voyages and travels of an Indian interpreter and trader*. Facsimile edition reprinted (1971). Toronto: Coles Publishing Company.
Lyons, John. 1968. *Introduction to theoretical linguistics*. Cambridge: Cambridge University Press.
Mackenzie, Alexander. 1801. *Voyages from Montreal ... to the frozen and Pacific Oceans in the years 1789 and 1793 ....* London: T. Cadell and W. Davies.
Matthews, G. H. 1955. A phonemic analysis of a Dakota dialect. *IJAL* **21**:56-59.
Matthews, G. H. 1970. Some notes on the Proto-Siouan continuants. *IJAL* **36**:98-110.
McCawley, James. 1970. Where do noun phrases come from? In Jacobs and Rosenbaum (eds.) 1970, 166-83.
McCawley, James. 1972. A program for logic. In Davidson and Harmann (eds.) 1972, 498-544.
McLean, John. 1849. Notes of a twenty-five years' service in the Hudson's Bay territory. London: Richard Bentley.
Michelson, Truman. 1912. Preliminary report on the linguistic classification of Algonquian tribes. *BAE-AR* **28**:221-90b.
Michelson, Truman. 1913. Contributions to Algonquian grammar. *American Anthropologist* (n.s.) **15**:470-76.
Michelson, Truman. 1914. Algonquian linguistic miscellany. *Journal of the Washington Academy of Sciences* **4**:402-9.
Michelson, Truman. 1919. Two proto-Algonquian phonetic shifts. *Journal of the Washington Academy of Sciences* **9**:333-34.
Michelson, Truman. 1920. Two phonetic shifts occurring in many Algonquian languages. *IJAL* **1**:300-4.
Michelson, Truman. 1935. Phonetic shifts in Algonquian languages. *IJAL* **8**:132-71.
Michelson, Truman. 1939. Linguistic classification of Cree and Montagnais-Naskapi dialects. *BAE Bulletin* **123**:67-95.
National Museum of Canada. 1963. *Contributions to Anthropology, Part II*. National Museum of Canada Bulletin No. 194.
National Museum of Canada. 1967. *Contributions to Anthropology: Linguistics I*. National Museum of Canada Bulletin no. 214.

Newman, Stanley. (ca. 1935) Bella Coola grammar. Franz Boas Collection. MS. 267.
Newman, Stanley. 1947. Bella Coola I: phonology. *IJAL* **13**:129-34.
Newman, Stanley. 1969. Bella Coola paradigms. *IJAL* **35**:299-306.
Oldmixon, John. 1708. *The British Empire in America*. London: J. Nicholson. 2 vols. "The history of Hudson's Bay . . . " (last chapter vol. 1) reprinted in J. B. Tyrrell, *Documents relating to the early history of Hudson Bay*. Champlain Society Publication 18.
Partee, Barbara Hall. 1972. Opacity, coreference, and pronouns. In Davidson and Harman (eds.) 1972, 415-41.
Peranteau, P., J. Levi, and G. Phares (eds.). 1972. *The Chicago which hunt*. Chicago Linguistic Society.
Perlmutter, David. 1971. *Deep and surface structure constraints in syntax*. New York: Holt, Rinehart & Winston.
Perlmutter, David. 1972. Shadow pronouns in French. In Peranteau *et al.* (eds.) 1972:73-105.
Perlmutter, David and Paul Postal. Forthcoming. Relational grammar.
Piggott, G. L. 1971. Some implications of Algonquian palatalization. In Kaye, Piggott and Tokaichi (eds.) 1971, 11-38.
Piggott, G. L. 1973. On a rule of dissimilation in Odawa. In Piggott and Kaye (eds.) 1973, 28-41.
Piggott, G. L. and J. D. Kaye (eds.). 1973. Odawa Language Project, second report. Linguistic Series 1, Centre for Linguistic Studies, University of Toronto.
Piggott, G. L. and B. Mossop. 1973. Inflectional endings of the transitive verbs in Ojibwa: a paradigmatic arrangement. In Piggott and Kaye (eds.) 1973, 51-80.
Pittman, Richard S. 1965. The fused subject and object pronouns of Red Pheasant Cree. *Linguistics* **13**:34-38.
Postal, Paul. 1968. *Aspects of phonological theory*. New York: Harper and Row.
Postal, Paul. 1971. *Cross-over phenomena*. New York: Holt, Rinehart and Winston.
Postal, Paul. 1974. *On raising*. Cambridge: MIT Press.
Reibel, D. A. and S. A. Schane (eds.). 1969. *Modern studies in English*. Englewood Cliffs, N.J.: Prentice-Hall.
Rice, S. A. (ed.). 1931. *Methods in social science: a case book*. Chicago: University of Chicago Press.
Riggs, Stephen Return. 1890. *Dakota-English dictionary*. Contributions to North American Ethnology 7.
Rigsby, Bruce. 1967. Tsimshian comparative vocabularies with notes on Nass-Gitksan systematic phonology. Paper read at the Second International Conference on Salish Languages. Seattle, Washington.
Rogers, J. 1963. Survey of Round Lake Ojibwa phonology and morphology. In National Museum of Canada 1963, 92-154.
Ross, J. R. 1967. Constraints on variables in syntax. Ph.D. dissertation. M.I.T.
Ross, J. R. 1969a. A proposed rule of tree pruning. In Reibel and Schane (eds.) 1969, 288-299.
Ross, J. R. 1969b. Guess who. Papers from the Fifth Regional Meeting, Chicago Linguistic Society, 252-286.
Sapir, E. 1915. The Na-Dene language, a preliminary report, *American Anthropologist* **7**:534-58.
Sapir, E. 1931. The concept of phonetic law as tested in primitive languages by Leonard Bloomfield. In Rice (ed.) 1931. Also reprinted in Sapir 1949,73-82.
Sapir, E. 1949. *Selected writings of Edward Sapir*. Ed. by D. G. Mandelbaum. Berkeley and Los Angeles: University of California Press.
Sapir, E. and M. Swadesh. 1939. *Nootka texts*. Linguistic Society of America, William Dwight Whitney Series.
Sapir, E. and M. Swadesh. 1955. *Native accounts of Nootka ethnography*. Indiana University Research Center in Anthropology, Folklore, and Linguistics.
Saunders, Ross and Philip W. Davis. 1972. Verbal categories in Bella Coola: reduplication. Presented to the XIth Conference on American Indian Languages. San Diego.

Shaw, P. A. 1974. Review of *Deep and surface structure constraints in syntax* by D. Perlmutter. *Canadian Journal of Linguistics* **19**:209-16.
Shuy, Roger (ed.). 1973. *Some new directions in linguistics.* Washington, D.C.: Georgetown University Press.
Siebert, F. T. 1967a. The original home of the Proto-Algonquian people. In National Museum of Canada 1967, 13-47.
Siebert, F. T. 1967b. Discrepant consonant clusters ending in *-k in Proto-Algonquian. In National Museum of Canada 1967, 48-59.
Taylor, A. R. 1967. Initial change in Blackfoot. In National Museum of Canada 1967, 147-156.
Taylor, A. R. 1969. A grammar of Blackfoot. University of California doctoral thesis. Berkeley.
Thomas, Alexander and Eugene Arima. 1970. *T'a:t'a:qsapa – a practical orthography for Nootka.* Ottawa: National Museum of Man.
Thomas, Alexander and Edward Sapir. 1910. Unpublished manuscripts in the west coast language of Vancouver Island. Ottawa: National Museum of Man.
Todd, E. 1970. A grammar of the Ojibwa language: the Severn dialect. Ph.D. dissertation. University of North Carolina.
Voegelin, C. F. 1940. The position of Blackfoot among the Algonquian languages. *Papers of the Michigan Academy of Sciences, Arts, and Letters* **26**:505-12.
Voegelin, C. F. and F. M. Voegelin. 1964. Languages of the world: North American. Fascicle one (= *Anthropological Linguistics* **6**:6).
Umfreville, Edward. 1790. *The present state of Hudson's Bay* . . . . London: Charles Stalker.
Warkentin, John and Richard I. Ruggles (eds.). 1970. *Manitoba historical atlas: a selection of facsimile maps, plans, and sketches from 1612 to 1969.* Winnipeg: Historical and Scientific Society of Manitoba.
Watkins, E. A. 1865. *A dictionary of the Cree language, as spoken by the Indians of the Hudson's Bay Company's territories.* London: Society for the Propagation of Christian Knowledge.
Weinreich, Uriel. 1963. Four riddles in bilingual dialectology. In *American contributions to the Fifth International Congress of Slavists.* The Hague: Mouton.
Wolfart, H. Christoph. 1973. Plains Cree: a grammatical study. American Philosophical Society, *Transactions*, n.s., vol. 63, part 5. Philadelphia.
Wolff, Hans. 1950. Comparative Siouan III. *IJAL* **16**:168-78.

PM 232 .L5

Linguistic studies of native
   Canada